IMPERIAL RUSSIA

1700–1917

MARC RAEFF   *(Photo by Catherine Raeff)*

IMPERIAL RUSSIA
1700–1917

State · Society · Opposition

Essays

in Honor of

Marc Raeff

Edited by

Ezra Mendelsohn *and* Marshall S. Shatz

NORTHERN ILLINOIS UNIVERSITY PRESS
DeKalb, Illinois 1988

© 1988 by Northern Illinois University Press
Published by the Northern Illinois University Press, DeKalb, Illinois 60115
Manufactured in the United States of America
Design by Julia Fauci

Library of Congress Cataloging-in-Publication Data
IMPERIAL RUSSIA, 1700–1917.
Bibliography: p.
1. Soviet Union—History—1689–1800.   2. Soviet Union—
History—19th century.   3. Soviet Union—History—Nicholas II,
1894–1917.   4. Raeff, Marc.   I. Raeff, Marc.   II. Mendelsohn,
Ezra.   III. Shatz, Marshall.
DK127.I47 1988   947   88-29067
ISBN 0-87580-143-9

C O N T E N T S

Editors' Introduction vii

Ezra Mendelsohn
  On Marc Raeff: *A Memoir* xi

PART I :   RULING IMPERIAL RUSSIA

Hans J. Torke
  Crime and Punishment in the Pre-Petrine Civil Service:
  The Problem of Control 5

James Cracraft
  Opposition to Peter the Great 22

Allen McConnell
  Catherine the Great and the Fine Arts 37

Richard Wortman
  Images of Rule and Problems of Gender in the Upbringing of
  Paul I and Alexander I 58

Richard G. Robbins, Jr.
  His Excellency the Governor: *The Style of Russian Provincial
  Governance at the Beginning of the Twentieth Century* 76

PART II :   IMPERIAL RUSSIAN SOCIETY

Elise Kimerling Wirtschafter
  The Ideal of Paternalism in the Prereform Army 95

Gregory L. Freeze
A Social Mission for Russian Orthodoxy: *The Kazan Requiem of
1861 for the Peasants in Bezdna* **115**

Samuel C. Ramer
The Transformation of the Russian Feldsher, 1864–1914 .... **136**

Martha Bohachevsky-Chomiak
Women in Kiev and Kharkiv: *Community Organizations in the
Russian Empire* **161**

PART III : OPPOSITION TO THE IMPERIAL ORDER

John Keep
The Sungurov Affair, 1831: *A Curious Conspiracy* **177**

Judith E. Zimmerman
Herzen, Herwegh, Marx **198**

Marshall S. Shatz
Michael Bakunin and His Biographers: *The Question of
Bakunin's Sexual Impotence* **219**

Jonathan Frankel
The Roots of "Jewish Socialism" (1881–1892): *From "Populism"
to "Cosmopolitanism"?* **241**

Abraham Ascher
German Socialists and the Russian Revolution of 1905 .... **260**

Paul Avrich
V. M. Eikhenbaum (Volin): *Portrait of a Russian Anarchist* **278**

Edward Kasinec with Molly Molloy and Elliot S. Isaac
Marc Raeff: *A Bibliography (1946–87)* **289**

Contributors **315**

EDITORS'
INTRODUCTION

For more than a quarter-century, Marc Raeff has been a commanding presence in the field of Russian history. His influence both as scholar and as teacher has been far-reaching, especially after he joined the faculty of Columbia University in 1961 (in 1973 he was appointed the first Bakhmeteff Professor of Russian Studies). The present volume honors him upon the occasion of his retirement from Columbia.

As the Bibliography of his writings included in this volume demonstrates, Marc Raeff's own interests have ranged over virtually the entire span of imperial Russian history, thematically as well as chronologically. His first book, *Siberia and the Reforms of 1822*, published in 1956, reflects his abiding interest in the Russian Empire's far-flung provinces and borderlands; the appearance in 1957 of his *Michael Speransky: Statesman of Imperial Russia, 1772–1839*, helped put the workings of the Russian state on the agenda of an entire generation of American scholars. The recently published *The Well-Ordered Police State* continues his examination of legal and institutional change in Russia, here moving back to the seventeenth and eighteenth centuries and comparing the Russian experience with that of the German territories. His *Origins of the Russian Intelligentsia*, on the other hand, probed the life of the eighteenth-century nobility in search of the intellectual and psychological roots of the nineteenth-century intelligentsia. In numerous edited works, which have made an abundance of historical and historiographical materials available in English to students and general readers, his subjects have included Peter the Great and Catherine the Great, the Decembrists, political reform projects, and Russian thought (in his invaluable *Russian Intellectual History: An Anthology*). This is to say nothing of his articles, several of which have been of seminal importance, and the astonishing number of incisive book reviews that continually stream from his pen. Though generally identified as an eighteenth-century historian, Raeff in his most recent book demonstrates how inappropriate such categorizing is in his case: *Understanding Imperial Russia* draws together in a lively and succinct synthesis his insights into the imperial order as a whole, from its formation in seventeenth-century Muscovy to its unraveling in 1917. Written and published originally in French, this book is also an example of his remarkable ability to read, write, and speak English, French, German, and Russian with equal effortlessness, a linguistic agility which has been nothing less than awe-inspiring to his American-born students and colleagues.

It is appropriate that a collection of essays honoring such a scholar not be confined to one particular period or theme of imperial Russian history. The scholars who have contributed to this volume represent several generations, but they have all shared the good fortune of knowing Marc Raeff, either as his doctoral students or as professional colleagues. They were asked to pursue their individual interests within the chronological time span of imperial Russia, roughly from Peter the Great to the Russian Revolution. Each article, therefore, develops its theme in its own way, breaking new ground or revising received ideas, and each stands on its own as a contribution to the understanding of Russian history.

The volume is more than the sum of its individual parts, however, for the fifteen essays form a distinct structure. They fall into three broad groups: those that deal with Russia's rulers and officials, those that focus on one or another social stratum or social group, and those that examine currents of opposition to the existing order. As such, they reflect what might be called—with appropriate apologies for resorting to such an over-worked term—the dialectic of modern Russian history. The first five articles reflect the double-edged nature of the imperial state: an authoritarian and repressive force on the one hand, as James Cracraft's study of Peter the Great, for example, makes abundantly clear, but also—and this is a theme to which Marc Raeff's work has particularly directed historians—a positive and progressive force. In such areas as culture and education, on which Allen McConnell has focused, the Russian state was capable of pursuing forward-looking and constructive policies. That the most common result of "enlightened autocracy" was irresolvable contradictions and ambiguities, however, is documented by Hans Torke's account of the government's early efforts to police its own officials, Richard Wortman's study of the upbringing of Paul and Alexander I, and Richard Robbins's examination of the provincial governors in the postreform period.

Part II moves beyond the state's rulers and officials and traces their impact on various elements of Russian society. As several of the contributors demonstrate, the autocracy was often the victim of its own best impulses. Elise Kimerling Wirtschafter demonstrates that within the army the regime's paternalistic principles often generated higher expectations than could be met. Gregory Freeze and Samuel Ramer, treating the Orthodox clergy and the new profession of feldshers, respectively, show how by the second half of the nineteenth century the government's own educational efforts had begun to breed a growing sense of independence in these two groups. Conversely, Martha Bohachevsky-Chomiak shows how the government's worst impulses, such as its treatment of ethnic and religious minorities, tended to backfire, in this case by lending political significance to grass-roots community organization.

Ultimately, the interaction of state and society and its attendant frictions gave rise to an array of opposition currents and movements, the subject of Part III. Perhaps because so much attention has been lavished on this aspect of modern Russian history, these articles are particularly concerned with revising the myths and misperceptions that have accumulated in the historical literature. As a group, the articles reflect the broad spectrum of opposition that the state eventually came to face. Though in itself a minor incident, the Sungurov conspiracy of 1831, which John Keep has reconstructed, was one of the earliest signs of unrest within the educated classes. In part involving military officers, it followed on the heels of the Decembrist uprising and was viewed with alarm by Nicholas I. The gentry intellectuals of the 1830s and 1840s were the next to be heard from, and Judith Zimmerman and Marshall Shatz retrace and revise elements of the biographies of two of the foremost among them, Herzen and Bakunin. By the end of the nineteenth century, opposition to the tsarist order had begun to feed on sources beyond Russia's borders: Jonathan Frankel takes a fresh look at the interaction between Russian-Jewish émigré centers and Russian Jewish Socialism, while Abraham Ascher investigates German Social Democracy's response to the 1905 revolution. The volume ends fittingly with Paul Avrich's profile of the anarchist Volin, whose political views (like those of Bakunin) were the exact antipode of the all-pervading influence of the autocratic state—and who lived long enough to experience the mixed blessings of imperial Russia's downfall.

Within the broad pattern reflected in the threefold division of the volume, the reader will find a number of dialogues taking place between some of the articles. For example, Elise Kimerling Wirtschafter illuminates the paternalistic relationship between officers and recruits in the prereform army, which was regarded as a paradigm of social and political relations within the country as a whole, and John Keep demonstrates that even this institution was not impervious to opposition sentiments. Jonathan Frankel's tracing of the profound impact of the 1881 pogroms on the thinking of Jewish political groups forms a companion piece to Martha Bohachevsky-Chomiak's study of another of the empire's ethnic minorities, the Ukrainians. The self-contradictions inherent in the personalized, paternalistic style of autocratic rule, glaringly evident in the education of Paul and Alexander I as described by Richard Wortman, are echoed in the behavior of the army officer corps and the provincial governors treated by Elise Kimerling Wirtschafter and Richard Robbins, respectively. The articles by Judith Zimmerman, Jonathan Frankel, and Abraham Ascher reflect the ever-widening international dimension of Russia's domestic opposition movement.

In referring to "the dialectic" of Russian history, we certainly do not mean to imply that the demise of the imperial order was predestined, or ineluctable. Marc Raeff's *Understanding Imperial Russia* cautions us against the teleological character of much of the historiography on prerevolutionary Russia and the Russian Revolution, and it is a warning we would do well to heed. The purpose of this volume is to shed further light on the complex forces that made and unmade imperial Russia, to enrich the discussion of, without attempting to resolve, the question of how and why it met its ultimate fate. That is the most fitting tribute its authors can pay to Marc Raeff, who has so greatly enriched our fund of knowledge and, no less important, has kindled our historical imagination.

Ezra Mendelsohn

Marshall S. Shatz

ON MARC RAEFF

A Memoir

Ezra Mendelsohn

I came to Columbia as a graduate student in history in 1961. In those days the professors at that august institution seemed all-knowing, very distant, and not very welcoming. New students were obliged to attend a lecture course on historiography, and at one of the first meetings a celebrated member of the department solemnly explained that most of us were probably not clever enough to become professional historians. An oversensitive and underconfident young man, I took this as a hint that I should change my mind about my future career. The same professor seemed very annoyed when I later went to see him—during office hours, of course. Most likely the question I asked him (about the attitude of the hero of one of his books toward Jewish nationalism) was not very intelligent. The man in charge of my M. A. seminar was cordial enough, in an absentminded way, but did not seem terribly interested in his students' activities. Of my time sitting in his office with my fellow students I can remember only his long telephone conversations in unintelligible languages. Yet another illustrious scholar faced the blackboard while lecturing, and so timed his discourses as to disappear into his office sanctuary just as time expired.

All this did not surprise me very much. My previous experience at both the University of Pennsylvania and the Hebrew University of Jerusalem had been much the same. I will never forget how, at the latter institution, I induced a state of panic in an economic historian by suggesting that I write a modest research paper under his supervision. True, my father, himself a professor at Columbia, appeared to enjoy a rather close relationship with his students, but he taught an arcane subject (ancient Semitic languages) in which only a devoted few took any interest. The history department was a different story.

I wanted to study Jewish history at Columbia, but Professor Salo Baron very wisely suggested that I specialize in something more marketable (he could not have foreseen that, twenty-five years later, Jewish historians would be in great demand at American universities). I thought of Russian history, for rather silly reasons. My parents were born in the Russian Empire, and they identified to some degree with the Russian or the Russian-Jewish revolutionary tradition. My uncles, New York artists, spoke Russian to each other. Russian literature was highly valued in the family, as was chess. I never heard a word of Russian at home, unfortunately, but was proud of our Russian connection, however vague it might be. In college I had taken a course in Russian history, given by an enthusiastic and excellent teacher (let me name him: Alexander Riasanovsky). I now decided to study Russian and went to see Marc Raeff to inquire whether he would have me as a student.

Whether I was right or wrong in choosing Russian history is not certain, but I knew early on that I was right in choosing Marc Raeff as my teacher. My first talk with him, a talk I remember well to this day, persuaded me that in at least two ways Marc was quite different from most of his colleagues. First, it appeared that he genuinely wanted to have students—he was glad to take me on, despite my near total ignorance of his field. Second, he seemed to enjoy talking to students and hearing their opinions on various subjects. I find it interesting, in retrospect, that these qualities, not his imposing scholarship, impressed me so much. I assumed that all Columbia professors were learned men and women, expert in their disciplines. Later on I realized that Marc's learning was truly extraordinary: he seemed to read everything and know almost everything. But in the beginning it was Marc's friendliness and openness—happily coexisting with his somewhat formal, European manner—that I found so remarkable.

I attended Marc's lecture course and a wonderful seminar devoted to Peter the Great. It seems to me that in that seminar I learned, for the first time, how historians work—how they decide what questions to ask and how they decide what can be compared with what. I still have my notes from his lectures, which I have to admit served me for much too long as the basis for my own lectures on Russian history. (If I am not mistaken Marc once told me that lecture notes have to be thrown away every couple of years so that the lecturer will not grow stale. In this, as in many other matters, I have not been a perfect disciple.) A few minor incidents stick in my mind. Once, after a lecture, Marc asked me whether I thought his course was too dull. I was astonished by this question. Another time the question arose as to when, exactly, the Mongols (or do I mean Tatars?) had converted to Islam. Marc was not entirely sure of the answer, and said so. This frankness—not the lack of knowledge—also astonished me.

As time passed I realized that Marc's attitude toward his students went deeper than "mere" friendliness and openness. He conceived of us as constituting a kind of community for which he took a special responsibility. This meant, for one thing, doing everything in his power to further our progress in graduate school. If my case is characteristic, Marc broke all records for the speed with which he read dissertations, for he read mine in the space of a week. Later he took all of two weeks to read a ponderous, eight-hundred-page book I had written on a subject of no great interest to him. He wrote recommendations gladly and did his best to place us after we had finished our degrees (in those days there were still jobs). He also invited us to his home in Tenafly, usually for dinner. At these occasions Marc would speak honestly of the strengths and weaknesses of his colleagues (usually, I think, of their weaknesses). It was quite interesting for us to hear that certain illustrious Russian historians were really "idiot savants." It became known to us that Marc did not suffer fools gladly, especially among his colleagues. But in my experience he was always intensely loyal to his students, and when he could not praise them (and he was too honest to deal in false praise) he said nothing. In fact we were not all geniuses, and not all of us entered academic life. There was some truth, after all, in the words of the unwelcoming Columbia professor I mentioned earlier. But all of us were, during our graduate school years, part of that community. We were spoken to seriously, and we were listened to. And we were encouraged.

Moreover, this community was maintained even after we had departed from the West Side of Manhattan. Marc, a great correspondent, wrote to us, read our manuscripts and recommended them for publication, and helped us to get grants, tenure, and promotion. It was expected that we would get in touch with him whenever we were in New York. And, in due course, as we became his colleagues (and the progression from student to colleague was remarkably smooth) we were able to reciprocate by inviting him to our universities.

I have emphasized Marc's loyalty to his students, but I also want to emphasize the great impact that his intellectual and personal integrity made on us. There is a good Hebrew word for this quality, *yosher*, which is related to the word meaning "straight." He did not bend his high academic standards, and he never tailored his personal opinions in order to find favor in our eyes. Indeed, our community of students and teacher was held together by, among other bonds, respect for Marc's integrity. I have rarely encountered its like.

I suspect that I am not alone among Marc's students in having made the

effort to model my professional behavior on his. I have found it very difficult, indeed, usually impossible, to do so. It is no easy thing, I have
discovered, to take a genuine interest in one's students and to relate to
them with that mixture of respect and authority that comes so naturally
to Marc. My failures in this respect have only increased my respect for
his achievement at Columbia.

My subject in this brief memoir has been Marc's *Menschlichkeit*, and not
his scholarship, though the two are intimately connected. As far as the
latter is concerned, the essays in this volume make clear his great scholarly
influence and reflect his scholarly standards and interests. The putting
together of this *Festschrift* has been a labor of love for its contributors and
editors. Some of us were fortunate to have studied with Marc, and all of
us feel privileged to be counted among his friends and colleagues. We hope
that he will derive satisfaction from reading this volume, itself a product
of his faith in us and of his encouragement of our work.

IMPERIAL RUSSIA
1700–1917

P A R T

I

RULING IMPERIAL RUSSIA

CRIME AND PUNISHMENT IN THE
PRE-PETRINE CIVIL SERVICE
The Problem of Control

Hans J. Torke

One of the most fundamental themes in the work of Marc Raeff is the idea that the personnel of the Russian civil service—until well into the nineteenth century—was inadequately trained and educated and therefore performed badly. This unsatisfactory state of affairs derived, ultimately, from the fact that Peter the Great, for sundry reasons, was simply not able to modernize the administration he inherited from seventeenth-century Muscovy. Implicit in this interpretation is a critical attitude toward the pre-Petrine officialdom, which Raeff held to be "essentially negative or passive in nature."[1] Within certain limits, and taking into account various exceptions (that serve to confirm the rule), it is quite possible to agree with this interpretation—notwithstanding the positive but one-sided portrait of the Muscovite chanceries recently offered by B. Plavsic.[2] Plavsic's incorrect assessment is, at least partly, explained by the fact that his research largely ignored the problem of crime and punishment in the civil service.

In general, the dismal performance of Muscovite officials has been explained in terms of inadequate salaries. The disorders in administration and justice were, to a considerable degree, caused by the economic condition of civil servants. This interpretation explains such phenomena as favoritism, incompetence in the collection of taxes,[3] and above all the corruption endemic in seventeenth-century Muscovy. The last of these was rooted in the *voevoda* system, in which the head of a province still practiced the notorious *kormlenie* ("feeding") that had been formally proscribed but never systematically abolished. Indeed, by granting *voevoda* appointments as a kind of sinecure, the Muscovite government actually helped to reinforce this traditional conception of civil service.

Hence it was that the material support of *voevodas* and provincial officialdom remained a primary obligation of local communities and a major
fiscal burden on them. These expenditures were not in the least concealed, but rather were recorded in special books that distinguished the
various forms of support. These included sundry payments—for the *voevoda's* original relocation to his new place of service (*v"ezzhii korm*),
for holiday celebrations (*prazdnichnyi korm*), but above all for daily or
monthly outlays in grain and other food products, wood, beer, spirits,
forage, and the like. The expenditures for the voevoda's relocation could
be quite considerable, amounting to as much as three hundred rubles. But
all these payments were acceptable to the populace so long as they remained within traditional bounds. An uprising broke out in 1635 in Khly-
nov (Viatka), for example, because the voevoda demanded five hundred
rubles to pay for his moving expenses. The government, on the other
hand, several times prohibited all kinds of bribery—at least in theory. As
Tsar Michael admitted in a decree of 10 August 1620: "It has come to
OUR attention that OUR *voevodas* and officials are doing all kinds of
things contrary to OUR order." On the counsel of Filaret and the boyar
duma, the tsar forbade the population to pay illegal perquisites (*posuly*),
which were often described euphemistically as "tokens of respect" (*po-
chesti*) and leniently regarded as such; also banned were name-day gifts
(*pominki*) and provisions or support in kind (*korm*), which included such
elements as cultivation of the *voevoda's* land and hay making.[4]

Perquisites and support in kind were doubtless a continuation of the
earlier *kormlenie* system, whereby the governor (*namestnik*) put the judicial
and administrative levies in his own pocket and likewise regarded the traditional payments in money, in kind, and in labor as his salary. The *pominki*, however, must be seen as a new abuse and an example of direct
bribery without any historical precedent. It would probably be fair to say
that the horrendous corruption that came to prevail in nineteenth-century
Russia had its inception not in the system of perquisites of the fifteenth
and sixteenth centuries, but in their preservation and elaboration in customary law by the *voevodas* in seventeenth-century Muscovy. The basic
cause for this was the weak financial condition of the state after 1613,
which forced the government to pursue a contradictory policy: even as
the government issued its threats of punishment (according to the decree
mentioned previously, those guilty of bribery were to pay a fine twice the
amount in question and to be declared beyond the protection of the law),
it was consciously dispensing *voevoda* positions as a living for the simple
reason that it could not provide a sufficient salary from its own coffers in
Moscow. Rarely were the *voevodas* given special state villages for their
support; equally rarely did the local people receive a written charter for-

bidding that the *voevoda* be supported by the inhabitants or meddle in the affairs of the locally elected government.[5] While the Siberian voevodas increased the levy from natives (*iasak*) by means of taxlike "gifts" (in return for tolerating proscribed games of chance), after 1613 district offices (*cheti*) again kept *kormlenie* books. And even if these financial books of central offices recorded only the expenditures for officials dispatched to that province, the very terminology used here recalled the customary payments before 1556.[6]

In the capital too it was impossible to achieve anything without money and above all connections (*zastup*), a system that naturally struck foreigners as particularly repugnant. Lorenz Rinhuber, a doctor from Saxony who served as secretary to Russian ambassadors, reported in his *Wahrhafte Relation Von der Moscowischen Reise und Occupation* (1685) of his difficulties with the secretary of the Foreign Office, Ukraintsev, who "acted coldly and severely in order to demand levies (*posul*) or gifts. I intended to give him something and afterwards did present a few things to him and six other tsarist officials, for it is especially true in Russia, *latranti cerbero offam. . . .*" Ukraintsev is also supposed to have embezzled fifty rubles from the monetary gift that the tsars gave Rinhuber in 1684, while some of the clerks illegally kept back another twenty-five rubles. Rinhuber finally grew tired of complaining, "because their salaries are quite meagre" and because he had experienced the same kind of behavior at the French court.[7] Most of the other travel accounts forgot to take note of this last point. Thus the Danish ambassador Giöe in 1672 offered only the categorical declaration that "tout est à vendre ici" ("everything is for sale here").[8] He also overlooked, for example, what the German pastor Johann Gottfried Gregory reported to the Brandenburg Elector at the end of the 1660s: "The Germans must often give the boyars *posuly* or presents, as a result of which some things are then put right; but all this must be done secretly, for if the tsar finds out, then the boyar who fixed up the matter will go to Siberia in disgrace."[9]

That the highest authorities refused to tolerate corruption is naturally important for assessing the legal conceptions of the state. But in Muscovy this refusal coexisted with the government's willingness to take into account custom and the attitude of the populace. A secret letter to Tsar Alexis upbraiding the leading officials of the Moscow Land Office (*zemskii prikaz*) for their concealment of the illegal trade in spirits by fugitive servitors, for sodomy, and even for murder[10] was really the exception, not the norm. As a rule, people were accustomed to the fact that they could not successfully do business or engage in litigation in Moscow unless they gave the requisite presents. This attitude is illustrated, for example, in the notes of a certain Ivan (a servitor of the Prilutskii Monastery) regarding

the gifts that he had to dole out in 1682 and 1683 to the officials of the
Streltsy Office and the Great Treasury so that the monastery's tithe for
1677–78 and 1678–79 could be deducted from the "coachman's tax" for
1679–80: up to ten rubles in money, as well as food products (for example,
sugar, geese, wine), went not only to the officials and scribes, but also to
their servants, drivers, and the like.[11] For the poor, including those of
good birth, the magnitude of sums required for bribes often represented
an insuperable problem, a point that repeatedly found expression in the
nobility's petitions to the tsars.

Giöe accused the officials not only of venality, but above all of procras-
tination and red tape, calling them formalists, blockheads, and procrasti-
nators.[12] Such emanations of bureaucracy, especially the notorious delays
and paperwork that one experienced in Moscow (*moskovskaia volokita*),
were naturally just as widespread at the provincial level. Chicherin lists a
whole series of abuses perpetrated only by the *voevoda*s, who ignored the
tsar's decrees and simply did not imprison criminals, who arbitrarily had
service people beaten or illegally called up for active service, who meddled
in ecclesiastical or communal affairs (hence the communities' fervent desire to have each new tsar confirm their privileges), who embezzled state
revenues and salaries, who subjected traveling merchants to extortion
(hence the rescinding of authority to issue travel papers [*proezzhie gramoty*]
from Siberian *voevoda*s in 1646 and from *voevoda*s all over Russia in 1667),
and who coerced Tatars to convert to Christianity.[13] The sources are full
of descriptions of such abuses and transgressions, but also describe occasional trials of those who committed them. As is shown by the eight-
month investigation of accusations against the notorious D. M. Pozharskii
(who, as *voevoda* of Pskov, provoked charges of treason, embezzlement,
and oppression of the local populace),[14] no one was absolutely free from
temptation. Especially great were the abuses in Siberia, where the *voevoda*s of Iakutsk, P. Golovnin (1644–45) and V. Pushkin (1646) were particularly reprehensible. In Siberia the *voevoda*s had jurisdiction over the sale
of alcohol, which provided a special source of income.[15] A complaint
(published by Solov'ev) from the inhabitants of Velikii Ustiug in 1627
against their five scribes shows that minor officials could also make their
presence felt.[16] But in the European regions of the empire the situation
was not much different. The tsarist steward (*striapchii*) I. A. Buturlin
lodged an impressive complaint in 1634 against the disorder, corruption,
and oppression of the populace that the Moscow officials in Mozhaisk had
perpetrated.[17] Not without reason did Alexis grant immunity charters in
1654 to the cities that he had conquered in his war with Poland-Lithuania—in an effort to shield them from new Muscovite *voevoda*s, from judicial delays, and from high-handed treatment by the *streltsy* and soldiers.

Nevertheless, the tsar was aware that the *voevodas* and officials in the Belorussian cities took "gifts" from the nobles and petty townsmen (*meshchane*), and on 14 March 1656 he once more prohibited these and certain other kinds of abuses.[18]

In the maze of bureaucratic malfeasance there were only a few men whose probity clearly set them apart. Of I. A. Khil'kov, a chancery head in the 1650s–1670s, it was said that he did not accept monetary bribes. And when A. S. Matveev was banished, he passionately and rightly defended himself against the accusation of self-enrichment by noting that the cities of the Novgorod, Vladimir, and Galich districts had not been ruined while under his direction and that the purchase of hereditary estates—for which he had been reproached—was entirely within the law.[19] A. L. Ordin-Nashchokin was a genuine paragon of virtue. When he complained to the tsar "Oh, Sire, things are dealt with so weakly in Moscow and there is too little zeal in state affairs," he was expressing not only his dissatisfaction with the structure and course of administration, but also his opposition to the superfluous regulations and red tape—and, simultaneously, his support for giving greater responsibility and independence to local authorities. He devoted considerable attention, by Moscow standards, to the local population. Thus, when he became the *voevoda* of Pskov in 1665 (where local prosperity had been undermined by the bureaucracy), he attempted to counteract the chief deficiency in administration—the subordination of economic interests to fiscal goals and exploitation of the people—by promoting communal self-government, trade, and handicrafts. In the long term, however, his ideas failed to take hold.[20] In essence, he had in mind a state of affairs that was to be achieved in Russia only in the second half of the nineteenth century: the surmounting of the *votchina* tradition (that is, the conception of state service as an extension of personal interests) and a certain self-restraint on the part of the bureaucracy in favor of greater initiative on the part of society.

Whether the evil could have been eliminated had it been seized at the very root is a highly speculative question. The tsarist government did in fact resort to comprehensive controls and a subtly differentiated, complex register of criminal acts. But the controls, partly because of the lack of a modern conception of what the state is, ultimately had little effect. The lack of a properly defined way of doing things made supervision utterly impossible: aside from regulations for particular cases, there were neither manuals with standardized forms, nor registers, nor time limits for the processing of documents. Even a response to a letter from the tsar followed no set form, and it actually came to pass that some *voevodas* let an entire year pass without responding. Admonitions too were often left unanswered. Such negligence stood in direct contradiction to the painstaking observance of external form in correspondence, the flouting of which was regarded as an insult to one's personal honor (*bezchestie*).[21] If a *voevoda* wrote, it was entirely up to him *what* he wrote, and the annual reports (*schetnye* or *smytnye i pometnye spiski*)—insofar as they were submitted at all—are of little relevance to the local situation. In rare instances the central government demanded the transmission of income and expenditure books, but not until 22 May 1685 did it order the submission of documents on the extraordinary revenues to the Office of Service Lists (*razriadnyi prikaz*), an office that also received reports on political secrets from the *voevodas*.[22]

The disorders and shortcomings noted here represented a violation of the officials' service oath, which was meant to exercise a certain control over an officialdom that, in ethical terms, regarded itself as a group of state servitors. This oath (identical for servitors and subjects) was not a new institution in the seventeenth century. From 1613 it contained formulations that Peter the Great later employed in his oath, which remained essentially unaltered until 1917.

After the oath of subjects had been given in February 1613, the clergy present at the election of Michael Romanov demanded on 11 April 1613 that the lay participants in the assembly of the land reinforce these views by swearing the new service oath. Thereupon the "boyars, chamberlains, princes, *voevodas*, nobles, and officials" swore, among other things, that they would not rise illegally above their birth and service rank, would possess only those hereditary and service estates that had been bestowed, would accept without question the tasks assigned by the tsar, and would cause the tsar no trouble.[23] It was also quite natural that the foreign officers who had been hired for "the troops of the new order" had to swear such an oath in July 1631.[24] In the first half of the 1650s Tsar Alexis made the oath more differentiated and rigorous. First of all, on 31 August 1651 the oath not only forbade service to another ruler if one were a native of Poland-Lithuania, Western Europe (*nemetskii*), or other countries, but also explicitly mentioned the duty to combat Muscovy's foes, who were explicitly named: the Crimean Tatars, the Nogais, the Lithuanians, and "West Europeans." The final oath issued in 1653 contained the same requirements, but in addition to the tsar included as well the entire tsarist family and, in particular, future children. Besides the usual formulas concerning the need to serve the ruler zealously, to wish him well, and to protect him from harm, it explicitly noted the ban on desertion and treason, robbery and murder, favoritism and perjury. Another innovation of 1653 was the inclusion of different supplements to the general oath for particular groups of officials. Hence the duma officials were specifically obliged neither to make public the thoughts of the sovereign and the decisions of the duma before a decree was published, nor to do anything without the tsar's knowledge. Similar obligations were applied to various groups of court officials, and particular caution was demanded with respect to foreigners. The secretaries and Moscow nobility were sworn to justice, silence, incorruptibility, and impartiality and, insofar as they had any role in financial records, honesty in matters pertaining to the treasury.[25] In 1654 *Three Rituals for Oath-Taking (Tri china prisiag)* was published in Moscow; it divided the oaths into three categories—for subjects, officials, and civil court proceedings—and described the accompanying liturgical acts. On 20 January 1658 and 10 April 1667 the tsar ordered that the ceremony be held in the presence of a secretary of the Office of Service Lists if a new promotion into the ranks of the Moscow nobility were involved. Indeed, this oath was to be sworn on the day of the promotion; no one was to assume office without first taking the oath.[26] The oath for the "sworn tax collector"—that is, the elected official (*vernyi, po vere, po vernosti*) responsible for the alcohol and customs administration and for the collection of fees and transport of money—had its own special character. Its wording included as sanctions the ecclesiastical punishments of anathema and eternal damnation—until Tsar Fedor proposed to a council in November 1681 that these punishments be abrogated. The clergy in fact decided to substitute secular punishments, "because many people [nevertheless] commit sins in service to the Sovereign and in the collection of taxes."[27]

Thus the ruler made ethical demands of his officials. But what means were at his disposal to check for violations ex post facto? In the 1650s–1660s the fiscal system was partially controlled from Moscow by the Accounts Office (*schetnyi prikaz*). Otherwise, central control was in general exercised by investigative officials (*syshchiki*), who were dispatched to investigate when something extraordinary had transpired in a province. These were usually officials of the ad hoc investigatory offices (*sysknye prikazy*). In political cases it was always a boyar, *okol'nichii* (lesser-ranking boyar), or *stol'nik* (chamberlain), sometimes along with an assistant, who was charged with conducting the investigation. For example, the provincial uprisings of 1648 were investigated in this manner. On 17 October 1687 the investigatory officials received the right to visit suburbs (*slobody*) without first contacting the central offices that held authority over these areas. But otherwise they traveled to a province only at the request of a *voevoda*, and the cases in which a *voevoda* came under investigation were in any event infrequent.[28]

We may conclude, then, that control from the center was insufficient. It should also be emphasized that the investigatory officials themselves were not immune to bribery. The latter problem was evident in the complaints of the townspeople of Shuia in 1618 against M. Beklemishev and again in 1639 against I. Tarbeev. A. F. Palitsyn, who was dispatched as the chief investigator of complaints against Tarbeev, used torture so extensively and so indiscriminately in his interrogations that he even provoked a complaint against him in 1640.[29]

Visits by the tsar to the central offices seem to have begun only with Peter the Great.[30] In the opinion of many historians the Secret Chancery (*tainyi prikaz* or *prikaz tainykh del*), established in 1654 and operative until 1676, was supposed to function as a supreme organ of control. That interpretation is suggested, in particular, by the report from Kotoshikhin that clerks from this office accompanied envoys on their missions and military commanders in their campaigns. It must be pointed out, however, that Epstein has questioned Kotoshikhin's credibility on this particular point.[31] Golikov has linked the establishment of this office with popular unrest over innovations from the West and the correction of liturgical books.[32] In general, the literature has offered four interpretations of the Secret Chancery: it has been depicted as a kind of religious inquisition, a secret police, a private chancery for the tsar, and a tsarist chancery with supervisory functions. Since Gurliand's study of the Secret Chancery, however, the last view has come to prevail—namely, that the Secret Chancery should be seen less as an intelligence department than as a "direct line" between the tsar and the populace, an instrument for dealing with administrative arbitrariness and abuse. For this purpose too Patriarch Filaret, according to Gurliand, created adjunct administrative institutions; although the sources disclose little about them, they did make their presence felt.[33] Platonov has suggested that the establishment of this office was linked with the demise of the assemblies of the land: when this mainstay of the government disappeared in 1653, the tsar acted to counteract the bureaucratization of administration by establishing a new power base.[34]

Establishment of this central office was in fact one of the early manifestations of Russian absolutism. But it seems rather hazardous to draw a causal connection between the rough chronological coincidence of the last "great" *zemskii sobor* and the establishment of the Secret Chancery, for rather than constituting a counterweight to bureaucratization in administration, the Secret Chancery probably served more to concentrate the tsar's affairs and hence meshed fully with the general course of bureaucratization. Tsar Alexis might well have welcomed the fact that this new institution enabled him to ignore the regular administration, because, as Solov'ev has suggested, he wanted to avoid a direct confrontation between the parvenu Ordin-Nashchokin and representatives of the older families (Odoevskii, Dolgorukii). Thanks to the new office, he was able to correspond with various individuals without fear that this correspondence would become known to others.[35] Veselovskii has added an interesting nuance to this idea: the tsar was too much a devoté of tradition (*starina*) to understand the new times and constructed a kind of *oprichnina*, which corresponded to his own interests. This would also explain the disappearance of this office after his death in 1676.[36]

Indeed, one can hardly avoid concluding that the Secret Chancery was, above all, designed to be the nerve center of the tsar's interests and hence could not function as an instrument of direct supervision, for it stood alongside, not above, the other central offices. This private office of the tsar also concerned itself with his economic administration and, after 1663, the court lands as well; it sought to enhance the economic security of the Moscow *streltsy*, the "bodyguards," whom Alexis rewarded generously after suppression of the uprising in 1662 and whom he placed directly under the Secret Chancery. In this conglomeration of tasks,[37] only a minor role could be accorded to financial control over central offices, supervision of international negotiations, and performance of other control functions. In general, the chancery, which was directed by a chief secretary (D. Bashmakov) and staffed by ten clerks, did not develop into a specialized institution. In the final year of its existence, the Secret Chancery had a collegium of chief clerks at its head: a single secretary, significantly enough, could no longer achieve an overall view of its work. Hence the Secret Chancery did not provide effective control over administration. Even in purely numerical terms, it was not the powerful central agency that was once envisaged in Soviet historical scholarship. Important investigations, such as the interrogation of Razin in 1671 and the false pretender Vorob'ev three years later, were performed by the boyar duma, as they had been previously. The Soviet historian Golikova has in fact acknowledged the accidental, unsystematic character of the Secret Chancery's activities.[38]

Because organs of effective control were thus wanting, it was necessary in Muscovy to proceed in a preventive fashion and to rely upon the impact of prohibitions (or the fear of exposure for abuses, through complaints and denunciations) and punishments. But complaints were only successful if they arose from less remote cities; complaints from Siberia, for example, rarely reached the capital. There were, moreover, some mutual denunciations by officials.[39] Insofar as complaints existed when a *voevoda* was replaced, his successors had to investigate these cases in the presence of the interested parties. Consequently, the replacement of officials was regarded as the best form of control. But it did not always work, as the case of a *voevoda* in Rzhevsk demonstrates: he met his successor on horseback outside the city, and had him jailed; two years elapsed before he could be dismissed.[40] In practice, one *voevoda* carried on just like another. As a means to defend the populace, in an extreme case the government resorted to the following measure: the *voevodas* of Pustozerskii Ostrog had to reside five hundred versts away from the town in the summer.[41] In general, the *voevodas* of Siberia were subjected to particularly severe treatment: Thus when they journeyed to or departed from their posts, they had to undergo the equivalent of a real customs inspection. Apart from the property that he declared upon entry, the chief *voevoda* could only take out an additional five hundred rubles; for other *voevodas* and secretaries, the sum was three hundred rubles. To be sure, there were always ways and means to circumvent such control: either the officials gave all their money to one of the group at the time of entry (who then, upon departure, could take out correspondingly large sums for the others), or they armed themselves with a tsarist charter that allowed them to leave their baggage sealed until arrival in Moscow—where friends were always on hand in the Siberia Office.

Other prohibitions for the entire realm sought to prevent favoritism and bias among officials. Thus one from 4 January 1663 forbade officials to sit in judgment against those who had filed a complaint against them. In such cases, an official from a different city—not less than 100 nor more than 150 versts removed—was to be substituted as the judge. On 5 March, 1672 installation of officials as *voevodas* in cities where they owned property was forbidden.[42] After 22 September 1680, the trial in complaints against a *voevoda* for bias was to be held in another city, and on 12 August, 1681 Tsar Fedor Alekseevich expanded a rule of the Ulozhenie (ch. 10, art. 3) to include central chanceries, directing that judges could not participate in trials of kinsmen. *Voevodas* (and their kinsmen) were not allowed to conduct business, even in matters of serfdom.[43]

The threat of capital punishment raised special problems of its own. Whereas in many instances the tsar prescribed the penalty at his own discretion (for example, when an official considered a simple petition or a justified complaint a conspiracy [Ulozhenie, ch. 2, art. 22]), the Ulozhenie, the law code of 1649, also prescribed execution for forging official signatures, letters, and seals.[44] It is, to be sure, quite another matter how far the death penalty, prescribed in fifty-four cases in the Ulozhenie, was actually applied, both in general and against officials in particular. In the final analysis, the weak system of control meant that control in individual cases depended upon the efficacy of sanctions—on how terrifying the punishments in Muscovy were. Collins (Tsar Alexis's personal physician) emphasized that, in contrast to England, "they put very few to death here, only whip them, which is worse than the pains of death."[45] In fact, there were relatively few spectacular executions, which, as a rule, were carried out against heretics and those who committed crimes of violence, false pretenders to the throne, and participants in popular uprisings. Of these the execution of Shein and Izmailov in 1634 (for alleged treason) probably evoked the greatest sensation.[46] It was precisely the personalized regime of Tsar Alexis that substantially reduced the deterrence value of capital punishment, which he used chiefly as a threat—for example, in a statute of 30 April 1654 that solemnly condemned abuses in the leasing of taxes and customs.[47] When an investigative official unmasked a crime in the provinces, he generally (after the usual tortures) cast all the suspects into prison to await the decision of the central government. But the tsar granted pardons to most offenders. Experience with this system impelled I. G. Romodanovskii, as he investigated a rebellion in Ustiug Velikii in 1648, to have four of the guilty executed at his own command. Of the remaining ninety-nine inhabitants whom he imprisoned without regard to degree of guilt, six died from the torture they had endured.[48] In that sense it was simply honest policy when on 22 March 1683 Sophia replaced the death penalty for seditious speech with the knout and banishment. This measure, which simultaneously meant an amnesty for the 1682 uprising, did not, however, extend to outlying regions of the realm.[49]

So far as punishments are concerned, an exceedingly broad range of measures could be applied to the same criminal act: in one case disgrace (*opala*); in another confiscation of property, known as "ruination" (*razorenie*); in a third "perpetual ruination" (*vechnoe razorenie*). Voevodas (and, after 16 June 1669, those clerks of central chanceries who kept account of the money on hand each month) bore financial liability. There were monetary fines, beatings with the rod, the knout, imprisonment, banishment, and—upon occasion—a homily from Tsar Alexis.[50] Ellersieck has tracked down a rare case in which this "most gentle" tsar did not grant a pardon but rather increased the punishment: when the director of the tsarist mint voluntarily revealed in August 1651 that he had taken fifteen thousand rubles from the treasury (which he later paid back with interest), Alexis at first lauded him for his honesty, but then himself participated in the investigation and torture that preceded the offender's demotion.[51] The tsar also endeavored, so far as possible, to ensure that banishment—essentially a quite mild punishment—was in fact implemented. On 26 December 1663 he sent an order to various monasteries to give no credence to those exiles who claimed to be the tsar's emissaries (in order to obtain exemption from monastic rules and regulations). In October 1673, similarly, Alexis ordered the *voevoda* of Turinsk to maintain stricter supervision in his area over political prisoners, who consisted chiefly of rebellious Ukrainians and of whom many had fled.[52]

In general, penal practice, if not the law itself, in no sense functioned as a real deterrent. Even the punishment that was supposed to be most acutely felt by servitors—the frequent confiscations of property—in reality had little effect, because these were confined to a fixed percentage of official salaries (which had only a negligible nominal value) and in fact rarely involved the seizure of land. And, in the worst case, bribes could help ameliorate the punishment, as Collins again bears witness: ". . . The dispensation of their Justice is commonly Arbitrary, for they have very few written Laws, they go much upon Presidents [sic] (but money is their best President, which overthrows all the Former)."[53] This observation also suggests that the transition from law based on precedent to codified law, which was being effected in various law books in the seventeenth century, evidently brought with it no great progress in the direction of greater legality.

Indeed, Collins's book appeared twenty-two years after the most significant of these law codes, the Ulozhenie of 1649. At least *one* goal of the Ulozhenie of 29 January 1649, as well as of its 23 July 1641 precursor (which was also the chief source for chapters 9 through 12 of the Ulozhenie of 1649) was the establishment of a uniform set of laws for the entire realm—as has been repeatedly stressed by such historians as Stroev, Shmelev, Zagoskin, Latkin, and Zabelin.[54] Although social demands were responsible for the impulse to systematization, at work too was the need to combine and integrate the many laws that had accumulated in the various books of decrees (*ukaznye knigi*) of central chanceries since the last general law code, Sudebnik of 1550. As a conference of the tsar, ranking clergy, and boyars concluded on 16 July 1648, such a collection of laws was supposed to mean that "justice and investigation in all trials will be the same for all people of all ranks in the Moscow state, from the highest to the lowest rank." The same words (which indeed also found their way into the preamble of the Ulozhenie itself) were used by Tsar Alexis when on 19 January 1650 he informed the various cities of the assembly of the land that had enacted the law code and sent each *voevoda* two copies of it.[55] It would, however, probably be going too far to see in this either legal equality (Alekseev) or a tendency toward democratization (Platonov), for the code neither spoke of the *equality* of all before the law nor applied to *everyone*: rather, it denoted only a similar—that is, uniform and fair—judicial procedure for all (with the exception of peasants).[56] How little even a qualified interpretation of the code corresponded to practice is evident from Matveev's futile citation of this principle in a memorandum sent from exile. Nikon's indignation that the clergy also supposed itself to be subject to this "equality" was perhaps not unfounded, even if not entirely credible (because, as archimandrite of the Novospasskii Monastery, he had himself participated in the *sobor* of 1648–

49, signed the Ulozhenie, and later, as archbishop of Novgorod, even purchased five copies of it). The criticism of the Ulozhenie and the Monastic Chancery that he voiced in 1658 to Streshnev and Paisii pertains solely to the limitations imposed on the Church's judicial competence. However, in objective terms he hit the mark when he declared that no fixed rules had been established for these judicial trials. Cases had already come to light of *voevodas*, evidently overly zealous in their interpretation of the Ulozhenie, who had begun to intercede in ecclesiastical affairs.[57]

In fact, as a codification of law the Ulozhenie—given its content and poor systematization—was essentially no better than the earlier *sudebniki*. Above all, it could not attain significance as a criminal law code, for it adhered little to real judicial practice. In the final analysis, it lacked the character of a fundamental law and said nothing about the essence of tsarist power, the organization and function of the boyar duma, and the workings of chanceries and *voevoda* administration.

In specific cases, the regulations on criminal law in the Ulozhenie (that is, in the long tenth chapter, "on Justice") pertained chiefly to those administrative crimes that concerned procedural law. For peasants and bondsmen, special regulations (chapters 11 and 20) applied. Chapters 21 and 22, which dealt with robbery, theft, and capital punishment, had to be expanded and modified—just twenty years after the Ulozhenie took effect—by a "Statute on Criminal Courts for Theft, Robbery, and Murder" (1669), followed by further decrees in 1669, 1677, and 1680. Finally, on 16 December 1681 Tsar Fedor ordered central chanceries to draft new articles to cover all those cases that had been overlooked by the Ulozhenie and its supplementary amendments. There are some indications, in fact, that a broader legal reform (for which twenty-six new articles were promulgated the same year) that would make more prominent use of Roman civil law was being planned.[58] But all this led only to a new decree of 11 November 1685 on the procedures and punishments for delays.[59] Roman law, which could probably have assured more efficacious control over the administration, was not adopted, and even a simple codification of law did not come to pass until 1832. Russia was to suffer from these deficiencies in its legal order until well into the second half of the nineteenth century.

The facts that Peter the Great could not deal with the great number of administrative crimes, that his control ultimately proved ineffective, and that his punishments did not constitute a deterrent probably arise from a variety of causes. But the most important of these was the lack of social estate institutions. In his comparison of Russia with "the well-ordered police states," Marc Raeff has recently made clear that in Russia "to a much greater degree than was the case in the West, [the bureaucracy] had no overall control and direction, for there were no constituted bodies to limit its capricious tyranny or to make abuses known to higher institutions."[60]

NOTES

ACKNOWLEDGMENT: *I would like to express my gratitude to Professor Gregory L. Freeze of Brandeis University for translating this article into English.*

1. M. Raeff, *Understanding Imperial Russia: State and Society in the Old Regime* (New York: 1984), 6. For an earlier statement of this perspective see Raeff's "The Russian Autocracy and Its Officials," in Hugh McLean et al. (eds.), *Russian Thought and Politics, Harvard Slavic Studies*, 4 (Cambridge, Mass.: 1957), 78.

2. B. Plavsic, "Seventeenth-Century Chanceries and Their Staffs," in W. M. Pintner and D. K. Rowney (eds.), *Russian Officialdom: The Bureaucratization of Russian Society from the Seventeenth to the Twentieth Century* (Chapel Hill: 1980), 19–45.

3. On the problem of favorites see H.-J. Torke, "Oligarchie in der Autokratie: Der Machtverfall der Bojarenduma im 17. Jahrhundert," *Forschungen zur osteuropäischen Geschichte*, 24 (1978), 179–201. On the inadequate tax collection, see Torke, "Gab es im Moskauer Reich des 17. Jahrhunderts eine Bürokratie?" ibid., 38 (1986), 276–98.

4. *Akty sobrannye v bibliotekakh i arkhivakh Rossiiskoi Imperii Arkheograficheskoiu ekspeditsieiu Imperatorskoi Akademii Nauk* (AAE), 3 (St. Petersburg: 1836), no. 115. See also S. M. Solov'ev, *Istoriia Rossii s drevneishikh vremen*, 5 (Moscow: 1961), 285–86, and, in general, M. M. Bogoslovskii, *Zemskoe samoupravlenie na russkom severe v XVII v.*, 2 (Moscow: 1912), 284–85. The relocation *kormlenie* may also have been nurtured by the fact that it conformed to popular custom, whereby "bread and salt" (*khleb-sol'*) were offered as a sign of welcome.

5. Such a letter of protection, issued on 17 May 1677 for the inhabitants of Cherdyn', is to be found in *Akty istoricheskie sobrannye i izdannye Arkheograficheskoiu Kommissieiu* (AI), 5 (St. Petersburg: 1841), no. 16.

6. A prohibition on increased *iasak* collection from 1636 is in *ibid.*, 3, no. 193. A *kormlenie* register has been published in A. N. Zertsalov, "Kormlenaia kniga Kostromskoi cheti 1613–1627," *Russkaia istoricheskaia biblioteka*, 15 (1894).

7. L. Rinhuber, *Relation du voyage en Russie fait en 1684 par Laurent Rinhuber* (Berlin: 1883), 218, 263–65.

8. Iu. N. Shcherbachev, "Iz donesenii pervogo datskogo rezidenta v Moskve (1672–1676)," *Chteniia v Obshchestve istorii i drevnostei rossiiskikh pri Moskovskom universitete* (ChOIDR), 2 (1917), II, 34.

9. Rinhuber, *Relation du voyage*, 10.

10. *Zapiski Otdeleniia russkoi i slavianskoi arkheologii Imperatorskogo Russkogo Arkheologicheskogo obshchestva* (ZORSA), 2 (St. Petersburg: 1861), 682–84.

11. *Akty iuridicheskie, ili sobranie form starinnogo deloproizvodstva* (St. Petersburg: 1838), no. 376. Similar lists from Shuia are available from the *zemskie starosty* Fedor Ivanov (1641) and B. I. Skomlev (1677): *Starinnye akty, sluzhashchie preimushchestvenno dopolneniem k opisaniiu g. Shui i ego okrestnostei* (Moscow: 1853), nos. 52 and 134.

12. Shcherbachev, "Iz donesenii pervogo," 33.

13. B. N. Chicherin, *Oblastnye uchrezhdeniia Rossii v XVII veke* (Moscow: 1856), 310–12.

14. I. Ivanov, "Sledstvennoe delo o kniaze Dmitrie Mikhailoviche Pozharskom, vo vremia bytnosti ego voevodoiu v Pskove," ChOIDR, 1 (1870), V, i–xii, 1–169.

15. In the years 1626–28 the Pskov chronicle complained of a violation of the alcohol law—namely, the arbitrary abrogation of the clergy's distillation rights by the *voevoda* V. Turenin. *Pskovskie letopisi*, 2 (Moscow: 1955), 281.

16. Solov'ev, *Istoriia Rossii*, 290.

17. A. K. Kabanov, "'Gosudarevo delo' striapchego Buturlina o zloupotrebleniiakh v Moskovskom gosudarstve," *Deistviia Nizhegorodskoi Gubernskoi Uchenoi Arkhivnoi Kommissii*, 8 (1909), 58–70.

18. *Russko-Belorusskie sviazi: Sbornik dokumentov (1570–1667 gg.)* (Minsk: 1963), no. 317 (letter of protection for Mogilev from 25 May 1655) and no. 349.

19. Solov'ev, *Istoriia Rossii*, 6 (Moscow: 1961), 620; A. S. Matveev, *Istoriia o nevinnom zatochenii Blizhnego Boiarina, Artemona Sergievicha Matveeva* (St. Petersburg: 1776), 38–40.

20. Solov'ev, *Istoriia Rossii*, 395; I. I.Ditiatin, "Iz istorii mestnogo upravleniia," in Solov'ev, *Stat'i po istorii russkogo prava* (St. Petersburg: 1895), 459–60.

21. Thus the communications from the *voevoda* to his subordinates were called *pamiati* ("memoranda"), and communications to the tsars (that is, central authorities) were called *otpiski*. To other *voevodas* he sent either a communication, or when a tsarist command was being communicated, a memorandum (Chicherin, *Oblastnye uchrezhdeniia*, 270, 283–85).

22. *Polnoe sobranie zakonov Rossiiskoi Imperii* (PSZ), series I, 2, no. 1122.

23. *Sobranie gosudarstvennykh gramot i dogovorov, khraniashchikhsia v Gosudarstvennoi Kollegii inostrannykh del* (SGGD), 1 (Moscow: 1813), no. 203.

24. Ibid., 3, no. 88.

25. PSZ, 1, nos. 69 and 114.

26. Ibid., nos. 218 and 406.

27. AI, 5, no. 75, pt. 5.

28. PSZ, 2, no. 1265. An example of the activities of such investigating officials (the inspection of prisons) is in ibid., no. 1271.

29. *Starinnye akty*, nos. 13, 41, 44.

30. For a report of a visit by Tsar Peter to the Foreign Chancery (*posol'skii prikaz*) and the Office of Service Lists on 16 March 1688, see S. K. Bogoiavlenskii, "Pis'mo d'iakov Posol'skogo prikaza kniaz'iam Vasiliiu Vasil'evichu i Alekseiu Vasil'evichu Golitsynym o poseshchenii tsarem Petrom Alekseevichem Posol'skogo prikaza: 17 March 1688 goda," ChOIDR, 4 (1911), III, 51–52. Already on 10 February 1688 the Swedish envoy Chr. von Kochen reported

that Peter had unexpectedly visited all the central administrative offices in the night; see Chr. von Kochen, "Moskva v 1687–1688 gg.," *Russkaia starina*, 23 (1878), 126.

31. G. K. Kotoshikhin, *O Rossii v tsarstvovanie Alekseia Mikhailovicha*, 4th ed. (St. Petersburg: 1906), 85; F. T. Epstein, *Die Hof- und Zentralverwaltung im Moskauer Staat und die Bedeutung von G. K. Kotošichins zeitgenössischem Werk "Über Russland unter der Herrschaft des Zaren Aleksej Michajlovič" für die russische Verwaltungsgeschichte* (Hamburg: 1978), 68.

32. I. I. Golikov, *Deianiia Petra Velikogo, mudrogo preobrazitelia Rossii, sobrannye iz dostovernykh istochnikov i razpolozhennye po godam*, 2d ed., 13 (Moscow: 1840), 92.

33. I. Ia. Gurliand, *Prikaz Velikogo Gosudaria Tainykh Del* (Iaroslavl': 1902), 3–5, 331; see also G. G. Tel'berg, *Ocherki politicheskogo suda i politicheskikh prestuplenii v Moskovskom gosudarstve XVII veka* (Moscow: 1912), 311–12.

34. S. F. Platonov, "K voprosu o tainom prikaze," in Platonov, *Stat'i po russkoi istorii (1883–1912): Sochineniia*, 2d ed., 1 (St. Petersburg: 1912), 229–31.

35. Solov'ev, *Istoriia Rossii*, 6, 623.

36. S. B. Veselovskii, *Prikaznoi stroi upravleniia Moskovskogo gosudarstva* (Kiev: 1912), 179.

37. What was of interest to the tsar is evident from an overview of the extant documentation of the former Secret Chancery, which was prepared between 1710 and 1713 by order of Peter the Great. Among the materials were two large boxes, in which "the documents were decomposed and eaten away by mice, so that it is impossible to decipher them" ("Opis' delam prikaza Tainykh del 1713 goda," ZORSA, 2, 1–43).

38. N. B. Golikova, "Organy politicheskogo syska i ikh razvitie v XVII–XVIII vv.," *Absoliutizm v Rossii (XVII–XVIII vv.)* (Moscow: 1964), 247–48. A. A. Preobrazhenskii still speaks of a central intelligence agency in *Istoriia SSSR s drevneishikh vremen do nashikh dnei v dvukh seriiakh v dvenadtsati tomakh*, 3 (Moscow: 1967), 64.

39. In 1630 this led to a military clash in the Western Siberian Mangazeia between the voevodas G. I. Kokorev and A. F. Palitsyn, with the involvement of the local garrisons and city population; see *Ocherki istorii SSSR: Period feodalizma: XVII v.* (Moscow: 1955), 338.

40. V. P. Alekseev, *Bor'ba za ideiu zakonnosti v Moskovskoi Rusi* (Moscow: n.d.), 87.

41. Chicherin, *Oblastnye uchrezhdeniia*, 301.

42. PSZ, 1, nos. 331, 508; Chicherin, *Oblastnye uchrezhdeniia*, 304–6.

43. PSZ, 2, nos. 837, 885; *Pamiati russkogo prava* (PRP), 6 (Moscow: 1957), 77–78, 343.

44. PRP, 6, 35, 43.

45. S. Collins, *The Present State of Russia, in a Letter to a Friend at London; Written by an Eminent Person residing at the Great Tzars Court at Mosco for the space of nine years* (London: 1671), 58. Collins is a highly reliable source. There is quite similar testimony from other travelers, for example, the Dutch sailmaker Jans Strauss, who was in Russia in 1668–69 and asserted that nowhere in Europe was justice more severe than in Moscow; see Ia. Ia. Striuis, "Puteshestvie po

Rossii Gollandtsa Striuisa," *Russkii arkhiv*, 1 (1880), 58. On the matter of capital punishment, see also N. D. Sergeevskii, *Nakazanie v russkom prave XVII veka* (St. Petersburg: 1887), 90–92, 291.

46. On this case, see Solov'ev, *Istoriia Rossii*, 5, 169–71.

47. PSZ, 1, no. 122.

48. *Gorodskie vosstaniia v Moskovskom gosudarstve XVII v. Sbornik dokumentov* (Moscow and Leningrad: 1936), 141–43.

49. PSZ, 2, no. 1002.

50. An example of the latter is in PSZ, 1, no. 123. The decree on the liability of secretaries is in ibid., no. 454.

51. H. E. Ellersieck, "Russia under Aleksei Mikhailovich and Fedor Alekseevich, 1645–1682: The Scandinavian Sources," Ph.D. dissertation, University of California, Los Angeles, 1955, 264.

52. E. V. Barsov, "Iz rukopisei E. V. Barsova," ChOIDR, 4 (1885), V, 2–3; SGGD, 4 (1828), no. 88.

53. Collins, *Present State of Russia*, 44.

54. On the historiography, see K. A. Sofronenko's introduction to PRP, 6, 11, and M. N. Tikhomirov and P. P. Epifanov, *Sobornoe Ulozhenie 1649 goda* (Moscow: 1961), 27–29.

55. SGGD, 3, no. 129; PSZ, 1, no. 23; PRP, 6, 20.

56. This is clear in chapter 10, article 1, of the Ulozhenie (PRP, 6, 77). See Alekseev, Bor'ba za ideiu, 106, and S. F. Platonov, *Moskva i zapad* (Berlin: 1926), 111. As an analogue, article 34 of Catherine II's "Great Instruction" might be cited, for it says that the equality of all citizens consists in the fact that they are all subject to the same laws; see PSZ, 18, no. 12, 949.

57. Matveev, *Istoriia o nevinnom*, 121–22; A. N. Zertsalov, "Novye dannye o zemskom sobore 1648–49 gg.," ChOIDR, 3 (1887), IV, 14–16; Nikon, "Mneniia patr. Nikona ob Ulozhenii i proch. (Iz otvetov Boiarinu Streshnevu)," ZORSA, 2, 444.

58. H. Neubauer, *Car und Selbstherrscher: Beiträge zur Geschichte der Autokratie in Russland* (Wiesbaden: 1964), 193–194; PSZ, 1, no. 441; 2, no. 900.

59. PSZ, 2, no. 1140.

60. M. Raeff, *The Well-Ordered Police State: Social and Institutional Change through Law in the Germanies and Russia, 1600–1800* (New Haven: 1983), 217.

OPPOSITION TO PETER THE GREAT

James Cracraft

The subject of opposition in Russia to Peter I "the Great" (born 1672, reigned 1682–1725) has not been ignored by historians. References to it abound in the extensive literature on the Petrine period while monographic studies have been devoted to major oppositional figures, "affairs," events, and movements, and to the governmental organs created to adjudicate cases of opposition.[1] Yet with one or two partial and quite limited exceptions,[2] no single study has focused on the whole phenomenon of opposition to Peter's government and policies and to Peter himself, although links between various of its occurrences have been posited. This neglect, if it may be so termed, is understandable. Indeed, it is a thesis of this essay that opposition to Peter I in Russia was both constant and pervasive, and that it therefore cannot be adequately described and assessed without detailed reference to the main developments of the time. The history of opposition to Peter is in effect the history of his reign; or so, with qualifications, it will be argued here.

Of course, the problem is in the first instance one of definition. Which of all the known instances of unrest, dissatisfaction, violence to persons or property, or hostility to the authorities, whether active or passive, whether by deed or by oral expression, are to be considered manifestations of opposition to Peter's government and policies or to Peter personally? Which, in other words, can be seen as having immediate political significance? One approach to answering this question is to adopt the view of contemporary Russian officialdom. But the difficulty with this method is that the basic legal provisions against political offenses enacted under Peter I exhibit a transcendent breadth and vagueness, reflecting, it might be suspected, less a lack of legal finesse than the breadth and complexity of the problem itself.

Thus a Senate decree of 1714 specified that by the traditional phrase *slovo i delo gosudarevo* ("the sovereign's word and deed") was to be under-stood anything written or spoken that related adversely to the "health of His Majesty the Tsar or to the high-monarchical honor" or that comprised "any [act of] rebellion or treason."[3] By the tsar's own decree of 25 January 1715 "all true Christians and loyal subjects" were to report directly to him or to the appointed officials anything relating to "grave matters . . . namely, the following: 1. Any evil design against the person of His Majesty the Tsar or treason; 2. Any sedition or rebellion; 3. Any spoliation of the treasury, and other such matters."[4]

Again, under the *Military Statute* of 1716, which declared that "His Majesty is an absolute monarch who need not account for his actions to anyone on earth, but as a Christian sovereign has the power and authority to govern his realm and lands in accordance with his own will and good judgment," we find that any act or even unfulfilled intention that might have infringed on the tsar's freedom of action or discomfitted the authori-ties was considered criminal. In addition to straightforward acts of treason or rebellion, the *Statute* required punishment of anyone "who transgresses by abusive words against the person of His Majesty, censures his actions or intentions, or discusses same in an unseemly [*nepristoinyi*] manner." Also proscribed here were "all unseemly and suspicious meetings and gatherings." Whole chapters of the *Statute* were similarly devoted to often trivial offenses that were nonetheless thought to be connected, somehow, with treason to the fatherland. And while the *Military Statute* was meant to apply to persons in the armed forces, the decree ordering its dissemi-nation extended its norms to practically everybody else.[5]

As well it might have. In the continued absence of an updated legal code the officials charged under Peter I with adjudicating political offenses could refer only to the *Sobornoe Ulozhenie* of 1649. There, both the death penalty and confiscation of property were prescribed for anyone who har-bored designs against the sovereign's life, raised an army for the purpose of taking over the state, consorted with or in any way aided the tsar's enemies, treacherously surrendered a town, or "banded together and plot-ted" against the tsar or any of his officials and caused "pillage and massa-cre." The same punishment was provided for anyone who concealed knowledge of such crimes or designs.[6]

The *Ulozhenie* of 1649 was the first code in the history of Russian law to designate political offenses as the most important form of criminal ac-tivity. But its inadequacies in this respect required that the actual defini-tion of a political crime, particularly in the earlier years of Peter's reign, be worked out in judicial practice, and by officials obliged to handle what seems to have been an unprecedented degree and variety of hostility to

the regime. And it is to this practice, especially the operations of the Preobrazhenskii Prikaz, that we now turn in an effort to discover the nature
and extent, as well as the historical significance, of opposition to Peter I.

The Preobrazhenskii Prikaz emerged in the 1680s as the administrative
office (headquarters) of the guards regiment founded by the youthful Peter
I at the royal retreat, near Moscow, of Preobrazhenskoe. In the 1690s,
following riots in Moscow, the regiment was assigned to the basic police
and garrison duties in the capital formerly carried out by the royal *strel'tsy*
(musketeers), who had become increasingly restive under Peter's regime.
In 1696 the Preobrazhenskii Prikaz was given jurisdiction over political
offenses committed anywhere on the territory of the Russian state, regardless of the offender's rank and regardless of where the case might
previously have been tried.[7]
Peter's decision to endow the headquarters of his favorite regiment with
such sweeping powers appears to have been inspired by several factors:
by the growing number of political offenses requiring adjudication; by the
jurisdictional confusion engendered by his own previous but only partial
grants of such authority to the Preobrazhenskii Prikaz; by the fact that
the Prikaz, his own creation, was headed by one of his most senior and
trusted lieutenants, Prince F. Iu. Romodanovskii; by distrust of the
strel'tsy (finally disbanded in 1698); and by Peter's concern, evident in
other decrees of the time,[8] to counteract the shortcomings of established
judicial procedure.[9] His decision also reflected a deeper trend in Russia
toward judicial centralization and accretion of power by the monarch
going back at least fifty years.

Between 1697 and 1708 the Preobrazhenskii Prikaz heard hundreds of
cases either brought to it directly or referred by other offices. These included plots against Peter I's life, outright rebellion, espionage, preten-
sions to the throne, despoiling of the tsar's image, distortion of his titles
or abuse of his name; "unseemly utterances" touching not only on Peter,
his personal conduct, or his relations with his entourage but on his wife,
children, and other family members; and complaints against persons suspected of having dealings with Peter's half sister, Tsarevna Sofia, deposed
as regent in 1689, or of sympathizing with other of his opponents. In these
years, as its records show, the Prikaz handed down convictions in some
507 such cases, prescribing for each punishment ranging from death by
dismemberment and decapitation to mutilation, floggings of one kind or
another, terms of hard labor, banishment to a monastery or distant settlement, and—in the case of some female convicts—obligatory spinning for
the state. These convictions do not include the many hundreds more for
participation in the *strel'tsy* revolt of 1698 and in the Astrakhan rebellion

of 1705–6.[10] Nor do these numbers include, obviously, the hundreds of additional cases found *not* to involve a political offense. Indeed, so large had the volume of business at the Preobrazhenskii Prikaz become that by a Senate decree of 1714 the initiators of cases that did not in fact touch on the "health" or "honor" of the tsar or "comprise any rebellion or treason," but dealt with "simple matters," were themselves made liable to harsh punishment, which in practice usually meant flogging with the knout. After promulgation of this decree,[11] and apparently as a result of it, the number of such "simple" cases handled by the Prikaz sharply decreased.

The actual practice of the Preobrazhenskii Prikaz in these earlier years of Peter I's reign reveals, then, that for his government, and indeed for hundreds of ordinary plaintiffs, political crimes included virtually any "word or deed" which infringed, however slightly it might seem to us, however innocently, on the absolute power of the monarch or which tended to undermine, however indirectly, the existing state order. The operations of the Prikaz also reveal that over the years the authorities had developed norms for distinguishing political from other offenses and for specifying, with respect to the former, the degree of punishment due. Moreover, it appears on close inspection that in the final analysis the author of these norms was Peter himself. Not only did he take a most active part in the work of the Preobrazhenskii Prikaz, but as tsar he was of course the ultimate source of both law and justice and could settle cases not covered by existing law or judicial practice. Officially and formally, the final and often the initial factor determining what constituted politically significant opposition to Peter I's regime was Peter himself.

For Peter, on the evidence once again of the records of the Preobrazhenskii Prikaz, the most serious political crimes were treason and rebellion (*bunt*). By the latter he understood, like his predecessors, any mass undertaking against the authority of the tsar or of his deputies or any conspiracy aimed at killing the tsar or overthrowing the government. The usual penalty for such crimes was death, the form depending on the degree of guilt; in some cases, however, as with lesser participants in the "Shaklovitii affair" of 1689,[12] the punishment was flogging and mutilation followed by perpetual banishment to Siberia. But Peter also considered *any* joint action against the authorities equivalent to rebellion and liable to similar punishment, even when this amounted to no more than the submission of a collective petition of grievances, a petition that in at least one instance he did not even bother to read before condemning the petitioners.

Under Peter, moreover, acts of treason to be punished by death came to include defecting to the enemy, divulging military secrets, spying, giving aid to the enemy, and engaging in any antigovernment agitation that led others to leave the country. "Unseemly utterances" and other individual actions reflecting adversely on the tsar's dignity or policies were in general treated as lesser crimes; yet even here, depending on what was said or done and on who might have seen or heard it, and sometimes also on the offender's social class, death or the harsher forms of corporal punishment were prescribed. Such "unseemly utterances," the records indicate, were by far the most common form of political offense tried at the Preobrazhenskii Prikaz between 1697 and 1708; and for the various grades of these and all other political crimes (and for false accusations of same) some thirty different punishments were defined under Peter I's supervision and systematically applied. It is worth noting that in supervising the Prikaz's work Peter himself showed a preference for work sentences or for banishment to a distant or new settlement, as distinct from the death penalty or the more severe forms of mutilation. He is reported as having once said, "Of course crimes and disorders must be punished; but at the same time my subjects' lives must be preserved as far as possible"[13]—preserved, there can be no doubt, for service to the state.

Our knowledge of the operations of the Preobrazhenskii Prikaz in these years (1697–1708) prompts several tentative conclusions. The first is that in thus adjudicating hundreds if not thousands of political offenses Peter's government devised various penal and procedural norms that were later applied elsewhere. The relevant provisions of the *Military Statute* of 1716 (referred to previously) would be one such instance; elements of the treatment of religious nonconformists (decrees of 1718), another;[14] the use of inquisitorial process in suppressing banditry (1710), a third;[15] some of the material gathered in preparing a new law code (1720s), a fourth.[16] A second, related conclusion is that in granting, late in 1696, comprehensive jurisdiction over political offenses to a single office, the Preobrazhenskii Prikaz, and in thus subordinating to it all other governmental agencies, Peter took his first decisive step on the road to greater administrative centralization and functional delineation. Here the history of his famous reorganization of the state properly begins. Third, the range of offenses judged by Peter's government to be of a political nature and requiring trial and punishment was obviously wide, wider than ever before in Russia; and this fact, coupled with the volume of such cases handled, indicates that from early on in the reign opposition to Peter was on an unprecedented scale. Finally, the records of the Preobrazhenskii Prikaz strongly suggest that opposition to Peter's regime was also widespread in society, since actionable political offenses were committed by persons of every rank and social condition: by members of the boyar class and service gentry, *strel'tsy*, clergy both high and low, simple townsmen and peasants, and officers as well as ordinary soldiers. Qualitatively if not quantitatively, it would seem, Peter I faced by 1708 a kind of national resistance.

The Preobrazhenskii Prikaz was not the only bureau charged by Peter I with adjudicating political crimes. There was also the Secret Chancellery or, in its full title, the "Chancellery for Secret Inquisitorial Affairs," a title that distinguished it from such lesser inquisitorial offices as those concerned with irregularities in recruitment or with routine "schismatic affairs." An examination of its activities tends to confirm the conclusions just noted with respect to the operations of the Preobrazhenskii Prikaz.[17]

The Secret Chancellery emerged in 1718 in connection with the trial of Peter I's son and heir, Tsarevich Aleksei, and as part of the office of P. A. Tolstoi, one of several such personal chancelleries founded under Peter and entrusted by him with various missions. Tolstoi had earned Peter's special favor by having retrieved the wayward tsarevich from his haven in Italy, and during the first six months of its existence the Secret Chancellery, headed by Tolstoi, was concerned almost exclusively with prosecuting the tsar's case against his son. There is, it seems, little of substance to add to the printed documentation and secondary literature on the whole Aleksei affair.[18] But with reference to the problem before us the trial of the tsarevich—undoubtedly the single most important political trial carried out under Peter I—is significant in at least several major respects.

In the first place, Aleksei's trial was relatively open. After the usual secret and lengthy inquisitorial process had done its work, and the evidence had been gathered, the case against the tsarevich was presented for judgment to an assembly of 128 notables specially convened for the purpose. Then, following Aleksei's condemnation by the assembly, a substantial selection of the evidence against him was published both at home and abroad, with the intention, clearly, of justifying the tsarevich's condemnation, of discrediting his sympathizers, and of warning the tsar's enemies whoever they might be. Such actions by Peter's government bespeak an anxiety that the conspiracy surrounding Aleksei was but the crest of a wave. Indeed, although relatively few persons were denounced in the course of the trial and eventually punished, the circle of the tsarevich's tacit or potential supporters against his father, to judge only from the evidence presented, was wide and threatened the destruction not only of Peter's grand projects, such as St. Petersburg or the fleet, but of Peter himself.

Second, the trial of Tsarevich Aleksei—his arrest, interrogation under torture, open condemnation for treason, and mysterious death before sentence could be imposed—itself became a cause of further opposition to Peter I. There is considerable evidence, for example in the records of the subsequent activities of the Secret Chancellery, that Peter's treatment of his son was generally perceived as a great scandal. More immediately, several prominent churchmen had been implicated to one degree or

another in the conspiracy surrounding Aleksei; in the case of the metropolitan of Rostov, the association led to his execution. And there is no
doubt that this revelation precipitated Peter's decision to abolish the ancient headship of the Russian church and to incorporate its administrative
apparatus in the administration of the state. Finally, the Tsarevich Aleksei
affair gave rise to the Secret Chancellery itself, which thereafter expanded
its operations under Peter and in fact was to endure, in one form or
another, until the nineteenth century.

Its records show that apart from the Aleksei affair the Secret Chancellery investigated some 370 "grave matters" between 1718 and 1725, sharing jurisdiction in this respect with the older Preobrazhenskii Prikaz. (The
exact relationship between the two offices is a subject of scholarly dispute,
but it seems that under Peter I the Secret Chancellery retained the character of an extraordinary commission, the Preobrazhenskii Prikaz that of
a permanent bureau. In 1722, it too was designated a "chancellery" and
between 1718 and 1725 it adjudicated roughly two thousand political
cases.) By far the majority of the "grave matters" investigated during these
years by the Secret Chancellery—upward of 75 percent—involved political offenses as these had come to be understood, although by now the
term included, its records show, such crimes as "unseemly utterances"
against senior officials and Peter's second wife, Catherine, and expressions
of sympathy for the deceased tsarevich. Moreover, in the first three years
of its existence some 70 percent of all cases lodged at the Secret Chancellery were referred to it directly by the tsar, some following an arrest that
he had personally made. It would seem that nearing the end of his reign
Peter was increasingly occupied with the problem of opposition to his
regime even as he pressed forward with new and far-reaching reforms—
administrative, military, economic, cultural—and in no way modified his
conduct to placate his opponents. The possibility that Peter had become
obsessed with what he took to be opposition, indeed that he had long
since, perhaps from the beginning, exaggerated its importance, should be
considered.

In other words, the records of both the Preobrazhenskii Prikaz and the
Secret Chancellery suggest that the problem of Peter I's opposition is also
the problem of Peter himself: of his motives, ambitions, and desires, if
not of his whole psychological makeup. This might be the moment to
place in evidence, as an example of what is at issue, Peter's "dream of the
bad animal." On 26 April 1715, as the written record, evidently dictated
by Peter himself, relates, he

> had a dream. It was as though an eagle were sitting in a tree, and beneath
> it had crept or crawled some sort of large wild beast, like a crocodile or a

dragon, onto which this eagle immediately leapt, and gnawed its head from its neck—that is, chewed away half the neck and killed it. And then, while many people gathered to watch, another such beast crept up, whose head this eagle also gnawed off, it seemed in plain view of everybody.

It was suggested elsewhere, after referring to the psychological literature and after establishing correspondences between the content of this dream record and known facts of Peter's conscious life, that what may well be symbolized here was an intense, not to say savage struggle raging deep within him between his baser and nobler selves—a struggle that was being acted out, as was everything in his conscious life, before a crowd of people. Peter's dream record (one of twelve to have survived) presents evidence of a fundamental inner conflict whose projection onto the outer world, one might add, facilitated his readiness to identify and punish opponents. Indeed in that earlier study, discussing possible sources of this dream's imagery, it was also suggested that

> The impression that something very basic in Peter is at issue here gains further ground when we reflect that the *raskol'niki* [schismatics], who were always a most troublesome problem for Peter, were wont to depict him, in both word and picture, as the "crocodile," as he no doubt knew. It was one of the ways in which the more aggressive of the religious dissidents taunted and reviled him, to which he would respond, with equal vigor, by denouncing them for ignorance and superstition, for obstinacy and plain wickedness, and by persecuting them in one way or another, sometimes violently.[19]

Turning to more conventional texts illustrative of a possible obsession with his opposition, we might consider Peter's directive to the clergy requiring them to violate the traditional and canonical secrecy of confession whenever they heard anything therein that could be construed as treasonable. In the spring of 1722, under Peter's direct supervision, the Holy Synod added to the recently promulgated *Ecclesiastical Regulation* a provision that reads in part:

> If during confession someone discloses to the priest an unfulfilled but still intended criminal act, especially [one] of treason or rebellion against the Sovereign or State, or an evil design against the honor or health of the Sovereign and the family of His Majesty, and disclosing such an evil intention shows that he does not repent of it but indeed justifies his intention and does not forsake it, and confesses it not as a sin but rather to be confirmed in his intention by the assent or the silence of his confessor, which [fact] may be discovered in this way: if the confessor orders him in the name of God wholly to desist from his evil intention and he is silent and

apparently dubious, or justifying himself appears unchanged in this respect; [in such cases] the confessor must not only not grant him absolution and remission of his openly confessed sins, but must promptly report him at the prescribed places. . . .

These "places," as the document specifies, were the Secret Chancellery and the Preobrazhenskii Prikaz, where "such crimes are tried" and where, at the time of trial, the confessor himself was to appear and "declare everything he has heard about this evil intention explicitly, without hesitation, and concealing nothing." The authors of this injunction went on to argue that in so acting priests did not really violate the secrecy of confession but rather fulfilled a larger Christian duty. And in a supplementary "Announcement" to the clergy of May 1722 the Synod, again with Peter's personal participation, recounted several "actual cases" in this connection for the purpose both of instructing (or admonishing) confessors and of justifying the Synod's injunction.[20]

One such case had arisen in the course of Tsarevich Aleksei's trial, when it was revealed that "during confession he had told his confessor that he wished his father were dead; and this confessor forgave him in the name of God and said that he too wished he were dead, which this former confessor himself admitted under inquisition. . . ; and for this evil deed he [the confessor] was put to a well-deserved death." The second and most recent case cited by the Synod in its "Announcement" had come to trial in March of that same year (1722), because

> a certain malefactor, on arrival at the town of Penza, publicly uttered many evil things against the most high honor of His Most Illustrious Imperial Majesty, and most pernicious words against the State, about which an inquisition is now under way in the Secret Chancellery. But from this inquisition it has already appeared that this malefactor had intimated these evil words to his priest in confession, who did not in any way forbid them but indeed assented to some of them, as now this unfrocked priest himself has confessed under inquisition.

The "malefactor" in question was later executed, essentially for the crime of publicly calling Peter the Antichrist. His trial also resulted in the informal trial by the Holy Synod of its own president, Metropolitan Stefan Iavorskii, who was alleged to have remarked to the defendant that Peter was not the Antichrist, but an "iconoclast"—a contemporary euphemism for "Protestant." And the third such case cited in the Synod's "Announcement" to the clergy of May 1722 involved "the criminal Talitskii," who

> intimated to his priest in confession his most wicked intention, namely: to write a letter by means of which he wished everywhere to incite sedition,

insisting that it was right and not to be forsaken; and the priest, although this [intention] disgusted him, nevertheless gave him communion, and did not report it to the appropriate authorities . . . and this criminal proceeded to carry out his intention. And should he not have been caught in the act, what blood and disasters would have issued therefrom! And to what wickedness the sacrament of penance had been put by Talitskii and his confessor!

This passage was written by Peter himself, as was another denouncing Talitskii in similar terms that Peter inserted into a synodal admonition to religious dissenters that had been promulgated a few months before (January 1722).[21]

In fact, we now know that in the spring of 1708, at the height of the Bulavin uprising,[22] Peter issued a secret order to the clergy obliging them in the course of their duties, including that of confessor, to be on the lookout for signs of treason or rebellion among other criminal acts or designs and to report them to the authorities. Here Peter cited instances in which clergy had been remiss in this regard in the revolts of the *strel'tsy* of 1682 and 1698, the Astrakhan rebellion of 1705–6, and the case of Talitskii.[23] Talitskii, it should be noted, had been tried and executed back in 1700–1701 for composing a leaflet in which the proximate end of the world was predicted, Moscow was called Babylon, Peter himself was denounced as the Antichrist, and the people were bidden not to serve the tsar or to pay his taxes. Talitskii evidently had planned, with a following thus aroused and with the help of disaffected *strel'tsy*, to depose Peter while he was away campaigning and to replace him with a certain, presumably sympathetic, boyar. Seventeen persons were named by Talitskii as his supporters and were also summoned to trial at the Preobrazhenskii Prikaz. Five of these were also executed in consequence; eight were condemned to flogging, mutilation, and banishment to Siberia; and one, the bishop of Tambov, was deposed and banished to the Solovetskii monastery in the far north, while his diocese was virtually abolished (by merger with the Moscow diocese). Observing how Peter would cite the case once in 1708 and twice again in 1722, it might be thought that Talitskii had become in his mind the personification of all who opposed him, and the touchstone of his obsession.

In any event, it was the Talitskii affair and other such cases of opposition to Peter I's regime, whether collective or individual, large-scale or apparently trivial, and spanning the whole of the reign, that gave rise to the judicial activities of the Preobrazhenskii Prikaz and the Secret Chancellery, to the death of the heir to the throne, and to some of Peter's more

radical and far-reaching "reforms." Opposition to Peter's regime, as we
see, was neither an isolated nor, in the eyes of the regime itself, a negligible phenomenon. But what exactly inspired such opposition? How
much of it is to be attributed to the actions of Peter I and his government,
and how much to events before his time or to factors over which he had
little if any control? No very precise answers can be given to these questions. Yet a sampling of the fairly abundant evidence at our disposal in
this connection yields, again, several tentative conclusions.

The first is that at least some of the opposition to Peter derived from
obvious structural, inevitable, or accidental causes. These would include
the displacement, as in the palace revolution of 1689, of certain grandees
and their kinsfolk, clients, and friends (who then plotted to regain, while
it still seemed possible, their lost power and privileges); the incompetence
or depredations of particular officials; the hostility of the official church
toward nonconformists (a policy initiated before Peter's time); or the burdens of serfdom (an institution about which Peter did, and perhaps could
have done, essentially nothing). But it is also apparent that much of the
opposition which surfaced during Peter's reign was directed against policies that were either initiated by him and his government or in some way
intensified or expanded by them. Among the causes of this more specific
opposition may be mentioned the unprecedented exactions of all kinds
occasioned by Peter's continual wars and building projects; the official and
sometimes forcible promotion of such practices as smoking tobacco, shav-
ing the beard, and calculating the year from the birth of Christ (instead of
from the creation of the world), all hitherto proscribed by custom or by
law; the official preference granted foreigners, almost uniformly scornful
of Russians and their ways; the often drastic curtailment of the clergy's
rights and immunities, sometimes without any justification; the imposition of new responsibilities on the service gentry; not just the suppression
of rebellious *strel'tsy* but the abolition of the *strel'tsy* as such; and the intensified persecution, albeit in moderated form, of religious nonconformity.

All of this is fairly well known, even if it has yet to be studied in a
systematic and comprehensive way. But the evidence under review also
reveals that still more of the opposition which manifested itself during the
Petrine period was directed against Peter himself. It was aroused not only
by the factors just mentioned, but by Peter's own "unseemly" words and
deeds: by his smoking and drinking; by his often shabby, unregal, or un-
Russian dress; by his frequent indulgence in extravagant jokes and pranks;
by his flouting of the sacred rites; by his divorce from Tsarevich Aleksei's
mother (a member of a prominent Muscovite clan) and then marriage to a
lowly foreigner; by his treatment of Tsarevich Aleksei; by his perpetual,
public, and seemingly unconcerned revelation of the many follies, vices,
and frailties of the tsar himself, hitherto a sacrosanct figure.

Indeed, the most common of the complaints lodged against Peter's regime, the common thread running through the endless depositions and denunciations brought to the appropriate offices, cutting across rank and social condition, was that in his personal conduct, as much as or even more than in his policies, Peter had early revealed himself to be a false tsar. He was a "tyrant," "impostor," "servant of Antichrist," or "Antichrist" himself; "heretic," "blasphemer," "Latinizer," or "iconoclast"; the "Magog" of Ezekiel's prophecy; really a "German" or a "Swede," even a "Musulman," in disguise. These charges were repeated again and again as each new impropriety (*bezchinnost'*), each fresh imposition, added fuel to the fire. We are back to Peter—and to the realization, once again, that without him the history of his times would have been unimaginably different.

Yet in closing this introductory and necessarily brief survey of the problem of Peter I's opposition, the difficulties in reaching any final conclusions should be stressed. The lack of access to certain archives is one such difficulty, obviously, as is the necessarily heavy reliance on official sources. The need also to rely on the testimonials of foreign observers, primarily Europeans whose hostile and uncomprehending bias against natives and native institutions or customs was endemic, is a third. But more serious perhaps than any of these is the difficulty of the voice of the opposition itself. How is the historian to translate or interpret hostility that is frequently expressed in terms that are not just unfamiliar, but utterly alien to his own sensibility? Too often the secondary literature reveals not so much an awareness of this difficulty as a willingness to put words in the mouths of Peter's opponents, a readiness to decide that what actually is being said manifests some underlying cause or some unconscious motive that historians themselves have invented.

To be aware of these difficulties, however, does not preclude advancing a kind of unifying hypothesis. We have perhaps isolated here a fundamental syndrome of action and reaction, of opposition to Peter I's regime engendering in turn innovations or even major "reforms" as well as its own punishment. Opposition to Peter's regime, continual and pervasive, manifesting itself in various ways and arising from various causes, was both cyclical and cumulative and as much relation to what happened of historical significance during the era as any other factor, whether it be the incursions of foreign enemies or the europeanizing ambitions of the ruler. To study the whole phenomenon is to become increasingly skeptical of the view which holds that the sole or even the main agent of change in Petrine Russia was a dynamic governing elite and which depicts the rest of society, whether intentionally or not, as largely inert or passive. And it is likely that when the full history of Peter's opposition has been written, our picture of a basically benign, enlightened, or at least progressive regime—of an era of great reform—will be fundamentally modified. However we might ultimately evaluate his achievements (another question altogether), it may well turn out that Peter I became "the Great" as a matter less of conviction than of simple self-preservation.

NOTES

ACKNOWLEDGMENT : *An earlier draft of this essay was read at a conference held in October 1977 at the University of Rochester. Marc Raeff was the commentator, and the essay has benefited greatly from his characteristically incisive remarks.*

1. See the various specialized works cited in the following notes. In the general literature, see the classic works of Kliuchevskii and especially of Solov'ev: V. O. Kliuchevskii, *Sochineniia*, 8 vols. (Moscow: 1956–59), 4, 225–34 and passim; S. M. Solov'ev, *Istoriia Rossii s drevneishikh vremen*, 15 vols. (Moscow: 1962–66), vols. 7–9 passim.

2. V. Ulanov, "Oppozitsiia Petru Velikomu," in V. V. Kallash, ed., *Tri veka: Rossiia ot smuty do nashego vremeni*, 3 vols. (Moscow: 1912), 3, 56–86; M. S. Anderson, *Peter the Great* (London: 1978), 140–56.

3. N. B. Golikova, *Politicheskie protsessy pri Petre I: Po materialam Preobrazhenskogo prikaza* (Moscow: 1957), 26.

4. *Polnoe sobranie zakonov Rossiiskoi imperii s 1649 goda.* 1st Series, 1649–1825. 46 vols. (St. Petersburg: 1830–43), 5, no. 2877 (hereafter cited as *PSZ*, followed by relevant volume and document number).

5. *PSZ*, 5, 3010. Peterson suggests that wide distribution of the *Military Statute* was ordered so as "to avoid controversies over jurisdiction between civil and military courts": C. Peterson, *Peter the Great's Administrative and Judicial Reforms: Swedish Antecedents and the Process of Reception* (Stockholm: 1979), 339–40; but he explicitly does not deny the importance of the latter's influence on the development, in Peter's time and thereafter, of the former (341 ff.).

6. *PSZ*, 1, 1.

7. Golikova, *Politicheskie protsessy*, is the basic work on the subject and our main guide here; see also her "Organy politicheskogo syska i ikh razvitie v XVII–XVIII vv.," in N. M. Druzhinin et al., eds., *Absoliutizm v Rossii (XVII–XVIII vv.)* (Moscow: 1964), 243–80. For more detail and extensive documentation, see the older works of M. I. Semevskii, *Slovo i delo 1700–1725 gg.* (St. Petersburg: 1884), Book 2 of his *Ocherki i razskazy iz russkoi istorii XVIII veka*; N. Novombergskii, *Slovo i delo gosudarevo*, 2 vols. (Tomsk: 1909–11); and a series of documentary studies by G. V. Esipov: *Dela Preobrazhenskogo Prikaza* (St. Petersburg: 1861); *Raskol'nich'e delo v XVIII veke* (Moscow: 1861); *Raskol'nich'i dela XVIII stoletiia: Izvlechennyia iz del Preobrazhenskago prikaza i Tainoi rozysknykh del kantseliarii*, 2 vols. (St. Petersburg: 1861–63); *Liudi starago veka: razskazy iz del Preobrazhenskago Prikaza i Tainoi Kantseliarii* (St. Petersburg: 1880); *Tiazhelaia pamiat' proshlago: Razskazy iz del Tainoi Kantseliarii i drugikh arkhivov*

(St. Petersburg: 1885). There is of course a large literature devoted to the history of the Schism (*Raskol*) in Russia, of which the most important titles for our purposes here are A. Sinaiskii, *Otnoshenie russkoi tserkovnoi vlasti k raskolu staroobriadstva v pervye gody sinodal'nago upravleniia* (St. Petersburg: 1895) and P. S. Smirnov, *Spory i razdeleniia v russkom raskole v pervoi chetverti XVIII veka* (St. Petersburg: 1909). I might note that I have twice been denied access to the archives of the Preobrazhenskii Prikaz: once, in person, at the Central State Archives (TsGADA) in Moscow, in 1979; the second time, in 1981, on application to same through the International Research and Exchanges Board (IREX) in New York, which elicited the telegrammed response, in English, that these archives "are closed to all researchers for a long time."

8. For example, *PSZ*, 2, 1491; 3, 1572.

9. See also R. Wortman, "Peter the Great and Court Procedure," *Canadian-American Slavic Studies*, 8, no. 2 (Summer 1974), 303–4; and Peterson, *Administrative and Judicial Reforms*, 303 ff.

10. For those events see M. M. Bogoslovskii, *Petr I: Materialy dlia biografii*, 5 vols. (Moscow: 1940–48), vols. 3 and 4, passim; V. I. Buganov, *Moskovskie vosstaniia kontsa XVII veka* (Moscow: 1969); V. I. Buganov and A. N. Kazakevich, *Vosstanie Moskovskikh strel'tsov 1698 god: Sbornik dokumentov* (Moscow: 1980); N. B. Golikova, *Astrakhanskoe vosstanie 1705–1706 gg.* (Moscow: 1975).

11. Golikova, *Politicheskie protsessy*, 26.

12. A. Truvorov, ed., *Rozysknye dela o Fedore Shaklovitom i ego soobshchnikakh*, 4 vols. (St. Petersburg: 1884–93); N. G. Savich, ed., *Vosstanie v Moskve 1682 g. Sbornik dokumentov* (Moscow: 1976).

13. Golikova, *Politicheskie protsessy*, 41, quoting an eighteenth-century Russian miscellany.

14. J. Cracraft, *The Church Reform of Peter the Great* (Stanford: 1971), 76–78.

15. Wortman, "Court Procedure," 304.

16. A. G. Man'kov, "Proekt Ulozheniia Rossiiskogo Gosudarstva 1720–1725 gg.," in S. L. Peshtich et al., eds., *Problemy istorii feodal'noi Rossii: Sbornik statei k 60-letiiu prof. V. V. Mavrodina* (Leningrad: 1971), 159–82.

17. The basic work is still V. I. Veretennikov, *Istoriia Tainoi Kantseliarii Petrovskago vremeni* (Kharkov: 1910); but see also J. L. H. Keep, "The Secret Chancellery, the Guards and the Dynastic Crisis of 1740–1741," *Forschungen zur osteuropäischen Geschichte* 25 (1978), 169–93, and works cited in note 7.

18. N. Ustrialov, *Istoriia tsarstvovaniia Petra Velikago*, 5 vols. (St. Petersburg: 1858–63), vol. 6; M. P. Pogodin, ed., "Tsarevich Aleksei Petrovich po svidetel'stvam vnov' otkrytym," *Chteniia v imp. obshchestve istorii i drevnostei rossiiskikh pri Moskovskom universitete*, 3 (1861), 1–374; R. Wittram, *Peter I, Czar und Kaiser: Zur Geschichte Peters des Grossen in seiner Zeit*, 2 vols. (Göttingen: 1964), 2, 346–405; A. Besançon, *Le Tsarévitch immolé* (Paris: 1967); O. F. Kozlov, "Delo Tsarevicha Alekseia," *Voprosy istorii* no. 9 (1969), 86–92.

19. J. Cracraft, "Some Dreams of Peter the Great: A Biographical Note," *Canadian-American Slavic Studies* 8, no. 2 (Summer 1974), 173–97 (especially 184–87).

20. Cracraft, *Church Reform*, 238–40.

21. Ibid., 240–42.

22. For which see V. I. Lebedev, *Bulavinskoe vosstanie 1707–1708* (Moscow: 1934); E. P. Pod"iapol'skaia, *Vosstanie Bulavina 1707–1709* (Moscow: 1962); and P. Avrich, *Russian Rebels 1600–1800* (New York: 1972), 131–77.

23. V. A. Petrov, "K voprosu o roli dukhovenstva v bor'be s antifeodal'nymi vosstaniiami (o nerazyskannom ukaze 1708 g.)," *Istoricheskii arkhiv*, 4 (1955), 196–200.

CATHERINE THE GREAT AND THE FINE ARTS

Allen McConnell

Catherine II is not generally appreciated in Western literature as a patroness of the fine arts, and in Soviet historiography the great flowering of the arts in her reign is attributed to Russian society alone, with the sovereign a mere bystander. The support of the arts of her fellow enlightened despot Frederick the Great was thoroughly treated in a monograph by Paul Seidel[1] two generations ago, but there is no comparable work in any tongue on Catherine, though her contribution was greater. A few years ago a scholarly collective work appeared, *The Courts of Europe: Politics, Patronage and Royalty, 1400–1800*, edited by Arthur Geoffrey Dickens. A dozen sovereigns are treated, and Russia's Peter the Great is included, although the editor concedes that this tsar's court was "in its harsh pragmatism almost deserving to be called a non-court."[2] Yet Catherine II has no chapter, though she ruled from 1762 to 1796, was the last major sovereign within the four centuries surveyed, and was the last and not the least of Europe's great royal patrons. Isabel de Madariaga's superb work, *Russia in the Age of Catherine the Great*, devotes but 1 of 588 pages to the fine arts. Even when Catherine is studied by an art historian, her support of the arts is often treated summarily or condescendingly. One recent scholar has written that "the contribution of her personal taste and intellect to the culture of the Russian Enlightenment was somewhat equivocal and ultimately disappointing."[3]

On the other hand Louis Réau wrote in a slim volume in 1912 that the works of art and architecture commissioned and collected by Catherine constitute "the most remarkable artistic achievement of any eighteenth-century sovereign."[4] Yet even Monsieur Réau did not credit her with taste, intelligence, or any motive beyond the crassly political:

> Catherine the Great is no less utilitarian than Peter the Great: even in her wildest extravagances she remained a shrewd calculator. In her essentially

practical mind art was not separate from politics. Patronage is for her a means of government. She finds in it not only gratification of *amour propre*, but also an admirable instrument of propaganda in favor of Russia. . . .

In his view Catherine, like her model Peter I, did not regard the fine arts as a source of pleasure or enlightenment.[5] And Alexander Radishchev, her harshest critic and one-time protégé, scorned her support of art as not only political but also tasteless: "In the erection of magnificent buildings, the waste was often accompanied by a misunderstanding of true art. I saw that their internal and external arrangements lacked even the slightest particle of taste."[6]

Both the angry Radishchev and the laudatory Réau—however much they differ on the value of her achievement—agree on her purely political motivation. But was the fostering of the fine arts in her reign inseparable from politics? Did she have no other motives? There were also, I suggest, her personal enjoyment of beauty and her didactic Enlightenment faith that the arts can refine and energize a people. As the *Encyclopédie*, which she had offered in the first weeks of her reign to publish, had put it:

> Every reasonable man knows that the arts and sciences are the leading reformers of the human race. The more a people cultivates them, the more its natural harshness is softened, laziness and idleness are destroyed, bad inclinations are removed; on the contrary the mind becomes clear, the civil order is established and commerce flourishes, giving pleasure and riches to the human race.[7]

No one today, with the example of Grofaz (Hitler) with his love of architecture and Beethoven in mind, can believe that the arts have such a civilizing effect. But Catherine, in so many matters the realist, fully shared the *Encyclopédie*'s naive and optimistic view. She believed that through education, the use of reason, and enlightenment she could create a "new race of men" in Russia.[8] In her early days of rule she believed education's grand object was nothing less than "the making of the ideal man and the perfect citizen."[9] Decades later Chekalevskii, conference secretary of the Academy of Fine Arts, wrote that this school was to stimulate "love of virtue" (mainly civic virtue) and "such conduct as is not found in any other state, to prepare artists to fix in their young hearts good morals and an inclination to the good . . . the real aim of the fine arts."[10]

Catherine had received no education in the fine arts from her tutors, family, or avid reading. Yet once on the throne she took vigorous practical steps to place the teaching of the fine arts on a sound footing by setting up new statutes for the Academy of Fine Arts established by Elizabeth in

1757 and ultimately housing it in one of the most impressive of the neoclassical buildings she had erected, making it the largest such academy in
Europe.

Count Ivan Shuvalov became the head of the academy two years after
he had set up the first Russian university, in Moscow. One of the best
educated Russians of his day; fluent in French, German, and Italian; a
friend of Helvétius; he had urged in somber terms before the Senate the
need for the academy. "Here we have almost no art, for there is not one
skilled national artist" (surely an exaggeration, but he identified a real
problem). He attributed the dearth of artists to the lack of knowledge of
foreign languages and of "the sciences necessary for the artist."[11] The enthusiastic hopes of the time were expressed by a French artist called to
Russia to instruct the Russians. He compared his and other Frenchmen's
role in Russia to that of the ancient Greeks in Rome or to Italians in
France after Leo X.[12]

Unfortunately Catherine obliged the young Shuvalov, whom Voltaire
had called the "Peter the Great of the arts," to retire and travel abroad.
He was replaced in March 1763 by Ivan Betskoi, the natural son of Field
Marshal Ivan Trubetskoi and a much less able figure, but one who had
Catherine's complete confidence for reasons still not satisfactorily explained. Probably his privileged access to Catherine derived from his
early contacts with philosophes (none of whom recalled him), his experience as an intendant of construction (implying supervision not only of the
construction of palaces and their gardens, but also of all major construction throughout the empire and all brick and glass factories), his complete
devotion to enlightenment ideals, and his faith in the power of education.
He was not gifted, but his devotion to education can be seen in his reform
of the Cadet Corps to make future officers "knowledgeable citizens" with
a broad education. His "General Plan for the Education of Young People
of both Sexes"[13] emphasized free and universal education to create a "new
kind of person," liberated by upbringing in a boarding school (from the
age of five to twenty-one) from his family and from a corrupt, backward
society. Education was to be by moral persuasion, not by the old methods
of corporal punishment.[14]

The Academy of Fine Arts reflected these lofty concerns in its statutes
and policies. Some students were enrolled at age five or six; others, with
some training elsewhere, started later. Except for serfs, students were accepted from all social classes. In one early class, of thirteen students in
architecture, thirteen in painting, and seven in sculpture, there were sons
of a sergeant, a soldier, a priest, a scribe, a stoker, a peasant, and a merchant.[15] One contemporary found the less affluent always preferred.[16] It
was *la carrière ouverte aux talents* there. The best students were destined to

go abroad for further education, though not in the numbers originally hoped. Between 1760 and 1789 over forty Russians studied in the most desired places, the Académie des Beaux Arts and the ateliers of Paris.[17]

The program was lengthy and demanding; discipline was severe. Of 850 students admitted in the course of twenty-seven years, only 418— less than half—finished the program.[18] Parents had to promise in writing not to ask for their children's return unless they were ill or failing.[19] Furthermore, no student even had the right to have visits from his parents.[20] Lest students see anything "base" (*podlyi*) they were not allowed to look at peasants or even skilled workmen.[21] To isolate them further, the Academy had its own library, apothecary, hospital, and church.[22] (It also had its own printing press, a privilege Catherine would later extend to the individual citizen in 1783, when by imperial edict anyone was free to open a press anywhere without special permission.[23]) To add to these hardships, corporal punishments—though prohibited by the statutes—were frequent: "they take place everywhere."[24]

Not surprisingly, there were many signs of poor student morale. There were reports of "great disorder" in students' rooms that Betskoi's biographer attributed to the "weak development of feelings of honor and duty" among the students. More likely causes were the rigid rules and poverty. Some were "barefoot and therefore do not go to class."[25] One infers a callous neglect of the youths' basic needs. Some students were unruly and placed under guard for drunkenness, brawling, theft, counterfeiting keys and passports.[26] The discipline was harsh for faculty as well. An instructor, Chemesov, one of the best Russian engravers of the eighteenth century, was dismissed because he sent a student to buy stamps from a shop on the first floor of the Academy building.[27] Little wonder that faculty were hard to find and retain. As late as 1775, Betskoi complained in a letter to the empress that "the present teachers were chosen by lot from over forty people wishing to take their places; it was scarcely possible to choose four acknowledged as capable . . . not one of them has shown real ability; not one is attaining the present goal of the institution; not one has understood its spirit; they think only of personal affairs . . . ." He hoped to replace them with "honest foreigners."[28]

The most appalling failure with regard to the Academy's provisions for its students may be seen in Betskoi's coldly factual, unapologetic report to the institution's governing council. During the years 1774–83, of the 380 students in the educational division (the lower division that prepared students for the advanced courses), 73 died. The deaths (and official indifference to them) probably resulted from the period's strange notions of hygiene as seen in an Academy of Sciences publication of 1768, which insisted that "From six to seven years [of age] one should not dress them warmly for in this way little by little from earliest years they learn to bear extreme cold."[29] We do not know of Catherine's reaction to this or indeed whether she knew of it, but she shared these Spartan ideas—no doubt in a more reasonable form—and saw to it that her grandsons slept on hard mattresses with few blankets and open windows.

We do know of Catherine's exasperation at Betskoi's management of the Academy of Fine Arts, for she thought he was spending too much. She disapproved of his requests for more money.[30] But the institution was chronically underfunded and had to rely on philanthropists to reduce the deficits.[31] Scholars differ on who bears the greater responsibility for the problems—Betskoi with his mismanagement or Catherine with her parsimony.[32] But the ultimate blame must fall on the empress, who inexplicably kept Betskoi on for years, during the last ten of which he was blind. As she wrote to Grimm on the ninety-three-year-old Betskoi's death, for the last seven years "he had reverted to infancy and sometimes into dementia."[33] She expressed neither gratitude nor sorrow upon the demise of a faithful and zealous if limited servant. The Soviet historian Iaremich appraised the Academy's long period under Betskoi as a "lethargic sleep" from which it was freed only at the end of the century. For twenty-five years Betskoi had employed professors without experience or talent.[34] During this time a high price was paid in human suffering and frustrations, in aborted careers, lost lives, and rubles (over the period 1765–82, 685,000 rubles was spent on the construction of the building, which was mainly completed in 1772).[35] At Betskoi's death in 1795 work was still unfinished on the church's interior, five stairways, and grand staircase.

Still, on balance the venture had not been a long sleep but a stunning success. Among the teachers and students, along with incompetents, were the leading Russian architects, painters, engravers, and sculptors of the generation, and the tradition held in the next century. The edifice itself was called by a French visitor in 1792 "the handsomest in Petersburg," and among all of Catherine's many institutions," none deserves more than this the admiration of travelers and the gratitude of her people."[36]

If we turn from this seedbed of talents to works of art themselves, we may find in a few examples from the three main fine arts further clues to Catherine's attitude to the fine arts. What follows will not be a survey of the fine arts in her reign, but a consideration of selected topics that bear on our subject.

Architecture is traditionally the preferred way for a ruler to display his dynasty's power and grandeur, its stability and legitimacy. But Catherine II did not need to launch a great building campaign for these purposes, for her predecessors had already built the great imperial residences of the northern capital.[37] The Winter Palace in St. Petersburg was already, in its fourth version, substantially what it is now in its sixth—one of the most grandiose of all the European imitations of Versailles. Elizabeth had spent 1.5 million rubles on it between 1755 and 1759, while fighting a major war against Frederick the Great.[38] Apple-green and white, richly decorated with its white columns in two tiers, and having more than 150 statues along the roofline, it remains the most impressive building in Leningrad.

Catherine did not attempt another grand residence in the capital,[39] although she added the Pavillon de l'Hermitage to the Winter Palace, for she wished, in addition to the royal apartments, a private retreat. It was in these rooms that she received distinguished guests such as Diderot and Grimm on their visits to St. Petersburg. Here she had her library—some thirty-eight thousand volumes—replete with the works of the philosophes.[40]

The first Hermitage building was designed in 1764 by the French architect Vallin de la Mothe, the first professor of architecture at the Academy of Fine Arts and also its main architect. The addition was built in five years, but six years later Catherine needed more room for her growing art collection. Iurii Veldten, a Russianized German, the son of Peter I's chief kitchen steward, was chosen for the task. A French traveler, Fortia de Piles, who had visited it in 1790–92, estimated that the art collection included at that time more than twenty-four hundred paintings.[41]

A third building was added to these in 1780, the Hermitage theatre, designed by an Italian, Quarenghi, who considered it his finest achievement. Its semicircular auditorium had seats for only two hundred spectators, but de Piles noted that often it housed performances for a mere dozen spectators.[42] Comedies written by the sovereign herself—gentle, didactic satires without personal targets—were performed in this elegant theatre.

These additions to the Winter Palace were strung out in a line along the Neva, making an impressive continuous neoclassical facade. The effect of order and grace was enhanced by the granite facings with which Veldten clad the quays and canals in Catherine's reign. These buildings and a half-dozen others (including the Academy of Fine Arts, across the Neva) were all in the neoclassical style and showed that Catherine was following the objective she had set in her public competition of 1763 for the rational planning of St. Petersburg—to give the city "such magnificence as befits the capital of a far-flung state."[43]

But in her personal requirements, as distinct from matters of state,

Catherine had no craving for magnificence. Fortia de Piles described her personal quarters in the last years of her reign:

> The Empress's apartments are quite simple: before the audience-chamber is a small glass cabinet, where the crown and diamonds of S. J. are kept; the audience-chamber is very simple: the throne beside the door is of crimson velvet; then comes a wooded and gilded salon, with two ridiculously small chimneys.[44]

The architecture of her buildings, even the largest, reflected a distaste for the elaborate. She dismissed Count Ivan Shuvalov's palace as looking "like cuffs of Alençon lace."[45] Nor did she seek to overwhelm by size. When the French architect Bourgeois de Tesnière presented a plan that was probably the genesis of Starov's Tauride palace Catherine found it too grandiose.[46] Similarly, in refusing a request from Betskoi's commission for construction for over sixty thousand rubles to improve two Moscow palaces, she wrote, "Since I go to Moscow not for magnificence but for the government's business, there is not the least necessity for pomp for me."[47]

Of course, Catherine loved to build. As she wrote to Grimm in 1779, "the rage to build here is stronger than ever . . . building is a devilish thing; it devours money, and the more one builds, the more one wishes to; it is a sickness, like drinking. . . ."[48] But she controlled this intoxication. She commissioned the Russian architect Starov, an Academy alumnus, to work out plans in 1772 to form a palace square with a monumental semicircle of colonnades and a high pavilion opposite the Winter Palace, but she later abandoned the idea.

Catherine had incredibly grandiose plans for the older capital, Moscow, despite her feeling that it was "the seat of sloth," where nobles "live in idleness and luxury and become effeminate."[49] The great art historian Igor Grabar contended that "from the very first day on the throne" she intended to build a "new court" there.[50] After two architects' work failed to satisfy her she had Bazhenov, another Academy graduate, draw up plans for enclosing the southern part of the Kremlin with a gigantic triangular palace surrounded with classical columns. It would have meant tearing down a great part of the southern Kremlin walls, as well as the Nikolskii gates. The main façade would face the Moscow River, whose embankment would be clad with granite. In a Western scholar's opinion this façade, with its great upper story colonnade, would have been comparable only to Diocletian's palace. Grabar called it "one of the greatest concepts in world architecture."[51] Part of the foundation was laid out in 1773, but in 1775 Catherine ordered the work stopped. Scholars differ as to why. Grabar in his prerevolutionary history simply noted that Catherine "cooled" to the idea.[52]

Soviet researchers find political reasons. One pointed to the potential risks of the great oval central square during the popular celebration of triumphs:

> Bazhenov's palace would not be an imperial palace in the strict sense of the word but a social edifice. . . . The huge scale, the breadth, the openness and the tie with the city, the country, and the people—all this would be too bold, too alien to the whole ideology of absolutism.[53]

But it is not certain that this would have been only a "social edifice" or that Catherine would have been bothered if it had been. The "openness and tie with the city" could hardly be "too bold, too alien" to absolutism, for the St. Petersburg palaces were as open as could be; the northern capital had no walls except for the fortress built in 1703. And surely absolutism historically had not been uncomfortable with edifices of "huge scale" but delighted in them as symbols of wealth, power, and stability, as witness Versailles, Schönbrunn, Caserta, the Winter Palace, and Peterhof. Grabar much later wrote that it was abandoned allegedly because of the instability of the buttresses of the Kremlin hill, but the real reasons were the Moscow revolt of 1771 and the Pugachev peasant wars, 1773–75. "Like all Catherine's undertakings of this time, the widely advertised construction of the Kremlin palace served as a screen for measures to strengthen autocracy and serfdom. As soon as the aim was achieved, she quickly quit the construction."[54] He cited no evidence for these suppositions, and it is unlikely that she paraded plans for what she intended to abandon. Her attitude remains a puzzle, an anomaly.

She showed the same distaste mentioned earlier for the grandiose in rejecting Clerisseau's plans for a *maison antique* at Tsarskoe Selo. She had wished a modest building with baths, atrium, triclinium , and Pompeian frescoes to indulge her love of Roman antiquity. But the French architect thought a Russian empress must have something gigantic, on the scale of Diocletian's palace and the baths of Caracalla.[55] Catherine was furious at being so misunderstood, but five years later she asked through Grimm that Clerisseau plan a triumphal gate in St. Petersburg. The architect again made his plan too grandiose for her taste.

After ordering the gigantic work on the Kremlin palace stopped, she commissioned Bazhenov to design a palace at Tsaritsyno in neo-Gothic style, but after his death in 1785 she found it like a catafalque, and the half-finished work was abandoned. Perhaps the work symbolized the old Moscow she hoped to supersede. This and Bazhenov's other projects may have been abandoned because of intrigues against the architect. Metropolitan Evgenii wrote of Betskoi's hostility to him because of his "independence of character."[56] Or they may have been considered not worth the cost, especially in the case of the proposed Kremlin palace. Fortia de Piles, who had seen the model, observed that Bazhenov had estimated the cost at 20 million rubles, but "it would have cost at least three times that much."[57] Grabar thought it would have cost over one hundred million rubles.[58] It would have extended for two miles. That would have been more like Hitler's megalomaniac future capital of a world empire than Catherine's second capital.

In fact the funds were available, for Catherine had ample revenues. But she spent them in a prudent way (except for bijouterie and gifts to favorites). Already in 1766 she boasted to one of her magnates of how she had reduced inflated accounts: "their accounts are already cut in half: I think that in giving them less money you will make them cut it yet again by half. . . . they do for less money all that they would have done with the sums which they were asking."[59] Despite her reputation for extravagance (merited with regard to her favorites) and her complaints of how building is intoxicating and "devours money," she used little of her enormous imperial revenues for construction.

Her expenditures for architecture are difficult to estimate. P. N. Maikov has cited with justified skepticism a German historian's estimate that they reached several million rubles per year.[60] This figure is high, for in the detailed analysis given by N. D. Chechulin government expenditures on construction at their peak, in 1795, only reached 484,000 rubles, which was almost twice the next costliest year, 1794. Other expenses for 1795 included 7,746,000 for the court (about 11 percent of all expenditures), 21,684,000 for the army, and 761,000 for schools. The outlays for construction were only 4.3 percent of the budget.[61] And these construction figures are for building throughout the empire.

Catherine's fiscal prudence in general may be seen from the fact that in her entire reign (1762–96) she spent 1,615,000,000 rubles while revenues were 1,415,000,000 rubles, resulting in a deficit of only about 200,000,000 rubles, which was made up by loans and the use of assignats.[62] Such a small deficit in comparison with total revenues and expenditures would be enviable in any Western nation today. A French historian has noted that at the end of the eighteenth century Russia was practically free of debts, one of the most remarkable financial performances in Europe, in great contrast to the record of Louis XV and Louis XVI.[63] One notes Catherine's pride in her fiscal self-restraint in a letter of 1773 to Falconet, the French sculptor she commissioned to make a monument to Peter the Great:

You will not believe me perhaps if I told you that after five years of war, I have no need to create ways to acquire money; however, that is true. I have refused forty million which they offered me four months ago.[64]

Frederick the Great, the other great enlightened despot of the age and self-styled "king of beggars" who was as famous for his parsimony as she for her profligacy—spent 10,573,000 thalers for buildings in 1768, three-quarters of his revenues for the year![65] Catherine never spent a remotely comparable portion of her revenues on buildings. Her patronage of the most public and costly of the fine arts was moderate in scale, discerning in judgment, and consistent in style.

In sculpture, Catherine did not receive such an impressive heritage from her predecessors as she had in architecture. Nor did she give many commissions to Russian sculptors, in contrast to the many she gave to her pleiad of Russian architects. The best Russian sculptor of her reign, Fedor Shubin, had to appeal to his alma mater for support because he could find no work. For reasons of space I shall treat only one sculptor, who produced the most impressive art work of her reign—Étienne Falconet's equestrian statue of Peter the Great. Falconet is the artist with whom she had the most extended contacts, and these reveal much of Catherine's attitude toward the fine arts.

Catherine was not satisfied with Rastrelli's equestrian statue of Peter, already finished in Elizabeth's reign. After eliminating many sculptors she boldly chose, on the recommendation of the philosophe Denis Diderot, Falconet, known at the time for his statues for several chapels in Paris, his erotic statues for boudoirs, and his directorship of the Sèvres porcelain factory.[66] He arrived in Russia in 1766 and left in 1778, four years before his statue was finished. His pupil, Mlle. Marie-Anne Callot, made the bronze horseman's head. The work was beset with frustrations typical of Russia, particularly the interference of Betskoi. The hiring, pay, and dismissal of craftsmen; the noisy erection of a building next to Falconet's studio (stopped at last only by Catherine's intervention); Betskoi's repeated heavy-handed but unsuccessful pressures for a change in design—all these factors made Falconet irritable and bitter.

For some time Catherine was very attentive and reassuring. Her summons was exquisitely tactful: "Monsieur Falconet, if this does not interrupt any of your pursuits, I pray you to call on me this morning. . . ."[67] She approved his design, with the rider's horse trampling a serpent (the only allegorical object in the work), and she allowed him the choice of assistants and location. She gently urged him to do the casting himself but she used no greater pressure than flattery. When he failed to receive comments from the public on his unveiled model she soothed him,[68] and when he complained of an opera singer, Coltellini, who had said he was stupid, unable to do the statue's head, and without the empress's confidence, she replied that Coltellini was mistaken and had not even seen Falconet's work. "I advise you to ignore all this gossip. . . . Make an armistice with your enemies as I with the sultan: follow my example."[69] She apologized when she was a few days late replying to a letter.

> Monsieur, do not conclude because I have not replied to you for three days that I have become proud or lazy; since the battle of Kagoul [1770] I have had a vile migraine which has not permitted me to do so.[70]

At times she may have been too attentive, as Falconet gaily complained: "I would never have believed Your Majesty so hard to please regarding sculpture. You do not leave my atelier at all and more than twenty times, Madame, you make me begin things again . . . ."[71] She immediately reassured him: "Do not pause at what I am saying, for I may speak poorly; go your way."[72] And again: "The merest schoolboy knows more than I about your art."[73]

But with the passing years Falconet's complaints tired his august patroness. In a letter to Grimm, her favorite correspondent, she referred to "Falconet le difficile."[74] She had originally prized Falconet both as an artist and as an adviser on all the arts, but he had often sought to intercede with her on behalf of mistreated artists, in particular a talented Russian, Losenko, whom a contemporary German traveler had called "the Lomonosov of painting."[75] Falconet urged that Losenko, the first Russian to paint Russian historical themes, be spared the administrative work that exhausted his energies:

> Pestered, fatigued, tormented, overwhelmed by a thousand academic trifles which have never concerned a professor in any academy in the world, Losenko cannot make a brush-stroke. He is the first capable painter in the nation; one is unconscious of this, one sacrifices him. One will only have mediocre artists so long as they are not better treated.[76]

Catherine, who had once asked Losenko whether she might see his work in progress (provided this would not disturb him),[77] replied at once that she was "very vexed" that Losenko was being pestered and would say that she needed him for her gallery, "and then he will very well have to be ceded to me."[78] This suggests that she felt she had to overcome bureaucratic resistance, no doubt the stubborn Betskoi's. But Falconet's intercession was fruitless. Three years later Losenko died destitute at age thirty-six, made dissolute through despair.

Catherine cooled toward Falconet. She acquired a new art adviser and agent who never made inconvenient pleas and never complained of Betskoi—Baron Melchior Grimm in Paris, with whom she was in constant correspondence from 1774 until her death in 1796. Falconet left St. Petersburg in 1778 without even taking leave of Catherine.[79] On learning of Falconet's stroke in that year she coldly wrote to Grimm that if Falconet were dead, Grimm should try to recover her portrait.[80]

If we turn from Catherine's callous treatment of Falconet to his work for her, we find that he projected a statue that he described as Catherine's giving laws to her empire to make her people happy (Catherina legislatrix was her favorite image for her portraits). The statue's idea had been Diderot's. A second sketch of a monument to Catherine, suggested by the ubiquitous and tasteless Betskoi, had two figures—Catherine's sustaining a tottering Russia. The Senate had already discussed a series of monuments glorifying her reign; its deliberations began the day after her coup d'état.[81] But within months she opposed the Senate's plan for a statue of her and instead called for one of Peter I (she later wrote that as for a statue of her, "it will not exist while I am alive").[82]

Designs proposed by senators and others were overly complicated and highly allegorical. Fortunately Falconet had his own plan. He had in mind something new, and while still in Paris he showed his sketch to Diderot—the hero on his horse, leaping across a symbolic crag.[83] In the completed statue Peter is shown in civilian dress, calmly reining in his rearing charger. Peter faces the Neva with his right arm outstretched, pointing to the city he had created by his indomitable will. The statue was mounted upon an enormous block of granite, brought from Finland by windlasses and rollers and then by boat, taking two years to reach the St. Petersburg quay.[84] The total cost, including the moving of the huge rock, was 424,610 rubles.[85]

Catherine wrote to Grimm of the public's and her reaction to the statue's unveiling in 1782: " . . . when I looked about me, I saw everyone with tears in their eyes. . . ." The statue's "air of contentment . . . encouraged me to try to do more in the future, if I can."[86] Not a word on the sculptor who had created the masterpiece and who was not invited to the ceremony.

Catherine's patronage of painting, especially the collecting of masterpieces, was one of her most distinguished contributions to the fine arts in Russia. Armed with the advice of Diderot, Falconet, and Grimm in Paris, and of Mengs and Reiffenstein in Rome, Catherine set about making her Hermitage a world-renowned depository of great works of art. One modern critic has suggested that spite may have been the "mainspring of Catherine's love of art collecting."[87] She may be charged with excessive ambition, vanity, falsity, dalliances, occasional callousness—but never spite. She loved these works and did not open them to the public. One could visit the Hermitage only when she was not in St. Petersburg, unless one was ready to go to a lot of trouble. Fortia de Piles explained:

> When she is in Petersburg, it is very difficult, not to say impossible, to gain entrance, because the sovereign comes at all moments of the day, so the prohibition on entry is continuous.[88]

An exception was made for students at the Academy of Fine Arts, who had permission to enter the Hermitage and make copies of the paintings.[89]

By contrast Maria Theresa, Catherine's contemporary and Empress of Austria, opened the Habsburg collection, especially rich in great Italian masters, to the public in the Belvedere. Not only students but also the general public was admitted free of charge—if their shoes were clean. With typical neoclassical didacticism, she wished the rooms of the palace to be used so that the gallery should "become 'a visible history of art,' providing lasting instruction rather than ephemeral pleasure."[90]

Within a year after her accession Catherine acquired her first great collection, that of the Berlin merchant Gotzkowsky. It was destined for Frederick the Great, who could not keep it because of the debts following the Seven Years' War.[91] Thereafter her pace did not slacken. In 1768 she bought from the Austrian minister, Count Cobenzl, paintings and drawings from the Gaignat collection; in 1769 the collection of Count Brühl, minister of Saxony and the King of Poland; in 1771 the collection of Crozat, Baron de Thiers, outbidding Horace Walpole. Seven years later Walpole had to sell the paintings of Houghton Hall in Norfolk to meet debts and she bought them. In 1781 she acquired the Count Baudouin collection. And still Catherine was enjoying it all in solitary glory: "only the mice and I can admire it all."[92] She wrote to Grimm in 1790 of her thirty-eight thousand books, ten thousand drawings, her pictures and the way the promenade of three thousand steps from her chamber through the Hermitage and back "past quantities of things I love" kept her in good health through the winter.[93]

She was not always pleased with the work of her agents, for she had her own views on art, however often she disclaimed any capacity to judge paintings. Even "the divine" Reiffenstein could blunder. Rejoicing at receiving copies of Raphael's Loges (for which a special gallery was built in the Hermitage) and some works of Mengs, she complained that "all the rest are wretched daubs. . . . Oh, damn! It is incredible how the divine one let himself be deceived this time."[94] Sometimes she refused to buy even a good work whose price she considered exorbitant.[95]

Catherine, like Frederick II, underestimated home talent and did less than she could have done to foster it. We have seen the tragic case of Losenko. And Levitskii, perhaps the most talented native-born painter of her time, received for his best portraits less than a tenth of what the Austrian portraitist Johann Baptist Lampi (in Russia 1791–97) was paid.[96] Only Losenko's historical portrait *Vladimir and Rogneda* and a few landscapes by Ivanov and Shchedrin were placed among the thousands of works in the Hermitage.[97] Falconet had exhorted Betskoi in 1771 that there was no Russian, even Her Majesty, more persuaded than he, Falconet, that "it is better to have the cabbages of one's garden in the pot than to go looking for them elsewhere."[98] But neither Betskoi nor the empress heeded. Indeed, this unsolicited advice may have added to her irritation with Falconet. She put more effort into collecting foreign masterpieces than encouraging native ones. But she did not neglect Russian painters altogether.

At the Academy of Fine Arts she fostered the students' interest in Russian history. She loved to read ancient documents, wrote *Zapiski o russkoi istorii* and published them regularly in *Sobesednik*, and wrote a historical drama about Prince Oleg.[99] Her aim was to cultivate Russian national pride and to demonstrate that Russia, except for the interruption of the Time of Troubles, was a European state. She welcomed a course at the Academy on historical painting (along with courses on landscapes, portraits, and later, domestic scenes and battles), and as early as 1766 she encouraged paintings on Russian historical narrative themes for the students' annual competitions.[100] These themes alternated with others, however, and judging by extant paintings, more chose mythological, classical, or biblical subjects than Russian history. Catherine did not press the matter.

She did not offer material support for Russian history painters, and it was only in portrait painting that Russian artists reached distinction, for here there was a ready market. The class that counted for Catherine was the nobility, particularly the *generalitet*, and they as well as the wealthier merchants turned to Russian painters for their portraits. The most successful portraitist, Levitskii, had a profound effect. He "invented the character of St. Petersburg society for some time to come, much as Van Dyck earlier in England had created an image of an aristocracy which the members were from that time onwards obliged to emulate."[101] Such a Europeanized elite, looking to the West, seeking distinction through service to the Westernizing monarch and wishing to preserve for posterity (and guests and visitors) an image of self-respect, *gravitas*, and civic virtue was an impressive measure of Catherine's success in educating her people—or more precisely the top half percent or so who constituted the nobility.

There were Russian painters who portrayed the peasants, usually in unreal happiness or affluence. But I. A. Ermenev's watercolors of the unfortunates, such as *The Destitute* and *The Blind Singers*, are realistic and harrowing. The son of a court groom, he entered the Academy of Fine Arts in 1761 and graduated in 1767 as a historical painter. He had received a second gold medal for a work on Prince Oleg's treaty with the Byzantine emperors. He left, however, with the low certificate of fourth degree with the notation "unworthy conduct" though "outstanding in talent." He was not permitted to travel abroad, but managed to, and Falconet took him under his protection.[102] He made a watercolor of the taking of the Bastille with the inscription "Sic virtus omnia obstacula vincit [Thus virtue overcomes all obstacles]."[103] Such an appeal to virtue—and civic virtue at that—was far from what Catherine had had in mind when she prescribed that the education of artists lead to virtue! Ermenev returned to St. Petersburg in 1790 and came to no harm. Little is known of him.

Of all the fine arts in Catherine's reign, Ermenev's work alone is implicitly critical of the northern Semiramis' society. And perhaps only so for modern sensibility, for his works in his time may have seemed poignant portrayals of an unchangeable reality, not denunciations of injustice. In belles lettres, which Catherine followed attentively, Radishchev's *Journey from St. Petersburg to Moscow* made an explicit, impassioned, and unmistakable call for drastic reform in all aspects of Russian life and branded the sovereign a hypocrite. In the fine arts, there was no such challenge to Catherine's image and system. There were no "repentant nobility" among the mainly soldiers', peasants', and *raznochintsy's* sons who constituted the artists, architects, and sculptors. They were upwardly mobile, suffering none of the alienation that Marc Raeff's works have revealed in the eighteenth-century intelligentsia of noble origin. The fine arts all contributed to Catherine's practical goals—the celebration of her dynamic Europeanizing monarchy and society. (They did not contribute to her utopian goals; no human institution could.) We may agree that Catherine's personal contribution to the culture of the Russian Enlightenment in the fields of literature, journalism, history, polemic, and drama was "equivocal and ultimately disappointing."[104] But in the fine arts, for all her mistakes, her contribution was in the final analysis wise, consistent, and impressive. Despite all the shortcomings noted—the incompetent president of the Academy of Fine Arts for almost her entire reign, the chronic underfunding, the rigid discipline and utopian pedagogic aims of the academy, the underestimation of native talents, the shabby treatment of distinguished artists—the academy became the center of Russia's artistic life for a century.[105] And she inspired in Russian society enthusiastic support for the arts as a matter of noblesse oblige. Magnates attended academy lectures and assemblies, served on its councils, and vied to become honorary members and donors.[106] In architecture she made some false starts and for a dozen years planned what would have been a great blunder—the megalomaniac Kremlin palace. But one modern scholar has called Leningrad "probably the most perfect classical city since ancient Rome,"[107] and much of that classical heritage was due to Catherine. Another notes that "the leading role played by Russia in the production of early neoclassical architecture is almost entirely due to Catherine II. Under her aegis St. Petersburg was transformed into an unparalleled museum of neoclassical building. . . ."[108] In sculpture the Bronze Horseman was a similar triumphant monument. (No one in her day could have foreseen that Russia's greatest poet would one day make it an evocative symbol of the ambiguities of power.) Its brilliantly laconic inscription summarized her legitimacy, her program, and her pride: "To Peter the First from Catherine the Second."

Yet it would be wrong to assume that Catherine cared only for symbols reinforcing power, stability, and prestige. In her later portraits, one can notice her concern for truth as well. True, most portraits had glorified her or flattered her, beginning with Torelli's grand allegorical composition with Catherine as *Minerva, protectress of the arts*. But in her last year of life a portrait showed her as she was and tells of another side of her patronage of the arts. It was by a Ukrainian, Borovikovskii, whom she discovered painting a mural in Kremenchug when she passed through the town. The mural showed Peter I plowing and Catherine II following, sowing. On the spot she invited the young painter to study at the Academy of Fine Arts. In 1796 he painted her likeness with none of the usual accessories of royal portraits—no impressive backdrop of crown, scepter, orb, regal gown, or book of laws or classical column. True, there is a rostral column, but in the far distance. We see an elderly lady in an unflattering but comfortable green dress, walking her favorite greyhound in a park. No royal patron had ever been so depicted. Here, at least, the empress showed that a royal patroness of the arts could appreciate art's highest calling: to tell the truth.

Notes

ACKNOWLEDGMENTS: *I would like to thank Professors John D. Browning and Paul Fritz, chairmen of the McMaster University Association for Eighteenth Century Studies, for the invitation to present this paper in an informal, simpler form and to thank faculty and students for comments on it. I would also like to thank Dr. Leonard Tarassuk, formerly curator of the Hermitage Collection on Arms, and my colleague, Professor Andrew G. Whiteside, for their comments and criticisms.*

1. Paul Seidel, *Friedrich der Grosse und die Bildende Kunst* (Leipzig and Berlin: 1922).
2. Arthur Geoffrey Dickens (ed.), *The Courts of Europe: Politics, Patronage and Royalty 1400–1800* (London: 1977), 8.
3. Robin Milner-Gulland, "Petersburg Baroque," in R. Auty and D. Obolensky (eds.), *A Companion to Russian Studies: An Introduction to Russian Art and Architecture* (Cambridge, England: 1980), 87.
4. Louis Réau, *Catherine la Grande, inspiratrice et Mécène des arts* (Paris: 1912), 7.
5. Ibid., 7–8.
6. A. N. Radishchev, *A Journey from St. Petersburg to Moscow*, trans. by Leo Wiener, ed. Roderick P. Thaler (Cambridge, Mass.: 1957), 75.
7. P. N. Petrov, *Sbornik materialov dlia istorii Imperatorskoi St. Peterburgskoi Akademii Khudozhestv za sto let ego sushchestvovaniia* (St. Petersburg: 1864–66), 1, 774.
8. Pavel N. Miliukov, "Educational Reforms," in Marc Raeff (ed.), *Catherine the Great: A Profile* (New York: 1972), 94–95.
9. Isabel de Madariaga, *Russia in the Age of Catherine the Great* (New Haven and London: 1981), 490.
10. Peter Petrovich Chekalevskii, *Razsuzhdenie o svobodynkh khudozhestvakh, s opisaniem nekotorykh proizvedenii rossiiskikh khudozhestv* (St. Petersburg: 1792), 38.
11. I. E. Grabar' (ed.), *Istoriia russkago iskusstva, 3: Peterburgskaia arkhitektura v XVIII i XIX veke* (Moscow: n.d., 1912?), 270–72.
12. "Discours sur le Progrès des Beaux Arts en Russie" (n.p.: 1760), cited in S. P. Iaremich, "Osnovatel' Akademii Khudozhestv," *Russkaia Akademicheskaia Khudozhestvennaia Shkola v XVIII v.* (Moscow and Leningrad: 1934), 63, n. 3. Hereafter cited as *R. A. Kh. Sh.*
13. DE Madariaga, *Russia in the Age*, 491. For a good account of Betskoi's ideas and their impact on the Academy, see Iaremich, "Vliianie vospitatel'nykh idei na khudozhestvennuiu shkolu prezidentstva I. I. Betskogo" in *R. A. Kh. Sh.*, 65–95.
14. DE Madariaga, *Russia in the Age*, 492.
15. Iaremich, *R. A. Kh. Sh.*, 93, n. 85.
16. Fortia de Piles, *Voyage de deux Français dans le Nord de l'Europe . . . en 1790–92* (Paris: 1796), 3, 22.
17. L. Réau, "Les artistes russes à Paris en XVIIIe siècle," *Revue des Études slaves* 3 (1923), 286–98. See also, for Russian art students in Paris and Rome, N. N. Kovalenskaia, *Russkii Klassitsizm* (Moscow: 1964), 90–99.
18. I. G. Georgi, *Opisanie rossiisko-imperatorskago stolichnogo goroda Sankt-Peterburga i dostopamiatnostei v okrestnostiakh onogo* (St. Petersburg: 1794), 438.
19. DE Piles, *Voyage de deux Français*, 188–89.
20. N. N. Kovalenskaia, *Istoriia russkogo iskusstva v XVIII v.* (Moscow and Leningrad: 1940), 82.

21. Iaremich, *R. A. Kh. Sh.*, 73, 88, n.36; Kovalenskaia, *Istoriia*, 83. These works cite different archival documents but do not indicate how common this offense was.

22. P. M. Maikov, *Ivan Ivanovich Betskoi; opyt ego biografii* (St. Petersburg: 1904), 318.

23. K. A. Papmehl, *Freedom of Expression in Eighteenth-Century Russia* (The Hague: 1971), 91–92.

24. De Piles, *Voyage de deux Français*, 189.

25. Maikov, *Ivan Ivanovich Betskoi*, 333.

26. Iaremich, *R. A. Kh. Sh.*, 73, 88, n. 35. n. 38.

27. Ibid., 80.

28. Letter of May 1775 in *Russkaia Starina*, 2 (1886), cited in Iaremich, *R. A. Kh. Sh.*, 72.

29. Ibid., 72 and 88, n. 32. Iaremich cited the passage from *Kratkoe nastavlenie vybrannoe iz luchshikh avtorov s nekotorymi fizicheskimi primechaniiami o vospitanii detei. . . .*

30. Maikov, *Ivan Ivanovich Betskoi*, 86–89.

31. George H. Munro, "The Academy of Fine Arts," in Joseph L. Wieczynski (ed.), *Modern Encyclopedia of Russian and Soviet History* (Gulf Breeze, Fla.: 1976–), 1, 20.

32. Iaremich's "Khudozhestva v periode prezidentstva Betskago," *R. A. Kh. Sh.*, 99–206, consistently assails Betskoi. Maikov defends him as doing the best he could, given the constant underfunding.

33. *Pis'ma Imperatritsy Ekateriny II k Grimmu (1774–1796) izdannyia s poiasnitel' nymi primechaniiami Ia. Grota*, in *Sbornik Imperatorskago Russkago Istoricheskago Obshchestva*, 23 (1878), 644–45.

34. Iaremich, *R. A. Kh. Sh.*, 83. Iaremich gives numerous examples of Betskoi's pomposity, aloofness, autocracy, confusion, and callousness.

35. Maikov, *Ivan Ivanovich Betskoi*, 312, n. 5.

36. De Piles, *Voyage de deux Français*, 198–99.

37. The achievements of the 1740s and 1750s "have a grandeur unparalleled in the history of Russian architecture." Milner-Gulland, "Petersburg Baroque," 81.

38. Michael T. Florinsky, *Russia: A History and an Interpretation* (New York: 1953), 1, 489.

39. Catherine added a splendid palace named after her first grandson, Alexander, in Tsarskoe Selo, with a graceful park around it. She also added to the palace built by Elizabeth the Cameron Gallery (named for Catherine's Scottish architect) to display her favorite statuary—almost all busts of classical statesmen, philosophers, poets, and so on. For her son, Paul, she built a neoclassical palace and ensemble in Pavlovsk, three miles from Tsarskoe Selo.

40. *Pis'ma imperatritsy Ekateriny II*, 499.

41. De Piles, *Voyage de deux Français*, 22.

42. Ibid., 16.

43. V. N. Bernadskii, S. S. Volk, M. P. Viatkin et al. (eds.), *Ocherki istorii Leningrada*, 1 (Moscow and Leningrad: 1955), 327.

44. DE Piles, *Voyage de deux Français*, 14–15.
45. Denis Roche, "Frantsuzskoe vliianie na khudozhestvennuiu shkolu," *R. A. Kh. Sb.*, 40.
46. Ibid., 41.
47. Maikov, *Ivan Ivanovich Betskoi*, 89–90.
48. *Pis'ma Imperatritsy Ekateriny II*, 157.
49. Dominique Maroger (ed.), *The Memoirs of Catherine the Great* (London: 1955), 363.
50. I. Grabar' and S. Kemenev (eds.), *Istoriia russkago iskusstva*, 6 (Moscow: 1961), 96.
51. Milner-Gulland, "Petersburg Baroque," 90; Grabar' and Kemenev, *Istoriia russkago iskusstva*, 6, 96.
52. Grabar', *Istoriia russkago iskusstva*, 3, 333.
53. Boris I. Krasnobaev, *Ocherki po istorii russkoi kul'tury XVIII veka* (Moscow): 1972), 262.
54. Grabar' and Kemenev, *Istoriia*, 7 (Moscow: 1961), 101–102.
55. Réau, "Les artistes russes," 17.
56. Mitropolit Evgenii [Bolkhovitinov] *Slovar' russkikh svetskikh pisatelei*, 1 (Moscow: 1838), cited in Petrov, *Sbornik materialov*, 3, 629.
57. DE Piles, *Voyage de deux Français*, 299.
58. Grabar', *Istoriia russkago iskusstva*, 3, 333. He gave no source in the first edition; the 1961 edition omits the cost.
59. Maikov, *Ivan Ivanovich Betskoi*, 89–90.
60. Herrmann, *Geschichte des russischen Staates*, pt. 2 (Gotha: 1866), 630, cited in Maikov, *Ivan Ivanovich Betskoi*, 82, n. 1. Herrmann's work was not available to me.
61. N. D. Chechulin, *Ocherki po istorii russkikh finantsov v tsarstvovanii Ekateriny II* (St. Petersburg: 1906), 297.
62. Ibid., 318, n. 5.
63. C. Morazé, "Finance et despotisme: Essai sur les despotes éclairés," *Annales. Sociétés. Economies. Civilisations* (July–September 1948), 288.
64. Bibliothèque de l'institut français de Petrograd, 7: *Correspondance de Falconet avec Catherine II, 1767–1778, publiée avec une introduction et des notes par Louis Réau* (Paris: 1921), 205. Hereafter cited as *Falconet*.
65. Rudolph Augstein, *Preussens Friedrich und die Deutschen* (Frankfurt a. M.: 1968), 106.
66. A circular letter to artists who had already served the Russian court elicited exorbitant estimates for sculptors' services. Pajon asked 600,000 livres and Cousteux 480,000 livres. A livre was worth about four rubles at the time. See Ilse Bischoff, "Étienne Maurice Falconet," *Russian Review* 24 (October 1965), 370. Falconet, offered 300,000 livres by Prince Golitsyn, Russian ambassador in Paris, would accept only 200,000 livres—25,000 livres per annum for eight years. See A. L. Kaganovich, *Mednyi vsadnik* (Leningrad: 1975), 29.
67. Catherine to Falconet, 14 March 1770, *Falconet*, 120.
68. Catherine to Falconet, 29 May 1770, ibid., 127.
69. Catherine to Falconet, 6 June 1774, ibid., 177.

70. Catherine to Falconet, 14 August 1770, ibid., 136.

71. Falconet to Catherine, 16 March 1767, ibid., 9.

72. Catherine to Falconet, 28 March 1767, ibid., 14.

73. Catherine to Falconet, 3 August 1767, ibid., 19.

74. Catherine to Falconet, 30 June 1775, *Pis'ma Imperatritsy Ekateriny II*, 27.

75. Heinrich Christoff von Reimers, cited by Iaremich, "Khudozhestva v periode prezidentstva I. I. Betskago," *R. A. Kh. Sb.*, 191, n. 10.

76. Falconet to Catherine, 27 October 1770, *Falconet*, 137.

77. Kovalenskaia, *Russkii Klassitsizm*, 78.

78. Catherine to Falconet, 29 October 1770, *Falconet*, 139.

79. Catherine to Grimm, 1 October 1778, *Pis'ma Imperatritsy Ekateriny II*, 104.

80. Catherine to Grimm, 29 June 1787, ibid., 416. Falconet died five years later; Catherine's only concern was that Grimm try to retrieve some letters she had written to Falconet during his first year in St. Petersburg. Letter of 6 June 1791, ibid., 548.

81. Kaganovich, *Mednyi vsadnik*, 12.

82. Catherine to Grimm, 21 September 1785, *Pis'ma Imperatritsy Ekateriny II*, 386.

83. Kaganovich, *Mednyi vsadnik*, 40.

84. A report on this astonishing engineering feat is given in Carburi de Ceffalonie, *Le Monument élevé à la gloire de Pierre le grand. . . . Relation des moyens méchaniques qu'ont été employés pour transporter à Pétersbourg un rocher . . .* (Paris: 1777).

85. Chekalevskii, *Razsuzhdenie*, 89. A similar figure—460,989 rubles—is given in Maikov, *Ivan Ivanovich Betskoi*, 347, n. 1.

86. Catherine to Grimm, 10 December 1782, *Pis'ma Imperatritsy Ekateriny II*, 265. Not all spectators were so impressed. Fortia de Piles thought the extended right arm lacked nobility and the slope so gradual as to make the horse's great exertions unnecessary: ". . . plus on l'examine, plus on le trouve détestable." de Piles, *Voyage de deux Français*, 194.

87. Pierre Descargues, *The Hermitage Museum: Leningrad* (New York: 1961), 22.

88. de Piles, *Voyage de deux Français*, 23.

89. Chekalevskii, *Razsuzhdenie*, 149.

90. E. Wangermann, "Maria Theresa: a Reforming Monarchy," in Dickens, *The Courts of Europe*, 303.

91. L. Réau, *I Musei di peitroborgo* (Bergamo: 1930), preface.

92. Nigel Gosling, *Leningrad* (London; 1965), 110.

93. Catherine to Grimm, 18 September 1790, *Pis'ma Imperatritsy Ekateriny II*, 499–500. Catherine's queries, orders, and comments to Grimm on matters of art are collected in L. Réau, "Correspondance artistique de Grimm avec Catherine II, " *Archives de l'art français, nouvelle période,*17 (1932).

94. Catherine to Grimm, 27 September 1781, *Pis'ma Imperatritsy Ekateriny II*, 221.

95. In 1779 she wrote to Grimm of seven Le Moine paintings priced at forty thousand rubles as "d'une cherté horrible" and boasted that she never, thank God, bought at such a price. Catherine to Grimm, 18 June 1779, ibid., 145.

96. Kovalenskaia, *Istoriia russkogo iskusstva v XVIII v.*, 3.

97. Chekalevskii, *Razsuzhdenie*, 151–54.

98. Falconet to Betskoi, 3 April 1771, *Falconet*, 144–45.

99. For her historical works on early Russia, see André Mazon, "Catherine II, historienne de la Russie médiévale," *Académie des incriptions et belles-lettres, Comptes-rendus* (Paris: 1944), 458–72.

100. For topics from Kievan times in the painting competitions of the 1760s, see Iaremich, *R. A. Kh. Sh.*, 110–11, and for sculpture, ibid., 132–35.

101. George Heard Hamilton, *The Art and Architecture of Russia* (Baltimore: 1954), 229.

102. Grabar' and Kemenev, *Istoriia*, 7, 255–64, gives a brief biography and appreciation of Ermenev, who was forgotten until Iaremich discovered him in 1934.

103. Iaremich, *R. A. Kh. Sh.*, 194, n. 30.

104. Milner-Gulland, "Petersburg Baroque," 87.

105. A. L. Kaganovich, *Ocherki istorii Leningrada*, 1 (Leningrad: 1955), 40.

106. Julius Hasselblatt, *Historische Überblick der Entwicklung der Kaiserliche Russische Akademie der Kunste in St. Petersburg.* (St. Petersburg and Leipzig: 1886), 95.

107. Zoe Bakeef Peterson, "The Architectural Heritage of Leningrad," *American Slavic and East European Review* 6, nos. 10–11 (December 1945), 18.

108. Sandra Millikin in *Encyclopedia Brittanica*, 19 (1972), 438b.

IMAGES OF RULE AND PROBLEMS OF GENDER IN THE UPBRINGING OF PAUL I AND ALEXANDER I

Richard Wortman

> Mentor, speaking thus, continued along the road to the sea; and Telemachus, not strong enough to proceed on his own, allowed himself to be led without resistance. Minerva, at all times concealed within the form of Mentor, covered Telemachus invisibly with her aegis, and extending over him a divine ray, gave him a sense of courage that he had not felt since he had come to this island.
>
> FÉNELON, *Les aventures de Télémaque, livre 6*

The strange changes and inconsistencies in the personalities of Paul I and Alexander I have prompted explanations focusing on their upbringing and their anomalous relations with their parents. Paul grew up as heir under the suspicious eye of his mother, Catherine, who had usurped the throne. Alexander's sympathies were divided between the court of his grandmother, Catherine, and his father's military camp at Gatchina. These circumstances were certainly crucial in shaping the personalities of the two emperors. But they are important only insofar as they influenced the heirs' own conceptions of their obligations and goals as monarchs. As boys and young men, Paul and Alexander were introduced to a series of Western images of rule that expressed the philosophical and political ideals of eighteenth-century Europe. The models of ruler presented to them by important figures in their lives were varied and often conflicting. Their upbringing, then, reflected not only the troubled family relations in the imperial house, but the divergent conceptions of the ideal ruler held by different elements in the court.

Western images of the monarch were decisive in shaping the heirs' notions in late-eighteenth-century Russia, for local tradition provided no acceptable model of rule. Elizabeth and Catherine were elevated to the throne by guards officers and officials seeking amenable rulers who would not abuse their power. In the treacherous politics of the Russian court, female rulers seemed more reliable and dependent, less subject to uncontrolled despotic whims. They represented benevolence and stability on the throne, a taming of autocratic authority. In this respect, notions of gender reinforced political calculations, and Paul and Alexander grew up in a setting dominated by the image of the benevolent empress. Peter the Great, whose memory was extolled in statutes, ceremonies, and verse, epitomized violent change and instability and could hardly serve as a model for a boy destined for the throne. Peter's model was invoked, but only after being transformed to fit ideals fostered by the reigning empress.

In the eighteenth and nineteenth centuries, it was always the empress who insisted on a rigorous civil education for the heir and concerned herself with his teachers and the organization of his instruction. Both Elizabeth and Catherine based their vulnerable claims to rule on the benefits they promised to bestow upon the nation. By educating the heir, they hoped to ensure the persistence of their achievements and the political progress of Russia. They removed the boys at birth from the care of their parents; Elizabeth took Paul from Peter Fedorovich and Catherine; Catherine took Alexander from Paul and Maria Fedorovna. When the heir reached the age of seven or eight, he came under the supervision of a learned tutor who followed Enlightenment theories of pedagogy.

Many of the men the boy encountered outside the classroom, however, entertained different ideals. They esteemed martial values of power and authority. They worshipped Frederick the Great, not Frederick the poet and flautist but Frederick the stern disciplinarian and epitome of military leadership. The heirs encountered two different and irreconcilable models, reflecting the radical separation between the male and female influences on their lives. Their feelings of ambivalence toward these models were later reflected in their varied personae, which so bewildered their contemporaries. Nicholas I, who originally was not destined for the throne, did not receive a humanitarian, enlightened education and assumed the unambiguous role of military officer. But the conflict would reappear in the life and reign of his son, Alexander II.

The tutors tried to present the heir with a model of a male ruler who exemplified the civil and humanitarian values of the Enlightenment. But the traits they emphasized, under feminine auspices, hardly corresponded to those prevalent in the male society of the court. Their teaching encouraged meekness and self-restraint. They tried to instill in the heir a sense of civic virtue, which would show him his duty to work for the good of his subjects. This duty required the mastery or denial of the ruler's personal impulses. Thus, although concepts of civic virtue did not carry feminine associations at the time, they came to the heir under feminine auspices and were not shared by many of the highly placed men he would meet. The heir had to learn to be a new kind of man, not the kind he saw around him in the court.

Paul's tutor, Nikita Panin, drew his ideas about education from the texts of Leibniz and tried to apply them to the education of the Grand Duke. Leibniz had taught that the prince should be a "good man," who exhibited "great sentiments of piety, justice, and charity" and applied himself "firmly to do his duty." The most important virtue for a prince, according to Leibniz, was prudence. Prudence "ordains the manner in which the prince must act in all sorts of circumstances." Other virtues the prince should exemplify were valor, moderation, justice, and generosity.[1] Panin too stressed the importance of teaching virtue. In his outline to the Empress Elizabeth on the education of the Grand Duke Paul, he asserted that the heir must have "a tender soul and heart" before he could learn to think and reason. He had to develop the virtues of a sensitive (*chuvstvitel'noe*) understanding of his creator and his intentions and of man's duty to God. But there was little emphasis on religion in Panin's memorandum. The education he recommended focused on political morality. A good monarch, he stressed, could have no true interest apart from the well-being of the people entrusted to him.[2]

Leibniz had taught that history would enable the prince to "be part of the council of former Emperors and Kings so that he one day will better preside in his own." Panin's plan too stressed the importance of history, which would present to the heir "examples of the great deeds of his sanctified ancestors." Henry IV and Frederick the Great were the principal Western models presented to Paul. Paul took notes on Sully's diary, and his library contained many volumes on Frederick's statecraft. The only "sanctified ancestor" made by his teachers into an example was Peter the Great, who, as David Ransel has shown, became the symbol of their hopes for reform. But the Panin group evoked a tamed and seemly Peter, devoted to law and sympathetic to their constitutional goals. Paul's teacher of mathematics and science, Semen Poroshin, distinguished between two types of courage: fearlessness and impudence. But, in his view, only fearlessness was governed by reason, and it was fearlessness that Peter exemplified. Peter's courage was an act of self-control. Peter, Poroshin informed his pupil, was not courageous by nature, but by reasoning (*razsuzhdeniia*) had overcome his weakness.[3]

Another source of models for eighteenth-century monarchs was literature, and the most popular tale of princely virtue, read by both Paul and

Alexander, was François Fénelon's *Les aventures de Télémaque, fils d'Ulysse*. Fénelon's tale appeared in numerous editions, four of them translations, in eighteenth-century Russia. The author presents a utopian vision of an austere life of labor led in an ideal kingdom. *Télémaque* was taken by intellectuals as a critique of the luxury of the imperial court, and Catherine's journal, *All Sorts of Things* (*Vsiakaia vsiachina*), treated the work unfavorably. But at the same time *Télémaque's* code of princely conduct very much suited the empress, and she later gave the book to her grandson, Alexander.[4]

Télémaque showed the boy how a good monarch should think and feel. The prince had to stand above entanglements. Family and personal attachments of any kind prevented him from giving total devotion to the commonweal. Telemachus cannot learn to be king from his missing father, but from Mentor, his "second father," who makes wisdom and virtue rather than instinct and tradition his guides to behavior. Thus Panin and the teachers under his supervision were to replace Paul's father. Telemachus's search for his natural father leads him into danger, and it is Mentor's advice that saves him. When the boy encounters a storm, he realizes his error and says, "Am I not unhappy for having believed myself at an age when one has neither anticipation of the future nor experience of the past, nor the moderation to improve the present! Oh! If ever we escape from this tempest, I will distrust myself as my worst enemy: it is you Mentor whom I will always believe."[5]

Patience is the most important virtue for Fénelon, just as prudence was for Leibniz. The gods made Telemachus wait to find his father as a lesson in patience. "One must be patient in order to be the master of oneself and of others." It was impatience that allowed passions to reign and kings to abuse their powers.[6]

The greatest danger in Fénelon's parable lay in Eros. "Love is to be feared more than shipwrecks." Like Ulysses, Telemachus falls in love with a nymph on Calypso's island. He begins to waste away from his passion. Mentor makes it clear that romantic love is the greatest danger. Modest beauty is far more dangerous than vice or brutality, for "in loving it, one believes that he is loving only virtue." Love diverts the monarch from true virtue, which can be attained only by ruling his people.[7] Fénelon here expresses the secular asceticism of his era. Love was not sinful or evil; it was selfish. It led the prince away from his obligations to humanity.

The prince must resist and deny his own sexual impulse, to become less masculine for the sake of the common good. In the final scene, reason assumes a feminine form. Mentor dematerializes and, in a blaze of azure and gold, reveals herself as Minerva. The goddess calls upon Telemachus to restore the age of gold and recites a final set of maxims. She exhorts him to love his people and to do everything to win their love—to live in simplicity for the good of the people and not for his own glory.[8]

Mentor is a goddess in male disguise, and the image of the good prince is in many respects a tamed, feminized image. Self-restraint, patience, and chastity characterize the good prince. Power is a dangerous possession. This was the lesson taught under the aegis of Catherine, when she came to the throne. Catherine herself was depicted as Minerva in art and celebration—Minerva in her pacific guise, who personified wisdom, prudence, reason, and the inner control of the stoic ethic. Though not everything Panin taught suited Catherine, the general lines of the education followed her prescriptions, and she attended all of Paul's examinations.[9] His tutors tried to convey this image by assigning, when he was older, writings of Montesquieu, Voltaire, Diderot, Helvétius, and Hume. At the dinner table, Paul heard Panin converse with leading officials, foreign dignitaries, and writers. Later, under Panin's influence, he wrote several memoranda which argued for the regularization and organization of government through the introduction of a rule of law and the reform of institutions. He held that legislative power should "repose in the hands of the ruler but with the agreement of the state, for otherwise it will turn into despotism." In these writings, Paul described a stoic image of a ruler who, subordinating his will to natural law, promoted the well-being of his people. The good ruler epitomized meekness, for he had it in his power to abstain from power, to refrain from abuse of the law.[10]

Minerva replaced Peter's image of Hercules as a guide and an ideal. But Paul did not adopt the ideal of his mother, seeking rather a strong masculine image in the male rulers of the past. From childhood, Paul admired the authoritarian, intimidating Peter, whose will brooked no limits, the second element in what David Ransel has described as Paul's "ambivalent legacy." Paul declared that "his greatest ambition was to resemble [Peter] one day and to continue the work he had begun."[11] The eulogy to Henry IV of France, which he wrote when he was about twenty years old, also reveals pronounced authoritarian predilections. The king Paul describes is devoted to the state; he seeks to improve his people, as befits Leibniz's and Panin's ideal ruler. But his devotion, in Paul's essay, is displayed as a distrust of everyone, a determination to take responsibility for everything himself, and a will to punish swiftly when disobeyed. Henry refused to be deceived, Paul writes, and made it his business to know everything, down to the pettiest detail. He banished vassals who did not do service, and he gave gifts and favors himself, not through ministers. He looked upon government not as an intellectual matter, but "as the well-being of a family." And this paternal concern for "the good order of domestic life" distinguished him from gifted people who had profound minds. We see in

Paul's vision of total control the impulse that led him as tsar to try to direct everything from the throne and to issue as many as forty-eight thousand orders in a single year.[12]

The quality Paul most esteemed in Henry was order, *poriadok*. Frugality came next on his list, followed by tenderness, patience, honesty, and fidelity to one's word. He admired Henry's ability to combine opposed characteristics, elevated feelings and simplicity, a soldier's courage and an abundance of love. But the strongest feeling expressed in this school exercise is a fear of weakness in the monarch. Paul saw Henry as the embodiment of strength. Though Henry was tender with friends, Paul emphasized, he had a strong will and was never weak. In a note on how a wise monarch could transform "the Russians," Paul suggests that he hoped, by civilizing his people, to turn them into a more effective weapon. Once the wise monarch had "softened their ferocious spirit, their cruel and unsociable manners, this people [the Russians] would become terrifying for all their neighbors."[13]

Warfare had the greatest appeal for Paul, and he found his principal examples of male behavior not in the classroom but at the military exercises he was allowed to attend. As a little boy, he fantasized about serving in the ranks in the cavalry and infantry. Riding in uniform, wearing a saber, participating in reviews and maneuvers at Krasnoe Selo captured his imagination. It was not only the glamour and color of the events that he found enchanting. On the drill field, he escaped from the world of admonition and piety and took his position as commander, issued orders, received reports, watched complicated exercises enacted for his approval. This was the real world of power that the abstract prescriptions of his classroom could scarcely rival. It is no wonder that his lessons suffered seriously in the following days.[14]

In military exercises and discussions, Paul found a common interest with men of high station. His tutors spoke to him as a pupil, preaching and admonishing. In military uniform, Paul, whom Catherine had appointed general-admiral at his birth, had to be treated on an equal footing. Over the dinner table, he heard talk of war and armies. He listened intently to serious conversations about military matters and the military resources of Russia conducted by leading generals of the realm, among them Nikita Panin's brother, Peter. From them, he learned that the armed forces lacked order and discipline and heard pleas for more powerful and assertive leadership.[15]

In these conversations, Paul heard many complaints about Catherine's neglect of the army and the superiority of Prussian military organization; Peter Panin spoke with great admiration of the Prussian army. In 1765, at age eleven, Paul was most impressed by Colonel Michael Kamenskii's

description of the Prussian military camp at Breslau. Kamenskii sneered
at the philosophical character of Paul's education. What good, he asked,
would the wisdom of Greece's philosophers have done at the battle of
Marathon? Kamenskii's Peter the Great gave "his subjects an example in
nearly all things, was not ashamed to be a soldier or sailor, but never was
a clerk, nor a protocolist in a single college or even the Senate." These
remarks deeply troubled Poroshin, but Kamenskii prevailed and later was
raised by Paul to the position of general-field-marshal. When Prince
Henry of Prussia visited Russia in 1770 Paul met him, and his fascination
with Prussian ways grew.[16]

Like his father, Peter III, Paul idolized Frederick the Great. But it was
Frederick the commander and disciplinarian who captured his imagination, not Frederick the statesman. This fascination only grew when he
met Frederick in Berlin in 1776. In discussions with Peter Panin and
Prince Nicholas Repin, a cousin of the Panins, Paul developed ideas about
the need to transform the Russian armed forces. He drafted plans for
more efficient recruitment of soldiers into the army and better deploy-
ment to protect Russian borders. He hoped to form a special army of
foreign soldiers under his own personal leadership.[17]

Catherine, fearing Paul as a potential rival for power, allowed him no
governmental responsibility. She even forbade petitioners to approach
him for assistance. He had little choice but to withdraw and occupy himself with his regiments at Gatchina, much as Peter the Great had done
when he was kept from power. But the model for Gatchina was Potsdam
and not Preobrazhenskoe. "As you entered Gatchina," one observer
wrote, "it was as if you were entering a Prussian territory."[18] At Gatchina
Paul indulged his love for drill, uniforms, and the trivial details of the
parade ground—the mania that dominated his reign and became his abiding legacy for future generations. The Russian imperial persona thus received its Western apotheosis in Frederick the Great, and the Prussian-
style officer drilling his troops became the symbol of the controlled but
dominating display of masculine power. Paul's sons, Alexander I and
Nicholas I, and his grandson, Alexander II, all shared his fascination with
military discipline, ceremony, and spectacle. Participating in parades,
playing drillmaster, fussing over the details of dress, grooming, and pos-
ture came to express the male ethos of the imperial family. The unceasing
displays of military elegance and discipline succeeded in impressing foreigners that the Russian imperial house fulfilled one current European
ideal of monarch: the stern and unrelenting military disciplinarian.

In Russia, the military ideal existed side by side, in uneasy balance,
with the Enlightenment ideal of civic virtue. Because of the division between the male and female influences on the heir's life, they represented

opposed, irreconcilable personal types. Paul responded by denying the feminine side of his upbringing. As an adult he revealed no trace of the "tender soul and heart" that Elizabeth and Catherine's tutors had hoped to instill in him. His pro-Prussian sympathies and fierce antagonism to all liberal thought led Catherine, during the last decade of her reign, to seek ways to remove him from the succession. When Paul ascended the throne at the age of forty-two, he turned violently against the principles of respect for law and self-restraint that she represented. He withdrew the Charter of the Nobility, restored the collegial system, and exercised a violent despotism that proved the antithesis of the compassion and tolerance his mother strove to display.

During his reign, Paul embodied a bizarre combination of the roles of the male ruler he had come to admire. He took on the authoritarian manner and principles of Peter the Great without, however, Peter's design or vision. He emulated Frederick the Great's parade-ground discipline. The daily watch parade became the ceremonial center of governmental life, as he tried to command government as he would the military. But he lacked Frederick the Great's strategic flair and his sense of the use of military forces. He also accepted the office of protector of the Knights of Malta and assumed the title in an elaborate ceremony.[19] But these roles did not fulfill his grandiose aspirations. He saw himself as the godlike emperor and tried to live up to the panegyric metaphors addressed to Peter. Paul was the only Russian emperor to command troops when dressed in imperial crown and mantle. In this guise, Lotman has suggested, Paul sought to show Russia "a spectacle of God."[20]

The response of Paul's son, Emperor Alexander I, to the dual images of absolute monarch was to strive to embody both images and satisfy all the expectations of him. Like many grandmothers, Catherine doted more on her grandson than she had on her son, and she played an extremely active role in organizing his education. She immediately withdrew him from his parents' supervision, just as Elizabeth had taken Paul away from her, and tried to shape Alexander according to her Enlightenment ideal of ruler. At his birth, in 1777, Gavriil Derzhavin delivered the stoic message in an apostrophe that would be cited as Alexander's guiding ideal through his life.

> Be the ruler of your passions,
> Be a human being (*chelovek*) on the throne.

To be human, according to Catherine, was to submit one's lower, animal impulses to reason; to ensure the triumph of one's higher intellectual faculties. Like Minerva disguised as Mentor, Catherine sought to replace the absent father and teach her pupil to be a better man and a good ruler. She set forth a series of maxims in a copy of *Télémaque* she gave Alexander. "Be mild, humane, accessible, compassionate, and liberal." Good people should love him, evil fear him, and all respect him. He should preserve the "ancient taste for honor and virtue." "Duplicity," she asserted, "is unknown to great people." She hoped he would become "a great person, a hero." But she did not want him to follow his father's military path. When he was four years old, she wrote in her notebook, "Listen, do not begin to imagine that I want to make of Alexander the one who cuts the Gordian knot. Literally, nothing of the kind. Alexander will be a splendid person but not at all a conqueror—he has no need to become one."[21]

The ruler Catherine envisaged stood apart from society. He made decisions on his own, prompted by his own conscience: "virtue does not make itself known in the crowd." He should avoid flatterers and contact with high society that might "darken the ancient taste for honor and virtue." Catherine dramatized this lonesome quest for virtue in her parable, "The Tale of the Tsarevich Khlor," her own version of *Télémaque*.

The tsarevich Khlor, in Catherine's tale, was the son of the kind tsar of Russia before the rise of Kiev. He was beautiful, intelligent, and lively, and his reputation spread far and wide. The Kirghiz Khan longed to have the wonderful boy. He had Khlor kidnapped, then gave him the task of finding the "rose without thorns," the symbol of virtue. It was Felitsiia, the personification of happiness, who helped him in his quest. Felitsiia, of course, represented Catherine herself, and Derzhavin later won her favor by extolling her in his ode, "To Felitsiia." Felitsiia's son, Reason (*Razsudok*), guides Khlor to find the correct path to the rose.

The central theme of the tale is caution. Felitsiia warns Khlor about those who entice him from his path by flattery and merry diversions. Only Reason gives sound advice. Reason points to a hill far in the distance, but Khlor, impatient, ignores his directions and seeks a shorter way. This leads him to grief—in the form of a marketplace—and, frightened, he returns knowing that he must curb his impulsive nature. Reason, like Mentor, emphasizes the importance of patience. "Only by patience is work conquered." On the hill, Khlor meets an old man and an old woman, representing honor (*chestnost'*) and truth (*pravda*). At the temple of the rose, horns blare, drums resound, extolling the boy who discovered the rose at so young an age.[22] Catherine even built a "temple of the rose" at Tsarskoe Selo for her grandson. The rose lay in an urn on an altar. The ceiling was decorated with frescoes of Peter the Great looking down upon an allegorical "Russia prospering," with symbols of wealth, science, and industry. Russia herself leaned on a shield carrying a picture of Felitsiia—Catherine.[23]

Catherine listed the "Tale of the Tsarevich Khlor" (mentioning the title twice) among the books she recommended in the memorandum she wrote to Count Nicholas Saltykov on the elementary education of Alexander and his younger brother, Constantine. The precepts of the memorandum were drawn from Enlightenment writers; many of them, like the articles of her *nakaz* to the codification commission, are direct quotations from her favorite philosophers, in this case Comenius, Locke, and Fénelon.[24] The heir's education, she wrote, should create a kind, good person. Virtue, respect, and good conduct should be the chief concerns of his teachers. He should grow up learning the golden rule, to feel "benevolence to humanity" and have "tender and sympathetic attitudes to all" and a "pure and grateful heart." The child should learn "justice," defined by Catherine as "not acting contrary to the laws," in addition to "love for truth, generosity, self-restraint, intelligence, based on reflection, wholesome ideas, and reasoning combined with diligence." Throughout her reign, Catherine defended Enlightenment ideas in her conversations with him, and in her last years she even read and explained to him the Declaration of the Rights of Man.[25]

Alexander's tutor, La Harpe, also emphasized the importance of moral over intellectual education. A ruler, he declared in a memorandum to Catherine, should not be a physicist or a naturalist or jurist, but an "honorable man and enlightened citizen." He should use his knowledge to become conscious of the obligations of one responsible for the fate of millions. Like Catherine and other Enlightenment pedagogues, he was convinced that history was only a means to teach principles derived from philosophy. History could provide examples of rulers who showed "the civic spirit," but, La Harpe emphasized, the instructor had to guide the heir to the proper models:

> One must never forget that Alexander the Great, gifted with wonderful genius and brilliant qualities, laid waste to Asia and committed so many atrocities merely from the desire to imitate the heroes of Homer. In the same way Julius Caesar, emulating Alexander the Great, committed a crime by destroying the freedom of his fatherland.[26]

La Harpe explained in his memorandum that philosophy would help the prince to understand "civil societies" and "the principles which are their bases." Alexander would learn that men were once equal, and that there have been absolute monarchs "so generous and true" that they vowed publicly, "We have the glory to say that we exist only for our peoples."[27]

To acquire virtue, to become a "public man," Alexander had to isolate himself from his environment and engage in diligent, solitary work. La

Harpe hoped that principles of philosophy and the examples of history would provide the guidance that would allow his pupil to escape traditional models of masculine conduct. The philosopher urged Alexander "to replace living friends by those who are dead, and these true friends you will find in the great models presented by history."[28] Peter the Great's name was conspicuously absent from La Harpe's recommendations, and, as Nicholas Riasanovsky has suggested, Alexander may have been the first Russian ruler not deeply concerned with Peter's image. The historical figures La Harpe approved of as Alexander's friends were not the conquerors but the great legislators, Solon and Numa, who had laid the bases of the institutions that had shaped their peoples' political life. La Harpe's principal exemplar was Marcus Aurelius, and he liked to think of himself as Marcus's tutor, Seneca. He taught Alexander the stoic notion of a supreme reason that would guide a philosophical elite to the natural law that would enable them to govern citizens equally. Alexander, enlightened on the throne, could realize the stoic ideal of virtue and introduce a just and egalitarian political order.[29] In a letter to Alexander of 1794, La Harpe quoted lines of Voltaire,

> Mortals are equal, it is not birth,
> But only virtue that makes them different.[30]

When Alexander was fifteen years old and about to be married, La Harpe provided him with a formidable reading list. *The Wealth of Nations* was prominent. "It is indispensable, sir, that you make the effort to read this classic, of which the principles, once well grasped, allow you to estimate what happens in matters of manufacture, trades, commerce, and taxation." He included a great number of histories of the ancient world by both ancient and modern authors, as well as histories of all the modern powers. He assigned Cicero's writings on the duties of man, Ferguson's "Essay on Civil Society," works of Montesquieu, Mably, and Rousseau. In a letter to Alexander he even recommended a collection of famous speeches in the English Parliament. But ultimately Alexander must seek the true promptings of reason in himself.

> The unshakeable bases of morality have been placed in your heart by the creator of myriads of worlds. Accustom yourself, sir, to consult the infallible oracle who dwells in this temple and lend him an attentive ear in the silence of the passions. Books will teach you to organize, according to different systems, the truth evident to anyone who has not been perverted by prejudices or bad education.[31]

But the prejudices of the environment continued to influence and tempt Alexander. His physical beauty, poise, and charm evoked sighs of admiration from Catherine and the leading figures at court. Potemkin compared him to Apollo. General A. Ia. Protasov, who supervised Alexander directly, lamented that the ease of the heir's social success distracted him from serious pursuits. His marriage to Princess Margaret of Baden, in 1793, ended his tutor's supervision and brought his education to an end.[32]

Yet Alexander claimed to take his tutor's admonitions seriously and constantly berated himself for failing to measure up. At the age of thirteen, he wrote to La Harpe: "Instead of urging myself on and doubling my efforts to profit from my remaining years of study, each day I become more nonchalant, more remiss, more incapable, and each day I surround myself with those like myself who stupidly consider themselves perfection only because they are princes." He castigated himself for being an egoist, uninterested in others, who out of excessive vanity wanted only to shine. "At thirteen, I am the same child as I was at eight, and the more I advance in age the closer I come to nil."[33]

Despite his efforts to please his tutor, Alexander found men he could admire at his father's military camp at Gatchina rather than in books of ancient history. As a child, during the 1780s, he visited Gatchina once a week; in his teens, his visits became more frequent and his love of the military more open. His enthusiasm troubled his teachers. In 1793, when Alexander was fifteen, General Protasov deplored his fascination for gun practice.[34] After his marriage, Alexander began participating in exercises at Gatchina four times a week and experiencing the same joy at the maneuvers at Krasnoe Selo that his father had experienced several decades before. He wrote to La Harpe that he was occupied from six in the morning until afternoon. "This summer, I can definitely say that I have served."[35]

Alexander's first understanding of state service was military service. But unlike his father, he continued to profess the civic principles he had learned in the classroom. Alexander tried to embody both images and to please the figures dominant in both settings of the court. Catherine remarked that Alexander contained many contradictions "as a result of which he is extraordinarily beloved by those around him." As he grew up, he developed the ability to take on all the characteristics expected of him by his teachers, friends, and the favorites of both his mother and his father. Protasov observed that Alexander would obediently repeat the principles he was taught, but gave little evidence of sincerity. His mathematics teacher, Masson, characterized him as "the ideal that enraptures us in Telemachus."[36]

Alexander developed extraordinary skill at dissembling. Catherine remarked how well he acted in children's plays. As emperor, he used this skill with great success, assuming the appropriate role for each occasion. He played the earnest reformer, calling for regularization of government, yet, Marc Raeff has observed, he was forever evasive and intriguing, displaying a suspicion of anyone who might oppose his autocratic will that was "almost pathological."[37] He advocated tolerance, while maintaining strict censorship, and, in the last years of his reign, introduced a barrack-like despotism that began to resemble his father's. It is no wonder that Napoleon called him "the Talma of the North."

Marc Raeff has shown us how little the dichotomy of "liberal" and "reactionary" helps us to understand Alexander's institutional reform. Such terms presume a concept of constitutionalism remote from his thinking, and a consistency that was alien to the entire behavioral pattern of a Russian monarch. Alexander understood his calling as a performance of varied and contradictory roles. By the end of the eighteenth century, the life of the nobility and the court had become especially theatrical. "The theater invaded life," Lotman wrote, "and actively restructured everyday behavior."

Alexander's "proteanism" was his effort to comply with the conflicting European images of monarch presented to him in the court. His hypocrisy and instability were more responses to the need to live up to contradictory expectations than causes of his inconsistent behavior. He endeavored at once to be the monarch shorn of violence and domination, governed by humanitarian impulse, and the ruler of men, who exercised his dominating authority untrammeled in the administration and on the parade ground. Many were disappointed, angered, or mystified by Alexander's shifting persona. Lotman observed that the verb "to dupe" appears repeatedly in descriptions of his behavior.[38]

Alexander also pretended to yearn to escape his imperial responsibilities. In 1796 he frequently expressed the wish to abdicate. In a letter to La Harpe, he went so far as to deplore his brother Constantine's obsession with the military. "As for me, though I am a military man I desire only peace and tranquillity, and I would gladly yield my rank for a farm near yours. . . ." He complained a few months later to Kochubei about the condition of the administration and confided his desire to retire with his wife to a farm on the Rhine, "where I will live tranquilly as a private person, finding happiness in the society of friends and the study of nature."[39]

But this was still another role he had learned to play—that of a character of the sentimental literature of the late eighteenth century, which he had read with his teacher, the sentimentalist poet Nicholas Murav'ev. The idyll of a bucolic private life came from the poetry of Solomon Gessner, whose grave Alexander went out of his way to visit on his return from Paris in 1815. Alexander liked to play the young man, overwhelmed by fate, forced to bear the stern responsibilities of life. "Politics dictate duties that the heart represses," he declared. Private virtue seemed more attainable than public. It was Télémaque's "private and peaceful state where virtue is less difficult."[40]

Alexander dealt with the conflicting masculine and feminine images of his education by acting in ways that reflected both. His ambiguous behavior both intrigued and exasperated his contemporaries. He captivated women and enjoyed their company more than that of men, but his relationships seemed to have begun and ended with flirtation. Men noted his feminine features. Metternich observed that Alexander's character presented "a strange mix of the qualities of a man and the weaknesses of a woman." Vigel', himself a homosexual, remarked that Alexander's attractive appearance was "nearly feminine." Varnhagen wrote in his memoirs, "His most essential features are vanity, or cunning and dissimulation; if he wore a woman's dress, he would seem an elegant woman."[41]

Marc Raeff has observed that Alexander, like Catherine, exerted an erotic attraction over his servitors. Vasilii Karazin's exalted praise of Alexander at the beginning of his reign expressed feelings that seized other men who became enraptured with Alexander's seductive charm and appearance. When Karazin fell from favor he felt, Herzen observed, like a "rejected lover." Other officials experienced the same feelings. Michael Speranskii, and the minister of justice, Ivan Dmitriev, both had tearful partings with the emperor when they left office. Speranskii described him as "a veritable enticer."[42]

Alexander presented an androgynous, incorporeal ideal. His idealized form, from the beginning of his reign, was the angel. When he ascended the throne, he promised in his accession manifesto that he would rule "according to the laws and the heart" of his grandmother. Nicholas Karamzin then wrote his famous lines:

> You shine like a divine angel
> With goodness and beauty,
> And your first words promise
> Catherine's golden age.[43]

Alexander maintained this appearance and manner throughout his reign. "What a majestic appearance," Zhikharev wrote in his diary in September 1806. "What a beauty and in addition, what a soul! A wonderful angelic face and platonic smile." At first, the metaphor of angel captured the elusive, somewhat spiritual beauty of Alexander's charm. Later in his reign, it expressed the mystical Christianity he hoped to propagate. Appropriately, he was memorialized as an angel. Montferrand's Alexandrine Column on the Palace Square is crowned by an angel over six meters in height, sculpted by B.I. Orlovskii with Alexander's features. The angel holds a cross, looks toward the ground, and points to the heavens.[44]

Ethereal and otherworldly when appropriate, Alexander could also play the stern and unyielding commander. He liked to view himself as a general and compare his skill with the military leaders of his time. We see Alexander's striking the pose of Napoleon, too, though his generals were able to keep him from actual combat. Instead, he commanded on the parade ground. There Alexander played the role of martinet, spending hours drilling his soliders. He insisted on precise definition of the length of the step, and the number per minute. He took every opportunity to drill his troops and even in 1812 reserved time for parades. His mother, the dowager, accused him of wasting his time on the concerns of a subaltern. It was this common devotion to discipline that bound him to Aleksei Arakcheev, a product of Paul's Gatchina detachments.[45]

At the same time, Alexander developed a preoccupation with the details of military dress and the general appearance of his troops. The military became a theatrical display, as well as a show of authority and discipline. Drill was elevated from a training exercise into a spectacle. Parades were Alexander's favorite form of spectacle, and "he kept the part of producer for himself and used his thousands-strong army as an enormous ballet company."[46] The parade ground provided a scene for the emperor to protest his masculinity when the demands of modern warfare ruled out his military leadership.

Neither a sympathy for humanitarian ideals nor a passion for military exercises was unique to Russian monarchy at the time. The distinctive feature, rather, was the effort to adopt the different ideals of European monarchy, simultaneously and without compromise. The ideals presented to the heir in the late eighteenth century by different circles in the court carried with them the tone and associations of the male and female figures who promoted them. Caught between the two, the heir was bound to disappoint the expectations of one or both. Paul responded with a series of fantastic caricatures of despotic male military authority. Alexander became the protean ruler, fulfilling the expectations of all for the moment, and no one in the end.

The dichotomy in royal imagery persisted in Russian princely education through the first half of the nineteenth century. Alexander's successor, his younger brother Nicholas I, was not expected to succeed to the throne and grew up under the supervision of military officers. He assumed the unambiguous role of military officer and revealed little doubt or, indeed, flexibility in his conception of his role as emperor. But the dichotomy appeared again in the education of Nicholas's son, the future Alexander II. Nicholas's mother, the dowager empress Maria Fedorovna, appointed the sentimentalist poet Vasilii Zhukovskii to plan and direct Alexander's education. Inspired by the theories of Pestalozzi, Zhukovskii tried to instill in the heir the romantic, humanitarian sensibility of the early nineteenth century. After the dowager's death in 1828, the heir's mother, Alexandra Fedorovna, continued to support Zhukovskii's efforts, while Nicholas I continued to train his son on the parade ground. The dualism of imperial imagery came to an end only with the upbringing of Alexander II's children. By then, the empress had come to share or at least accept the emperor's conception of the role of monarch. The last tsars, Alexander III and Nicholas II, did not have to choose between contradictory models fostered within the imperial family. But, by the same token, they were deprived of the liberating influence of an alternative personality, a feminine side with a vision of benevolent and sympathetic rule that could temper the exercise of autocratic power.

NOTES

1. Leibniz's *De educatione Principis commentatio*, in French, in *Magazin für das Kirchenrecht die Kirchen und Gelehrten-Geschichte* (1787), 178, 191–92, 195–96; Patrick Riley (ed.), *The Political Writings of Leibniz* (Cambridge, England: 1972), 92–103.

2. N. I. Panin, "Vsepoddanneishee pred"iavlenie slabogo poniatiia i mneniia o vospitanii Ego Imperatorskogo Velichestva Pavla Petrovicha," *Russkaia Starina* 36 (1880), 315–17; for a summary of the entire proposal, see David L. Ransel, *The Politics of Catherinian Russia: The Panin Party* (New Haven: 1975), 207–11.

3. Semen Poroshin, *Zapiski* (St. Petersburg: 1881), 97–98, 292; Leibniz, *De educatione*, 192; Panin, "Vsepoddanneishee," 316; Ransel, *Politics of Catherinian Russia*, 268, 282-83.

4. Ransel, *Politics of Catherinian Russia*, 220; Walter J. Gleason, *Moral Idealists, Bureaucracy and Catherine the Great* (New Brunswick, N. J.: 1981), 97–98. The view presented by A. S. Orlov that Catherine objected to the content of *Télémaque* seems absolutely unfounded. A. S. Orlov, "'Tilemakhida' V. K. Trediakovskogo," *XVIII Vek* (Moscow-Leningrad: 1935), 5–57. Catherine as well as other educated individuals found Trediakovskii's translation ponderous and impenetrable. Indeed, according to Karamzin, it was prescribed as a playful punishment for those who did not speak Russian in the Academy (Orlov, 23). But Catherine certainly approved of the work in general, and it remained an important intellectual influence during her reign. See Isabel de Madariaga, *Russia in the Age of Catherine the Great* (New Haven: 1981), 490.

5. *Les aventures de Télémaque* in François de Fénelon, *Oeuvres complètes* (Paris: 1851–52; reprinted Geneva, 1971), 6, 401–2.

6. Ibid., 564.
7. Ibid., 436–44.
8. Ibid., 565–66.
9. "Tsesarevich Pavel Petrovich; istoricheskie materialy khraniashchiesia v biblioteke dvortsa goroda Pavlovska," *Russkaia Starina* 9 (1874), 674.
10. Hugh Ragsdale (ed.), *Paul I: A Reassessment of His Life and Reign* (Pittsburgh: 1979), ix; Ransel, "An Ambivalent Legacy: The Education of the Grand Duke Paul," in Ragsdale, *Paul I*, 4–5, 8–11. On the reception of stoic and natural law theories in Russia, see Gleason, *Moral Idealists*, 87–91. The theme of self-restraint is set forth most effectively in the works of Denis Fonvizin, and particularly his "Discourse on Permanent Laws of State." See Marc Raeff, *Russian Intellectual History: An Anthology* (New York: 1966), 101. For comments on the text, and other writings of Fonvizin, see Walter Gleason, *The Political and Legal Writings of Denis Fonvizin* (Ann Arbor: 1985).
11. Ransel, "Ambivalent Legacy," 13–14.
12. "Tsesarevich Pavel Petrovich; istoricheskie materialy. . . ," 676–82; John L. H. Keep, "Paul I and the Militarization of Government," in Ragsdale, *Paul I*, 100. Ragsdale has argued that Paul's tendency to subject everything to rule and control fits the obsessive-compulsive personality type. Such traits are undoubtedly evident in his character, but it is important to note that the pattern of control from above exemplified by Frederick the Great was widely admired in Europe at the time. Paul merely took it to insane extremes. See Ragsdale, "The Mental Condition of Paul," in Ragsdale, *Paul I*, 17–30.
13. "Tsesarevich Pavel Petrovich; istoricheskie materialy," 682–83.
14. Poroshin, *Zapiski*, 327–33, 416, 517–18; N. K. Shil'der, *Imperator Pavel Pervyi* (St. Petersburg: 1901), 61–64.
15. Poroshin, *Zapiski*, 516; Shil'der, *Imperator* 59–60.
16. Shil'der, *Imperator*, 60–61; I. Bozherianov, *Detstvo, vospitanie, i leta iunosti Russkikh Imperatorov* (St. Petersburg: 1914), 45–46.
17. Dmitrii Kobeko, *Tsesarevich Pavel Petrovich (1754–1796)* (St. Petersburg: 1887), 171–79.
18. Ibid., 102; N. K. Shil'der, *Imperator Aleksandr Pervyi, ego zhizn' i tsarstvovanie*, 4 vols. (St. Petersburg: 1897–98), 1, 94.
19. Christopher Duffy, *Russia's Military Way to the West: Origins and Nature of Russian Military Power, 1700–1800* (London: 1981), 202–3; Keep, "Paul I and the Militarization," 92–94; Roderick E. McGrew, "Paul I and the Knights of Malta," in Ragsdale, *Paul I*, 50.
20. Iu. M. Lotman, "The Theater and Theatricality as Components of Early Nineteenth Century Culture," in Iu. M. Lotman and B. A. Uspenskii, *The Semiotics of Russian Culture* (Ann Arbor: 1984), 156.
21. Shil'der, *Aleksandr Pervyi*, 1, 27–28, 21.
22. Catherine II, *Skazka o tsareviche Khlore* (St. Petersburg: 1787).
23. Shil'der, *Aleksandr Pervyi*, 1, 59–60.
24. J. L. Black, *Citizens for the Fatherland: Education, Educators and Pedagogical Ideals in Eighteenth Century Russia* (Boulder, Colo: 1979), 177.
25. Shil'der, *Aleksandr Pervyi*, 1, 32; "Sobstvennoruchnyi imennoi ukaz i nastavlenie Imp. Ekateriny II gen.-an-shefu Nikolaiu Ivanovichu Saltykovu o vos-

pitanii velikikh kniazei Aleksandra i Konstantina Pavlovichei," *Sbornik imperatorskogo russkogo istoricheskogo obshchestva*, 27 (St. Petersburg: 1880), 307–20; A. Kornilov, *Kurs istorii Rossii XIX v.*, 3 vols. (Moscow: 1918), 1, 78–79.

26. Shil'der, *Aleksandr Pervyi*, 1, 36.

27. Ibid., 1, 37–39; Jean Charles Biaudet and Françoise Nicod, *Correspondance de Frédéric de la Harpe et Alexandre Ier* (Neuchâtel: 1978), 1, 12–13.

28. Shil'der, *Aleksandr Pervyi*, 1, 39; Biaudet and Nicod, *Correspondance*, 1, 15, 90.

29. A. Fateev, "Le Problème de l'individu et de l'homme d'état dans la personnalité historique de Alexandre I, empereur de toutes les Russies," in Russkii Svobodnyi Universitet v Prage, *Zapiski nauchno-issledovatel'skogo ob"edineniia*, 3 (1936), 150–51.

30. Biaudet and Nicod, *Correspondance*, 1, 90.

31. Ibid., 135.

32. A. Ia. Protasov, "Dnevnye zapiski o vospitanii velikogo kniazia Aleksandra Pavlovicha," *Drevniaia i Novaia Rossiia* (1880), 3, 773–75; Shil'der, *Aleksandr Pervyi*, 1, 44–46, 51–56.

33. Biaudet and Nicod, 73–74.

34. Protasov, "Dnevnye zapiski," 773.

35. Shil'der, *Aleksandr Pervyi*, 1, 91–95, 98; Biaudet and Nicod, *Correspondance*, 1, 179.

36. Shil'der, *Aleksandr Pervyi*, 1, 92; Protasov, "Dnevnye zapiski," 765; A. N. Pypin, *Obshchestvennoe dvizhenie pri Aleksandre I* (Petrograd: 1918), 38.

37. Marc Raeff, *Michael Speranskii: Statesman of Imperial Russia, 1772–1839* (The Hague: 1969), 40–42.

38. Lotman, "Theater and Theatricality," 145, 159.

39. Shil'der, *Aleksandr Pervyi*, 1, 111–14; Biaudet and Nicod, *Correspondance*, 1, 158.

40. Pypin, *Obshchestvennoe*, 36–37; V. K. Nadler, *Imperator Aleksandr I i ideia sviashchennogo soiuza*, 5 vols. (Riga: 1886–92), 1, 15; Fateev, "Le problème de l'individu," 5, 5–8.

41. S. Mel'gunov, *Dela i liudi Aleksandrovskogo vremeni* (Berlin: 1923), 42, 49, 98–104.

42. Marc Raeff, *Origins of the Russian Intelligentsia: The Eighteenth Century Nobility* (New York: 1966), 53, 190; Mel'gunov, *Dela i liudi*, 42; A. I. Gertsen, *Sochineniia*, 9 vols. (Moscow: 1955–58), 7, 446; Richard Wortman, *The Development of a Russian Legal Consciousness* (Chicago: 1976), 124–25.

43. N. M. Karamzin, *Polnoe sobranie stikhotvorenii* (Moscow-Leningrad: 1966), 261.

44. Mel'gunov, *Dela i liudi*, 43; A. Ricard de Montferrand, *Plans et détails du monument consacré à la mémoire de l'Empereur Alexandre* (Paris: 1836), 36; N. I. Nikitin, *Ogiust Monferran; proektirovanie i stroitel'stvo isaakievskogo sobora i aleksandrovskoi kolonny* (Leningrad: 1939), 254.

45. Mel'gunov, *Dela i liudi*, 43–44, 58.

46. Lotman, "Theater and Theatricality," 155.

HIS EXCELLENCY THE GOVERNOR

*The Style of Russian Provincial Governance at the Beginning
of the Twentieth Century*

Richard G. Robbins, Jr.

When the Provisional Government abolished the office of provincial governor in early March 1917, few expressed regrets about the demise of a two-hundred-year-old institution.[1] In the eyes of many Russians, governors were the local embodiments of the discredited autocracy, practitioners of an authoritarian and arbitrary style of rule that the revolution was supposed to end forever.

The passage of seven decades, however, enables us to take a more detached look at the institutions and officers of the old regime. Recent studies of the tsarist bureaucracy have demonstrated that many of the long-accepted characterizations of prerevolutionary officialdom were based on a significant degree of misconception and prejudice.[2] In the case of the provincial governors, a closer examination of their activities in the last years of the old regime reveals that despite their reputation for *proizvol* (arbitrariness), the *nachal'niki gubernii* (provincial chiefs) no longer ruled chiefly by command. Although arbitrariness was never absent from provincial government, gubernatorial style was more likely to be marked by negotiation, persuasion, and compromise. In order to be effective, the tsar's viceroy could not act as a satrap but had to display at least some of the skills of a modern politician.

The altered character of gubernatorial rule, and the coexistence of traditional authoritarianism with a more modern, less arbitrary style of administration, reflected the evolution of the governorship during the course of the eighteenth and nineteenth centuries.[3] As conceived by Peter the Great in the early years of his reign, the governor was to be a genuine viceroy, the representative of the emperor in the newly created gubernias (*gubernii*), who could wield great power by virtue of his direct connection to the sovereign. And although the rights and duties of the governors changed many times in the course of the century, the central administration regularly sought to place local governance in the hands of an official who would truly be the "master of the province."

In the nineteenth century, however, a number of developments combined to transform the Russian governorship significantly. The first was the creation of the ministries in the reign of Alexander I. These institutions stood as intermediaries between the governors and the sovereign. Soon they began to extend their control over portions of the gubernia administration and weaken gubernatorial authority at the local level. Power in the provinces became increasingly fragmented, and governors had to contend with independent representatives of various central agencies.[4] More important, the Ministry of Internal Affairs (MVD) sought to reduce the governors' autonomy and to turn them into direct subordinates within a growing bureaucratic hierarchy. These threats to the governors' viceregal position were never fully realized, however. The emperors did not want ministerial power to subvert their own authority, and, as a result, they sought to maintain the independence of the governors and to use them as a direct link with the provinces and the people. At the same time, however, the tsars did not completely exempt the governors from the developing bureaucratic system. Nicholas I's *nakaz* to the governors issued in 1837 stressed their dual role as personal representatives of the autocrat and ministerial functionaries.[5]

Despite the rise of ministerial authority, the prereform governor remained a commander, and the term "master of the province" continued to be employed in the sections of the law codes that outlined his rights and duties.[6] But the position of the governors changed greatly in the 1860s and 1870s. The establishment of the zemstvos and urban institutions of self-government, the restructuring of the judiciary, and the growing emphasis on legality (*zakonnost'*) in all aspects of government combined to produce a new situation. As a result, governors lost most of their powers of positive command, except in the area of police functions, and were transformed into general supervisors of a gubernia administration that they could no longer fully control.

The diminution of the governors' powers resulting from the reforms proved unsatisfactory to the tsarist government. Beginning in the late sixties, it sought to restore a significant portion of gubernatorial authority. New legislation asserted the governors' role as the chiefs of provincial administration and expanded their ability to take actions protective of order and the political status quo. The most notable of these laws was the infamous decree on "measures to preserve state order and public tranquillity" issued on 14 August 1881. In addition, the "counterreform" legislation of the late 1880s and early 1890s expanded the control the *nachal'niki gubernii* could exercise vis-à-vis the zemstvos, urban dumas, and peasant institutions.

Yet central officials understood that these and other measures could never restore the powers of the prereform governorship. Authority at the local level was now thoroughly fragmented among institutions of self-government, the gubernia agencies of the several ministries, and the administrative apparatus subject to the governors. If effective rule in the provinces were to be maintained, then governors who could work within the confines of the new system, using the power of command they still possessed in combination with other, more subtle techniques, would have to be found.

In its search for "new model" governors, the MVD began to alter its selection processes and to reshape the gubernatorial corps during the late-nineteenth and early-twentieth centuries. Central to this transformation was a process that might be called professionalization through provincialization. Before the great reforms, the majority of governors were drawn from the military and central institutions, and selection procedures were often haphazard. Now, governors' careers became more regular and, with growing frequency, the Ministry of Internal Affairs picked governors from the ranks of those who had worked extensively in provincial administration as either appointed or elected officers. Between 1879 and 1913, the average length of prior provincial service by the governors of European Russia rose from 11.5 years to almost 15 years. During the same period, the number of governors who had previously worked for over 15 years in the gubernias climbed from 20 to 54 percent.

The kinds of jobs future governors held varied—vice-governor, *uezd* or provincial marshal, zemstvo delegate, permanent member of a provincial committee, land captain—but almost always they required a combination of administrative and political skills. The men who would be governors acquired, as a result of their service, an extensive knowledge of the workings of local government; they also gained a broad understanding of the way the game of gubernia politics was played. Of perhaps equal significance was the fact that at some time in their careers more and more governors held posts that gave them direct experience in dealing with the peasantry and its problems. And although the MVD's selection criteria clearly emphasized practical on-the-job training, formal education was not neglected. The educational levels of the governors rose in the reigns of the last two tsars, and the number of governors with training in the law increased from 10 to 34 percent.[7] By the start of the new century, the governors were increasingly well adapted to the circumstances caused by the changes begun in the 1860s.

There is, of course, no way to prove conclusively that alterations in the education and career patterns of governors had a direct bearing on the way they ruled. Yet an extensive examination of gubernatorial memoirs, private papers, and a variety of other official documents strongly suggests that a large number of turn-of-the-century governors were confident, competent, aware of the restraints on their power that the law imposed, and sensitive to local needs and concerns.[8] Efforts by governors to use the power of positive command did not cease, but inconsistency rather than arbitrariness seems to have been their major failing. Slowly and with some difficulty, the *nachal'niki gubernii* began to modify the techniques of provincial governance.

The style of gubernatorial administration that now emerged was a mixture of the old and the new. On one level it was archaic—personal and patriarchal governance in the manner of a *tishaishii tsar* ("most gentle tsar"). On the other, it was quite modern, involving the skills of a practical politician. Confronting a situation in which they were relatively powerless, governors sought to make use of the prestige that their viceregal status provided. At the same time they had to display political acumen and the ability to maneuver and persuade in order to attain their desired ends.

The personal and patriarchal aspects of gubernatorial rule are the easiest to document. In keeping with their status as the tsar's viceroys, governors frequently became involved with the problems and needs of the people of their gubernias. They assigned great importance to the official reception (*priem*) at which citizens from all walks of life could come forward to make requests of the *nachal'nik gubernii*. Most governors held a reception for several hours each day; few would let a week go by without one. And the kinds of things that petitioners asked governors to do show that in the eyes of the people they ruled they were indeed surrogates for the *tsar izbavnik* ("tsar-deliverer"). "The children did not have tea today, and I cannot buy provisions for supper," wrote Evgeniia Lapitskaia to Viatka's N. A. Troinitskii. "Your Excellency, I turn to you as a man and a governor. We are in a terrible situation."[9]

Requests from provincial citizens involved governors in a wide variety of personal, even intimate, problems. A distraught mother begged N. P. Sinel'nikov to help break up a romance between her son and a soldier's wife. Karl Boi, a teacher of German in Kurland who had been accused of molesting his students, asked Governor D. D. Sverbeev what to do about the "slander." And when Gerasim Golovkov, a hired worker at the Academy of Arts in St. Petersburg, lacked the money necessary for the purchase of a railway ticket to Belostok, to whom did he turn? To Governor I. V. Lutkovskii, of course![10]

As far as can be determined, governors responded positively to these appeals, making, at the very least, good faith efforts to satisfy them. The *nachal'niki gubernii* took considerable pride in their role as local problem solvers. Even when passing on a request to other hands, governors appended notes to guide subordinates in handling the case.[11]

The personal and patriarchal style of the governors was also frequently evident in the way they treated members of their staffs. Governors commonly regarded many of their closer subordinates as family, affording them special solicitude and protection. Governors S. V. Shakhovskoi, G. A. Tobizen, and N. M. Baranov were well known for the kindness they showed to lesser officials.[12] While governor in Grodno, M. M. Osorgin developed the practice of finding out what particular local *chinovniki* liked to eat. If, by chance, the favorite dish of one of these officials was being served at the governor's lunch, Osorgin sent a servant to bring the man to table.[13] On a less intimate level, governors were often directly involved in helping officials obtain pensions or posts in other provinces.[14]

Solicitude toward subordinates was more than a reflection of the governors' humanity, however. It had an important practical significance. Competent staff was hard to find, and governors had to treasure the gems that came their way. Moreover, because local officials were easily demoralized given their inadequate pay and low status, governors had to lift their spirits whenever possible in order to mobilize them and inspire their best efforts. Forming a kind of family group was an important means to this end.

The personal and patriarchal approach extended far beyond the confines of the governors' mansions and the gubernia offices. When forced to deal with matters such as labor unrest, peasant disturbances, and urban riots, governors often sought to be present at the scene and to handle matters directly. In part, the governors were responding to the expectations that surrounded their office. The *nachal'niki gubernii* represented the tsar, and the Russian autocrats had always fostered the myth of the emperor's intimate concern with the needs of his subjects. As a tsar-surrogate, the governor was supposed to be an embodiment of this ideal. At the same time, in handling manifestations of lower-class violence, governors often operated on the principle "If you want the job done right, do it yourself." Because lower officials, especially the notoriously corrupt and inefficient police, could not always be relied upon, governors felt that when matters reached a flash point, their physical presence was required.

Gubernatorial style is best demonstrated in the treatment of strikes and other forms of labor unrest.[15] Governors saw such disturbances as being highly dangerous and worked diligently for a rapid restoration of order. At the same time, however, circumstances often permitted governors to become involved in resolving the causes of disputes, and they could cast themselves in a protective and mediating role.

N. S. Brianchaninov's handling of a strike at the Khludov textile mill in Egor'evsk during the summer of 1893 provides a useful demonstration of the many techniques governors might employ. Although the strike was a large one, involving three thousand workers, and had been accompanied by considerable violence, Brianchaninov chose not to rely exclusively on force. At the outset, he dispatched troops to the scene and terminated the disorders. But the next day His Excellency appeared at the factory to begin the complex and lengthy task of negotiating a settlement. Toward the workers, the governor was firm. He met with strike leaders and told them that their walkout was illegal and that their demands for better pay, reduction in the workload, and curtailment of night work would never be met as long as they refused to go back to the bench. At the same time, however, Brianchaninov held out the prospect that changes could be won by less strident means.

After this, the governor moved in two directions. He had a number of the strike leaders forcibly removed to their native villages. Simultaneously, he turned to the employers and persuaded them to pay the workers more frequently, reduce the length of the night shift, and eliminate it entirely before Sundays and holidays. Later Brianchaninov induced the factory owners to remove the plant manager, fire some of the more abusive lower echelon supervisors, and institute a regular review of workers' complaints. In the end, his efforts restored calm and allowed the factory to reopen. And although the strike flared again in October, the governor was convinced that the reforms he had promoted laid the basis for a peaceful resolution of future disputes.[16]

The way in which Brianchaninov and other governors coped with instances of labor unrest suggests that they were not sympathetic to the management of industrial firms. In their reports to the Ministry of Internal Affairs, governors frequently portrayed factory conditions in a negative light and described the exploitation of the proletariat in terms similar to those found in socialist propaganda.[17] The workers, apparently, sensed this bias and for that reason often sought to involve the *nachal'niki gubernii* in their disputes with management. According to Daniel Brower, workers used industrial violence in order to bring the governor to the scene. Experience led factory hands to believe that a governor's intervention was likely to produce desirable results. Individuals might be arrested or sent home, but as a group the workers would benefit.[18]

On the whole, governors tended to be much more stern in dealing with peasant disturbances, and they seldom became involved in mediating disputes.[19] Still, they sought to bring the peasants into submission by persuasion and, on occasion, could be quite successful. During the summer of 1884, for example, Chernigov's Governor S. V. Shakhovskoi brought the inhabitants of a mutinous village to their knees by means of a lengthy harangue that skillfully played on their religious beliefs and their intense loyalty to the tsar. In the end, the governor formalized the peasants' submission by arranging a strange communion service in which each of them received from his hand a piece of bread dipped in salt after which they pronounced the words "May God be witness to my repentance and to the truth of my promise."[20] Governor S. D. Urusov, too, advised persuasion when dealing with peasant disorders. Approach the offenders as rational human beings, he suggested. Display "a certain amount of bonhomie" and try to appeal to the peasants' basic respect for law and order. But governors' rhetorical powers were often insufficient, and when they failed to persuade, they readily made use of compulsion, including the birch. Even Urusov admitted that a governor should always be prepared for trouble and have available, "as a sort of *ultima ratio*," disciplined military units.[21]

It would be easy to explain the governors' differing approaches to workers and peasants in terms of economic interest and class prejudice. As large landholders themselves,[22] most governors desired to maintain existing agrarian relations. Moreover, their upbringing and training had convinced them that the existing system on the land was basically just. Thus although the governors, as outsiders, quickly saw the flaws in factory conditions, they viewed the problems of the peasantry with less sympathetic eyes.

But when giving due weight to the factors of class and self-interest, we should not ignore the practical difficulties that agrarian disputes presented to the governors. An industrial strike was a situation that contained a wide variety of possible concessions regarding wages, hours, or conditions. Thus it was easy for a governor to play the mediator. In a peasant disturbance, however, issues were more tightly joined. The conflict usually concerned ownership of a piece of land, payment of a tax or fee, matters about which there could be little compromise. If the peasants refused to be persuaded, the governor had few means besides force to break their resistance.

The patriarchal style was useful in handling the demands of ordinary citizens and instances of lower-class violence. Until the first years of the twentieth century, at least, governors could count on the traditional conservatism of the Russian common people and on their respect for constituted authority. More modern techniques had to be employed, however, when His Excellency sought to cope with clearly political situations such as conflict with gentry marshals, institutions of self-government, and field agents of the central ministries. Here the governors had to deal with representatives of educated society who enjoyed social prestige, a degree of independent power, and a recognized sphere of activity. The viceregal status of the *nachal'nik gubernii*, although helpful, was not sufficient. Denied the power of command in most cases, a governor would succeed or fail largely on the basis of his ability to maneuver and persuade.

In their political efforts, governors would rely heavily on something called "service tact" (*sluzhebnyi takt*). This term had no precise definition, but in a broad sense it meant the ability to maintain authority without giving offense; a willingness to cultivate and, when necessary, to appease powerful local forces; a knack for reconciling conflicting parties and resolving differences. Service tact had not been a dominant characteristic of provincial administration in the prereform era, when the style of rule resembled more closely that of a military command. But the papers of governors and central directives from the late-nineteenth and early-twentieth centuries reveal the frequency with which the term came to be used and the great significance assigned to it. "Service tact" was a code word that described the kind of political skills that had become indispensable for gubernatorial success.

The importance of service tact was most clearly demonstrated in those circumstances when it was either wanting or insufficiently displayed. Consider the sad case of Sergei Ivanovich Golikov, governor of Voronezh from 1909 to 1914. On paper Golikov was almost perfect for the job. A graduate of the University of Moscow Law School, he had been an assistant procurator, an *uezd* marshal of the nobility, and a permanent member of the provincial committee on zemstvo and urban affairs. He should have known the field of provincial politics and the way to play the game. Yet his governorship was something of a disaster.

Two years after Golikov's posting to Voronezh, an MVD inspector, N. Ch. Zaionchkovskii, visited the gubernia. He found the governor to be young, energetic, and well prepared. There was only one problem. "In Voronezh," Zaionchkovskii wrote, "I have not encountered a single individual who has a good word to say about the local governor. He is surrounded by those who wish him ill, [these include] those on the Right, the Center and the Left." All the powers of the capital city, the provincial and *uezd* marshals, the chairman of the zemstvo executive board, the procurator, and even the head of the gendarmes could not abide the *nachal'nik gubernii*.

What had Golikov done? Nothing, it would seem, that was terribly serious. His Excellency was not very personable, and his police chief and head of chancellery cut him off from provincial leaders. There had been some tactless statements. When giving his opinion on the work of the *uezd* conference of land captains, Golikov had used the phrases "the conference should have . . ." and "the conference has not attended to . . . the question . . . carefully enough. . . ." As a result the Voronezh *uezd* marshal took umbrage. And Golikov compounded tactical blunders by personal indiscretion. Zaionchkovskii learned that another basis for enmity between the governor and the *uezd* marshal was "their simultaneous pursuit of one and the same lady, who had shown a decided preference for Golikov." Having offended local honor, the governor became the victim of a series of petty slights to which, apparently, he replied in kind. Tensions grew, and ultimately Golikov was politically isolated.[23]

Obviously, provincial life provided more serious grounds for tension and conflict. Governors and the institutions of self-government clashed regularly over a wide range of issues. Yet we can infer from recent studies of relations between the zemstvos and the bureaucracy that most issues of dispute between the *nachal'niki gubernii* and elected institutions concerned practical issues about which men could honorably disagree and which could be handled by established institutional channels with a minimum of hard feelings.[24] The kind of conflict that tended to be most disruptive occurred when one of the parties, most often the governor, overstepped the bounds of decorum, thereby giving matters a personal dimension.

Thus, for example, when Kharkov governor I. M. Obolenskii publicly criticized the accounting procedures of the provincial zemstvo, and Vologda Governor A. A. Musin-Pushkin inadvertently used the terms *obmer* and *obves* ("false measure" and "false weight") in reference to local merchant practices, explosions took place.[25] Below the surface, of course, lurked more serious problems—the tension and indignation produced when Obolenskii suppressed peasant disturbances in 1902 and the resentment caused when Musin-Pushkin tried to clean up the gubernia capital and reform commercial practices. Yet these substantive questions could not be voiced. Matters came to a head only when the governors allowed their personalities to become the issue.

If personality defects, most notably a want of tact, could produce gubernatorial difficulties, then positive qualities could also be the source of a governor's success. The governorship of A. I. Kosich in Saratov (1887–91) provides a useful example. When Kosich, an army general with little civilian experience, arrived in the province he found aspects of the local economy in disarray and the zemstvos in a state of somnolence. The governor's task was to point out the deficiencies of zemstvo work and to encourage more initiative. Given zemstvo sensitivities and resistance to gubernatorial pressure, this was no easy matter. But Kosich had his way and, at the same time, acquired considerable local popularity.

Available materials do not enable us to follow all of the governor's activities. But the speeches he made to various zemstvo assemblies give us a sense of his style. Kosich was quite blunt about zemstvo shortcomings, and he freely gave advice about what needed to be done. Yet at the same time, he displayed considerable solicitude for the zemstvo as an institution and skillfully mixed his criticisms with praise and expressions of optimism about the zemstvos' future.[26] As a result of this display of tact, Kosich moved the zemstvo to action in a number of important areas. Of particular significance were his efforts to encourage the reluctant zemstvos to make peasants build up their local grain reserves. Kosich's success in this field helped the province weather the disastrous crop failure and famine of 1891–92.

Relations between the governors and the field agents of the several central ministries also required liberal amounts of political savvy. Governors were constantly engaged in negotiations with local military commanders, directors of the fiscal chambers, gubernia procurators, managers of state properties, bishops, and school superintendents. Because these officials were not really subordinate to the *nachal'niki gubernii* and jealously guarded their independence, attempts to coordinate their activities with those of the provincial administration had to be carried out with extreme caution and tact. Even an improperly phrased invitation to meet on a matter of mutual interest could produce an affront. Thus when acting governor P. M. Boiarskii asked Saratov bishop Germogen to attend a session of the provincial board to consider arrangements for celebrating the fiftieth anniversary of the emancipation, the imperious cleric penned an angry letter of protest to Prime Minister Stolypin. "One need not have an exaggerated opinion of the prestige of Episcopal power and dignity," Germogen asserted, "in order to understand that inviting a bishop [to a meeting] without preliminary negotiations . . . , as if he were a simple official, is either [an act of] disrespect or a conscious desire to insult the bishop."[27] Similarly, maintaining good relations with the military, so necessary for the order and security of the province, often required governors to employ "the cunning of the serpent and the mildness of the dove."[28] The tsar's viceroys had to be extremely careful lest they offend the army officers' prickly sense of honor. P. P. Stremoukhov noted that on occasions he had hushed up many scandals involving military men; frequently, he helped officers escape the clutches of local moneylenders as part of an effort to keep the peace with the army leadership.[29]

By the beginning of the twentieth century, then, the governors were no longer real commanders, but managers and persuaders who based their power on a combination of viceregal status, acquired administrative skills, and arts of maneuver, compromise, and palaver. Gubernatorial arbitrariness had not been totally eliminated, but it had been mitigated.[30] The emergence of governors who were knowledgeable about provincial administration and often were experienced local politicians had important consequences for imperial governance in the late-nineteenth and early-twentieth centuries. Because they had served extensively at the gubernia level before assuming their high office, many governors began their job with the strong conviction that they knew how gubernia affairs ought to be managed. Sometimes confidence bordered on arrogance, as in the case of Riazan governor N. N. Kisel'-Zagorianskii, who, having held a variety of lower posts, described his qualifications with a disarming lack of modesty:

> I not only knew the law, but I could also carry out the duties of all of my subordinates starting with the *volost'* scribe and the secretary of the provincial board, and finishing . . . with members of all the existing provincial committees, the chairman of the [zemstvo] *uprava*, the marshal, and . . . the vice-governor. And I could fulfill these [duties] better than any of them.[31]

Other governors were less strident in expressing the conviction that they knew how to rule, but this attitude influenced their political style. Frequently, it made them reluctant to follow unquestioningly the directives from the center. S. D. Urusov, for example, decided at the outset of his tenure in Bessarabia that he would never let the minister of internal affairs treat him as a direct subordinate, justifying his position by reference to the statutes that defined the governors' powers.[32] But Urusov's feeling that he could function independently of central directives and his determination to act on the basis of the needs of the gubernia, not the policies of St. Petersburg, were also undoubtedly based on the confidence he gained from long prior experience in provincial affairs.

Outright gubernatorial defiance of orders from the MVD was rare, but it did occur.[33] Much more common was the practice of ignoring the demands of the St. Petersburg bureaus or of implementing them selectively. Governors often saw capital officials as ignorant and their orders misguided, and when conflict developed with the center the *nachal'niki gubernii* often simply went their own way, even if it involved a degree of risk. During his tenure in Perm, I. F. Koshko, who had earlier served as a land captain, permanent member of the provincial committee on peasant affairs, and vice-governor, became involved in a dispute with the Minister of Internal Affairs over a complex question of land redistribution. When the governor failed to convince his superior of the correctness of his view, he broke off the discussion. Koshko pursued what he believed to be the proper policy, guided by his conscience, experience, and the law as he understood it.[34]

Familiarity with local administration and self-government also helped to determine the attitude of governors toward the work of lesser officials, the zemstvos, and urban institutions. For example, many governors were critical of the land captains. Often their negative assessments were based on the fact that they themselves had held that post or some other office that gave them extensive contact with the peasant world.[35] By way of contrast, governors who had served in the zemstvos or had worked closely with them tended to be supportive if not indulgent.[36] Most conflict, when it occurred, did not stem from a reluctance of governors to cooperate with the zemstvos but from the almost unavoidable friction that developed as state and societal institutions sought to define and adjust their mutual relations. As provincial "politicians," governors realized that their ability to manage gubernia affairs depended to a considerable degree on the goodwill of key local figures, many of whom were associated with the zemstvos. The pursuit of a modus vivendi might even lead a governor to modify or oppose a central order that seemed bound to produce serious discontent. Stephen Sternheimer's claim that governors sabotaged the Stolypin land reform in order to keep on the good side of gentry leaders is probably exaggerated,[37] yet it is very likely that in implementing the reform the governors were quite sensitive to local opinion.

Despite governors' efforts to avoid conflict, their style of rule could, in certain circumstances, cause disputes. No politician, however skillful, can keep the interests of all groups in perfect balance; satisfying one faction might produce unhappiness in another quarter. In addition, the personal character of gubernatorial rule tended to make it highly inconsistent. Governors frequently intervened in a host of matters, bypassing official channels and sometimes bending, if not breaking, the law. They behaved this way because they accepted their status as the autocrat's viceroy and because they knew that many local people expected them to act directly and personally. But governors could not hope to handle all questions themselves, so they were selective about the issues to which they gave attention. This practice made gubernia administration seem uneven and arbitrary, especially to the educated public. It perpetuated the image of the governor as a satrap at a time when his power of command was rapidly eroding.

Gubernatorial rule at the end of the nineteenth century appears to have been relatively mild and fairly effective. But it rested on fragile foundations. Because gubernia institutions were inadequate and power was fragmented among various independent agencies, the governors' control over their provinces depended on the degree of consensus they could achieve with the educated classes and on the lower orders' passive acceptance of constituted authority. By the start of the twentieth century, however, both of these bases of provincial administration were beginning to crumble. In 1905 large segments of the elite deserted the system, and the workers and peasants rose in open revolt. Governors did not meet this challenge very well. In part they simply lacked the instruments of force needed to maintain law and order. But equally serious appears to have been the psychological inability of the *nachal'niki gubernii* to cope with an unprecedented situation.

Schooled in the system of provincial "politics" that placed great emphasis on decorum, tact, and persuasion, governors were ill prepared to deal well with a rude, elemental storm that rendered their style of rule useless. Although confronting massive agrarian disturbances, many governors refused to see their economic and social roots, blaming instead revolutionary agitators.[38] When an increasingly desperate central administration ordered them to take the most extreme repressive measures, governors often hesitated, preferring to negotiate rather than shoot. But such moderation availed them little. During the summer of 1905, Vladimir governor I. M. Leont'ev sought to end a workers' strike in Ivanovo-Voznesensk by using the traditional methods of limited force, persuasion, and compromise. He was repeatedly frustrated. The workers were emboldened by the rising tide of revolution and resisted the governor's efforts to bring them back to the job. The factory owners, on the other hand, were increasingly fearful. They refused to go to the scene of the disturbances and were reluctant to engage in serious bargaining with their employees. Meanwhile, the MVD, and especially the Department of Police, demanded immediate, decisive action, including the use of force. Even when the strike ended without serious violence or major loss of life, Leont'ev received little credit. The workers remained alienated and discontented, the factory owners felt that they had not received adequate protection, and the governor's superiors in St. Petersburg continued to fault him for being insufficiently firm.[39]

When governors took steps to end disturbances, however, they found the social opprobrium that their actions generated difficult to understand or accept. Despair was common. Samara governor I. L. Blok captured the mood of many of the *nachal'niki gubernii* when he complained to his co-workers:

> You risk your life, you wear out your nerves maintaining order so that people can live like human beings, and what do you get? Not only is there no support . . . , but also at every step you encounter condemnation; you go about the city and catch glances filled with hatred as if you were some kind of monster, a drinker of human blood. . . .[40]

After order was at last restored, governors were encouraged to return to the patterns of rule they had employed before the upheaval.[41] In the main, these proved effective with reference to the educated classes, for whom the experience of the years 1905–7 had been decidedly chastening. But if we can judge from published materials, the governors were far less involved in dealing with the lower classes than they had been prior to the revolution. This can be explained in part by the growing importance of other, intermediary institutions: the factory inspectorate, trade unions, and radical parties for the workers, and the land reform agencies in rural areas. Yet the effacement of the governors also reflects the fact that despite the return of civil peace, the *nachal'niki gubernii* could not continue to administer the provinces as they had done before. As a result of the revolution, traditional patterns of deference to authority had been disrupted or destroyed, and the workers and peasants increasingly failed to respond to the personal and patriarchal style of rule. At the same time, cultural barriers and chronic weakness of government institutions made it impossible for governors to employ the more sophisticated political techniques that were proving at least moderately successful with the upper classes. In the end, the events of February 1917 would show that the limited modernization of the practices of gubernia administration effected by the start of the twentieth century had not been sufficient to give the governors a firm local base or to meet the needs of a rapidly changing society.

NOTES

1. This decree is published in English in Robert P. Browder and Alexander F. Kerensky (eds.), *The Russian Provisional Government 1917: Documents*, 3 vols. (Stanford, Calif.: 1961), 1, 243.
2. For some useful surveys of this literature see Daniel Orlovsky, "Recent Studies on the Russian Bureaucracy," *Russian Review* 34 (October 1976), 448–67, and Marc Raeff, "The Bureaucratic Phenomenon of Imperial Russia, 1700–1905," *American Historical Review* 84 (April 1979), 399–411.
3. For a brief, lucid discussion of the development of the Russian governorship see S. A. Korf, "Ocherk istoricheskogo razvitiia gubernatorskoi dolzhnosti v Rossii," *Vestnik prava* 31 (November 1901), 130–48. The standard treatment of the subject is I. Blinov, *Gubernatory: istoriko-iuridicheskii ocherk* (St. Petersburg: 1905).
4. N. P. Eroshkin, *Istoriia gosudarstvennykh uchrezhdenii dorevoliutsionnoi Rossii*, 2d ed. (Moscow: 1968), 180–92.
5. PSZ, 2d ser., 3 June 1837, no. 10303.
6. See "Obshchee gubernskoe uchrezhdenie," *Svod zakonov rossiiskoi imperii*, 2 (St. Petersburg: 1857), article 358.
7. For a more complete discussion of the changes in the MVD's selection policies and the transformation of the gubernatorial corps in the period 1879 to 1913 see my book, *The Tsar's Viceroys: Russian Provincial Governors in the Last Years of the Empire* (Ithaca, N.Y.: 1987), 25–38.

8. Among the sources that form the basis of this impression are the memoirs and papers of V. F. Dzhunkovskii (Tsentral'nyi gosudarstvennyi arkhiv oktiabr'skoi revoliutsii [TsGAOR], fond 826); N. A. Bezak's papers (Tsentral'nyi gosudarstvennyi istoricheskii arkhiv SSSR [TsGIA], f. 895); V. V. fon Val"s memoir of his governorship in Vilna (TsGIA, f. 916, opis' 1, delo 13) and his papers in TsGAOR, f. 542; M. M. Osorgin's memoirs in Otdel rukopisei gosudarstvennoi biblioteki im. Lenina (GBL), f. 215; the memoirs of A. N. Mosolov in TsGAOR, f. 1463, op. 1, d. 1115; the papers of N. A. Troinitskii, TsGIA, f. 1065, esp. the letters from his son, A. N. Troinitskii, found in d. 57; the papers of A. D. Sverbeev in Tsentral'nyi gosudarstvennyi arkhiv literatury i iskusstva (TsGALI), f. 472. S. D. Urussov's (spelled *Urusov* in the text) account of his governorship in Bessarabia, *Memoirs of a Russian Governor*, trans. by H. Rosenthal (London and New York: 1908) is very useful, as is I. F. Koshko's *Vospominaniia gubernatora (1905–1914): Novgorod, Samara, Penza* (Petrograd: 1916). This latter work can be supplemented by the unpublished segment "Vospominaniia gubernatora, chast' II: Perm'," which is held in the Bakhmeteff Archive at Columbia University (BAR). Of considerable value, too, is the section of N. N. Kisel'-Zagorianskii's memoirs that deals with his governorship in Riazan (BAR, Kisel'-Zagorianskii papers), and the memoir-essay of P. P. Stremoukhov, "Administrativnoe ustroistvo imperatorskoi Rossii po vospominaniiam gubernatora," (BAR, S. E. Kryzhanovskii papers).

9. Letter dated 2 August 1879, TsGIA, f. Troinitskogo, op. 1, d. 52, "Pis'ma Troinitskim ot raznykh lits," 1.

10. N. P. Sinel'nikov, "Zapiski senatora N. P. Sinel'nikova," *Istoricheskii vestnik* 59, no. 3 (1895), 729–30; Karl Boi to D. D. Sverbeev, 16 February 1900, TsGIA, f. Kantseliarii Ministra vnutrennikh del, op. 1, d. 1175, "Kurliandskaia guberniia," 22–23; Letter of Governor Lutkovskii to P. A. Gresser, 30 April 1884, Leningradskii gosudarstvennyi istoricheskii arkhiv (LGIA), f. Kantseliarii petrogradskogo gubernatora, op. 3, d. 1950, "Po lichnoi perepiske . . . ," 29.

11. Koshko, *Vospominaniia*, 145; Dzhunkovskii "Vospominaniia za 1909–1910," TsGAOR, f. Dzhunkovskogo, op. 1, d. 49, 158.

12. Osorgin, "Vospominaniia," GBL, f. Osorgina, papka II, d. 2, 28–30; S. I. Umanets, *Vospominaniia o kniaze S. V. Shakhovskom i baltiiskie ocherki* (St. Petersburg: 1899), 19; A. V. Ovchinnikov to N. A. Bezak, 26 October 1882, TsGIA, f. Bezaka, op. 1, d. 18, "Pis'ma . . . Ovchinnikova . . . Bezaku," 8.

13. Osorgin, "Vospominaniia," 148–49.

14. N. A. Troinitskii to L. S. Makov, 13 May 1880, TsGIA, f. Troinitskogo, op. 1, d. 86 [untitled *delo*], 1–4; letters of fon Val' to G. Khokhuli, 11 March and 4 April 1880, TsGAOR, f. fon Valia, op. 1, d. 103, "Prosheniia . . . i dr. materialy ob ustroistve, uvolnenii, peremeshchenii po sluzhbe chinovnikov," 7–15.

15. Generalizations about the governors' activities in labor disputes is based primarily on the materials contained in A. M. Pankratova and L. M. Ivanov (eds.), *Rabochee dvizhenie v Rossii v XIX veke: Sbornik dokumentov i materialov*, 4

vols. (Moscow: 1950–63), esp. vols. 3 and 4, and *Rabochee dvizhenie v Rossii v 1901–1904 "gg."* (Leningrad: 1975).

16. On Brianchaninov's response to the Khludov strike see *Rabochee dvizhenie*, 3, pt. 2, 315–42, and the governor's report for 1893, TsGIA, f. Departamenta obshchikh del (hereafter *DOD*,) op. 223, 1894, d. 207, 13–16.

17. Osorgin, "Vospominaniia," 168–75; see also the comments of Tver governor Akhlestyshev on factory conditions, *Rabochee dvizhenie*, III, pt. 2, 150–51.

18. Daniel Brower, "Labor Violence in Russia in the Late Nineteenth Century," *Slavic Review* 41, no. 3 (Fall 1982), 417–31.

19. Numerous examples of the governors' treatment of peasant disturbances can be found in the multivolume collection of documents *Krest'ianskoe dvizhenie v Rossii*. Of special value were the volumes covering the period 1881–1889, ed. by A. V. Nifontov and B. V. Zlatoustovskii, and the years 1890–1900, ed. by A. V. Shapkarin.

20. *Krest'ianskoe dvizhenie v Rossii v 1881–1889 gg.* (Moscow: 1960), 394–96.

21. Urussov, *Memoirs*, 105–11.

22. Until after 1905, roughly two-thirds of the governors were *pomeshchiki*, and nearly half of those held more than one thousand desiatinas (Robbins, *The Tsar's Viceroys*, 31).

23. TsGIA, f. DOD, op. 47, 1911, d. 305a, "Otchet . . . Zaionchkovskogo po obozreniiu deloproizvodstva voronezhskogo gubernskogo pravleniia i kantseliarii gubernatora," 80–82.

24. The excellent article by Thomas Fallows, "The Zemstvo and the Bureaucracy," in T. Emmons and W. Vucinich (eds.), *The Zemstvo in Russia: An Experiment in Local Self-Government* (Cambridge and New York: 1982), 184–93, shows clearly the complexity of governor-zemstvo relations. Conflict and cooperation between provincial administrators and zemstvos is also discussed in my study *Famine in Russia, 1891–1892: The Imperial Government Responds to a Crisis* (New York: 1975), esp. 124–48, and in *The Tsar's Viceroys*, 155–66.

25. On Obolenskii, see Fallows, "Zemstvo and the Bureaucracy," 213; on Musin-Pushkin, TsGIA, f. Kantseliarii Ministra vnutrennikh del, op. 2, d. 2171, "Delo po zhalobe vologodskikh kuptsov na oskorblenie ikh grazhdanskim gubernatorom."

26. A. I. Kosich, *Tsirkuliary, ukazanii i rechi* (Saratov: 1891), 53–64.

27. Letter dated 20 January 1911, TsGIA, f. DOD, op. 47, 1906, d. 64, "Sekretnoe po saratovskoi gub.," 31–32.

28. Urussov, *Memoirs*, p. 58. The author is quoting Matthew 10:16.

29. Stremoukhov, "Administrativnoe ustroistvo," sec. 1, 8–9, BAR, Kryzhanovskii papers.

30. This is not to suggest that the incidence of conflict between governors and the institutions of self-government had declined; indeed, disputes with the zemstvos in particular increased at the start of the twentieth century. But conflict should not be identified with *proizvol*.

31. "Mémoires," 180, BAR, Kisel'-Zagorianskii papers.

32. Urussov, *Memoirs*, 2.

33. Such cases usually took place during crises. The famine of 1891–92 produced several examples. See *Famine in Russia*, 55–57, 227.

34. Koshko, "Vospominaniia," 553–54.

35. Osorgin, "Vospominaniia," 187–89; Koshko, "Vospominaniia," 230–36. See also Saratov governor B. B. Meshcherskii's annual report for 1895, TsGIA, f. DOD, op. 223, 1896, d. 28b, 11. Osorgin and Koshko had been land captains; Meshcherskii had served as both *uezd* and gubernia marshal.

36. Urussov, *Memoirs*, 70–72; B. B. Meshcherskii's annual report for 1896, TsGIA, f. DOD, op. 223, 1897, d. 30b, 4; A. P. Engel'gardt's address to the Saratov zemstvo assembly, 1 December 1901, reprinted in A. P. Engel'gardt, *Chernozemnaia Rossiia: Ocherk ekonomicheskogo polozheniia kraia* (Saratov: 1902), xi–xiv. The generally friendly attitude of governors toward the zemstvos was not, by and large, extended toward urban institutions. Although it cannot be proved, this may reflect the fact that very few governors had prior experience working with city dumas.

37. "Administration and Political Development: An Inquiry into the Tsarist and Soviet Experience," Ph.D. dissertation, University of Chicago, 1974, 206–7, 220–21, 238, 247–48.

38. See the report of P. N. Durnovo, minister of internal affairs, to Nicholas II, 29 January 1906, in N. Karpov (ed.), *Krest'ianskoe dvizhenie v revoliutsii 1905 goda v dokumentakh* (Leningrad: 1926), 94–97.

39. See the relevant documents in A. M. Pankratova et al. (eds.), *Revoliutsiia 1905–1907 gg. v Rossii: Dokumenty i Materialy* (Moscow: 1955–63), the volume titled *Revoliutsionnoe dvizhenie v Rossii vesnoi i letom 1905 goda (aprel'-sentiabr')*, pt. 1, 403–65.

40. Koshko, *Vospominaniia*, 83.

41. See Stolypin's circular to the governors dated 15 September 1906, *Krasnyi arkhiv* 32 (1929), 163–68.

PART

II

IMPERIAL RUSSIAN SOCIETY

The Ideal of Paternalism
in the Prereform Army

Elise Kimerling Wirtschafter

T aking their cue from the historiographical tradition of the nine-teenth-century Russian "statist" school, historians have long focused upon the central role of the state in Russia's social de-velopment. This is no surprise, considering the weakness and structural amorphousness of Russian society as compared to the absolute political authority of the autocracy.[1] But despite this unlimited political power, prereform Russia remained an undergoverned country, and the modernizing policies of the "well-ordered police state" had little influence on the mass of servile society.[2]

The desire of the imperial government to reeducate and discipline its subjects through law was nowhere more visible than in military society.[3] The limited size of the military with its hierarchical bureaucratic struc-ture allowed a significant (though by no means absolute) degree of govern-mental control. An examination of the relationship between the state and the lower ranks of military society may therefore illuminate some impor-tant aspects of tsarist social policy.[4] In its dealings with military society, the government sought to impose on authority relationships a set of values best described as paternalistic. Most simply, this meant that persons in positions of authority played the role of father to their subordinates, who were in turn viewed as the children of their superiors. The first task of this essay is to define the various aspects of the paternalistic ideal as de-fined by the state. The second is to examine how that ideal operated in military society. What did it mean in practice? What was its role in defin-ing social norms? To what extent did the social groups affected absorb its message? Indeed, how consistently did the state actually project this mes-sage? Although the paternalistic ideal operated at all levels of military society, the focus here is upon the lower ranks in the prereform army.

THE PATERNALISTIC IDEAL

Through education and bureaucratic regulation, the autocracy actively sought to mold social relations in the prereform army according to a paternalistic ideal. Just as the tsar posed as "affectionate father" (*batiushka*) to his people, so too commanders in the army were seen as fathers to their subordinates.[5] Conversely, subordinates were viewed as children who needed guidance and protection. The notion of a father-child relationship applied primarily to relations between commanders and the lower ranks. But official proclamations also instructed senior commanders to approach young and inexperienced junior officers in a like manner. Official sources compared relations between the regimental commander and his subordinate officers to those between father and child. Similarly, the society (*obshchestvo*) of officers was portrayed as a family.[6] The paternalistic ideal thus extended from the very top of the military hierarchy down to the noncommissioned officers and *diad'ki* ("uncles"), who exercised the most direct supervision over the common soldiers.

Because the term of service (twenty-five years for most soldiers) was lengthy and because conscription brought juridical emancipation from serfdom, young recruits experienced a sudden and usually final break from family and village. In the eyes of the peasantry, recruitment was tantamount to death, as it was highly unlikely that a son sent to the army would ever return home.[7] For the recruit himself, entry into military society was a physical and psychological shock.[8] To help ease the transition to military life, the *diad'ka* acted as a kind of surrogate parent. The *diad'ka* was supposed to be an older, experienced soldier who had served irreproachably for at least ten years. As the "foundation of his regiment," the old soldier was also a teacher of young recruits.[9] When a recruit reached his assigned regiment, he was first placed under the supervision of a *diad'ka*, who taught him to dress correctly and care for his equipment. The authorities also expected the *diad'ka* to exert a moral influence on his charge; to explain to him the meaning of commands, the order of service; and in general to instruct him in the rules of military behavior. Because officials believed that the recruit's earliest experiences in the army played a crucial role in the formation of his overall attitude toward the service (especially in the light of widespread popular hostility toward conscription), they ordered the *diad'ka* to treat him with patience, affection, and understanding.[10] After about two years of close guidance by his *diad'ka*, the "recruit soldier" became a "young soldier" held fully accountable for his actions.[11]

The government assigned an important pedagogical role to *diad'ki* and noncommissioned officers, but in accordance with the paternalistic ideal the real father to the soldier was his commander. Commanders of individual units and their subordinate officers were supposed to take the place of the recruits' parents. Homesick and mournful, young recruits required the special concern and attention of their superiors. Just as the monarchy served as moral teacher to its people, it was especially important for commanders to supervise the moral development of their men. Reflecting this view, one midcentury observer attributed the moral failings of soldiers to their separation from parental influence and from the social norms of the village community.[12] It was the commander's duty to fill this moral and social void. Not surprisingly, officials who advocated the spread of literacy among the lower ranks tended to see it as a means for improving the moral quality of the troops.[13]

As father to his men, the commander was supposed to be feared and loved, severe but just.[14] In the image of the biblical God, he was to be both merciful and "awful." The ideal of paternalism combined fatherly concern for the welfare of the lower ranks with strict discipline and punishment, for purposes of teaching and protecting. In his 1774 instructions to company commanders, Count Vorontsov described the ideal commander:

> If it is necessary that the captain, as the head of a company, be feared and honored by all [his subordinates], it is just as necessary that they love and completely trust him. He should conduct himself like a father with [his] children, admonishing the dishonorable [and] correcting them with advice. [He should] punish the unworthy with charity, single out and love the good, so that they themselves and all others see that evil will be punished and meticulousness and virtue rewarded. He should involve himself in all the details of the company economy, help [his men] with advice, seek out for them all those [economic] benefits that depend solely upon his actions, without, however, violating the order of service. He should assure the safety of all that belongs to the soldiers. As often as possible he should visit his sick and ensure that they receive sufficient care. In a word, [he should] care for [his] soldiers as if they were his children.[15]

The ideal of paternalism thus required that a commander concern himself with the material and moral well-being of his troops. In return for this concern, the lower ranks owed their superiors unquestioning obedience, for the commander knows better than his men what is beneficial to them and "for this answers to God and Monarch."[16]

In addition to paternal concern and affection, the ideal relationship between commander and soldier also contained a strong punitive aspect. Compulsion for purposes of correcting was considered basic to the relationship between father and child. Thus Peter the Great compared the task of modernizing the Russian people to teaching children to read and write: both required compulsion.[17] Commanders were expected to enforce strict discipline and to punish severely, though not cruelly, any violations of the service order.[18] There existed an official belief that the lower ranks did not trust "weak" commanders, but rather respected severity (*strogost'*), as long as it was just.[19] Still, the military elite was aware that severity could easily degenerate into cruelty and repeatedly proclaimed that the commander should be a father, not a tyrant.[20]

Although the government stressed the need for a fatherly approach to the exercise of authority, it was also concerned that paternal affection not turn into excessive familiarity. Military discipline required a respectful distance between commanders and their subordinates. The government and many officers feared that intimacy with the lower ranks undermined discipline.[21] Thus one of the charges against the future Decembrist V. F. Raevskii at his court-martial in 1822 was inappropriate friendliness and familiarity with the lower ranks.[22] The authorities had difficulty distinguishing Raevskii's friendly attitude toward his subordinates from his democratic ideas and subversive intentions. Both were deemed pernicious to order and stability. Just as the Russian people owed absolute obedience to the "*tsar-batiushka,*" the lower ranks were expected to submit unconditionally to their commanders.

THE PATERNALISTIC IDEAL IN PRACTICE

To understand how the paternalistic ideal functioned in military society, one must consider the degree to which officers and soldiers incorporated this ideal into their behavior and worldview. In fact, most officers seem to have been relatively indifferent toward their men.[23] The scant attention paid to the lower ranks in officers' memoirs reflects this indifference.[24] But more than a few enlightened individuals took the ideal of paternalism to heart. The military writer Denis Davydov, a partisan leader in 1812, expressed deep feelings of affection for his men:

> Whoever has at one time been torn away from his subordinates with whom he has for so long shared hunger and cold, joy and sorrow, hardships and danger—that person will understand the emotions I felt when I turned over my party to another [commander]. From the battle of Borodino until [our] entry into Dresden, I tied my fate to their fate, my life to their lives. I was parting already not with subordinates. I was leaving a son in every hussar [and] in every cossack, a friend—in every officer [*chinovnik*].[25]

Davydov's condescending but affectionate attitude toward his men closely corresponded to the paternalistic ideal presented in official sources.

While serving in the Second Army, the future Decembrists M. F. Orlov, V. F. Raevskii, and P. I. Pestel' worked to alleviate the condition of the lower ranks by opposing abuses and softening punishments.[26] As commander of the Sixteenth Infantry Division, Orlov urged his subordinate officers to treat their men "with fatherly solicitation" (*popechitel'nost'*), reminding them "that soldiers are people, just as we are, that they can feel and think and have virtues . . . , and that it is possible to rouse them to all that is great and glorious without sticks and beatings."[27] Heeding the spirit of Orlov's words, A. G. Nepenin abolished corporal punishment in the Thirty-second Jager Regiment (where Raevskii served as a company commander).[28] The Decembrists combined the most humanitarian and pedagogical aspects of the paternalistic ideal with the democratic principles of the French Revolution, especially belief in the equality of all men and the dignity of the individual. In a sense, as military commanders they tried to put the ideal into practice. Still, their interpretation of the ideal exceeded governmental intentions, and, more important, their own ultimate goals were openly subversive.

It was not just poets and revolutionaries who in their thoughts and behavior embodied the paternalistic ideal. Officers and senior military officials with no trace of oppositionist sentiment—men such as M. S. Vorontsov, Sabaneev, and Kiselev—expressed enlightened attitudes toward the lower ranks, exhorting commanders to protect their men from unnecessary hardships and cruel treatment.[29] In a rescript of 1804 the tsar himself expressed concern about widespread cruelty and forbade excessively severe punishments for minor violations of the service order.[30] Similarly, in 1820 Major General P. D. Kiselev, then commander of main headquarters of the Second Army, placed some modest limits on the use of corporal punishment, attributing desertions, deaths, immorality, evasion, and fear of service to excessive cruelty. Although cruelty was still a serious problem, Kiselev also felt that it no longer won praise or "served as cause for bragging." Morality had changed "to the honor of Russian officers."[31] Clearly, the ideal of paternalism, emanating from the very pinnacle of political power, found some resonance at lower levels of the military hierarchy. Consistent with the image of father and child, officers who exhibited a paternalistic spirit tended to view soldiers condescendingly but affectionately. According to one allegedly factual account, honorable soldiers, who were always ready to sacrifice their own immediate needs, confided in their superiors and looked to them for protection. With kind and just treatment even the worst soldiers could be inspired to serve zealously.[32]

Despite the enlightened attitudes found among some commanders, the reality of military life fell far short of the government's paternalistic ideal.

The efforts of Alexander I, Kiselev, and others to restrain cruel commanders only testified to the persistence of the problem. There was a
relentless undercurrent of brutality affecting social relations in the prereform army. In the larger universe of military society, authority relationships conceived as a personal bond between "father" and "child" led
inevitably to arbitrariness and abuse. The government itself promoted
this abuse by its failure to enforce consistently the ideal it professed. The
notion of the commander as father to his men cast authority relationships
in a personalized mold that left much to the discretion of individual officers.[33] Although the government sought to contain the cruel treatment of
soldiers through repeated pronouncements of paternalistic values, it continued to define the legal norms of punishment very loosely and imposed
no formal limits on the frequency of punishment.[34] Actual governmental
practices, reflected in the decisions of military courts, were also ambiguous. Officers faced court-martial, conviction, loss of rank, and expulsion
from the service for cruelty toward their subordinates. But at the same
time, beatings for drunkenness, mistakes during military drills, and minor
violations of the service order and dress code were common practice.[35]

Military judicial records involving officers who were tried for abusing
their men reveal the irregularity of official policy. In April 1800 Second
Lieutenant Sviatikhin of the Plutalov Garrison Regiment was convicted
of excessively punishing his orderly with birches and ropes. The orderly
had died as a result of these punishments, so the issue of cruelty was fairly
clear-cut. The court concluded that although the orderly was slow and
derelict in fulfilling his duties, Sviatikhin should have first tried means
other than beatings to reform him.[36] Similarly, in 1810 Major Shchigolev
of the First Orenburg Line (Garrison) Battalion was deprived of all ranks
and demoted to private for repeated drunkenness and physical abuse of
his subordinates.[37] In obvious cases of repeated cruelty, the government
did indeed take steps to limit the severity of punishments and to protect
soldiers from depraved commanders.[38]

Even in cases of definitely proven abuse, however, the government did
not always steer a steady course. In 1820, the emperor himself ordered
the court-martial of Ensign Epanchin for abusive treatment of Private Nikanov. On 21 and 22 May, Nikanov had been on guard duty in Kherson
under the command of Epanchin. During that time Epanchin punished
him twice with sticks and rods (*fukteli*), allegedly for tardiness and for
card playing with a convict. Eleven days after the punishment blood
marks were still visible on Nikanov's body, an indication of excessive punishment. In addition, the use of rods was forbidden. The court found
Epanchin guilty of cruelty, but his sentence was not severe. He suffered
no punishment beyond the year he had already spent under arrest during

the investigation and trial.[39] The outcome of this case reflected the government's inconsistent position on the issue of cruel punishment. In a formal sense, the authorities condemned Epanchin's excessive severity. Yet the ambiguous sentence imposed did not leave the impression that cruelty would always be severely punished.

In a significantly more extreme case of abuse, Major Pavlov, commander of the eighth Black Sea Line Battalion, was found guilty of beating lower ranks who were exempt from corporal punishment and of forcing them to remain in full parade uniform for up to twelve hours during guard duty and military drills. Because of these excesses, eight men had died.[40] Pavlov also allowed his subordinates to inflict cruel and unjust punishments on the men.[41] There was, then, a clear pattern of abusive treatment and excessive punishments in the battalion. Consequently, an order of 7 April 1855, confirmed by the emperor, sentenced Pavlov to five months' arrest in the casemate and expulsion from the service without privileges of rank.[42] But despite Pavlov's extreme cruelty, the emperor soon softened his sentence: an order of 31 January 1856 reduced the period of arrest to two months and allowed Pavlov to remain in the service without, however, assignment to a command. Then, in November 1857, he was appointed Tsebel'dinsk police officer, and in 1861 the tsar ruled that he was eligible to receive all service awards and privileges except for the order of St. Vladimir and decorations for irreproachable service.[43] So even in cases in which the authorities saw definite evidence of abusive behavior, they did not always uphold the ideal of fatherly concern for the lower ranks with strict punishment of guilty officers. At the same time, the mercy shown Epanchin and Pavlov was consistent with the tsar's paternal affection toward his personal servitors among the bureaucratic nobility and officer corps.

Additional contradictions in the enforcement of paternalistic values resulted from ambiguities in the definition of cruel treatment. Legal ambiguity (which inevitably produced arbitrariness) was, of course, inherent in autocratic authority; for precise legal definitions implicitly limited the absolute power of the sovereign. The definition of cruel treatment depended upon a host of circumstances, including the overall condition of a particular unit and the conduct of the lower ranks. During an 1818 investigation ordered by the emperor, General Adjutant Baron Dibich reported that the lower ranks of the Astrakhan Grenadier Regiment had voiced complaints about their former commander, Major Kridner. Dibich found some of the claims justified. Many lower ranks holding military decorations had been subjected to corporal punishment. Although the punishments were not excessive, they did violate laws exempting decorated lower ranks from such penalties. A few men also testified that they had been severely punished: 500 blows with sticks and 100 to 150 blows with broadswords (which were forbidden). Dibich, however, considered these complaints exaggerated, for each time he questioned the men, they increased the number of blows.[44] In general, when he interrogated the soldiers individually, only a few expressed any really legitimate claims. On the contrary, most of the complaints concerned legal punishments of 25 to 50 blows with sticks for neglect of duty.[45]

Although the reported punishments had been relatively frequent and severe, in Dibich's opinion they rarely exceeded legal norms. Furthermore, the well-being of the regiment, which lagged behind the rest of the division and which was noted for its "spirit of laziness and insubordination," demanded strict measures.[46] Still, there was evidence of abuse by Major Kridner. Despite some inconsistencies in the specifics of their testimony, the lower ranks were almost universally dissatisfied with their former commander, whom they accused of excessive severity.[47] In addition, even before the investigation began, the corps commander had removed Major Kridner from his post for inappropriate and abusive verbal orders that showed contempt for his men. Dibich admitted that Kridner was guilty of strict and sometimes careless acts, but he felt that loss of command was sufficient punishment. For Kridner's guilt consisted "solely of excessive zealousness in the immediate reform of the regiment and the inability to use better means for that purpose."[48] Where discipline and performance were judged weak, severity was accepted. If commanders considered a more paternal approach ineffective, they could justify frequent beatings to their superiors.[49]

Economic conditions in the prereform army also revealed the government's inability to cast social relations in a paternal mold. Commanders were supposed to provide for all the material and spiritual needs of their men. Economic officials and military commanders were notoriously corrupt. But even an honest commander could not always observe the rules governing provisioning and supply. The army's (and society's) economic infrastructure was so inadequate, the troops' ability to meet daily economic needs so precarious, that commanders were frequently forced to make ad hoc adjustments and reallocations in direct violation of legal norms. There was a fine line between corruption and the continual improvisation required to provide for a regiment on a daily basis.[50] So in addition to the abuses of avaricious economic officials and commanders, shortages and inefficiency in the military economy made paternal care for the lower ranks' basic needs practically impossible. Military courts consistently and severely punished economic crimes (even sometimes with deprivation of noble status), and soldiers repeatedly received satisfaction for claims against their commanders. Still, abuses were so widespread and so difficult to control that the prosecution of economic crimes failed to improve significantly the material condition of the lower ranks.[51] The paternal dictum to protect and preserve brought few concrete benefits to the economic plight of the common soldier.

The paternalistic ideal, so eloquently espoused in official proclamations, evaporated in the face of the harsh realities of military life. Although the tsar and some enlightened commanders incorporated the ideal into their orders and instructions, the basic brutality of social relations in military society was never eliminated. In their dealings with the lower ranks, most officers had little in common with the ideal affectionate father. The government allowed brutality to continue by its demand for strict discipline at all costs from the lower ranks, by its inability to formulate precise legal norms of punishment, and by its failure to control economic abuses. Governmental enforcement of the paternalistic ideal was ambiguous and inconsistent. The personal nature of autocratic authority left legal definitions deliberately vague and placed vast discretionary power in the hands of individual commanders. The relatively weak institutionalization of Russian society and government together with the limitations of a preindustrial subsistence economy forced the authorities to rely extensively upon corrupt local officials to carry out policies emanating from above. Army, corps, and divisional commanders faced similar difficulties when they tried to implement policy at the regimental or company level. Even the efforts of an enlightened regimental commander could be thwarted by the dispersal of his unit over a large area.[52] Whatever the government's concerns and intentions, it is clear that the ideal of paternalism failed either to contain cruelty or to prevent officers from plundering their men.

SOLDIERS' RESPONSE TO THE PATERNALISTIC IDEAL

Daniel Field has shown that despite its falsity, the myth of the "*tsar-batiushka*" persisted in nineteenth-century peasant society and that it even generated rebellion and social instability.[53] Echoes of the myth were also found in military society, where the "*tsar-batiushka*" and the "father-commander" remained vibrant images. Soldiers' songs and stories expressed the theme of the "father-commander," though their genuinely popular character is not always certain.[54] More convincing evidence comes from the words and actions of soldiers in active service, as reported in court-martial records. Sometimes soldiers did indeed develop warm feelings of affection for their commanders. In a report on the Sixteenth Infantry Division, commanded by M. F. Orlov, a secret police agent quoted the lower ranks as saying, "The divisional commander is our father; he educates us." The agent also noted that the soldiers referred to the sixteenth division as "the *orlovshchina*."[55] In a similar show of affection, the lower ranks of the Second Burgskii Uhlan Regiment failed to press claims against Captain Tishchenko, because he was poor and had been a good squadron commander.[56] Reflecting the personalized nature of authority relations, an important element of autocracy and the paternalistic ideal, soldiers forgave the abuses of a commander they liked.

The personal affection that soldiers felt for particular commanders did not necessarily guarantee stability. In 1850 at the Kinburn Artillery Garrison, the lower ranks of Half-company 1 became frustrated and disobedient when they were subjected to extraordinary roll calls on two consecutive nights. The second time they marched off to their garrison commander, Lieutenant-Colonel Loman, for an explanation. Loman denied any knowledge of the reason for the extra roll calls, and at his request the men returned to their barracks. But when questioned subsequently by the duty officer, they again became unruly. At this point the Kinburn commandant sent Loman to pacify the men, who agreed to return to their duties.[57] As a result of this incident, eight lower ranks were court-martialed and Loman was dismissed from the service.[58] The trial revealed that the lower ranks were heavily involved with Loman in mutually beneficial private economic pursuits.[59] Their special affection for him thus had an economic basis. It is significant that when the men felt persecuted they appealed to Loman, and at his urging they immediately returned to good behavior. This suggests a close personal relationship between Loman and his men. Other officers even complained that Loman's relations with the lower ranks undercut their authority. They charged him with releasing soldiers from service duties to engage in private work.[60] It seems that through lax discipline and the pursuit of mutually beneficial economic gain, Loman had developed a warm, harmonious relationship with his men. Their personal identification with him was reflected in repeated proclamations during the investigation and trial "that they serve only the commander of the garrison, Lieutenant-Colonel Loman."[61] At Kinburn the reality of a beloved commander concerned with the welfare of his men clearly clashed with the interests of the service.

The vitality of the paternalistic ideal was perhaps most apparent in the social norms and expectations of the lower ranks. Soldiers expected two things from their commanders: that they provide for their material needs and treat them fairly. These expectations were consistent with military regulations and with the rhetoric of paternalism. Not surprisingly, then, soldiers deserted, rebelled, and committed disobedience on grounds of cruel treatment and economic abuse, using the paternalistic ideal to justify their behavior.[62] In 1820 Private Tutorin of the elite Pavlovskii Regiment claimed he had deserted to inform superiors of the frequent persecutions and beatings he suffered at the hands of a particular noncommissioned officer.[63] Similarly, in 1832 a private from the Dneprovskii Infantry Regiment fled to Austria, because "they beat me during training."[64] In a more significant case, one noncommissioned officer and ten privates from the First Orenburg Line Battalion deserted into the Kirghiz steppe in June 1849. At their trial, eight of the privates tried to justify their actions as a response to abusive treatment and unjustified punishments.[65] Although the battalion's commanders were cleared of any wrongdoing, the soldiers seem to have felt genuinely abused.[66] But even if their grievances were only a clever ploy, they are still indicative of popular beliefs and expectations. At the very least, the soldiers hoped to gain the sympathy of the authorities and perhaps soften their punishment by advancing such claims.

The military authorities themselves encouraged the popular belief that accusations against officers could be used to justify desertion. Military regulations unequivocally held officers responsible for desertions by their men. Commanders faced fines and arrest if desertions from their units exceeded acceptable limits.[67] They were also tried when a large number of desertions occurred.[68] Clearly, there existed among high-level military officials an underlying assumption that officers' abuses might provoke desertion. In cases of frequent desertion, the government's first impulse was to investigate the behavior of commanders. In an 1820 memorandum on corporal punishment, Major General Kiselev noted that "the loss of men from desertion and death, the lack of morality, evasion and fear of service often originate from arbitrary punishments." Cruel punishment, concluded Kiselev, accounted for the increase in desertions from the Second Army.[69]

Even where officers were ultimately found innocent of any abuses (and more often than not this was the case), their treatment of the lower ranks was always investigated. Thus an 1822 report on the reasons for desertions from the Second Battalion of the Thirty-second Jager Regiment explicitly addressed the possibility of provocation, concluding that there was no evidence of "excessive severity by the commander," training exercises that "exceeded human strength," or persecutions by anyone in a position of authority.[70] In cases of desertion, the authorities always considered the possibility of provocative abuses, but that in no way excused the action. Irrespective of any crimes committed by commanders, desertion was severely punished. The ideal of paternalism required strict discipline and obedience from the lower ranks, just as it required fatherly concern and fair treatment from their commanders.

Acts of disobedience by the lower ranks reveal both official and popular patterns of behavior similar to those found in cases of desertion.[71] The main difference was that in cases of disobedience, the responsible commanders were usually found guilty of abuses or, at the very least, of negligence or inefficiency. But this too did not justify insubordination by the lower ranks. Whatever abuses a commander committed, disobedience (like desertion) was never tolerated, and the guilty soldiers were always severely punished. Still, the most frequent cause of disobedience was cruel or unjustified punishment. In 1797 the Grenadier Company of the Azov Regiment rebelled against their commander, Captain Pisanskii, declaring that they could no longer bear his cruelties and intended to complain directly to the regimental commander.[72] In the final decision of the military judicial authorities, confirmed by the tsar, Pisanskii was acquitted of any wrongdoing, whereas the "instigators" of the "rebellion" were punished with the knout and exiled to Siberia.[73] Although the emperor concluded that the punishments inflicted by Pisanskii were just and proper, the grenadiers clearly felt they had been abused. There was, it seems, an obvious contradiction between the degree of punishment that the lower ranks considered just and that permitted by the law.

The gap between popular expectations of justice and official definitions of cruelty appeared time and again, even in cases involving commanders found guilty of definite abuses. In 1831 the first Grenadier Company refused to serve under Captain Okerman, whom they accused of unjustified severity. Okerman had clearly abused his men, punishing them with swords, sticks, and sabers. In addition, he had burdened them with excessive training (by candlelight on winter evenings) and had inspected their outfitting on holidays. But because his company was always in good condition and because the soldiers' dissatisfaction "arose only from his use, out of zealousness toward the service, of means that did not correspond to military regulations," the authorities sentenced him only to two months' arrest in the guardhouse. This would be followed by transfer to the army without the right to command a company, before being recognized for "outstanding service."[74] Once again the authorities concluded that the needs of the service demanded severity. And once again the soldiers' expectations of fair treatment were disappointed.

To be sure, the government repeatedly recognized a connection between popular disobedience and commanders' abuses. Captain Kniazhnin of the Keksgol'mskii Musketeer Regiment was dismissed from the service in 1810 for economic abuses and inappropriate punishments leading to disobedience by his men.[75] The Semenovskii rebellion of 1820 also illustrates the point. The regiment objected to the excessive severity of their commander, Colonel Schwarz. Upon taking command of the regiment, which in the past had enjoyed a liberal regime, Schwarz set out to impose the strictest discipline. He introduced an intensive training regimen and inflicted severe punishments for minor violations of the service order.[76] The military court investigating the incident actually found him guilty of cruelty and negligence, but because of his good record, his only punishment was dismissal from the service.[77] It is clear from the cases of disobedience provoked by excessively severe commanders that the lower ranks took to heart and interpreted in their own way official exhortations concerning fair and just treatment.

Soldiers also expected that their commanders would provide for their economic needs. Failure to do so frequently prompted complaints and in extreme cases led to outright disobedience. In the fall of 1856 four companies at the Sveaborg Artillery Garrison refused to work, because they had not received money for provisions for three days.[78] When their commander, Ensign Shchetinin, tried to punish three instigators, the men of Company 4 (which had been the most unruly and outspoken) refused to allow it, "for they did not steal anything" and as one gunner put it: "The tsar did not order us to starve." Although Shchetinin had not committed any crime and had sent a noncommissioned officer to Åbo for supplies, he was still guilty of "inefficiency" in provisioning his unit and was confined to the guardhouse for two weeks.[79] The authorities did not excuse the lower ranks' behavior, and they were punished severely. But their commander was also held responsible for their insubordination.

Soldiers guilty of desertion and especially of disobedience regularly pointed to abuses by their commanders in an effort to justify their own rebellious acts. Most of the time, it seems they genuinely felt abused. It is significant that they did not object to corporal punishment per se, but rather demanded that it be justified and not excessively severe. They also insisted that commanders fulfill their economic obligations to feed and clothe their men. In this respect the soldiers' expectations were consistent with the rhetoric of paternalism. The government encouraged these expectations by assuming that commanders' abuses often provoked desertion and disobedience. For this reason, soldiers could use the paternalistic ideal to their benefit. But they must also have known that no degree of cruelty or corruption would justify these crimes. The government consistently imposed severe punishment on lower ranks guilty of desertion or insubordination. Thus the soldiers' persistent efforts to explain their actions as a response to abuses by commanders suggest that there was a basic discrepancy between their own understanding of fair treatment and official definitions.

In practice, the paternalistic ideal was first and foremost a statist conception imposed upon military society from above. As such, it reflected the primacy of the state's interests in Russian society. Soldiers and officers alike were punished for any disruptions deemed harmful to the service. This does not mean, however, that soldiers and officers were treated equally, though in most cases all parties to a dispute were found guilty of some violation. In the absence of a modern professional outlook to regulate behavior, the paternalistic ideal of father and child (an extension of the myth of tsar and people) became the proclaimed basis for social relations and the primary ideological means through which the autocracy attempted to exercise social control. The ideal allowed the government to couch the need for strict discipline and absolute obedience in terms of affection and tenderness. In this way the government hoped to soften the brutalities of daily life by containing cruelty and rousing commanders to greater concern for the material and spiritual welfare of their men. But in the face of harsh realities, it was the punitive aspects of the father-child relationship that reigned supreme. Few officers internalized the lessons of the paternalistic ideal, and soldiers who independently demanded its implementation were severely punished. In the realization of its proclaimed goals, the state expected the soldier to remain a passive, malleable object to be molded and directed by enlightened social superiors. Russia's rulers believed that like children, soldiers needed supervision and moral guidance if they were to develop properly.

NOTES

ACKNOWLEDGMENTS: *The research for this article was funded by grants from the International Research and Exchanges Board, the Fulbright-Hays program for dissertation research abroad, and the Fulbright-Hays program for faculty research abroad. I am grateful to the officers and staff of the Central State Military Historical Archive of the USSR (TsGVIA) and the Lenin Library, where I conducted the research.*

1. By "structural amorphousness" I have in mind Marc Raeff's comments on the absence of constituted bodies or "estates" in Russia. In Raeff's view, these bodies were crucial to the process of modernization in seventeenth- and eighteenth-century Western and Central Europe, whereas their absence in Russia prevented comparable development of the country's material and spiritual productivity. See Marc Raeff, *The Well-Ordered Police State: Social and Institutional Change through Law in the Germanies and Russia, 1600–1800* (New Haven and London: 1983). On the weakness of Russian society vis-à-vis the state, see Richard Pipes, *Russia under the Old Regime* (New York: 1974).

2. Raeff, *The Well-Ordered Police State*, 216–57.

3. On the goals of the "well-ordered police state" in Russia, see ibid., 181–257.

4. The term *lower ranks* is a literal translation of *nizhnie chiny* and refers to both privates and noncommissioned officers. Because the sources often do not distinguish these two groups, I have chosen to use the term despite its awkwardness.

5. On the popular myth of the *"tsar-batiushka"*and its hold over the peasantry until 1905, see Daniel Field, *Rebels in the Name of the Tsar* (Boston: 1976), 1–29. On the origins and implications of the epithet *"tsar-batiushka,"* which was only one aspect of the complex and diversified myth of the ruler, see Michael Cherniavsky, *Tsar and People: Studies in Russian Myths* (New Haven and London: 1961).

6. *Russkii invalid*, 5 August 1841, no. 184, 722. According to one observer, the "father-commander" took the place of a young officer's biological father. Krestovskii, *Istoriia 14-go ulanskogo Iamburgskogo eia imperatorskogo vysochestva velikoi kniazhny Marii Aleksandrovny polka* (St. Petersburg: 1873), 103–4.

7. On the popular dread of recruitment, see Elise Kimerling, "A Social History of the Lower Ranks in the Russian Army, 1796–1855," Ph.D. dissertation, Columbia University, 1983, chap. 1.

8. For a literary depiction of the difficult transition from peasant to military society, see N. A. Polevoi, *Rasskazy russkogo soldata* (St. Petersburg: 1852). See also the review of this book in *Voennyi zhurnal* no. 2 (1853), 104–13.

9. "Obshchee znachenie soldat," *Chtenie dlia soldat* no. 6 (1855), 59–61; I. Trike, *Pamiatnaia knizhka dlia nizhnikh chinov, napominaiushchaia im o znachenii i dolge russkogo soldata i o glavnykh obiazannostiakh ego v razlichnye periody sluzhby* (St. Petersburg: 1853), 37–38; *Svod voennykh postanovlenii* (hereafter *SVP*) (St. Petersburg: 1838), ch. 3, kn. 1, st. 642. For a literary depiction of an old, literate soldier who is teacher, model, and inspiration for the young soldiers who love and respect him, see I. Skobelev, *Podarok tovarishcham, ili perepiska russkikh soldat v 1812 godu* (St. Petersburg: 1833).

10. Not all *diad'ki* and noncommissioned officers lived up to this paternalistic ideal in their relations with new recruits. See B. P., "Vzgliad na postepennoe obrazovanie rekruta i soldata," *Voennyi sbornik* no. 2 (1859), 504–5, 513–16; "Instruktsiia rotnym komandiram, za podpisaniem polkovnika grafa Vorontsova, 1774 goda ianvaria 17 dnia, v 17 punktakh sostoiashchaia, na 13 listakh," *Voennyi sbornik*, 82, no. 11 (1871), 39; Trike, *Pamiatnaia knizhka*, 37–39; "Obshchee znachenie soldat," 56, 60; *SVP* (1838), ch. 3, kn. 1, st. 642.

11. "Obshchee znachenie soldat," 55–57.

12. D. A. Miliutin, *Karmannaia spravochnaia knizhka dlia russkikh ofitserov* (St. Petersburg: 1856), 614. M., "O pol'ze obucheniia gramote vsei massy russkikh voisk," *Voennyi sbornik*, 1, no. 2 (1858), 357–58.

13. This was the view of Alexander I. See Judith Cohen Zacek, "The Lancastrian School Movement in Russia," *The Slavonic and East European Review* 45, no. 105 (July 1967), 355–56. See also, B., "Izvestie o zavedenii pri shtabe gvardeiskogo korpusa uchilishcha vzaimogo obucheniia," *Voennyi zhurnal* no. 1 (1819), 67–70, and M., "O pol'ze obucheniia gramote," 356–58.

14. *Stoletie voennogo ministerstva* (hereafter *SVM*) 4, pt. 1, bk. 2, sec. 2, app. 14 (St. Petersburg: 1902), 73. Major General Khatov 1, "O voinskoi distsipline," *Voennyi zhurnal* no. 3 (1827), 41–50. Vorontsov, "Instruktsiia rotnym komandiram," 46. L. K., "Soldat i ofitser," *Voennyi sbornik* 4, no. 8 (1858), 346.

15. Vorontsov, "Instruktsiia rotnym komandiram," 46. For a much later, but almost identical depiction of the paternalistic ideal, see Colonel Chernevskii, "O voennoi distsipline. Izvlechenie iz stat'i: nastavlenie molodym liudiam,

zhelaiushchim vstupit' v voennuiu sluzhbu," *Voennyi zhurnal* no. 3 (1856), 53–54: "The commander loves his subordinates like his own children, indefatigably worries about furnishing them with all that is needed, impartially encourages and rewards those who have excelled, gives to all [his men] the judgment and punishment necessary to preserve order, teaches them by his example, leads them to glory and victory. In return [his] grateful subordinates repay a good commander with warm love, deep devotion, unconditional obedience, and a continual readiness to die, if necessary, defending their commander in dangerous situations."

16. "Nachertanie o polevoi egerskoi sluzhbe," *Voennyi zhurnal* no. 5 (1810), 15–16.

17. Raeff, *The Well-Ordered Police State*, 247.

18. On the importance of strict discipline see, for example, Khatov 1, "O voinskoi distsipline," *Voennyi zhurnal* no. 1 (1827), 90–129; no. 3, 41–79; no. 4, 38–57. "Nachertanie o polevoi egerskoi sluzhbe," 15–17.

19. L. K., "Soldat i ofitser," 345. Joseph Tanski, *Tableau statistique, politique et moral du système militaire de la Russie* (Paris: 1833), 268–69.

20. "Pravila dlia obkhozhdeniia s nizhnimi chinami 12-i pekhotnoi divizii (prikaz nachal'nika 12-i pekhotnoi divizii general-leitenanta, grafa Mikhaila Semenovicha Vorontsova," *Voennyi sbornik* 5, no. 2 (1859), 501–2. See also the letter (dated 14 February 1821) from the commander of the Sixth Infantry Corps, General I. Sabaneev, to the general orderly officer (*dezhurnyi general*) of main headquarters, A. A. Zakrevskii, in *Sbornik IRIO* 73 (1890), 577–79.

21. In the aftermath of the Crimean War this attitude came under criticism by liberal military writers. L. K., "Soldat i ofitser," 334–35; Chernevskii, "O voennoi distsipline: Izvlechenie iz stat'i: nastavlenie molodym liudiam, zhelaiushchim vstupit' v voennuiu sluzhbu," 53–54; B. P., "Vzgliad na postepennoe obrazovanie rekruta i soldata," 506–7; N. F. T., "Golos iz armii," *Voennyi sbornik* 1, no. 1 (1858), 77–82; N. Glinoetskii, "Voennaia statistika i soldatskii byt," *Voennyi sbornik* 1, no. 2 (1858), 452–58.

22. *Tsentral'nyi gosudarstvennyi voenno-istoricheskii arkhiv SSSR* (hereafter *TsGVIA*), f. 801, op. 70/11, d. 42, vol. 2, 7-V.

23. L. K., "Soldat i ofitser," 336–37, 341–43; Glinoetskii, "Voennaia statistika i soldatskii byt."

24. See John Keep, "From the Pistol to the Pen: The Military Memoir as a Source on the Social History of Pre-reform Russia," *Cahiers du monde russe et soviétique* 21, nos. 3–4 (July–December 1980), 295–320.

25. Denis Davydov, *Voennye zapiski* (Moscow: 1982), 283–84. A later critic of the general indifference of officers to soldiers observed that in wartime shared experiences created a temporary intimacy between commanders and their subordinates. L. K., "Soldat i ofitser," 336.

26. S. S. Volk and P. V. Vinogradov, "Dva prikaza M. F. Orlova po 16-i divizii (1820–21)," *Literaturnoe nasledstvo* 60, no. 1 (1956), 7–12. *TsGVIA*, f. 801, op. 70/11, d. 42 (delo Raevskogo). On Decembrist plans addressing the needs of the lower ranks, see E. A. Prokof'ev, *Bor'ba dekabristov za peredovoe russkoe*

voennoe iskusstvo (Moscow: 1953). See also V. F. Raevskii, "O soldate," *Krasnyi arkhiv* 13 (1925), 309–14.

27. Volk and Vinogradov, "Dva prikaza M. F. Orlova," 8–9. *TsGVIA*, f. 801, op. 70/11, d. 42, vol. 12-V, ch. 1, 11, 75–76.

28. Volk and Vinogradov, "Dva prikaza M. F. Orlova," 7–8. For a copy of Nepenin's *prikaz* forbidding corporal punishment, see *TsGVIA*, f. 801, op. 70/11, d. 42, vol. 7-V, ll. 104–104 ob.

29. Vorontsov, "Instruktsiia rotnym komandiram"; M. S. Vorontsov, "Pravila dlia obkhozhdeniia s nizhnimi chinami 12-i pekhotnoi divizii"; letter from Sabaneev to Zakrevskii in *Sbornik IRIO*, 73, 577–79; Volk and Vinogradov, "Dva prikaza M. F. Orlova," 12, n. 9; corps *prikaz* of Sabaneev from 12 September 1820 in *TsGVIA*, f. 801, op. 70/11, d. 42, vol. 12-V, ll. 282–83. F. A. Leev, "Doreformennaia armiia. (Po zapiskam gr. P. D. Kiseleva)," *Vestnik vsemirnoi istorii*, no. 11 (1901), 96–125.

30. Elise Kimerling Wirtschafter, "Military Justice and Social Relations in the Prereform Army, 1796 to 1855," *Slavic Review* 44, no. 1 (April 1985), 74–75. Alexander I's rescript is printed in *Stoletie voennogo ministerstva*, 12, pt. 1, bk. 1, app. 4 (St. Petersburg: 1902), 29–30.

31. Wirtschafter, "Military Justice and Social Relations in the Prereform Army," 75–76. Kiselev's remarks are found in *TsGVIA*, f. 16231, op. 1, d. 430, ll. 1-1ob.

32. N., "Vyderzhki iz soldatskoi zhizni," *Voennyi sbornik* 34, no. 11 (1863), 139–68; 35, no. 2 (1864), 289–305; "Zametka polkovogo sviashchennika o russkom soldate," *Voennyi sbornik*, 36, no. 3 (1864), 135–44; L. K., "Soldat i ofitser"; Glinoetskii, "Voennaia statistika i soldatskii byt," 452–53.

33. On the importance of personal authority in Russian government, see Raeff, *The Well-Ordered Police State*, 203–8, 240–42.

34. Wirtschafter, "Military Justice and Social Relations in the Prereform Army," 68, n. 3, and 74–76.

35. Ibid., 76. For instances in which commanders were cleared of inflicting cruel punishments during military drills, see the 1799 court-martial of Field Captain Lachin (*TsGVIA*, f. 801, op. 62, d. 720 and op. 60, d. 11, ll. 449–50) and the 1818 investigation into the behavior of Major Kridner, former commander of the Astrakhan Grenadier Regiment (*TsGVIA*, f. 36, op. 1, d. 605).

36. As a result of his conviction, Sviatikhin lost his patents and was dismissed from the service. At the time he was twenty-six. He had entered service from the ranks of the *ober-ofitserskie deti* in 1786 and had reached the rank of second lieutenant in 1799. *TsGVIA*, f. 801, op. 60, d. 11, ll. 29–29ob.

37. Shchigolev, aged thirty-one, had entered service from the Russian nobility in 1795. *TsGVIA*, f. 801, op. 61, d. 34, ll. 254–62. For a similar case of a drunk officer abusing his men, see *TsGVIA*, f. 801, op. 61, d. 34, ll. 351–53.

38. The problem of cruel treatment will be fully discussed in my forthcoming book. For a less developed account, see Kimerling, "A Social History of the Lower Ranks," 342–81.

39. *TsGVIA*, f. 16231, op. 1, d. 360, ll. 1–17.

40. Pavlov had beaten and punished other lower ranks without justification and had imposed excessively harsh labor demands on two noncommissioned officers. *TsGVIA*, f. 801, op. 91, d. 28, ll. 15–16, 65–70.

41. Ibid., ll. 48, 66–67 ob.

42. Ibid., l. 65. Pavlov entered service in 1828 from the *vol'noopredeliaiushchie* ("volunteers") of Tauride province. Three months later he was promoted to noncommissioned officer; he reached the rank of ensign in 1837 and major in 1848.

43. Ibid., l. 85 ob.

44. *TsGVIA*, f. 36, op. 1, d. 605, ll. 4–7 ob., 21–25.

45. Ibid., ll. 8 ob.–12.

46. Ibid., ll. 8–9.

47. Ibid., ll. 8 ob.–13, 21–25.

48. Ibid., ll. 8–9, 12 ob. For some of the punishments inflicted by Kridner, see ibid., ll. 31–37 ob., 39–41.

49. On 12 May 1818 Kridner informed his regiment that because "the kind and tender treatment of the lower ranks did not offer any hope of bringing them to the degree of preciseness and knowledge of military drill demanded by superior commanders," it was necessary "to put them on the right footing with strict measures and punishment, for the slightest negligence." Thus Kridner ordered company commanders to punish any laziness during training with sticks and birches. Ibid., ll. 31–37 ob.

50. On the prereform regimental economy, see Elise Kimerling Wirtschafter, "The Lower Ranks in the Peacetime Regimental Economy of the Russian Army, 1796–1855," *The Slavonic and East European Review* 64, no. 1 (January 1986), 40–65. See also Wirtschafter, "Military Justice and Social Relations in the Prereform Army," 71–74. For a broader analysis of the pre- and postreform regimental economy as it relates to Russia's general economic backwardness, see the admirable study by Dietrich Beyrau, *Militär und Gesellschaft im vorrevolutionären Russland* (Cologne and Vienna: 1984), esp. 309–432. For the postreform army, see also John Bushnell, "The Tsarist Officer Corps, 1881–1914: Customs, Duties, Inefficiency," *The American Historical Review* 86, no. 4 (October 1981), 753–80.

51. For the courts-martial of officers accused of economic crimes, see Kimerling, "A Social History of the Lower Ranks," 317–42. Some of these cases are also discussed in Wirtschafter, "The Lower Ranks in the Peacetime Regimental Economy."

52. Regiments spent most of the year dispersed in small groups among peasant villages, usually at considerable distances from regimental headquarters.

53. Field, *Rebels in the Name of the Tsar.*

54. I mention soldiers' folklore with some reservations. L. N. Pushkarev has correctly warned that it is necessary to distinguish official folklore (found in journals such as *Chtenie dlia soldat*) from the genuine popular folklore—a judgment that only a trained folklorist is in a position to make. See L. N. Pushkarev, "Soldatskaia pesnia—istochnik po istorii voennogo byta russkoi reguliarnoi armii XVIII-pervoi poloviny XIX v.," *Voprosy voennoi istorii Rossii*

(Moscow: 1969), 422–32. For some folkloric references to the "father-commander,"see N. M. Lopatin, *Polnyi narodnyi pesennik* (Moscow: 1885), nos. 99, 117, 134. In peasant speech the soldier was a "slice cut off"(*otrezannyi lomot'*), his wife was his weapon, his brother was his knapsack, his father was his commander, and his mother or stepmother was the service. See L. V. Evdokimov, "Russkii soldat i ego sluzhba v narodnykh vozzreniiakh," *Voennyi sbornik*, no. 3 (1916), 135–36. For soldiers' songs that describe the cruelty and economic abuses of commanders, see L. Voitolovskii, "Soldatskie pesni i skazki," *Krasnaia nov'*, no. 5 (15) (August–September 1923), 130; G. A. Gukovskii, "Soldatskie stikhi XVIII veka," *Literaturnoe nasledstvo* 9–10 (1933), 112–52; and Pushkarev, "Soldatskaia pesnia."

55. Quoted in Volk and Vinogradov, "Dva prikaza M. F. Orlova," 8. In this instance the suffix -*shchina* does not carry its usual negative connotation.

56. In 1829 Tishchenko was convicted of misappropriating 520 rubles that should have gone to his men as money for munitions (*ammunichnye den'gi*). *TsGVIA*, f. 801, op. 61, d. 71, ll. 20–38. This case is discussed in Wirtschafter, "Military Justice and Social Relations in the Prereform Army," 72–73.

57. *TsGVIA*, f. 395, op. 286, d. 389, ll. 4–7; f. 801, op. 61/2, d. 250, ll. 514–19; f. 801, op. 87/32, d. 9, ch. 1–3.

58. *TsGVIA*, f. 801, op. 61/2, d. 250, ll. 518–19; f. 395, op. 286, d. 389, ll. 4–7.

59. The economic aspects of this case are discussed in Wirtschafter, "The Lower Ranks in the Peacetime Regimental Economy."

60. *TsGVIA*, f. 801, op. 87/32, d. 9, ch. 3, ll. 148–52.

61. Ibid., l. 149.

62. In a parallel phenomenon, peasants used the myth of the tsar as an excuse for insubordination. See Field, *Rebels in the Name of the Tsar*, 208–15.

63. In a rare action, Tutorin subsequently admitted that he lied about the beatings in hopes of justifying his absence. *TsGVIA*, f. 36, op. 1, d. 1109, ll. 21–22 ob. For a similar confession, see the case of Private Sheniavskii in *TsGVIA*, f. 801, op. 61, d. 202, ll. 390–93.

64. *TsGVIA*, f. 14414, op. 10/291, sv. 60(273), d. 326, ch. 26, l. 2. I am grateful to Professor Walter Pintner for sharing with me the files from fond 14414.

65. *TsGVIA*, f. 801, op. 61, d. 202, ll. 472–519 ob.

66. The court found no evidence of wrongdoing by the officers involved and was less inclined to believe the defendants, because nine of them had records of previous misconduct.

67. Likewise, they were rewarded when desertions did not occur. For the legislative norms, see *Polnoe sobranie zakonov Rossiiskoi imperii* (hereafter *PSZ*) (I) 24: 17588; 25: 18319; (II) 18: 16455 and 16834; 19: 17805. See also *TsGVIA*, f. 801, op. 61, d. 11, l. 192; op. 62, d. 746, l. 15 ob. and d. 787, l. 21 ob.

68. See the 1800 case of Colonel Dreniakin, who, although acquitted, still had to furnish evidence that his men had not been mistreated. *TsGVIA*, f. 801, op. 60, d. 11, ll. 350–51.

69. *TsGVIA*, f. 16231, op. 1, d. 430, ll. 1–3.

70. The commander in chief of the Second Army, General Wittgenstein, ordered the investigation after twenty men deserted from the battalion in December

1820. *TsGVIA*, f. 16232, op. 1, d. 142. For similar investigations revealing a suspicion of possible abuses, see *TsGVIA*, f. 801, op. 62, d. 746 and 787; f. 14414, op. 10/291, sv. 60, d. 326, ch. 4, l. 2.

71. Limitations of space prevent any discussion here of the soldiers' underlying attitudes and motivations. For example, what were the circumstances that prompted desertion? How did the soldiers themselves define abusive treatment? I will treat these issues fully in my forthcoming book.

72. The grenadiers actually did march off to the regimental commander without an order. *TsGVIA*, f. 801, op. 62, d. 226, ll. 375–82 ob.

73. Ibid.

74. *TsGVIA*, f. 395, op. 286, d. 250, ll. 57–58.

75. *TsGVIA*, f. 801, op. 61, d. 34, ll. 509–18, 533–37 ob. This case is discussed in Wirtschafter, "Military Justice and Social Relations in the Prereform Army," 77–79.

76. Anatole G. Mazour, *The First Russian Revolution, 1825* (Stanford: 1937), 518–63. V. A. Fedorov, *Soldatskoe dvizhenie v gody dekabristov, 1816–1825 gg.* (Moscow: 1963), 72–160.

77. In 1823 Schwarz was reappointed to service as a captain in the military colonies. In 1850 he was again found guilty of cruel treatment, permanently dismissed from the service, and forbidden to reside in the capitals. Mazour, *The First Russian Revolution*, 60, and Fedorov, *Soldatskoe dvizhenie*, 157.

78. *TsGVIA*, f. 801, op. 73, d. 32, ll. 138–72, 180–94. This case is discussed in greater detail in Wirtschafter, "Military Justice and Social Relations in the Prereform Army," 79–81.

79. *TsGVIA*, f. 801, op. 73, d. 32, ll. 190–94.

A SOCIAL MISSION FOR RUSSIAN ORTHODOXY

The Kazan Requiem of 1861 for the Peasants in Bezdna

Gregory L. Freeze

Despite the prominence of clerical offspring in the revolutionary and liberation movements in postreform Russia, historians have given scant attention to the internal, ecclesiastical origins and dynamics of this phenomenon. For the most part it has been assumed that the Russian Church was too otherworldly, or too servile, to address secular questions, and that radical *popovichi* owed their views to secular influences, not to Church tradition or the clerical culture. Although that view conveniently satisfies the desiderata of Soviet historiography, it has enjoyed equally broad currency in Western scholarship.[1] Curiously, the Church itself, even in prerevolutionary times, tended to concur that "the main source of rot" in the seminaries was "agitators from outside the seminary."[2] Although some observers have tried to discern roots within the Church,[3] for the most part the historiography has disregarded the ecclesiastical origins of the radicalism of its seminarians or the liberalism of its priests.

To explore that problem, this essay will examine one of the first and best-documented cases of collective social activism—a requiem for peasants slain during disorders in the village of Bezdna in Kazan province. The disorders in Bezdna on 12 April 1861 were among the bloodiest of the numerous confrontations that followed announcement of the emancipation statutes in that year and resulted in the death of scores of peasants and many more casualties.[4] But the violence in Bezdna gained lasting notoriety four days later when several hundred students in Kazan—from the university and local ecclesiastical academy—held a requiem to mourn the slain peasants. It was, however, not the typical requiem ordered by kinsmen for a single departed soul. Arranged by complete strangers and collectively dedicated to an anonymous group of slain peasants, the service struck nervous officials as more political than pious. Even more provocative than the demonstrative march to the cemetery chapel and the requiem itself was the brief eulogy delivered by a professor of the ecclesiastical academy, A. P. Shchapov. Not only did Shchapov express grief for the peasants as victims of their own ignorance and self-delusion, but he also predicted the approach of Russia's liberation and purportedly even said "something about a constitution."[5]

Although considerable attention has been given to both the peasant disorder in Bezdna and the requiem in Kazan, the role of the local ecclesiastical academy has been curiously overlooked.[6] This essay, which draws upon materials from Church archives, seeks to elucidate the academy's role in the requiem and to reconsider the motives and significance of participation by ecclesiastical students. Why the academy's students appeared at the requiem, and what they subsequently revealed about their motivation and values, form the central focus of this essay. As I shall attempt to show, the students' involvement was neither an accident nor the result of university influence, but rather derived from a new theology and a new secular definition of the clergy's mission. It was a fundamental reorientation toward social issues, seeking to secularize the clerical role, that underlay the academy's unexpected involvement in the affair.

Although rumblings of dissent and discontent had appeared in other academies and seminaries by the late 1850s, the academy in Kazan aroused particularly strong and widespread suspicions of "liberalism" and "freethinking." Although a member of the imperial family visited it in November 1857 and officially pronounced himself "pleased" by what he found,[7] most reports about the school were far less flattering. Particularly critical was a confidential communication in 1857 from the Third Section, which warned that "students at the Kazan Ecclesiastical Academy visit lectures at will, choose courses as they see fit," fail to take regular examinations, appear especially indifferent to religious subjects, neglect to attend church services, and even borrow "proscribed books" from the school's library.[8] Similar reports circulated inside the Church as well. Thus even a prelate in remote Kamchatka had heard of the problems in Kazan: "There is not the slightest doubt that our academies, above all the one in Kazan, are infected with the spirit of free-thinking."[9] Given the fact that the academy trained future elites for the Church, its next generation of bishops and academy professors, the alarm in ecclesiastical circles was hardly surprising.

It is, however, important to stress that the troubles in Kazan were not due to harsh conditions or to a lack of discipline—the explanations routinely adduced by Church authorities to explain seminary disorders. On the contrary, as an elite institution (with small, select enrollments) the Kazan Academy offered relatively luxurious conditions by the standards of the time. Nor did the school suffer from weak or diffident supervision.

Although the inspectorship of Archimandrite Fedor (Bukharev) in the mid-1850s provoked criticism for its excessive leniency, the appointment of Archimandrite Ioann (Sokolov) as rector in 1857 reestablished a regime of unrelenting disciplinarianism. Ioann had previously earned an unenviable reputation as a severe, uncompromising censor,[10] and soon after his arrival in Kazan he assumed a dominant role in the academy, intervening in virtually every aspect of its life and imposing his will upon faculty and students alike. To establish order in the school, he resorted to a host of severe measures—humiliating espionage, terrifying interrogations, and draconian punishments. The result, as observers later testified, was unbounded dread before the very visage of the rector, and though that was no guarantee of a change in views or values, it produced the trappings of external discipline and order much admired by the authorities in St. Petersburg.[11] Indeed, his imperious manner was so oppressive that on the very eve of the requiem his own faculty rose in revolt.[12]

What concerned Church conservatives was not the lack of discipline in the academy, but the appearance of modernistic, socially relevant stirrings in theology. Hardly anything could have been better calculated to conflict with the norms of prereform Orthodoxy, according to which the Church quite literally constituted a "spiritual domain" (*dukhovnoe vedomstvo*), empowered to regulate the sacred but categorically excluded from the profane.[13] The most famous propagator of the new theology was the former inspector, Archimandrite Fedor, whose theology of contemporary relevance held that, as Christ had represented the unity of the divine and profane, so too must the Church seek to fuse the sacred and worldly. No liberal in social or political questions, Fedor nevertheless believed that the Church must play an active role in the world, that such an involvement stood at the heart of its ecclesiology, and that only in this manner could Orthodoxy be fully infused into contemporary life. Although some critics held that Fedor sought to "modernize" and even "secularize" the Church and its mission, in fact he held that the central task was not to modernize Orthodoxy, but to make modernity Orthodox.[14] Still, the very fact that Fedor urged attention to temporal issues was significant, for that clearly implied a break with the Church of prereform Russia and its focus on the "otherworldly" role of Orthodoxy. To judge from later accounts, Fedor, through his personality and teaching, exerted a major influence upon the academy, where he quite consciously used the classroom to propagate his ideas on the interrelationship of "Orthodoxy and contemporaneity."

Fedor's departure in early 1858, however, did not put an end to such teachings, because Archimandrite Ioann—for all his authoritarian ways as rector—espoused the same theological ideas. As in Fedor's case, Ioann was in no sense a social or political radical, but simply believed that the

Church should have a greater role in temporal affairs. Although Ioann did little teaching himself, he tolerated dissemination of such ideas in the academy and actively popularized the new theology in his published works. Most interesting of all, he specifically linked the new principle of relevancy to ecclesiastical scholarship and, indeed, to his own institution. As Ioann wrote in 1857: "Our church scholarship should not be foggy abstractions and contemplation, but should be placed as the foundation of life, not only our own [in the Church], but more generally, not only in ecclesiastical but also external society, for religious principles form the basic foundations of the general life of the people." Most interesting of all, Ioann believed that the Kazan Academy was peculiarly well suited to be the pathbreaker for the new movement: "Perhaps this academy will be able to participate more quickly than others in regenerating life in Russia, because the very youth of our academy means that as yet it does not have much routinism—its spirit has not become petrified, its own life has not become frozen." [15]

The main vehicle for the academy's new role was its journal, *Pravoslav-nyi sobesednik*, which Ioann proclaimed "a fresh organ for interaction with the social life of the fatherland." [16] Indeed, within a year after Ioann's arrival in Kazan, he had given the journal an entirely "new direction" and proceeded to publish a series of articles that shocked conservative readers throughout the country—not least because the journal boldly addressed even so sensitive an issue as the emancipation of serfs. One of the more notable essays came from Shchapov, who described the attempts by the Church in medieval Russia to ameliorate the plight of the poor. Inoffensive as that might seem, the article equated serfdom with slavery (*rabstvo*) and pointedly stopped short of modern times—an implicit rebuke to the Church for having abandoned its mission and responsibilities. [17] But the most controversial piece in the journal came from the pen of Ioann himself, an article published in March 1859, bearing the title "A Sermon on the Emancipation of Peasants." The essay's main thesis was that the Church must not remain silent on the question of serf emancipation, above all because this issue was now of such contemporary importance. Ioann decried the injustices and abuses of serfdom and offered a host of Scriptural references to prove his contention that "Christianity does not support slavery [serfdom]." But he warned that emancipation would not be easy, chiefly because of almost certain resistance from the serf-owning nobility: "Alas, when one person has become the property of another, how difficult his emancipation becomes!" [18]

Even before Ioann's sensational article appeared in print, however, Church authorities in St. Petersburg had determined to put a bridle on the academy's journal. In a resolution of February 1859, the Holy Synod castigated *Pravoslavnyi sobesednik* and specifically objected to its efforts to make the Church more "relevant" to contemporary issues and values. Although the Synod expressed particular dismay over the substance of Shchapov's work on the Old Belief, it found that to be merely a more salient example of the pernicious "direction" of the journal. Indicative of the journal's unseemly proclivity toward contemporaneity, declared the Synod, was its use of fashionable new diction: "Foreign words abound in all the articles—humanity, idealism, progress, civilization, nightmare, paralyze, harmonize, area, etc., which do not at all correspond to the dignity of an ecclesiastical publication." To eliminate such "harmful" tendencies and to establish strict control over the style and substance of the journal, the Synod annulled the academy's authority to oversee the journal and transferred censorship responsibility to the Committee for Ecclesiastical Censorship in Moscow.[19] The Synod's resolution not only represented a humiliating reproof, but also severely impeded regular production of the journal, for all its articles now had to be sent first to Moscow for review and approval, a process that greatly complicated publication and distribution. The archbishop of Kazan, Afanasii, attempted to intercede on behalf of the academy and even defended the journal's use of "modern" diction and its interest in contemporary problems—striking evidence, once more, of the contemporary ecclesiastical interest in a more socially engaged Church. But Afanasii's argument carried little weight with the conservatives in the Synod, who flatly refused to modify its recent decision.[20] Although Afanasii eventually persuaded the Synod to return control over the journal to the academy,[21] the affair reinforced suspicions of liberalism and freethinking in the Kazan institution.

A routine inspection of the academy in May 1860 did nothing to restore confidence. Although the report by Nikodim (the vicar-bishop of Kazan diocese) was generally favorable, praising the quality of instruction and student work, it did hint of unhealthy tendencies in student interest and values.[22] But Nikodim evidently shared the new theology, for he urged not less, but greater engagement in temporal questions and problems, and specifically proposed to encourage "contemporarization" of the academy by giving the students greater access to secular newspapers.[23] Of greater potential concern to the Synod, however, was his admonition that the rector's imperious ways had had a pernicious effect upon morale, even discipline, in the institution. The criticism, uncommonly acerbic, derived at least partly from personal pique, for the tactless Ioann had denied Nikodim even a modicum of respect during his official inspection. Nikodim took retribution in his final report. While conceding Ioann's "breadth and profundity of erudition," Nikodim reproved him for excessive severity and urged that the rector show more paternal compassion, that he evince "less authoritarian sternness and greater accessibility" to those in his charge. As an example of the rector's harshness, Nikodim's report cited the summary expulsion of two students the previous year for having accompanied an acquaintance swimming (the latter had accidentally drowned). As Nikodim observed, "the decision shows a lot of harshness, but I see no love of fellow man." Such practices, he warned, had led to an exceedingly demoralized atmosphere in the academy, pervading faculty and students alike: "The students appear to be modest, even despairing and depressed. . . . Even the teachers are timid, as if frightened. It seems that they too feel the influence of the harsh administration." And recently, warned Nikodim, the haughty rector had withdrawn increasingly into his own quarters, appearing sporadically to cow faculty and students, but no longer able to exercise real control and supervision over daily life in the academy.[24] But such criticism of Ioann had no effect. Though rumors of his impending transfer circulated, it seems fair to assume that the Synod was not overly disturbed by reports about Ioann's tyrannical style, which had apparently established order and discipline in the academy.[25]

The initial response of Church authorities—both in St. Petersburg and in Kazan—to news of the requiem was surprisingly low-keyed. Church authorities first learned about the incident not from the local prelate or rector, but from the minister of internal affairs, who transmitted a report from the local governor that "two monks" from the academy had conducted a requiem for the peasants of Bezdna and that Shchapov had delivered a eulogy saying "something about a constitution." The report not only was vague about the substance of Shchapov's eulogy, but also incorrectly described the two students from the academy (only one of them was a monk) and failed altogether to mention the two local clergymen from the chapel who actually conducted the service. After receiving this report, the chief procurator, A. P. Tolstoi, went no further than to demand an explanation from academy authorities in Kazan.[26] Nor did the Synod take any immediate action. Perhaps most peculiar of all was the casual response of Archimandrite Ioann: despite his reputation as an uncompromising disciplinarian, he took no immediate action and even appeared to misgauge the political import of the affair. To quote his jejune notation on the official report for that day: "Although there was no disorder in the academy, it is impossible to term this day a good one."[27] The rector evidently believed it possible to bury the whole nasty business by issuing a mere reproof to the students and, through postdated approval of Shchapov's letter of resignation, by dissociating the academy from the most political aspect of the incident.[28]

Emperor Alexander II, however, assigned far greater importance to the incident and personally escalated the requiem into a cause célèbre. The reasons for the emperor's response are hardly discernible behind the cryptic words of the archival record, but it probably derived from his visceral fear of radicalism, his deep concern about the violent disorders in Bezdna, and the special importance he attached to Shchapov's political eulogy. Whatever the motive, Alexander categorically demanded vigorous action: "It is necessary to arrest Shchapov and to incarcerate the two monks in Solovetskii Monastery."[29] Now appreciating the gravity of the case, Tolstoi launched a full-scale investigation not only of the requiem itself, but of "the spirit and direction of the entire academy." The objective, as he explained, was partly to purge the school of any "harmful teachings"—a clear allusion to concerns about the theological modernism of the school— and, at the same time, to take measures that would "serve as an instructive example for other ecclesiastical schools."[30]

Significantly enough, Church authorities decided that the investigation must be conducted by special investigators and should not be delegated to Archimandrite Ioann, as first intended. This decision, taken well before Ioann's letters defending the school had reached St. Petersburg, derived from a general distrust of the modernistic spirit of the school, and, especially, from the recent inspection report by Nikodim, who had warned of Ioann's withdrawal and ignorance of daily affairs in the academy. Chief Procurator Tolstoi, for example, observed that because of Ioann's peculiar personality, especially his harshness and arrogance, "he could remain wholly uninformed about internal damage to the minds of the students entrusted to him."[31] Persuaded that only an outside investigation could establish the true state of affairs, the Synod and chief procurator decided to dispatch the Synod's chief secretary (N. I. Olfer'ev) and an archimandrite to be designated by Metropolitan Filaret of Moscow. The task, as Tolstoi explained to Olfer'ev, was to investigate "the present condition of the spirit among both students and faculty in the academy" and to decide "whether this does not suggest reasons to anticipate further disorders."[32]

Metropolitan Filaret, deeply shocked by news of the incident,[33] was still more perplexed by the demand that *he* designate a "reliable" archimandrite to conduct the investigation. Though the incident occurred outside his diocese, St. Petersburg's decision to invoke Filaret's assistance was not all that surprising, given his reputation as a theological conservative and his ability (through the Moscow Academy) to recruit and promote the best archimandrites in the empire. Though Filaret at first demurred (saying that he had but his single diocese from which to choose an archimandrite, whereas the Synod had the whole empire at its disposal), he abandoned resistance when told that Alexander II himself was relying upon his cooperation. Although the written record does not confirm the emperor's interest, it is not unlikely that Alexander, alarmed by liberal tendencies in the Church, preferred to rely upon a stalwart like Filaret. Metropolitan Filaret designated a member of his own consistory (Archimandrite Iakov, head of Danilov Monastery in Moscow) and also prepared a list of questions to guide the investigation.[34] Because Shchapov had been arrested and was now in government hands,[35] the Church concentrated entirely upon the ecclesiastical academy to determine how and why so many of its students became embroiled in the requiem.

Indicative of anxiety in Petersburg about the academy was the decision to adopt a special telegram code, which would enable the Synod's investigators to report, in full confidentiality, their preliminary findings on the academy. As soon as they had assessed the mood and atmosphere in the academy, they were to telegram the chief procurator to indicate whether conditions were "tranquil," "rather unsettled," or "dangerously disturbed."[36]

Long before the two investigators arrived, however, Rector Ioann launched a vigorous defense of the academy. In a long letter to the chief procurator, Ioann contended that the real instigators of the requiem were university students and that the whole affair, "from beginning to end," had been the handiwork of the university. The students of the academy, he claimed, had been only chance participants: the requiem had coincidentally been held in a cemetery chapel opposite the academy, and the students happened to be strolling in the area only because of the holiday and attended the requiem out of mere "curiosity." Sensitive to suspicion of a conspiracy to organize a "political demonstration," Ioann averred that the students had neither prior knowledge of the requiem nor even an awareness of the political implications of the incident until he explained them to them. Although it was plainly more difficult to downplay the fact that two academy students—a widowed priest, Iakhontov, and a hieromonk, Meletii—had helped conduct the requiem itself, Ioann contended that their role in fact had been only a secondary one. The two students arrived belatedly at the service and did no more than assist the priest and deacon of the chapel. The rector stressed that even the most compromising aspect of the service, Shchapov's political eulogy, was not to be laid at the academy's door, for Shchapov's resignation had been accepted the day before the requiem.[37] And even after the synodal investigators had arrived in Kazan, Ioann continued in his efforts to exonerate the students (and the academy) through missives, reiterating his view that the entire affair had been engineered "from the side of the university."[38]

Unfortunately for Ioann, however, the scandal was no longer to be sanitized by such reassurances. Quite apart from the emperor's personal demand for a thorough investigation, the two clergymen of the cemetery chapel refused to accept responsibility for the affair and, worse still, accused the academy of helping to organize the requiem. According to the local priest (Nikolai Bal'butsinskii), Iakhontov had arrived at the chapel together with the university student leaders and had played a key role, persuading the local staff to conduct the requiem with claims that the service—for "kinsmen" of his and the university students'—was entirely legal. Moreover, the priest claimed, it was the academy students who modified terminology and referred to the rebels as "those slain for freedom and the fatherland." The assertion, if true, provided strong evidence that the requiem had in fact been not a display of compassion, but an outright political demonstration.[39]

Confronted by such incriminating testimony and the arrival of outside investigators, Archimandrite Ioann made a frantic last-minute effort to short-circuit the whole scandal by appealing once more to St. Petersburg. In two lengthy letters to the chief procurator, Ioann reiterated his contention that the university bore sole responsibility for the affair and attempted to discredit the testimony of the clergy from the cemetery chapel. For example, he challenged the credibility of the chapel priest's testimony that the students had claimed the slain serfs as kinsmen. Given the rigid, hereditary social order, observed Ioann, it was hardly possible for the students to advance so ridiculous a claim—or for the priest to have believed it.[40] In addition to his own letters, the rector also sent the chief procurator what was surely the academy's last hope for a swift termination of the affair: a collective letter from the school's students to the chief procurator that attempted to explain their participation in the requiem and to solicit a general pardon. Given the animus of contemporary authorities toward "collective" declarations of any variety (and especially from lesser-status groups), the letter could only have been submitted with Ioann's permission, if indeed not upon his initiative. Nevertheless, the letter was clearly compiled without his assistance. It included the signatures of seven students not even involved in the requiem (the kind of meddling by "outsiders" so opprobrious to nineteenth-century Russian officialdom), and, more important, contained ideas directly contradictory to those of the prereform Church.

To be sure, the primary aim of the letter was to dispel such distrust and to demonstrate the students' political reliability. Hence they reaffirmed their general commitment to the traditions of the clerical estate and, following Ioann, flatly denied any political motives behind their participation in the requiem. They also deftly attempted to exploit stereotypes about the apolitical mentality of the clerical estate: "The entire direction of our upbringing, from our very childhood, instills in us a spirit of humility and submission." Underlining their faith in the tsar's determination to make significant reforms, they declared that "any meddling in government decrees would be an obstacle to the realization of its intentions." Under the present circumstances, they conceded, more than anything else the government required "public tranquillity." At the same time, the students affirmed their commitment to serve the best interests of the tsar and people. Noting that "millions of people are now, thanks to the all-merciful Sovereign, placed in new conditions of life," the clergy, like other service groups, wished "to promote the Sovereign's will and to be useful to the fatherland," above all by "taking an active moral-spiritual part in improving the people's condition, by drawing ever more closely to them, and by explaining to them their new rights and new life in a Christian spirit." Like the rest of their estate, declared the students, they were filled with a sense of their "high mission" and hence solely preoccupied with "the study of those subjects which prepare us for service to benefit our Holy Orthodox Church and beloved fatherland." The students avowed their commitment to this spiritual mission and assured the chief procurator that they were "utterly alien to any political matters, and we consider it inappropriate and improper to meddle in these." They had attended the requiem only because of "Christian compassion for those who perished" and professed deep regret for any misunderstanding that their participation may have caused.[41]

The students' collective letter is extremely suggestive as to their political attitudes and self-conception. Thus their optimistic expectations of impending reform, if wholly ingenuous, must have been irritating to the chief procurator, top officials, and especially the emperor—who had no such ambitious plans and could discern little evidence of apoliticism in these hopes for a radical transformation of the existing order. More important, the students did not take refuge in the "accidental" theory espoused by Archimandrite Ioann's letters, but candidly admitted that they had quite consciously joined in a service to express compassion for the slain peasants. Indeed, most striking was the frank statement of pity for the peasants, who had perished from their own "ignorance" and delusions. Although these feelings were consonant with clerical paternalism, the letter was surprisingly similar to Shchapov's eulogy, which had decried the serfs' futile death and reproved educated society for failing to enlighten the people. The students' bald statement of this idea in no sense served to allay suspicion of their political unreliability. Furthermore, the letter went on to affirm the students' intent to enlighten the people, and not merely in a narrowly spiritual sense. The letter was, above all, a clear statement of a new, this-worldly "service ethic," which redefined the clergy's role in a manner that transcended the narrowly liturgical, spiritual sphere of the prereform era. Fused with paternalistic condescension, the more secular service ethic conformed wholly with the "this-worldly theology" propagated at the academy from the mid-1850s and represented the logical application of those teachings to clerical service. For all the students' reaffirmation of apoliticism, they had nevertheless repudiated the asocial, other-worldly focus of the prereform Church.

The two investigators in Kazan, apprised of the collective letter, sent a telegram to St. Petersburg requesting that the Synod disregard it and that it take no action until their investigation was completed.[42] As that telegram implied, the investigators regarded the situation at the academy as sufficiently serious to warrant a full-scale investigation that should not be terminated by this clever ruse. Indeed, three days after their arrival in Kazan, Archimandrite Iakov and Olfer'ev sent a coded telegram to Petersburg and reported that, though further disorders were not imminent, the situation was nevertheless "rather unsettled"—that is, they gave the middling estimate of the state of affairs in the academy.[43] The investigators proceeded to examine various academy records (such as the daily "class reports" on student conduct), subjected the students to protracted interrogations, and informally solicited additional information from various laymen and clergy in the diocese.[44]

But the main focus of the investigation was on the students themselves, especially Iakhontov and Meletii, who had directly participated in the requiem and who bore the most obvious responsibility. The investigators subjected the two students to detailed questions and sought to elucidate any connection with the university, their precise role in the liturgy, and information on Shchapov and his eulogy.[45] Whereas Iakhontov's replies were evasive and disingenuous (he denied any wrongdoing, collaboration with university students, or knowledge of Shchapov's speech),[46] Meletii's proved more candid. He not only declared it to be "the sacred duty of every Christian to pray for the unfortunate," but confessed that he had participated in the requiem partly to counter the nobility's festive glee over the bloody repression in Bezdna—a motive that Ioann and the students had so far categorically denied. The hieromonk further revealed that Iakhontov had been the first to call the peasants "those slain for the faith and love of the fatherland"—in emulation of soldiers fallen in battle. Meletii contended that he had "prayed for the peasants not as rebels, but as Christians," and argued that he had no grounds to withhold Christian rites from them. He recalled that when peasants had been slain in the 1840s (in confrontations over the government's demand that they cultivate potatoes), they had not been denied a Christian burial, and Meletii saw no reason to deny a requiem for the victims of Bezdna. Meletii's testimony proved especially compromising for his fellow student, Iakhontov,[47] but it also suggested that the students' participation was far more political than previously admitted, far exceeding the mere "chance" or "curiosity" that had predominated in Ioann's explanations.

The Synodal investigators also subjected the other students to written interrogation. Their aim was to discover the students' real motives in attending the requiem, their precise knowledge of events at Bezdna, the content of Shchapov's eulogy, and their general opinion of him.[48] Despite the students' dissimulation, their responses in fact did little to exculpate them or the academy. Although a few students claimed that they had attended through sheer chance or uninformed curiosity,[49] most professed a motive of "Christian compassion" for the slain victims. Given the fact that the peasants died while resisting the government, that kind of compassion could very easily be equated with sympathy for "rebels" (*miatezhniki*). Hence what the students understood of the events in Bezdna was important, but their answers did little to improve their standing with the investigators. Although they denied any detailed knowledge, and although some did have rather garbled impressions of events there, virtually all knew the basic facts—that peasants had died in a confrontation with government troops.[50] In their own defense the students argued that they had prayed for the peasants qua victims of ignorance, not rebels against the government,[51] but this was a fine distinction that could not have done much to reassure the authorities of their innocence. As the investigators and Metropolitan Filaret subsequently noted, it was simply impossible to believe that the students did not grasp the political significance of their act. Finally, with respect to the questions about Shchapov, the students proved surprisingly strong-willed and, doubtless to the chagrin of the two investigators, refused to betray or compromise their former instructor. Thus, to avoid testifying about the substance of Shchapov's speech, they claimed that they had been unable to hear it despite the tiny size of the chapel. Again their assertions that the size of the crowd and Shchapov's poor diction made his speech inaudible struck the investigators as simply incredible.[52] Nor did they fail to praise Shchapov as an effective teacher at the academy; apart from complaints about his absenteeism in recent months, the students unanimously lauded him as a brilliant teacher and scholar and rebuffed attempts to obtain information about his private life, especially his reputed alcoholism.[53]

When the two investigators filed their final report in late June, they drew a far more incriminating picture than that offered in Nikodim's earlier reports. The interrogation, in particular, had been exceedingly important, not only because of what the students had said, but still more because of how they had behaved during the interrogation—in some cases, with undisguised insolence and impatience. Thus one student, in their view, manifested "hatred and ridicule toward monks" and was generally "irritable and insolent." Moreover, the investigators found evidence of close ties between the academy and university, not only from secondhand reports, but also from the alarming similarity exhibited in the "liberty in their manner of thought and living." The fact that a group of nine university students had volunteered a collective letter, claiming exclusive responsibility for the requiem and denying any organizational role by academy students, did nothing to weaken suspicion of collusion.[54] Though Ioann had been loath to admit any ties and later had conceded only occasional contact, the two investigators argued that the interaction had increased sharply over the last year, especially after Shchapov had begun to teach jointly in both institutions. It is important to stress that, rather than seek internal intellectual or social sources for the students' apparent "radicalism," the investigators preferred to find the source of contamination outside the Church—the university. That exogenous influence, they added, had also had a pernicious effect upon the students' spiritual and religious well-being. "To our great distress," wrote the two investigators, "we heard from many (including some firsthand witnesses) that of late only a few students perform their obligation to attend the church liturgy properly; the rest either do not go to church at all or, if they do, not as they should."[55] In short, though they did not judge the academy to be on the verge of major disorders (a fear paramount in the minds of ranking prelates and the chief procurator), the investigators discovered major shortcomings in the moral and political attitudes of its students.

Their findings, accepted fully by the procurator,[56] provided the basis for a harsh Synodal resolution on the whole case. Iakhontov, who had been most severely compromised by the entire affair, was dispatched to Solovetskii Monastery for an unspecified period of incarceration. Meletii, more contrite and candid, fared significantly better: in lieu of incarceration in Solovetskii Monastery (as Alexander II originally ordered), he was sent to a more comfortable monastery in Tobol'sk. Most noteworthy, however, was the severe punishment meted out to students who had only attended the requiem: the Synod ordered that they be reduced to the "second rank" (vtoroi razriad) in their class lists, a status that effectively disqualified them from an advanced degree in the academy (including that of "student" or full graduate), thereby spoiling their chances for a good career in the Church. That, of course, was precisely the purpose of the punishment—to prevent such people, deemed suspect and unreliable, from attaining positions of power and responsibility. Finally, six students, primarily because of their conduct during the interrogation, suffered still more severe penalties: three were forced to leave the academy and enter diocesan service; three others were expelled altogether from the clerical estate and excluded from future service in the Church.[57]

This essay has attempted to revise conventional assumptions about social attitudes within the postreform clerical estate (including both the parish clergy and their seminarian sons). As the materials on the Kazan requiem suggest, the academy's involvement was neither accidental nor exogenous, but rather reflected the emergence of a significant new current in Russian Orthodoxy. Although authorities (ecclesiastical as well as secular) preferred to blame the affair on either the university or the influence of secular philosophy, these factors possessed only marginal significance at the time and, in any event, cannot explain the specific content of attitudes and ideas prevailing in the elite academy. Far more important in the Kazan affair was the students' new belief in the Church's social mission, in the clergy's responsibility to teach and realize moral principles, not merely to administer sacraments. Such earthly Orthodoxy contradicted not only the government's efforts to exclude the clergy from the emancipation process,[58] but also connoted a radical shift from the prereform Church, in which the priest's role was strictly sacramental and nonsecular.

The primary dynamic behind the redefinition of role, moreover, was the new theology propounding a more relevant Orthodoxy. Although the change may have been influenced by a long-standing desire to reassert traditional prerogatives,[59] and by the Church's call for a greater involvement by the priest in parish life,[60] the Kazan students were inspired by this new theology. Firmly rooted in the teachings of the academy, the new theology shattered prereform inhibitions and assumptions and encouraged a fundamental reevaluation of the clergy's place and function in society. The theology of relevant Orthodoxy, moreover, aroused official distrust of the academy and probably explains why Kazan—where the new theology was so strongly entrenched—produced something so notorious as the requiem. Indeed, the new theology seems to have been virtually predominant in Kazan, where it was espoused by such influential, even mutually antagonistic, figures as Archimandrite Fedor, Archimandrite Ioann, Vicar-Bishop Nikodim, and Archbishop Afanasii. Although all these figures anticipated a conservative application of the new idea, they inadvertently provided the intellectual tools for a liberal, activist theology. Though as yet only crudely adumbrated and devoid of concrete political and social ideas, the students' basic vision of a more this-worldly church was the fundamental reorientation that would inform subsequent radical, liberal, and populist tendencies within the Church.

In essence, the reorientation meant a "secularization" of the clergy's traditional service ethic, which had become narrowly liturgical in the prereform era. It was a process not entirely unique to the clergy; as Marc

Raeff has argued, reformulation of the nobility's traditional service ethic
provided a key emotive and intellectual dynamic in their transformation
from a privileged elite into an important source of the revolutionary intelligentsia.[61] A roughly similar process—the redefinition of service to apply
to the "people"—affected the clergy as well, but with some significant
differences. In the clergy's case it not only came later, but was markedly
different in substance, for the clergy redefined their service not from tsar
to people, but from heaven to earth, from spiritual to temporal. All this
suggests that the revolutionary movement attracted clerical progeny in
such disproportionate numbers not merely because of the exogenous influence of secular schools and philosophical currents, but because of the
specific structure of their original subculture, in which the clergy's traditional service ethos was given a more worldly, secular definition in the
reform and postreform eras. The new ethos had to overcome significant
obstacles but steadily gained momentum in the decades after 1855, finally
culminating in powerful movements of clerical liberalism and seminary
radicalism in the early twentieth century.

NOTES

ACKNOWLEDGMENTS: *For financial support the author wishes to express his
gratitude to the Alexander von Humboldt-Stiftung, the International Research
and Exchanges Board, and the American Council of Learned Societies.*

1. For a good Soviet account, see P. S. Tkachenko, *Uchashchaiasia molodezh' v
   revoliutsionnom dvizhenii 60–70 gg. XIX v.* (Moscow: 1978). For an extreme
   statement in Western scholarship, see Richard Pipes, *Russia under the Old Regime* (London: 1974), 221–45.
2. Pobedonostsev to V. K. Plehve, July 1882, Tsentral'nyi gosudarstvennyi arkhiv Oktiabr'skoi revoliutsii, f. 586 (V. K. Plehve), op. 1, d. 1017, l. 14–14
   ob.
3. Most notable was an 1870 analysis by the Third Section, which sought to
   explain why former seminarians were highly prominent in nihilist, revolutionary ranks. It adduced a number of potential variables, including the fact
   that their "special philosophical education" gave them an advantage over students from secular schools. More abstract arguments were subsequently advanced by Nicholas Berdiaev, who suggested that the seminarians' religious
   mentality disposed them to absolutize secular ideas; see his *The Origins of
   Russian Communism* (Ann Arbor: 1955).
4. For a recent analysis of the Bezdna conflict and references to sources and
   earlier literature, see Daniel Field, *Rebels in the Name of the Tsar* (Boston: 1976),
   chap. 2.
5. Telegram from the governor of Kazan, 20 April 1861, in Tsentral'nyi gosudarstvennyi istoricheskii arkhiv SSSR (hereafter TsGIA SSSR), f. 797 (Kan-
   tseliariia Ober-Prokurora), op. 31, otd. 1, st. 2, d. 149, l. 6–6 ob.

6. For the most part, the literature focuses upon Shchapov's speech and the role of university students; see, for example, such standard Soviet accounts as G. Vul'fson and E. Bushkanets, *Obshchestvenno-politicheskaia bor'ba v Kazanskom universitete v 1859–61 gg.* (Kazan:1955), and G. Vul'fson, *Raznochinskoe demokraticheskoe dvizhenie v Povolzh'e i na Urale v gody pervoi revoliutsionnoi situatsii* (Kazan: 1974), 242–50; Field, *Rebels*, 94–103. The only substantial discussion of the affair with respect to the academy is found in P. V. Znamenskii's history of the school, which despite its value is too old-fashioned and archivally limited to shed much light on the affair. See his *Istoriia Kazanskoi Dukhovnoi Akademii za pervyi (doreformennyi) period ee sushchestvovaniia (1842–1870 gg.)*, 3 vols. (Kazan: 1891–92).

7. For the impressions of Prince Petr Georgievich Ol'denburgskii, see TsGIA SSSR, f. 796, op. 138, g. 1857, d. 1786.

8. TsGIA SSSR, f. 797, op. 27, otd. 1, st. 2, d. 227, l. 1.

9. I. Barsukov (ed.), *Pis'ma Innokentiia, mitropolita moskovskogo i kolomenskogo*, 2 vols. (St. Petersburg: 1897–98), 2, 99 (30 March 1858).

10. For Ioann's performance as a vigilant censor in the early 1850s, see the comments of an irate author quoted in A. Kotovich, *Dukhovnaia tsenzura v Rossii, 1796–1855 gg.* (St. Petersburg: 1907), 414–17.

11. See, for example, the material quoted in Znamenskii, *Istoriia Kazanskoi Akademii*, 1. 170.

12. The conflict had been building for several years and ultimately derived from the rector's authoritarian policies and condescending treatment of the teaching staff at the academy. Most of the faculty were either laymen or white (parish) clergy, who not unnaturally took offense at the rector's unabashed preference for monks as instructors. Archimandrite Ioann believed that the academy should primarily serve the monastic ideals of the Church, and, in any event, he believed monks made better scholars. In Ioann's view, a man must choose "one thing or the other: either a woman or scholarship" (quoted in ibid., 1, 158). Thus in 1858 he recommended that the academy seek the appointment of additional monks to its faculty, given "the special importance and usefulness of service by monks in the academy" (ibid., 1, 163). Still more oppressive for the faculty was Ioann's authoritarian manner, manifested, for example, in peremptory reassignment of faculty members to teach new courses. Driven to despair by the rector's tyrannical rule, the faculty prepared and sent a secret petition to authorities in Petersburg requesting that Ioann be replaced as rector. Although the imbroglio of the requiem caused them to retract the plea, their willingness to take such a desperate step suggests the kind of tension building within the academy itself. For the collective petitions, together with individual testimony against Ioann, see the documents in TsGIA SSSR, f. 796, op. 142, g. 1861, d. 1350, ll. 42–61; and Znamenskii, *Istoriia Kazanskoi Akademii*, 1, 164–66.

13. See Gregory L. Freeze, "Handmaiden of the State? The Church in Prereform Russia," *Journal of Ecclesiastical History* 36 (1985), 82–102.

14. Later historiography, much influenced by the accounts of his former students, tended to idealize Bukharev and, indeed, to depict him as a lone hero

against the Church hierarchy; not only is the idealization of Bukharev over-drawn, but such accounts fail to appreciate how widespread the theology of ecclesiastical relevance had become. For an analysis of Fedor's views, stress-ing the various nontheological issues in the controversy about his work, see Gregory L. Freeze, "Die Laisierung des Archimandrits Fedor (Bucharev) und ihre kirchenpolitischen Hintergründe: Theologie und Politik in Rußland Mitte des 19. Jahrhunderts," *Kirche im Osten* 28 (1985), 26–51.

15. Ioann, "Vera—osnovanie istinnoi nravstvennosti," *Pravoslavnyi sobesednik*, chap. 3 (1857), 690.

16. Ibid.

17. Shchapov also adumbrated what the Church's current role must be: it should not simply seek to ameliorate the people's material condition, but to "explain to the people the lofty meaning of freedom, and to develop and inculcate a spirit of true, moral-Christian freedom." It is to this "moral importance in popular life," he concluded, that "the contemporary pastors of the Russian people are summoned." See A. P. Shchapov, "Golos drevnei russkoi tserkvi ob uluchshenii byta nesvobodnykh liudei," *Pravoslavnyi sobesednik* 1 (1859), 73–74. No less inflammatory, especially for conservative churchmen, were Shchapov's concurrent publications on the Old Belief, which he explained by social conditions and implicitly related to the Church's failure to assume its proper social responsibilities. For conservative reactions to his work, see the comments by Chief Procurator A. P. Tolstoi, who conceded that Shchapov's *Russkii raskol staroobriadchestva* was well informed and cogently written, but gave the false impression that the Church had caused the seventeenth-century schism. Tolstoi proposed to ban circulation of the work, to reprimand the censor who authorized its publication, and to publish a rebuttal by an expert on the subject. See his letter to Metropolitan Filaret in TsGIA SSSR, f. 832 (Filaret [Drozdov]), op. 1, d. 83, ll. 128–29.

18. Ioann, "Slovo ob osvobozhdenii krest'ian," *Pravoslavnyi sobesednik* 1 (1859), 339–40. This article, which appeared just as censorship controls tightened and tensions over impending emancipation grew especially acute, provoked a torrent of rumors—and furious indignation in gentry circles. Ioann subse-quently denied any such sensational intent and professed shock and surprise over the public reaction to his article; see Ioann's letter in 1862, where he argued that readers had grossly misunderstood his article and asserted that he aimed not to preach the contemporary forms of progress but to "view the questions from a Christian point of view" (Ioann to A. A. Akhmatov, 9 Au-gust 1862, in Otdel rukopisei, Gosudarstvennaia biblioteka im. V. I. Lenina, f. 230, k. 10802, d. 127, ll. 4 ob.–5).

19. Synodal resolution of 13 February 1859/2 March 1859 in TsGIA SSSR, f. 796, op. 140, g. 1859, d. 254, ll. 1–2.

20. The archbishop stressed primarily the demoralizing effect of the Synod's res-olution but did reply to its critique. Thus, responding to the Synod's com-plaints about the journal's "modern" diction, Afanasii explained that such language—and the entire thrust of the journal—was designed "to entice the contemporary world to comprehend truth under its mantle, and thereby

more effectively to influence it in the spirit of the Faith." (Petition from Afanasii to the Synod, 26 March 1859, ibid., ll. 4–5 ob.) Even if that promised to
increase Orthodoxy's influence in secular matters, the prescription was nonetheless too deviant from the prereform "otherworldly Orthodoxy" for the
Synod. See its resolution of 30 March 1859 in ibid., l. 6–6 ob.

21. Despite his initial failure, Afanasii did not abandon the fight and a year later
finally prevailed upon the Synod to reverse its original decision. See the Synodal resolution of 30 July 1860 in TsGIA SSSR, f. 796, op. 141, g. 1860, d.
1405, ll. 1–3.

22. Ever sensitive to the intrusion of secular philosophical ideas, Nikodim did
complain of an undue familiarity with contemporary philosophical currents
and warned that, in some instances, it bordered on outright sympathy. After
perusing one class's student papers, which were supposed to rebut hostile
philosophical views, Nikodim observed that they appeared neither cogent
nor zealous in their defense of Orthodoxy and complained that one student
even manifested unorthodox opinions: "He regards the impudent thoughts of
the most recent philosophers as not only excusable, but even acceptable"
(TsGIA SSSR, f. 796, op. 141, g. 1860, d. 1042, l. 16 ob.). But this complaint formed a minor note in his formal report, which generally endorsed
the intellectual and moral condition of the academy.

23. Ibid., l. 28.

24. Ibid., ll. 34–36.

25. The rumors alarmed Ioann, however, and in October 1860 he wrote to the
influential deputy chief procurator, Prince S. N. Urusov, to defend himself
against the criticism and to plead that he be left in Kazan for reasons of health
(see his letter of 10 October 1860 in TsGIA SSSR, f. 797, op. 30, otd. 1, st.
2, d. 205, ll. 49–50).

26. TsGIA SSSR, f. 797, op. 31, otd. 1, st. 2, d. 149, l. 3–3 ob.

27. Ibid., f. 796, op. 142, g. 1861, d. 779, l. 43 ob.

28. Zhurnal Dukhovnoi akademii, 19 April 1861, TsGIA SSSR, f. 797, op. 1,
otd. 2, st. 2, d. 149, ll. 52–55. The ruse regarding Shchapov did not deceive
Ioann's superiors or, especially, the perspicacious metropolitan of Moscow,
Filaret, who immediately recognized the fortuitous resignation for what it
was. See his acerbic memorandum of 21 May 1861 in Filaret, *Sobranie mnenii
i otzyvov mitropolita moskovskogo i kolomenskogo Filareta*, 5 vols. in 6 (Moscow:
1885–88), 5, pt. 1, 60.

29. Imperial order of 20 April, cited in a memorandum from the minister of
interior to the chief procurator on 21 April (TsGIA SSSR, f. 797, op. 31,
otd. 1, st. 2, d. 149, l. 7).

30. Tolstoi to Filaret, 27 April 1861, in ibid., l. 14–14 ob.

31. Ibid.

32. TsGIA SSSR, f. 796, op. 142, g. 1861, d. 779, l. 2 ob. Tolstoi to Olfer'ev,
27 April 1861.

33. Given the academy's role in preparing intellectuals for Church schools and
"learned monks" for the episcopate, the participation of academy students in
the scandalous requiem was bound to appear extremely serious and danger-

ous. Little wonder, then, that when the conservative metropolitan of Moscow, Filaret (Drozdov), learned of the Kazan requiem, he could only shake his head in stunned disbelief (TsGIA SSSR, f. 796, op. 162, g. 1861, d. 779, l. 8).

34. Olfer'ev to the chief procurator, 3 May 1861, in TsGIA SSSR, f. 797, op. 31, otd. 1, st. 2, d. 149, ll. 44–45 ob.; Filaret to Olfer'ev, 2 May 1861, f. 796, op. 142, g. 1861, d. 779, l. 7.

35. In accordance with the emperor's order, Shchapov was arrested as he traveled to St. Petersburg (in a desperate attempt to explain his case personally to Alexander), and thereafter remained in government hands (TsGIA SSSR, f. 797, op. 31, otd. 1, st. 2, d. 149, ll. 24–26; see Znamenskii, *Istoriia Kazanskoi Akademii* 1, 198). Prior to Shchapov's departure from Kazan, both Ioann and the local archbishop attempted—without result—to obtain a copy of the speech, and the Synodal investigators also endeavored to gather additional information about the eulogy. But Shchapov's arrest gave the government jurisdiction over a key participant, and, as the chief procurator wrote with evident disappointment, "only the monks and people who prove more or less implicated in this affair are all that remain in our hands" (quoted in Olfer'ev to Urusov, 1 May 1861, TsGIA SSSR, f. 797, op. 31, otd. 1, st. 2, d. 149, l. 9 ob.).

36. The code was concealed in an ostensible report on the conditions of their journey, which was to be described as "bad," "satisfactory," or "good," in fact referring to the general state of the academy. TsGIA SSSR, f. 796, op. 142, g. 1861, d. 779, l. 6.

37. Ioann to Tolstoi, 28 April 1861 and 1 May 1861; Zhurnal Pravleniia Dukhovnoi Akademii; and "Ob"iasnenie" by Ioann Iakhontov and Hieromonk Meletii in TsGIA SSSR, f. 797, op. 31, otd. 1, st. 2, d. 149, ll. 50–59 ob.

38. Evidently responding to rumors that the requiem had been a counterdemonstration, intended to censure the gentry for jubilation over the violent suppression of the peasants in Bezdna, Archimandrite Ioann argued that "students of the academy had no special motives or goals in attending the requiem, for they had no previously thought-out plan or relations with the university." In a supplementary letter Ioann took pains to stress that most responsibility rested with Shchapov, who, especially once he began teaching jointly at the university the previous year, had begun to develop dangerous ideas and to sunder his ties to the academy. See Ioann's letters of 10 May 1861 and 11 May 1861 to Archimandrite Iakov in TsGIA SSSR, f. 796, op. 142, g. 1861, d. 779, ll. 11–14, 15–18 ob.

39. See the letter from the Archbishop of Kazan, Afanasii (4 May 1861), in TsGIA SSSR, f. 796, op. 142, g. 1861, d. 869, ll. 1–2 ob.; the statement by Bal'butsinskii is in ibid., f. 796, op. 142, g. 1861, d. 779, l. 25–25 ob.

40. TsGIA SSSR, f. 797, op. 31, otd. 1, st. 2, d. 149, ll. 62–63 (letter of 5 May 1861) and 66–66 ob. (letter of 8 May 1861).

41. TsGIA SSSR, f. 796, op. 142, g. 1861, d. 779, l. 27–27 ob.

42. TsGIA SSSR, f. 797, op. 31, otd. 1, st. 2, d. 149, l. 72.

43. TsGIA SSSR, f. 796, op. 142, g. 1861, d. 779, l. 32.

44. In addition to conversations with authorities and nobles in Kazan, the investigators obtained a further statement from Vicar-Bishop Nikodim, who had inspected the academy in the previous year. As in his earlier report, Nikodim placed primary blame upon its rector, whose administration had had a deleterious impact upon academic standards, morale, and spiritual conditions. Although primary responsibility for "moral conditions" normally rested with the inspector, Nikodim argued that here the inspector "merely had the misfortune to be inspector under a rector like Ioann, whose authoritarian spirit and arrogance deprive his colleagues of the proper exercise of their rights and responsibilities." But, apart from the rector, Nikodim—perhaps out of conviction or loyalty to his home diocese—defended the school against sweeping charges of "freethinking" and radical tendencies. He admitted that such accusations had a "grain of truth" but generally tried to dismiss them as "an exaggeration, which was due to envy, hatred (among some) of ecclesiastical education, a European conception of the foundations of religion, a fuzzy, narrow, and shallow grasp (among some) of the essence of Orthodoxy" (ibid., ll. 30–40, 22 May 1861).

45. For the questions, see ibid., l. 46–46 ob.

46. Iakhontov's written responses, dated 16 and 18 May, are in ibid., ll. 47–48.

47. Ibid., ll. 49–50 ob.

48. Ibid., l. 51–51 ob.

49. Ibid., ll. 53, 72.

50. Ibid., ll. 54, 55, 56, 57, 58, 59, 61, 62, 63, 64, 65, 67, 69, 73, 74, 79. Only in minor details—for example, one student had heard that a priest was slain as well—was the students' information defective.

51. Ibid., ll. 58, 62, 63, 65, 66, 67, 69, 70, 76, 78 ob., 79, 81, 83.

52. For example, see the statements in ibid., ll. 54 ob., 55 ob., 56 ob., 58 ob.

53. Ibid., ll. 54 ob., 55 ob., 56 ob., 57 ob., 60 ob., 61 ob., 63 ob., 64 ob., 67 ob., 70 ob., 75 ob., 78 ob., 79.

54. Ibid., d. 779, ll. 110–11.

55. TsGIA SSSR, f. 796, op. 142, g. 1861, d. 1350, ll. 3–36.

56. See his report to the emperor on 8 July 1861, in TsGIA SSSR, f. 797, op. 31, otd. 1, st. 2, d. 149, l. 122–122 ob.

57. Given the relative innocuousness of their conduct, and given the total failure to prosecute any of the students at the university, the penalties set for the academy students seem inordinately harsh and indeed provoked criticism as intolerably cruel and unfair (see, in particular, P. Dolgorukov, "Zhestokost' Sinoda," *Pravdivyi*, no. 3 [1862], 1). But the Synod's decision must be considered within the context of the academy's role in the Church, where it served as a specialized institution for the recruitment and training of future ecclesiastical elites. See TsGIA SSSR, f. 797, op. 31, otd. 1, st. 2, d. 149, ll. 137–40 ob. (Synodal resolution of 22 September 1861/4 December 1861).

58. For the state's attempt to restrict the clergy's role, see the materials in TsGIA SSSR, f. 797, op. 30, otd. 1, st. 2, d. 278, and I. Gurskaia, "Tserkov' i reforma 1861 g.," *Krasnyi arkhiv* 52 (1935), 182–90.

59. In good measure, the "new" clerical liberalism sought to reassert lost rights and prerogatives, as the clergy sought to reclaim the traditional former prerogatives as a "spiritual father" (*dukhovnyi otets*) exercising broadly defined leadership over his flock. In medieval Russia, the priest's spiritual authority had extended to secular matters as well; his powers to impose penance and to withhold vital sacraments (such as communion) gave him considerable leverage over his parishioners, whatever their rank and wealth. But from the early eighteenth century that clerical autonomy and authority had gradually atrophied, partly because of the state's desire to secularize administration and reduce clerical influence, and partly because of the nobility, whose social predominance and prerogatives as serf owners had severely restricted the role and competence of the Orthodox clergy. As the more candid expression of clerical views in the period of the Great Reforms demonstrates, the clergy nourished strong grievances about their diminished status and, especially, about the nobility's arrogance and predominance; see, for example, I. S. Belliustin, *A Description of the Clergy in Rural Russia*, trans. and ed. Gregory L. Freeze (Ithaca: 1985).

60. Most notably, from the late 1850s the Synod vigorously encouraged the clergy to establish parish schools, which would help prepare the emancipated serfs for full and responsible citizenship. Likewise, in the early 1860s many bishops favored greater roles for the clergy in parish and local affairs, whether it be giving the priest power of attorney for illiterate peasants or the legal right to participate in city and village government. See the discussion and references in Freeze, *Parish Clergy*, chaps. 5–6.

61. Marc Raeff, *Origins of the Russian Intelligentsia: The Eighteenth-Century Nobility* (New York: 1966).

THE TRANSFORMATION OF THE RUSSIAN
FELDSHER, 1864–1914

Samuel C. Ramer

The title *feldsher*, adapted from the German term for a military corpsman or paramedic, was introduced into Russia during the reign of Peter the Great. The first Russian feldshers served as medics in the army, and the title retained its military connotation throughout most of the eighteenth century. Feldshers in civilian practice did not become numerous until the second half of the nineteenth century, when they came to play a central role in every organized system of health care in the Russian empire.[1] Although a significant portion of these civilian feldshers worked in urban hospitals, the majority practiced in the countryside, and the predominant image of the feldsher was rightly that of a rural practitioner, the "muzhik's doctor."[2]

Under Russian law feldshers were licensed only to carry out a physician's specific instructions, and then only under his direct supervision. In practice, the scarcity of physicians in the countryside and the desperate need to provide the peasantry with some kind of trained medical personnel combined to make full compliance with this law impossible. Many feldshers were assigned to remote rural outposts where, despite the periodic visits of a supervising physician, they were essentially on their own. Even feldshers who worked alongside a physician in a rural clinic had to treat many emergency cases by themselves, because the physician was frequently absent either treating another patient or routinely visiting another part of his bailiwick. Even at the beginning of the twentieth century about one-third of those who sought modern medical care were treated first (and often only) by a feldsher. In the nonzemstvo provinces this proportion was almost a half, and in many individual provinces feldshers treated the majority of patients.[3]

Given the importance of the feldshers' role in rural life, it is remarkable how little we know about them as a group. Medical histories have devoted considerable attention to the evolution of the feldshers' medical role, and also to the passion with which growing numbers of physicians opposed independent feldsher practice, or "feldsherism."[4] But social historians of late-nineteenth and early-twentieth-century Russia have for the most part ignored feldshers, at best mentioning them in passing as part of the zemstvo's "third element."[5]

The reasons for this neglect are not hard to understand. The earliest feldshers were marginal figures whose limited education, plebeian (primarily peasant) origin, and low prestige among the educated classes placed them on the bottom rungs of the rural intelligentsia. Indeed, few contemporaries prior to the 1890s would have included them in any kind of intelligentsia at all. Certainly many feldshers managed to win the respect of physicians and patients alike because of their individual attributes, but few outside the medical community itself gave any thought to feldshers as a group. They were geographically dispersed, politically powerless, and professionally subordinate to physicians. In historiography, as in life, they have understandably been overshadowed by the physicians, and particularly the zemstvo physicians, with whom they served.[6]

This tendency to mention the feldsher only in passing, if at all, overlooks a whole series of questions that, once addressed, can enrich our understanding of the dynamics of Russian rural life. For example, what kinds of people became feldshers, and why? What was the nature of their training? In answering these questions one quickly discovers that the social and educational profile of the Russian feldsher underwent a profound transformation between the creation of the zemstvo in 1864 and the outbreak of the First World War.[7] The nature of this transformation, the reasons for its occurrence, and the information it can give us about social change in late imperial Russia constitute the subject of this article.

THE FELDSHER PRIOR TO THE ZEMSTVO

Although the exact number of feldshers practicing in Russia in 1864 is not known, it was certainly small and probably no greater than about two thousand.[8] This meant that most peasants in rural areas had no access to any kind of modern medical care, not even that of a feldsher. Physicians' reports lamented this shortage of qualified feldshers, which left rural medicine almost entirely in the hands of traditional peasant healers. Responding to this situation, the state made significant efforts to train feldshers for rural practice during the 1850s and 1860s, and these efforts were beginning to bear fruit when the zemstvo appeared.[9]

Several institutions were concerned with rural health care prior to the zemstvo, and all of them hired and sponsored the training of feldshers. The Public Welfare Board (*Prikaz obshchestvennogo prizreniia*), created by

Catherine the Great's provincial reform of 1775, was theoretically responsible for the welfare of the whole provincial population and maintained a
variety of institutions to this end, from schools and almshouses to hospitals in the provincial and district (*uezd*) capitals. In practice the Public
Welfare Board was primarily an urban institution that served the needs of
the towns and their immediate environs. This was especially true in the
field of medicine, in which physicians and their hospitals served an almost
exclusively urban population.[10]

The Public Welfare Board hired most of its early feldshers from military feldsher schools. By 1861, however, it had established five feldsher
schools of its own in Moscow, Kazan, Kharkov, Kiev, and Odessa. It also
subsidized twenty feldsher students at the Obukhov hospital in St. Petersburg. Altogether these schools produced about two hundred trained
feldshers per year by 1861, a number evidently regarded as insufficient
given the constant demands to open new feldsher schools.[11] Most feldshers employed by the Public Welfare Boards worked in provincial or
district hospitals, which were not located in rural areas.

A number of other institutions also sponsored feldsher training and
hired feldshers during the prezemstvo era. By the 1860s, for example, the
Ministry of the Court and Properties of the Imperial Family (*Ministerstvo
dvora i udelov*), which was in charge of peasants on the imperial family's
lands, had hired around three hundred feldshers and midwives.[12] But it
was the Ministry of State Domains (*Ministerstvo gosudarstvennykh imu-
shchestv*), which presided over the state peasants, that made the most significant strides in training feldshers for rural service. Under the leadership
of Count P. D. Kiselev, the ministry sought to improve the state peasants'
overall condition, including their health. During the 1840s and 1850s it
made the first serious efforts to supply some form of modern medicine to
the peasant in his village.[13] The number of physicians working for the
Ministry of State Domains was always small. During the 1840s and 1850s
there were sometimes as few as forty salaried physicians in its employ,
and never more than two hundred.[14] In practice this meant that there
were at best two or three salaried physicians per province. Other local
physicians often served without pay,[15] but the number of physicians at the
ministry's disposal was never large enough to make a significant impact
on rural areas. How, then, was the peasantry to be reached? The ministry
tried a number of measures. Its physicians and feldshers trained peasant
boys as vaccinators in an effort to combat the ravages of smallpox. It also
sponsored the training of some peasant women as midwives.[16] In addition,
it did what it could to use parish priests as auxiliary medical personnel.[17]

But the cornerstone of the ministry's plans to reach the peasantry was
the village feldsher. The ministry's successive chief physicians were un-

able to envision a time when there would be enough physicians in rural practice to provide the state peasants with reliable access to a physician's care. Therefore, they concentrated their efforts on providing those peasants with ready access at least to a feldsher.[18] Even this goal seemed ambitious at the time, given the small number of available feldshers and the difficulty of recruiting and training more.

By actively encouraging and subsidizing the training of feldshers, the Ministry of State Domains was able to expand the number of feldshers it hired from 372 in 1853 to 1,149 in 1864, a threefold increase in little more than a decade.[19] Most of these feldshers were sent after their training to serve a particular rural area, ideally a single peasant *volost'* consisting of several villages. In practice, it was more common for a feldsher in the prezemstvo period to serve two or three *volosti*.[20] The provincial or *okrug*[21] physician would visit such a feldsher periodically, often as rarely as once a year. The difficulty of traveling even short distances over existing roads, especially in the spring or fall, coupled with the fact that medical emergencies required immediate treatment, meant that these early village feldshers were for the most part engaged in independent practice.[22]

Who were these early feldshers? When we survey those working in 1864 for the Ministry of State Domains we find a number of distinguishing traits. They were all male, to begin with, a situation that would change after women were admitted to feldsher practice in 1871.[23] The majority were state peasants who had been recruited from their villages while still quite young, between the ages of twelve and sixteen. Among them, however, were also children of townsmen, of the clergy, and of a sprinkling of other groups, including the nobility.[24] Many of them were orphans, and early legislation on feldsher recruitment specified that feldshers should be "primarily orphans."[25] Their prior education had been minimal; judging from the difficulties many of them experienced in training they were at best barely literate. This would continue to be the case well into the zemstvo period, particularly where peasant children were concerned. For this reason the early zemstvo feldsher schools included in their programs a substantial amount of primary education.

The early feldshers of the Ministry of State Domains were trained in various ways. The most common practice was for an individual physician, usually the provincial physician of the ministry, to teach "the feldsher's art" to several (from two to twenty) peasant boys over a period of three to four years.[26] Ideally such boys had their practical training in a large hospital such as the provincial hospital of the Public Welfare Board, where the number and variety of patients were considerable. In such a large hospital they could gain experience caring for the sick and injured, and the range of illnesses they encountered naturally broadened their

diagnostic capabilities. Many peasant boys, however, studied with an
okrug physician of the ministry in a much smaller district hospital, which
had very few patients.[27]

Arranging feldsher training with an individual physician posed numerous difficulties. Housing was a problem, because there were no accommodations for such students in provincial or district hospitals. Renting an apartment for such boys in the provincial capital was only the beginning. The apartment had to be furnished, however austerely, and the boys needed food, clothing, and supplies. Some kind of supervision had to be provided, by the physician himself, a feldsher, or a governor hired to keep the boys out of trouble.[28] The forty rubles per year that the ministry allotted for each feldsher student at best barely covered these expenses. Small wonder that many provincial physicians professed themselves unable to assume the responsibility of teaching and looking after such feldsher students. Others volunteered to teach peasant boys what they could, and some actually took such boys into their own homes and combined the functions of teacher and surrogate parent.[29]

What evidence we have about the way in which provincial physicians conducted feldsher training suggests the following general picture. The physician himself usually assumed responsibility primarily for his young charges' "theoretical" training and did the best he could to teach them something about the human body and guide them through the textbooks provided by the ministry. Just how much they were able to comprehend naturally varied from case to case. Certainly their studies were constantly interrupted by the physician's own unpredictable schedule, so that nothing like regular classes seems to have been held.[30]

No one in the Ministry of State Domains expected these teenage feldshers to have a very deep understanding of medicine. The very textbook they studied was less a tract on medical principles than a by-the-numbers manual on patient care filled with commonsense injunctions.[31] The ministry hoped that during their training feldsher students would develop practical skills that would compensate for their limited theoretical knowledge. For this reason experience working in a hospital was always regarded as the most crucial part of feldsher education. But it was here that the early training was most flawed. Although the provincial physician occasionally took his feldsher students with him as he made rounds, most physicians were too harried by patient demands to spend much time explaining to students the reasons behind their diagnosis and treatment. Some in fact delegated this instruction to the hospital's senior feldsher.[32]

The Ministry of State Domains was gradually persuaded by its own physicians' reports that future feldsher training should take place only in specialized feldsher schools attached to major hospitals.[33] Such feldsher schools existed in a number of cities prior to the zemstvo, and they constituted the second major training ground for feldshers at the time. The most important of these schools for the Ministry of State Domains was that affiliated with the Moscow Foundling Home.[34] In 1854 approximately half of all the feldshers employed by the ministry had received their training at the home's feldsher school.[35] Many of these were orphans from the foundling home, for whom feldsher training opened up a career. Others had been selected by their villages and by the provincial offices of the Ministry of State Domains to attend the home as boarding students. Their expenses were covered for the most part by the ministry, with supplementary contributions from their villages.

The Moscow Foundling Home feldsher school provided a more structured course of study than that provided by a provincial physician, and the ministry consistently expressed a preference for hiring its graduates. If the percentage trained at the Moscow Foundling Home had fallen to one-quarter by 1864, it was because the ministry was hiring more feldshers than the foundling home could supply.[36] Recognizing this, the chief physician of the ministry urged the establishment of regional feldsher schools with a uniform standard of training as the best way to provide enough qualified feldshers for rural practice.[37] This is the path that provincial zemstvos would follow in the 1870s and 1880s, when they organized feldsher schools around the provincial hospital.

There were two other important sources of civilian feldshers in the prezemstvo era besides the various training programs of the Public Welfare Board and the Ministry of State Domains. The first was a large but indeterminate number of retired military feldshers who had been trained as corpsmen while serving in the army. These rotnye or "company" feldshers (not to be confused with those military feldshers who had completed a military feldsher school affiliated with a hospital) had never trained in a large hospital. They were generally acknowledged to be unqualified for civilian practice, and particularly unsuitable for independent practice in rural areas. The Ministry of State Domains hired almost no "company" feldshers, but reports from other physicians indicate that there was a large number of such feldshers working in the countryside during the 1860s.[38] Physicians made continuous efforts to eliminate them from civilian practice throughout the zemstvo era, but their numbers would remain substantial as long as the supply of feldshers trained in schools was insufficient to meet the country's demands. By the turn of the century, however, zemstvo and state institutions would hire almost exclusively the graduates of accredited feldsher schools.[39]

In addition to these "company" feldshers, whose incompetence and propensity for alcohol did much to give the very title feldsher an unsavory ring, there were more than a few feldshers who had no training whatso-ever. These feldshers simply called themselves such on the basis of certif-icates they had managed to acquire either from physicians in private practice or even from local government authorities. The absence of a uni-form licensing system for feldshers made it difficult to eliminate this kind of self-appointed practitioner, and one early zemstvo physician recalled that he had frequently encountered such "feldshers" working for the zem-stvo in the 1870s.[40]

Feldshers practicing in Russia in the 1860s were thus a diverse group, whether one considers their education, their practical skills, or their actual effectiveness as medical practitioners. This diversity notwithstanding, it is clear that the quality of feldsher education in the 1860s was extremely superficial no matter where a feldsher got his training. Provincial physi-cians evaluating the feldshers under them consistently made two general points in this regard. The first was that almost none of these early feld-shers had any real understanding of the nature of modern medicine.[41] The second was that, although many were quite capable as physicians' assist-ants working in hospitals, none was prepared for the burdens of indepen-dent practice. Here physicians blamed the nature of even the best feldsher training, which had encouraged feldsher students in hospitals to function as obedient assistants rather than to develop the sorts of diagnostic skills and therapeutic techniques that they would need as independent practi-tioners working alone in the countryside.[42] Finally, of course, most of these early feldshers' shortcomings as medical practitioners were made all the more serious by their meager primary education, the limited character of their overall cultural development, and the absence of any sense of calling among them.

FELDSHER RECRUITMENT AND TRAINING DURING THE ZEMSTVO ERA

When the zemstvo was introduced during the second half of the 1860s, it reaffirmed the importance of the feldsher's role in rural health care.[43] District zemstvo assemblies and boards looked to the feldsher to deliver primary care in rural areas, while early zemstvo physicians—whose num-bers were few—spent much of their time riding from one independent feldsher outpost to another in what came to be called the "circuit" (*raz*"-*ezdnaia*) system of health-care delivery. [44]

That even the best-trained feldshers of the time were unfit for this kind of independent practice was a point provincial physicians had made prior to the zemstvo's creation. The use of feldshers as independent rural prac-titioners was rendered even more unsatisfactory by the fact that the best feldshers tended to remain in cities, working either in hospitals or in private practice, despite the comparatively higher salaries offered for work in rural areas. Feldshers trained by the Ministry of State Domains constitute an exception, but by no means all of them remained in rural practice after 1864. The bulk of the trained feldshers who went to the countryside for the zemstvo in the 1860s were, in the colorful words of one early zemstvo physician, "decrepit old men, chronic alcoholics, or moral degenerates" who had been rejected for employment by other institutions.[45] They also included many "company" feldshers, who were barely competent to work even in hospitals, where they were often used as sanitary personnel rather than as physicians' assistants.[46]

The need to train a much larger body of qualified feldshers was therefore one that the zemstvo quickly recognized. Provincial zemstvos began to establish feldsher schools for this purpose as early as the 1860s. The Kazan and Kharkov zemstvos had inherited feldsher schools from the Public Welfare Board, and these continued to function as they had before.[47] In the nine years between 1867 and 1876 nineteen additional provinces set up schools for feldshers and midwives, a flurry of activity that then abated, only to be resumed in the 1890s.[48]

Some of these schools closed after only a few years in operation,[49] but the majority survived, gradually expanding their curricula and raising their entrance requirements as the provincial zemstvos sponsoring them sought to upgrade the quality of the feldshers they were training. In the nonzemstvo provinces there was a growing number of government schools, and by the early twentieth century a substantial number of private schools for feldshers and midwives had also appeared.[50]

All of these schools were subject to the control of the Medical Department of the Ministry of Internal Affairs, which set licensing requirements and had authority to approve even minor changes in curriculum. Faced with a proliferation of zemstvo feldsher schools in the late 1860s and early 1870s, each with its own curriculum and standards, the Ministry of Internal Affairs decided to simplify its own task by issuing a model charter (*normal'nyi ustav*) whose standards would be binding on all such institutions. This model charter of 1872, through which the ministry hoped to raise as well as standardize the level of feldsher training, deserves attention here because it tells us what the ministry thought achievable and desirable in feldsher education.

The model charter raised the minimum age of boys entering feldsher school to fifteen, somewhat older than had been the earlier practice, whereas the maximum age at matriculation was set at twenty. Entrants had to "be able to read and write in Russian and know the main prayers."[51] The course of study was set at three years, the first of which was devoted to what was essentially elementary education. In their second year students were introduced to medical subjects such as descriptive anatomy (including autopsies); physiology, which entailed general notions about the circulation of the blood, diet, and so on; and surgery, which emphasized the feldsher's role as an assistant. In their surgery course feldsher students learned how to perform minor procedures such as bloodletting, vaccinating, and tooth pulling. A pharmacology course included a general description of the plant, mineral, and animal worlds, but its primary purpose was to teach students how to make simple medicines out of available plants. Finally, a course on hygiene and forensic medicine offered a brief introduction to preventive medicine and practical advice on how to deal with drownings, suffocations, burns, wounds, and surface bleeding.

During these first two years of instruction feldsher students were to spend at least thirty hours per week in formal classroom study. In their third year this number was cut to twelve, as a review of all their second-year subjects was to be combined with more extensive practical application of their knowledge in hospitals. Feldsher students had to pass an annual exam, plus a final graduation exam at the end of three years. Graduates were obliged to serve four and one-half years working for the district zemstvo that had subsidized their education, after which they were free to seek employment wherever they wished or even to change professions. One incentive to continue working as a feldsher was their draft status. Those who finished four and one-half years in zemstvo service were exempt from the draft as long as they continued to serve as feldshers until they were thirty. Those who quit before thirty reverted to eligibility for the draft along with all the other males from their home village.[52]

The model charter of 1872 specified that feldsher students were to be chosen by district zemstvo boards "primarily from persons belonging to village communes."[53] There were several reasons for this initial preference for peasants as feldshers (a preference reflected in early recruitment to zemstvo schools). For one thing, medical planners thought that peasants, because they were already accustomed to the rigors of rural life, would tend to remain in rural practice. Moreover, it seemed likely that peasants with medical problems would most readily seek the help of someone who "spoke their language" and understood their way of life. In this vision the feldsher of peasant origin would be the ideal link between the world of modern medicine and that of the village.

Recruiting feldshers from the peasantry, however, posed two major problems. The first was that by no means all village communes were willing to provide candidates for feldsher training. This was particularly true in areas where profitable nonagricultural work was readily available to supplement peasants' agricultural incomes. Yielding an able-bodied male, even a minor, to a feldsher school in these areas represented a tangible economic loss without any clear guarantee of compensating benefits.[54] Second, and more important, was the fact that peasant boys—and almost all peasant recruits were male—had such a rudimentary education prior to entering feldsher school that they were difficult to train to an acceptable standard.

Physicians' reports on the performance of these early peasant feldshers are remarkably diverse. Some found their work "entirely satisfactory," whereas others saw them as worse than useless. To some degree this diversity of opinion merely registered the real differences that existed in feldshers' abilities, and even more so in their dependability, conscientiousness, and sobriety. It obviously reflected as well the diverse standards that individual physicians applied in evaluating feldshers. Some simply reported whether they found a particular feldsher's work acceptable given the limits of what they could expect. Others, particularly those concerned with the quality of zemstvo medicine as a system, seem to have measured their work against a higher and more abstract standard. What is certain is that during the 1870s growing numbers of zemstvo physicians rejected the feldsher's independent role as unacceptable, little more in fact than "licensed znakharstvo" (quackery).[55]

Had peasants been the only potential or acceptable feldsher recruits, zemstvo and other feldsher schools would simply have had to make do with the situation. But this was not the case. To the contrary, there was a growing number of applications to all feldsher schools from candidates of urban origin, many of them women, who had a much more extensive secondary education than their peasant counterparts. Some had actually completed classical gymnasia, and others had at least two or three years of gymnasium training. As feldsher schools began to train these applicants, they found them much more capable as students and, ultimately, much better qualified as medical practitioners.

As a result, peasant origin in and of itself gradually ceased to be the primary consideration in feldsher recruitment. Peasants remained an important contingent of feldsher recruits, particularly in zemstvo feldsher schools, and the question of social origin was never completely dismissed as irrelevant in training feldshers for rural practice. But it gradually took second place to a candidate's overall educational qualifications, not simply in admissions to feldsher schools but, more importantly, in the hiring decisions made by individual physicians.[56]

The availability of large numbers of better educated urban, and particularly female, applicants allowed feldsher schools to raise the educational requirements for admission and also to make the feldsher's training more extensive and demanding. Medical courses, both theoretical and practical, could be made more sophisticated as the students to whom they were addressed were more capable of absorbing the material. Much of this change in feldsher training was gradual, as individual feldsher schools made piecemeal adjustments in their programs after lengthy consultation with the Ministry of Internal Affairs. A new model charter of 1897, however, codified these new standards.[57] The primary education that had taken up the first year of feldsher training in the model charter of 1872 was eliminated in 1897, replaced by higher admissions standards. The normal training period was increased from three to four years in most schools, largely to accommodate an expanded curriculum and provide students with more practical experience in hospitals. By the beginning of the twentieth century the combination of better educated applicants and more elaborate training had begun to produce feldshers who were vastly superior to their predecessors of a quarter-century earlier.

FELDSHER STUDENTS IN 1910:
THE GROWING DOMINANCE OF URBAN WOMEN

Who were these urban applicants to feldsher schools? In answering this question it is useful to look at the statistics on enrollment in feldsher schools in 1910, the most complete that we have on the prewar period. These statistics, embodied in the following five tables, record the number of feldsher students, their sex, their social origin, their religion, the kind of education they had received prior to feldsher school, and their age. The tables also break down this information according to the kind of feldsher schools involved. By 1910 there were five basic types of feldsher school. The first provided feldsher training for men only. The second provided the same training for women only, although the admissions standards for women were slightly higher than those for men. The third trained both male and female students, although classes as a rule were segregated by sex. The fourth trained women not simply as feldshers, but as feldsher-midwives, a combination that physicians and zemstvos increasingly preferred. The main reason for this preference was a desire to cut infant mortality by improving the quality of obstetric care in the countryside; trained midwives had had almost no success in developing a practice among peasant women, and physicians reasoned that peasant women who had been successfully treated by a feldsher-midwife for minor injuries or illnesses would be more likely to trust such a practitioner, particularly a woman, in childbirth.[58] Finally, a number of schools trained both men and women as feldsher-midwives. Let us begin by looking at the enrollment in feldsher schools in 1910 (Table I).

The figures in Table I demonstrate that the total number of feldsher schools of all kinds had literally exploded to 66 by 1910, with a total

=========== T A B L E I ===========

ENROLLMENT IN FELDSHER SCHOOLS IN 1910

Type of School	Number of Schools	Enrollment	
		Male	Female
Feldsher (men only)	13	1,764	—
Feldsher (women only)	6	—	648
Feldsher (mixed)	13	381	544
Feldsher-midwife (women)	23	—	3,589
Feldsher-midwife (mixed)	11	201	935
TOTAL	66	2,346	5,716

Source: *Spisok srednykh i nizshikh meditsinskikh shkol grazhdanskogo vedomstva v Rossii* (St. Petersburg: 1910), xvi.

enrollment of 8,062 students. But the most striking fact is the overwhelming preponderance of women among feldsher students: just over 70 percent were women, the majority training to become feldsher-midwives. The growth in importance of the feldsher-midwife is also evident: 60 percent of all feldsher students were training to become feldsher-midwives, almost all of them women. Finally, it is interesting to note that three-quarters of all male students were enrolled in the thirteen feldsher schools for men only. Information on the social origin of these feldsher students helps to bring these raw figures into focus (Table II).

The figures in Table II demonstrate that the largest single group of feldsher students in 1910 was of *meshchanstvo*, or urban petit bourgeois, origin. Peasants still constituted almost a third of all feldsher students, but they were a majority only in the thirteen (primarily zemstvo) schools training men as feldshers. In schools training feldsher-midwives *meshchanstvo* women made up almost one-half of the student body, and they were joined by another 20 percent who were daughters of nobles, priests, clerks, teachers, and physicians. Put otherwise, the significant fact is that men and women of peasant origin made up less than one-fifth of the students training as feldsher-midwives.

Statistics on the education feldsher students had received prior to entering feldsher schools testify dramatically to the increase in overall

===== T A B L E I I =====

SOCIAL ORIGIN OF STUDENTS IN FELDSHER SCHOOLS IN 1910
(Percentages)

School	Peasant	Meshch-anstvo	Nobility	Clergy	Children of Teachers, Clergy, Physicians	Other
Feldsher (men)	62.7	19.9	3	1	1	12.3
Feldsher (women)	13.9	24	6	18.5	17	20.6
Feldsher (mixed)	37	35.6	6.7	5.4	7	8.3
Feldsher-midwife (women)	18.4	44.5	7.6	7.6	6.1	15.8
Feldsher-midwife (mixed)	18.4	53.2	8.1	3.3	5.9	11.1
TOTAL (Percentage of all feldsher students)	29	38.1	6.6	6.2	6.1	14

Source: *Spisok srednykh i nizshikh meditsinskikh shkol grazhdanskogo vedomstva v Rossii* (St. Petersburg: 1910), xvi.

educational preparation that the influx of urban women had brought about (Table III).

Thus almost 15 percent of all feldsher students had graduated from classical gymnasium, and over half had completed four or more years of gymnasium. Both of these figures are stunning when one recalls the feldsher students of only a few decades before. As a group women students had more education than most of their male counterparts, and indeed they account for almost all feldsher students with any degree of gymnasium education. Over 80 percent of the women studying to be feldsher-midwives had completed at least four years of gymnasium. If we

=========== T A B L E   I I I ===========

PRIOR EDUCATION OF FELDSHER STUDENTS IN 1910
(Percentages)

School	Gymnasium Completed	Gymnasium 6–7 Class	Gymnasium 4–5 Class	City School	Village School	Other
Feldsher (men)	—	—	0.4	31.4	61.2	7
Feldsher (women)	19.3	60.5	19.1	0.5	0.3	0.3
Feldsher (mixed)	20.3	3.1	33	22.4	18.3	2.9
Feldsher-midwife (women)	21.7	6.8	53.9	3.8	2.1	11.7
Feldsher-midwife (mixed)	13.6	6.5	44.7	14.9	6.2	14.1
TOTAL (Percentage of all feldsher students)	14.6	10	32.7	14.7	19.4	8.6

Source: *Spisok srednykh i nizshikh meditsinskikh shkol grazhdanskogo vedomstva v Rossii*
(St. Petersburg: 1910), xvi–xvii.

look at the men being trained in exclusively male feldsher schools, we see
that almost all of them had finished either a village school (61.2 percent)
or its slightly more sophisticated urban counterpart (31.4 percent). Both
of these offered at best what amounted to a junior high school education,
but even this was a vast improvement over the rudimentary education that
the earliest zemstvo feldsher students had received prior to entering
feldsher schools.

Records of feldsher students' religious affiliation in 1910 are shown in
Table IV. An astonishing 20 percent of all feldsher students were Jewish,
the overwhelming majority of them Jewish women studying to become
feldsher-midwives. Many of these Jewish women were studying in large
private schools for feldsher-midwives that had been established since the

=========== T A B L E   I V ===========

RELIGIOUS AFFILIATION OF FELDSHER STUDENTS IN 1910
(Percentages)

Type of school	Orthodox	Jewish	Roman Catholic	Other
Feldsher (men)	90.2	4.9	2.2	2.7
Feldsher (women)	89.9	5.9	2.9	1.3
Feldsher (mixed)	82	15.6	1.7	0.7
Feldsher-midwife (women)	69.5	27	1.4	2.1
Feldsher-midwife (mixed)	62.8	33.3	1.4	2.5
TOTAL (Percentage of all feldsher students)	76.2	20	1.7	2

Source: *Spisok srednykh i nizshikh meditsinskikh shkol grazhdanskogo vedomstva v Rossii* (St. Petersburg: 1910), xvi–xvii.

turn of the century. In feldsher schools for men and even for women the percentage of Orthodox students remained high, whereas the overall percentage for the empire was only three-quarters.

Finally, Table V shows the age structure of feldsher students in 1910. The majority of feldsher students in 1910 were young adults, over twenty years old at the time of their training. This alone is a dramatic change from the prezemstvo and early zemstvo periods, when most were peasant boys in their midteens. The disparity between the ages of male and female feldsher students is also marked. The tendency of male feldshers to embark on their studies at a considerably younger age than most female feldshers is directly related to the questions of social origin and prior education as well as gender: peasant boys, for example, entered feldsher schools when they were still in their teens because this was when they finished either a village or city school. The overwhelming majority of women of all social backgrounds, on the other hand, tended to enter feldsher schools somewhat later, usually after they were twenty, and significant numbers (many of whom were the wives or widows of soldiers, teachers, feldshers, and physicians) began their studies in their thirties.

To return to our original question regarding the identity of urban ap-

======= T A B L E   V =======

AGES OF FELDSHER STUDENTS IN 1910
(Percentages)

Type of school	Under 20	20–30	30–40	Over 40
Feldsher (men)	84.8	15.2	—	—
Feldsher (women)	16.5	73.1	10.3	0.16
Feldsher (mixed)	45.2	45.9	8.8	—
Feldsher-midwife (women)	26	66.2	7.5	0.22
Feldsher-midwife (mixed)	25.8	62.6	10.9	1.3
TOTAL (Percentage of all feldsher students)	41.6	51.6	6.5	0.29

Source: *Spisok srednykh i nizshikh meditsinskikh shkol grazhdanskogo vedomstva v Rossii* (St. Petersburg: 1910), xvi–xvii.

plicants to feldsher schools, we can see clearly that the largest single contingent by 1910 consisted of women of *meshchanstvo* origin, most of whom had at least some gymnasium education, and many of whom were Jewish. This wave of urban women seeking to become feldshers was the central reason for the marked improvement in feldsher qualifications that took place between 1864 and 1914. Three traits tended to set these women apart from their peasant male counterparts: a superior education, an overall cultural sophistication that was part of their urban experience, and a generally greater commitment to medicine that we find reflected in their voluntary choice to become either feldshers or feldsher-midwives and in their willingness to pay for their studies themselves.

Statistics on feldsher students alone, of course, do not give us an accurate picture of the entire body of practicing feldshers. Despite the predominance of women among feldsher students during the decade before the war, for example, 80 percent of the thirty thousand feldshers in civilian practice in 1913 were still male.[59] But the student statistics are indicative of important trends that had already had a significant impact on the feldsher community in Russia, and that would have remade it entirely within a few years had the war not intervened. The most significant trend was the feminization of the feldsher calling that occurred as part of the search for better qualified feldshers. This feminization, interrupted by the training of large numbers of male "company" feldshers during the war, was resumed under the Soviet regime during the 1920s.

Given the relatively unattractive nature of feldsher employment (low pay, limited prestige, difficult working conditions), how can we explain the fact that so many young urban women wanted to become feldshers? There is no simple answer to this question, but several factors that could encourage such a choice deserve mention. In the first place feldsher school prepared one for a job that provided a living and for which there was a demand. If practicing feldshers complained unendingly of their lot, it was always in comparison to that of schoolteachers, clerks, physicians, and other white-collar occupations. Certainly working as a feldsher was a more inviting prospect for most women than working in a factory, or as a seamstress, or hiring out as a domestic servant or tutor.[60]

For women in particular the number of occupations that offered the possibility of an autonomous existence was limited.[61] Many women, from the young and idealistic to widows more concerned with survival, were drawn to feldsher schools precisely because they offered the possibility of an independent career and job mobility.[62] The position of feldsher had an additional attraction for Jewish women, who made up a disproportionately large number of students, because the feldsher's diploma allowed them to leave the Pale of Settlement and work wherever they wished.

The feldsher's position could also appeal to anyone with even vaguely populist sentiments. One could go to the countryside and serve the people as a feldsher and in doing so identify oneself with the social ideals of the Russian intelligentsia. It would be a mistake to underestimate the power of this particular appeal. By the beginning of the twentieth century the civic spirit of the intelligentsia was part of gymnasium life, and most gymnasium students sought to become part of the intelligentsia, however they chose to define that term. Career choice was obviously an important step in reaching this goal. Many of the urban women who became feldshers would doubtless have become physicians had their means and circumstances permitted. The number who quit gymnasium after four or five, or even seven classes, suggests that many were unable to afford completing their studies, much less to attend a university. For these women becoming a feldsher or feldsher-midwife was an acceptable second best to a loftier but unrealizable goal.

By the 1890s women who were drawn to feldsher schools were also aware that physicians and hiring institutions such as the zemstvo had begun to express a positive preference for women as feldshers, and particularly as feldsher-midwives. The reasons for this preference, which brightened women's job prospects and enhanced their professional mobility, were numerous. To begin with, the urban women who applied to feldsher schools, as we have seen, were on the whole better educated and more mature that their predominantly peasant male counterparts. Physicians described them as "more cultured," a term that referred not only to their education but to what was perceived as their overall trustworthiness and sobriety.[63] Finally, it seems that many physicians felt more comfortable working with female assistants. Their education, maturity, and sense of commitment made them seem more likely to be able to constitute real colleagues whose judgment and expertise one could trust.[64]

THE IMPACT OF HIGHER QUALIFICATIONS ON FELDSHER EXPECTATIONS

The changes in recruitment and training that brought about such a radical improvement in feldshers' overall qualifications between 1864 and 1914 had a profound effect on the way feldshers viewed themselves, their work, and their place in society. As a result of their more formalized schooling, during which their teachers tried to imbue them with a sense of mission, feldshers were increasingly aware of their importance. The most sensitive saw themselves as part of the Russian intelligentsia by virtue of their calling, a self-image their schooling had fostered.

Many feldshers went to their first rural posting fully expecting to serve as partners with physicians in the great task of healing the Russian people. When they arrived at these posts, however, they often encountered physicians for whom the notion of any real partnership with feldshers was foreign. For most physicians the feldsher was at best a qualified and obedient assistant who would carry out instructions without error or improvisation. By definition he (or she) was a subordinate, and no amount of improvement in his qualifications or attitude could change this fundamental reality.

The more educated feldshers became, the more difficult it was for them to accept this "mechanical" definition of their task. More important, they resented the brusque and frequently tactless way in which many physicians treated them and interpreted this bosslike behavior as evidence of social discrimination. They never challenged the physicians' professional superiority, but they did seek a greater sense of collegiality in working together that was in line with the democratic ideals of the intelligentsia itself. When that collegiality and respect were lacking, as they often were, the growing sense of professional and personal dignity that their education had encouraged was offended.

Formal training also raised feldshers' expectations concerning their position in society. Here, as in their day-to-day relations with the physicians with whom they worked, they were frustrated time and again. Their pay remained low, usually about one-quarter of what physicians received. Their social status did not rise as rapidly as their increased qualifications and the nature of their work warranted. Indeed, it appeared to many feldshers that "the shabbiest clerk enjoys more humane relationships with the authorities and a more certain social position than the feldsher."[65] Certainly the indignities they suffered at the hands of hiring authorities suggested that their work was not valued. One senses in their writings a longing for respect and recognition that is even more powerful than their bitterness over bread-and-butter issues.

They were particularly offended by the indiscriminate nature of physicians' repeated attacks on "feldsherism," an unfortunate label for independent feldsher practice that inadvertently brought the feldsher's very legitimacy into question every time it was applied. They sought a clearer definition of their legal rights as medical practitioners that would eliminate their ambiguous status in Russian law and protect them from arbitrary treatment by physicians and hiring agencies. Finally, aware that the position of feldsher itself was professionally a dead end, they urged that the medical faculties be opened to those feldshers who had proved themselves to be gifted and committed healers. This access to the medical faculties remained closed to all but graduates of classical gymnasia until after 1917 on the grounds that only those with the broad humanistic education that gymnasium provided could be full-fledged physicians.

When the rewards and social status generated by their professional activity failed to match the expectations that both their education and the evolving democratic ethos in the country had helped to develop and justify, feldshers organized themselves into local and eventually national societies dedicated to improving their professional position. Although this is not the place to discuss the history of these societies, we should note that they constituted an impressive example of organization that is indicative of how much not only the Russian feldsher but Russian society itself had changed in the forty years prior to the revolution.

Despite the considerable improvement in the feldshers' abilities and dedication that occurred in the half-century prior to 1914, neither the medical profession nor society at large was prepared to honor their corporate professional claims to the extent that they wished. Feldshers lacked several of the classic prerequisites for professional recognition, from a uniform standard of training and supreme expertise in their field to institutionalized autonomy in their practice.[66] This was of little consolation to feldshers, who wanted greater social and professional recognition. As a result they, like many other groups in Russian society, entered an era of revolutionary upheaval filled with resentment over the continual frustration of what they saw as legitimate demands.

NOTES

ACKNOWLEDGMENTS: *I would like to thank the Tulane University Senate Committee on Research, the National Endowment for the Humanities, the International Research and Exchanges Board, the Fulbright-Hays Fellowship Program, the Kennan Institute for Advanced Russian Studies of the Wilson Center, and the University of Illinois for their generous support in the preparation of this essay.*

1. For a review of the origins of feldsher practice in Russia see my article "Who Was the Russian Feldsher?," *Bulletin of the History of Medicine* 50 (1976), 213–14.

2. As of 1907, almost two-thirds of the feldshers in the Russian empire were still employed in rural areas, most of them in clinics where they worked alongside physicians. This general figure is applicable whether one considers only the zemstvo provinces, all of European Russia, or the empire as a whole. *Otchet o sostoianii narodnogo zdraviia i organizatsii vrachebnoi pomoshchi v Rossii za 1907 god* (St. Petersburg: 1909), 60, 92.

3. B. B. Veselovskii, *Istoriia zemstva za sorok let*, 4 vols. (St. Petersburg: 1909–11), 1, 429.

4. See, for example, E. A. Osipov, I. V. Popov, and P. I. Kurkin, *Russkaia zemskaia meditsina* (Moscow: 1899), 71–97, and M. Ia. Kapustin, *Osnovnye voprosy zemskoi meditsiny* (St. Petersburg: 1889), 28–41. Beginning in the 1890s feldshers themselves generated a huge literature on their problems, much of it as part of their effort to improve their professional status. For a survey of the evolution of feldshers as a professional group written by a feldsher see P. A. Kalinin, *Profdvizhenie srednego meditsinskogo personala v Rossii* (Moscow: 1927).

5. B. B. Veselovskii is a major exception in this regard. His *Istoriia zemstva za sorok let* devotes considerable attention to the feldsher's place in zemstvo medical programs (vol. 1, 326–55, 426–34). See also his "Fel'dshera i vrachi," *Saratovskaia zemskaia nedelia* 8 (1903), 75–80, which is a sensitive and informed treatment of the professional conflicts between physicians and feldshers. The most recent exception is N. M. Pirumova, *Zemskaia intelligentsiia i ee rol' v obshchestvennoi bor'be* (Moscow: 1986), which deals with feldsher recruitment, social origin, education, and political involvement. Two other studies that briefly treat feldshers in the larger framework of the prerevolutionary intelligentsia are Pirumova, "Zemskaia intelligentsiia v 70–80-e gody XIX v.," *Istoricheskie zapiski* 106 (1981), 156–57, and V. R. Leikina-Svirskaia, *Russkaia intelligentsiia v 1900–1917 godakh* (Moscow: 1981), 58–59.

6. The Russian medical profession itself has only recently begun to receive the kind of thorough attention it deserves. See Nancy M. Frieden, *Russian*

Physicians in an Era of Reform and Revolution, 1856–1905 (Princeton, N. J.: 1981), and John F. Hutchinson, "Society, Corporation or Union? Russian Physicians and the Struggle for Professional Unity (1890–1913)," *Jahrbücher für Geschichte Osteuropas* 30 (n.s.), no. 1 (1982), 37–53.

7. By creating an immediate demand for large numbers of military feldshers, the First World War radically altered existing patterns of feldsher recruitment and training in Russia. For this reason I have concluded this essay in 1914 rather than extending it to 1917.

8. This is an estimate based on calculations set forth in the following discussion. There are no precise statistics available. Osipov's classic work on zemstvo medicine states that the zemstvo inherited around two thousand auxiliary medical personnel of all kinds, including midwives and pharmacists as well as feldshers. This estimate appears low when compared to the archival material cited here. See Osipov et al., *Russkaia zemskaia meditsina*, 89–90. Professor Frieden's figure of fifty-five hundred trained paramedics working for the Ministry of State Domains in 1867, based on the ministry's published figures for that year, is far larger than any numbers I encountered working with the same ministry's physicians' reports. The term paramedic in her text seems to include midwives as well as feldshers, so our estimates may not be so far apart. Frieden, *Russian Physicians*, 85–86.

9. For recent studies of rural medicine on the eve of the zemstvo see I. D. Strashun, "Polveka zemskoi meditsiny (1864–1914)," in P. I. Kal'iu (ed.), *Ocherki istorii russkoi obshchestvennoi meditsiny (K stoletiiu zemskoi meditsiny): Sbornik statei* (Moscow: 1965), 30–36; M. M. Levit, *Stanovlenie obshchestvennoi meditsiny v Rossii* (Moscow: 1974), 44–75; Frieden, *Russian Physicians*, 77–87; and my own article, "The Zemstvo and Public Health," in Terence Emmons and Wayne S. Vucinich (eds.), *The Zemstvo in Russia: An Experiment in Local Self-Government* (Cambridge, England: 1982), 282–86.

10. On the Public Welfare Board see Isabel de Madariaga, *Russia in the Age of Catherine the Great* (New Haven and London: 1981), 285, and Robert E. Jones, *Provincial Development in Russia: Catherine II and Jakob Sievers* (New Brunswick, N. J.: 1984), 141–44.

11. Tsentral'nyi Gosudarstvennyi Istoricheskii Arkhiv (TsGIA), fond (f.) 1297, opis' (op.) 216, delo (d.) 262, ll. 1–2.

12. N. A. Bogoliubov, "Udel'nye krest'iane," in A. K. Dzhivelegov, S. P. Mel'gunov, and V. I. Picheta (eds.), *Velikaia reforma: Russkoe obshchestvo i krest'ianskii vopros v proshlom i nastoiashchem*, 6 vols. (Moscow: 1911), 2, 246. Bogoliubov does not specify exactly how many were feldshers.

13. On Kiselev's goals as minister of state domains see W. Bruce Lincoln, *In the Vanguard of Reform: Russia's Enlightened Bureaucrats, 1825–1861* (DeKalb, Ill.: 1982), 30–34.

14. N. M. Druzhinin, *Gosudarstvennye krest'iane i reforma P. D. Kiseleva*, 2 vols. (Moscow: 1946–58), 2, 263–64.

15. Such volunteers did acquire service rank and could thereby earn a pension. Ibid., 2, 264.

16. Ibid., 2, 267.

17. TsGIA, f. 1297, op. 97, d. 69, ll. 49–49 ob., and Olga Crisp, "The State Peasants under Nicholas I," in Olga Crisp, *Studies in the Russian Economy before 1914* (New York: 1976), 88.

18. As the chief physician of the Ministry of State Domains stated in his annual report of 1853, the ministry's goal was to assure "that all *volosti* and village societies are supplied with feldshers who are sufficiently knowledgeable about their business." TsGIA, f. 1297, op. 97, d. 69, l. 1 ob.

19. TsGIA, f. 1297, op. 97, d. 69, l. 1 ob (1853) and f. 1297, op. 110, d. 73, vols. 1–2, passim (1864). Druzhinin's figures on feldshers employed by the Ministry of State Domains show great fluctuation with no tendency toward growth in the years 1847–56. He bases his figures on the ministry's annual reports of its personnel (Druzhinin, *Gosudarstvennye krest'iane*, 2, 265). My own impression after working with the annual reports of the ministry's physicians is that all these figures are at best approximations, but that there had been a significant increase in the number of feldshers employed by 1864.

20. The size of the peasant *volost'* had been increased under Kiselev to about eight thousand souls, with villages ideally no more than twenty-five miles from the *volost'* center. See Crisp, *Studies in the Russian Economy*, 86. For the distribution of feldshers on the eve of the zemstvo see Osipov, et al., *Russkaia zemskaia meditsina*, 61.

21. An *okrug* was the equivalent of several *uezdy* or districts. Crisp, *Studies in the Russian Economy*, 86.

22. Traveling even short distances was a difficult undertaking in most rural areas until well into the Soviet period. In September 1917, for example, the young physician Mikhail Bulgakov took exactly twenty-four torturous hours to travel by wagon from the district capital to his first posting in a village clinic. The distance covered was twenty-six miles. M. A. Bulgakov, *Zapiski iunogo vracha* (Letchworth, England: 1970), 9.

23. Alexander II's decision to allow women to train and practice as feldshers was based in part on the success that female nurses had experienced practicing in hospitals. L. F. Ragozin (ed.), *Svod uzakonenii i rasporiazhenii pravitel'stva po vrachebnoi i sanitarnoi chasti v imperii*, 3 vols. (St. Petersburg: 1895–98), 1, 218.

24. There are no complete statistics on the social origin of feldsher students in the prezemstvo period. All correspondence between the chief physician of the Ministry of State Domains and his provincial physicians during the 1840s and 1850s simply presupposes that these students are for the most part peasant boys. Two 1853 reports from Grodno and Minsk tend to confirm this, although they also record some townsmen and nobles. The latter were evidently drawn from the numerous poor *shliakhtichi* in Grodno and Minsk provinces. TsGIA, f. 1297, op. 98, d. 134, ll. 72–86.

25. "Polozhenie o shkolakh dlia obrazovaniia fel'dsherov," *Polnoe Sobranie Zakonov Rossiiskoi Imperii*, 2d ser., 4, no. 2862 (10 May 1829). Later correspondence within the Ministry of State Domains ritualistically repeats this emphasis on orphans. See, for example, TsGIA, f. 1589, op. 2, d. 223, ll. 1–1 ob.

26. TsGIA, f. 1297, op. 98, d. 134, l. 24.

27. TsGIA, f. 1297, op. 98, d. 102, vol. 2, ll. 84 ob.–85.

28. TsGIA, f. 1297, op. 98, d. 101, vol. 1, ll. 327–29.

29. Ibid., ll. 182, 200, 338 ob.–339.

30. Ibid., ll. 238–238 ob.

31. Feodor Zauer [Sauer], *Polnoe nastavlenie kak dolzhno khodit' za bol'nymi* (St. Petersburg: 1841). A more thorough textbook that went through many editions and was used by feldsher schools throughout the nineteenth century was I. Meisner and [—] Eisenakh, *Kratkoe rukovodstvo dlia fel'dsherskikh shkol*, 2d ed. (St. Petersburg: 1854). On the Ministry of State Domains' efforts to provide practicing feldshers with both these books see TsGIA, f. 1297, op. 100, d. 23, ll. 1–11.

32. TsGIA, f. 1297, op. 98, d. 101, vol. 1, l. 204.

33. Ibid., ll. 231–231 ob., 237–237 ob., 338–39.

34. *Imperatorskii Moskovskii Vospitatel'nyi Dom*, founded by Catherine the Great in 1763. There was also a feldsher school attached to the St. Petersburg Foundling Home, but the number of graduates working for the Ministry of State Domains was extremely small.

35. TsGIA, f. 1297, op. 100, d. 23, ll. 8–98 ob.

36. TsGIA, f. 1297, op. 110, d. 73, vols. 1–2, passim.

37. Chief Physician M. Konstantinovich's proposal, made in 1859, was that several extremely large (800 to 900 students) feldsher schools be set up to remedy "the *extreme* shortage of feldshers from which the ministry suffers" (in 1859 it had only 588 feldshers for the 1,868 slots available). Konstantinovich argued that these schools would only be a temporary necessity, and that after three to four years it would be possible to close them. He also wanted to send greater numbers of civilian feldsher students to existing military feldsher schools. His proposal, which was never acted upon, is important here because it explicitly rejected training with individual physicians and urged that schools be affiliated with large hospitals. TsGIA, f. 1297, op. 98, d. 102, vol. 2, ll. 84–89.

38. TsGIA, f. 1297, op. 216, d. 262, l. 3.

39. *Vysochaishe uchrezhdennaia mezhduvedomstvennaia Komissiia po peresmotru vrachebno-sanitarnogo zakonodatel'stva*, vol. 10, *Zakonoproekty. Prilozhenie 5-oe* (St. Petersburg: 1916), 280. For a general discussion of the conflict between "company" feldshers and those who had finished civilian feldsher schools see my article "Who Was the Russian Feldsher?"

40. TsGIA, f. 1297, op. 216, d. 262, l. 3.

41. Ibid., ll. 3–4 ob.

42. V. I. Radulevich, "Orlovskoe gubernskoe zemstvo," in D. N. Zhbankov (ed.), *Zemsko-meditsinskii sbornik*, 7 vols. (Moscow: 1890–93), 6, 5 (pagination by province).

43. When the zemstvo first assumed responsibility for public health, many district zemstvos appropriated little or no funding, and feldshers were often left to be supported directly by the peasant villages they served. Veselovskii, *Istoriia zemstva*, 1, 327. For a broader conceptualization of the early zemstvo's dilemma concerning personnel see S. Frederick Starr, *Decentralization and Self-Government in Russia, 1830–1870* (Princeton, N. J.: 1972), 293–315.

44. For a review of the controversy over the "circuit" system see Peter F. Krug, "The Debate over the Delivery of Health Care in Rural Russia: The Moscow Zemstvo, 1864–1878," *Bulletin of the History of Medicine* 50 (1976), 226–41.

45. TsGIA, f. 1297, op. 216, d. 262, l. 4.

46. Ibid., l. 4 ob.

47. The Moscow and Odessa schools of the Public Welfare Board had been closed prior to the zemstvo's creation.

48. TsGIA, f. 1297, op. 216, d. 262, ll. 4 ob.–5.

49. Ibid.

50. In 1907 there were ten such private schools throughout the empire. Three were in Moscow, three in Kiev, and the remaining four in Vitebsk, Odessa, Chernigov, and Saratov. Their total enrollment was 1,481 students, all female. Those schools located in the Pale of Settlement trained a high proportion of Jewish students. *Otchet o sostoianii narodnogo zdraviia i organizatsii vrachebnoi pomoshchi v Rossii za 1907 god*, 204–7. The number of private schools for feldshers, and particularly for female feldsher-midwives, more than doubled by 1914. TsGIA, f. 1288, op. 13, d. 9, passim.

51. TsGIA, f. 1297, op. 254, d. 316, l. 2 ob.

52. Ibid., ll. 2 ob.–5.

53. Ibid., l. 2 ob.

54. In 1853, for example, not one peasant in Moscow province was willing to send a son to feldsher school, primarily because of the sacrifice to peasant family income that such study entailed. TsGIA, f. 1297, op. 97, d. 69, ll. 145 ob.–146.

55. For a review of the debates over feldsherism and the larger issues involved see my article "The Zemstvo and Public Health," 292–98. The phrase "licensed *znakharstvo*" occurs in A. Malaksionov, "Zemstvo i meditsina," *Arkhiv sudebnoi meditsiny i obshchestvennoi gigieny* 2, no. 4 (December 1866), 55. Malaksionov was a physician.

56. TsGIA, f. 1297, op. 216, d. 262, l. 8.

57. Ibid., ll. 8–11.

58. On the development of the feldsher-midwife as a means of improving obstetric care in the countryside see my article "Childbirth and Culture: Midwifery in the Nineteenth-Century Russian Countryside," in David L. Ransel (ed.), *The Family in Imperial Russia: New Lines of Historical Research* (Urbana, Ill.: 1978), 233–34.

59. *Statisticheskie materialy po sostoianiiu narodnogo zdraviia i organizatsii meditsinskoi pomoshchi v SSSR za 1913–1923 gg.* (Moscow: 1926), xix.

60. For a detailed examination of the lot of working-class women see Rose L. Glickman, *Russian Factory Women: Workplace and Society, 1880–1914* (Berkeley, Los Angeles, London: 1984), chaps. 1–4.

61. For a good discussion of this problem see Richard Stites, *The Women's Liberation Movement in Russia: Feminism, Nihilism, and Bolshevism, 1860–1930* (Princeton, N. J.: 1978), 157–78.

62. The great demand for female feldsher-midwives allowed those with such diplomas to change jobs frequently. Many physicians saw this rapid turnover

rate as an important drawback in developing a rural practice, particularly for midwives. So physicians in the same area could be divided between those who preferred female feldsher-midwives on principle as better-trained and more conscientious practitioners and those who saw them as a "wandering element," unlikely to stay long in one place, and hence not necessarily preferable to the less mobile male feldshers. For a contemporary discussion that captures this division see "Protokoly meditsinskoi komissii pri Saratovskoi uezdnoi zemskoi uprave, 20-go maia i 17-go iiulia 1903 g.," *Vrachebno-sanitarnaia khronika Saratovskoi gubernii* 9 (September 1903), 528.

63. For a forceful early statement on the superiority of women as feldshers see I. V. Bertenson, "Vrachebno-professional'noe obrazovanie zhenshchin v Rossii," *Vestnik Evropy* 25, no. 11 (November 1890), 240–42.

64. Not all physicians either welcomed or worked in harmony with well-qualified female feldshers. For one female feldsher's account of her conflicts with the physician she served see Anna A., "Iz zapisok zemskoi fel'dsheritsy," *Vestnik Evropy* 25, no. 12 (December 1890), 549–93. Her experience was more the exception than the rule, however, because most physicians valued and respected the educated feldsher-midwife.

65. A. Lits, "Bol'nichnye fel'dshera i fel'dsheritsy," *Feldsher* 6, no. 13 (1896), 363.

66. On the more general dilemma faced by paramedical personnel in achieving professional recognition see Eliot Freidson, "Paramedical Personnel," David L. Sills (ed.), *International Encyclopedia of the Social Sciences*, 17 vols. (New York: 1968), 10, 114–20; and Amitai Etzioni (ed.), *The Semi-Professions* (New York: 1969).

WOMEN IN KIEV AND KHARKIV

Community Organizations in the Russian Empire

Martha Bohachevsky-Chomiak

Community organizations in the Russian Empire constitute an aspect of that "civil society" that Marc Raeff has made the subject of a number of his works. The study of communities beyond the capitals reveals a greater heterogeneity within the empire than one would expect to find, given the continued efforts of the tsarist government to centralize the administration and standardize its realm. Yet, works on imperial Russian society outside the Russian center have rarely focused on community organizations. Rather, because they have usually been written by members of the intelligentsia, they often overlook the organic process of local organization and concentrate on political developments. This is true, for example, of studies of women's organizations in non-Russian areas, which subordinate the story of women to that of the intelligentsia. With very few exceptions, studies of non-Russian women concentrate on their contributions to the cause that forms the subject of the book in question. Moreover, the pioneering works on women in the Russian Empire as a whole concentrate on women from the Great Russian milieu and approach the women's movement from the vantage point of philanthropic activity, feminist thought, and political activism.[1]

The work of women's organizations in the last fifty years of the Russian Empire helps to explain the functioning of civil society, for women were more likely to join community than overtly political organizations. A study of Kiev, the historical capital of Ukraine, and Kharkiv, the most dynamic city of the area, provides us with regional and ethnic dimensions that are not readily evident when studying the Russian women's movement as a whole. In this article I will focus on the establishment of the higher educational courses for women in Kiev, on the Sunday literacy schools for adults in Kharkiv, and on the attempts of activist women in Ukraine to establish closer links with feminists in Russia. Except for women who functioned in politically oriented organizations, such as the Slavic Benevolent Society or the Social Democratic party, or in philanthropic ones, women in Ukraine, compared to Russian women, showed little interest in traditional feminine causes such as the struggle against prostitution, conventional philanthropy, and public discussion of women's equality, including the right of women to education. Rather, organizations in Ukraine focused on concrete activities, self-help rather than philanthropy, although more research will have to be done before a definitive generalization can be made. Even branches of all-Russian women's organizations were significantly modified outside ethnic Russia. One can speak of the phenomenon of feminist regionalism, or, more accurately, of a pragmatic feminism whose major characteristics were an emphasis on self-help, cooperation among the socioeconomic classes and sometimes among the local nationalities, avoidance of ideology, and, in the last analysis, subordination of women's goals to those of the nation. The definition of the nation implicitly accepted by the women, however, was not always that used by the intelligentsia.[2]

Both Kiev and Kharkiv were imperial cities in the sense that their populations were predominantly Russian-speaking and the outlook of their leading classes was shaped by Moscow or St. Petersburg. But Kiev, the eldest of the cities of Rus', and Kharkiv, a bustling metropolis that emerged partly as a result of the Ukrainian move eastward when the empire incorporated the Ukrainian cossack lands in the eighteenth century and partly because of rapid industrialization in the nineteenth century, were surrounded by Ukrainian villages that provided a large part of the work force for the industries and shops of the cities. Both cities had a significant number of individuals who, although sharing the political and social sensibilities of the Russian ruling elite, nevertheless maintained an attachment to their narrower homeland, Ukraine. This patriotism manifested itself, for instance, in the work of Vasyl Karazin, the founder of the University of Kharkiv, and that of Mykhailo Maksymovych, founder of the Ukrainian school of historiography. The first Institute for Girls of the Nobility in Kharkiv was organized in 1812 at the initiative of the Ukrainian writer Hryhor Kvitka-Osnovianenko, who was a close friend of Taras Shevchenko. These representatives of imperial Ukrainian society are often viewed through a prism of Ukrainian nationalist historiography and are presented as a weak, conservative flank of the national revival movement. Less charitably, they are at other times described as epigones of that Ukrainian gentry that willingly contributed to the expansion and growth of the Russian Empire.

The history of Ukraine in the nineteenth century is usually restricted to the analysis of the views of the self-proclaimed Ukrainian intelligentsia.

This group shared much of the radicalism of the Russian intelligentsia and generally considered itself to be in the same camp as the Russians in the struggle for human rights and, by implicit extension for the Ukrainians at least, national rights. In fact, because it was fiercely democratic, the Ukrainian intelligentsia refused to maintain close ties with the upper classes. Its radicalism prevented it from recognizing the moderate gentry's interest in Ukraine. Moreover, because the Ukrainian intelligentsia often defined adherence to the national cause in terms of the use of the vernacular language, it further distanced itself from the gentry. The gentry for the most part spoke Russian and did not see language as an identifiable mystical force uniting the nation.

Nevertheless, the Ukrainian gentry and the Ukrainian intelligentsia shared common characteristics in that neither group was alienated from the peasants. They considered the peasants part of their own community. Unlike their Russian counterparts, neither the Ukrainian gentry nor the Ukrainian intelligentsia were conscience-stricken. The Ukrainian intelligentsia, coming from the land and very dependent upon it, offered a particularly strong example of an intelligentsia with ties to the historical land and the people.

The women, although not exactly part of the intelligentsia, shared its deep interest in the people and had an even greater "rootedness" in the local environment. The Ukrainian intelligentsia's outlook was fashioned by the central forces of education and ideology, and it defined itself in terms of opposition to the centralized regime rather than within the context of the local society. Women from the socially privileged segment of Ukrainian society preserved more of the flavor of local society and were less assimilated into the imperial mode than were the men. The women generally spent more time in the villages, where their families had estates. Thus they were often more familiar, at least through observation if not participation, with the folklore and language of the land. Unlike the men, women did not leave the area for the extended periods necessary for either schooling or obligatory state service. Close ties to the people, specifically to the villagers who were Ukrainian, were reinforced by the elements of romanticism that formed an integral part of the women's education. Hence, whereas the intelligentsia devoted itself to political activities, the type of work performed by the women was generally community work, to fulfill certain needs or to perform certain useful functions. We know less about the women than about the intelligentsia, for by upbringing the women were not in the habit of recording their experiences, articulating their positions, or generalizing their activities into policy statements.

Let us now turn to some specific examples of women's organizations in Ukraine. The most active women in Kiev and in Kharkiv worked in community rather than political organizations, although local government officials credited the former organizations with political significance. Thus the establishment, or rather the difficulties in the establishment, of the women's courses in Kiev was closely linked to the nationality issue not so much in the minds of the proponents of the scheme as in the assessment of the situation by *Okhrana*, the Russian secret police.

Ukraine had a tradition of community-supported schools lacking in Russia. After the incorporation of the Ukrainian lands into the Russian Empire, in the seventeenth and eighteenth centuries, many of the schools were closed, but the tradition was maintained. Whenever they could, Ukrainians tried to establish schools that would serve the needs of their communities. The struggle for schooling in the mother tongue was so pervasive that it subsumed the discussion on the education of women.

The drive for higher education for women in the empire came in the 1850s and 1860s. It was part of the demand to reform society, abolish serfdom, introduce a parliamentary system, reform the judiciary, and establish local autonomy. Ukrainian territories were especially responsive to the issue of women's education. The Kharkiv, Poltava, and Rivne educational districts went on record as favoring the creation of women's high schools that would assure women's entry into the universities.[3]

Still, special courses for women in Kiev were not organized until 1878, almost a decade after such courses had been founded in Moscow and St. Petersburg. None of the standard objections to higher education for women—such as the adverse effect higher education would have on the ability of young women to bear healthy children, or the possible increase in immorality that the presence of women in academia might engender— seems to have played a role in the opposition to establishing these courses in the capital of Ukraine. Nor did the problem seem to be one of the provinces lagging behind the center. The Kievan gentry women wanted to acquire an education as much and as early as the women in the other cities. They attended public lectures and patronized events that fostered the intellectual life of the city. The very idea of systematizing the various lectures into a coherent program at the local university originated among the liberal middle-aged women whose secure positions in society were determined by birth or marriage.

To be sure, the committee to develop such a program was composed of the luminaries of St. Vladimir University in Kiev. A faculty committee developed a plan for a two-year sequence of courses that were to be part of the regular curriculum of the university but that would be attended by female students. The first chairman of the committee, Prof. Alexander Ivanovich Selin, a literary scholar, patterned his suggestions on the program developed by V. I. Guerrier of Moscow University. His plan was

supported by the two major Kievan women's gymnasia.[4] After initial informal negotiations with the government it was formally presented in
1874, but the Ministry of Internal Affairs succeeded in blocking its implementation by pointing to the growth of the popularity of revolutionary
views among young women and by arguing that expanding educational
opportunity would strengthen the impact of revolutionary ideas. The ill-
ness and death in 1877 of Professor Selin provided a further excuse for
postponing the opening of the courses.

Permission to open the courses was finally granted by the government
in 1879, and the university senate elected Prof. Sylvestr S. Gogotsky to
chair the women's courses. His conservative reputation and his lack of
charisma allayed the fear that he might use the podium for the promotion
of liberal politics. Gogotsky, three years Selin's senior, was a Hegelian
philosopher who had also taught at the Kievan Spiritual Academy. His
scholarly output was solid but uninspired, qualities that made it acceptable to the authorities. The few articles he wrote on contemporary topics
centered on the differences between character development and education
and touched upon contemporary issues, such as the Ukrainian question,
only very gingerly. The Third Section nevertheless objected. The police
did not challenge the university administration's assessment of Gogotsky
as "an elderly man of stable political convictions." Rather, the analyst of
the Third Section, Chertkov, warned that Gogotsky was being used as
a front for an incipient nationalist opposition. Chertkov was especially
perturbed by Gogotsky's wife, Evdokia, "a woman of doubtful political
reliability [blagonadezhnost']."[5] Gogotska was suspected of holding a combination of socially progressive and Ukrainian national views.

Evdokia Gogotska has not become part of either the Soviet revolutionary or the Ukrainian national iconostasis. Politically she belonged to the
moderate wing of imperial society, and the fear her politics engendered in
the local Third Section seems to be unfounded. She did not fit the image
of the Ukrainian activist, nor did she identify herself with the "people" in
either the populist or the democratic-national sense. She also did not pass
the basic test of the Ukrainian national activists—devotion to the language
of Ukraine. Unlike most Ukrainian women activists of the time, she did
not write poetry, did not collect peasant artifacts, and did not yearn for
the simplicity of village life. She was a member of that part of Ukrainian
society that saw the empire in terms of diverse regions with local rights
and local organizations. The development of suitable means of enlightenment, the fostering of culture, the recognition of the importance of informed public opinion were the prime goals of such people. Gogotska had
been in the forefront of the efforts of Ukrainians to circumvent the ban on
publication in Ukrainian by publishing Russian language journals with

Ukrainian content rather than challenging the ban through publications abroad. In the 1870s, she acted as the legal publisher of the *Kievskii telegraf*, which collapsed under the usual dual pressure of lack of funds on the one hand and police harassment on the other. Gogotska's identification with the "Ukrainophile" tendency was used by the Third Section as proof that the courses for women at the University of St. Vladimir would serve as a front for another attempt by Ukrainians to undermine the stability and homogeneity of the empire. The local government authorities considered her dangerous precisely because she functioned within the confines of existing civil society and therefore attracted many influential individuals.

The police, like much subsequent Ukrainian historiography, identified the cause of Ukraine with that of democracy, even revolution. In this case it was more than a decade ahead of the Ukrainian intelligentsia itself, which in the 1880s and 1890s was for the most part neither revolutionary nor separatist. The logic of the police was very clear. They identified Ukrainianism with populism. The police were under the influence of the success the terrorist *Narodnaia volia* group had in Chernyhiv in drawing upon the cossack past, local autonomy, and more recent traditions in spreading their revolutionary views.

Furthermore, although mistrust of women by the all-male police was only to be expected, it was not entirely unfounded. Throughout the 1870s, women were in the forefront in the elaborate terrorist preparations to assassinate the tsar. And the fact that Sofiia Perovskaia, one of the tsar's assassins in 1881, was a descendant of the last hetman of Ukraine, and the daughter of a high government official, seemed to justify the analysis of the Third Section. The Kievan police chief complained that because he could not send his own agents to observe the meetings of the committee on women's higher courses, he found it difficult to assess the situation properly. Once the courses opened he could only hope that the inspectorate and the matrons assigned to care for the women would ensure both proper decorum and the desired political climate.[6] In fact, the Kievan courses attracted women who, in later life, were active both in the radical camp and among the Ukrainian nationalists. A number of women expelled from courses in Moscow and St. Petersburg because of their political activity were permitted to continue their studies in Kiev. They contributed to the popularization of radical ideologies and supplied police with additional ammunition.[7]

The police were also perturbed that fund-raising for the women's courses included concerts by popular Ukrainian ensembles. The popularity of the Ukrainian amateur theater groups was legendary, and even the tsars attended performances of the better known troupes, but the Kiev police successfully blocked all theatrical performances of Ukrainian groups in Kiev and even succeeded in barring concerts by Ukrainians from the Austrian Empire. Lack of theatrical performances in Kiev ensured good attendance at the choir concerts. Better known ensembles, such as the Lysenko choir, were closely monitored by the police, and when they performed to raise funds for the women's higher courses police mistrust of these courses increased.[8] The local authorities feared that Ukrainian language presentations would rouse the Ukrainian population to actions that the police would not be able to control. Indeed, the police seem to have been more diligent in rooting out Ukrainian organizations than the Ukrainians have been in chronicling them. A cooperative Kievan coffee shop, run by Elena P. Horska, was closed by the police because the women involved were allegedly active in the Ukrainian national movement. Yet neither Horska nor the venture itself is mentioned by any of the Ukrainian writers of the period.[9]

Neither the radicals nor the acknowledged activists among the Ukrainian intelligentsia attached much importance to the women's courses. Gogotska faded from view, and at any rate most women saw education not as a goal but as a preparatory step to more important activity.

The single most significant achievement of women in Kharkiv was the literacy school run by Khrystyna Danylivna Alchevska. Alchevska, like Gogotska, cannot easily be characterized. She was known as a pioneer of adult literacy schools and of the use of literary works for effective teaching of adults. She was generally presumed to have been a Russian, or at least her own national loyalty was not considered to be an issue. Yet she raised her three children as Ukrainians; one, Khrystia, become a Ukrainian poet. Alchevska began her successful venture in literacy schooling in Ukrainian, and when that language was banned she developed ways of introducing elements of Ukrainian literature and folklore into her programs. She was perhaps the first woman in the empire to make a political statement in print. In 1863 she spoke out in Herzen's *Kolokol* on behalf of the Poles, whose cause was not popular among the Russian intelligentsia and cost Herzen much of his popularity.[10]

Raised in Russia by russified parents, Alchevska discovered her heritage after her marriage to a Kharkiv merchant. She appears to have been singularly free of the tensions that plagued the imperial intelligentsia, and even her husband's suicide did not affect her equanimity.[11] Using the family fortune but relying heavily on help from like-minded women and from women factory workers, Alchevska opened a literacy school for adults in Kharkiv and taught in Ukrainian. After the ban on that language she switched to Russian. Some Ukrainian patriots, such as the writer Borys Hrinchenko, criticized her decision vehemently, but others shared her contention that schooling in Russian was better than illiteracy.

Alchevska herself wrote in the emotional style prevalent among many upper-class women. She was proud of cultivating contacts with the great writers of Russia but was equally assiduous in developing and maintaining close relations with Ukrainian writers. She developed effective ways of introducing Ukrainian culture and folk traditions into the public programs her pupils put together almost weekly. She popularized the wearing of peasant costumes in public and used poetry recitation and choral singing as means of demonstrating Ukrainian patriotism. In this manner she lessened the strangeness of city life for workers who had barely left the village. Making use of the fact that the school was on private property, she put up the first statue to the Ukrainian poet Taras Shevchenko. She also wanted to name the school in that poet's honor, and it was only the sensible argument of her daughter that prevented her from taking this rash step.[12] But the same daughter fought to prevent the removal of Ukrainian books from community libraries.[13]

Alchevska's school, which functioned from the 1860s to the outbreak of World War I, was the most successful and the longest-lasting of the adult literacy schools in the empire. Alchevska was a natural spokesperson on the subject of illiteracy nationally and internationally, most prominently at the Paris International Exhibit in 1889.[14] After the initial statement in Herzen's *Kolokol* supporting the claims of the Poles to both freedom and independence from Russia, she does not seem to have expressed her views on politics or nationalism in print. The fact that she raised her children to be Ukrainians, however, in itself constituted a political statement.

The women in Kharkiv did not show much interest in the nationality issue as such. They sought to meet the needs created by the rapid industrialization of the city through self-help and educational ventures. Some of these, such as the Association of Mutual Aid for Working Women, were composed of Ukrainian, Russian, and Jewish women whose interests in administering summer camps for children of the workers and setting up emergency care transcended national differences. This society was instrumental in opening the first coeducational secondary school in the city.[15]

Women's organizations in Kiev were also characterized by a practical and popular bent and by cooperation among its many ethnic groups, despite the national tensions that characterized much of the city's life. For instance, the Kievan branch of the Russian Society for the Protection of Women was part of the imperial umbrella organization for combatting prostitution. In St. Petersburg and Moscow it had a titled patrician membership that financed its work by charitable donations. The Kievan branch was composed of women of the intelligentsia dedicated to self-help efforts among the poor. Its membership was Russian, Jewish, and Ukrainian, and it was especially active in recruiting Jewish women, although its successes were limited to upper-class Jewish women and included few

Jewish women workers. Its leadership reflected the national mix of its members: for years it was headed by Dr. V. G. Kliachkina, a Russian woman whose daughter became a Ukrainian activist. Rosalia I. Margolina and Sofiia A. Sats, Jewish middle-class women, were repeatedly on the board, along with descendants of the Ukrainian cossacks. Initially, the organization had its headquarters in the fashionable part of town, but it moved to the working-class district to be closer to its base of operations. The women were primarily engaged in administering the sewing school for working and peasant women who moved into town looking for work. Along with the school, the women ran literacy courses, a cafeteria, a dormitory, an employment office, and a legal aid clinic. They held weekly meetings and organized entertainment programs into which they incorporated some Ukrainian folk culture in much the same fashion as Alchevska did in Kharkiv. The two hundred women who constituted the core membership of the organization were so successful that the police at times would not let them hold fund-raising lotteries because the finances of the organization were in such good shape.[16]

Organizations with a distinctly Ukrainian character, on the other hand, generally did not develop a separate women's branch or develop as women's associations. Rather, in keeping with the democratic and often socialist orientation of these groups, their female members saw little need for a separate women's agenda. A Ukrainian Women's Community (*Zhinocha hromada*) was nevertheless established by an informal gathering of some Kievan Ukrainian women and after 1905 served as a model for about twenty similar organizations in other cities. These organizations, although directed toward work with the peasants, were connected with the Revolutionary Ukrainian party and sought to organize Ukrainians. They encouraged peasant girls to attend secondary schools, discussed political subjects with them, and taught them how to disseminate political literature. They also set up libraries in the villages, taught adults to read, and worked for the establishment of child care centers. Their work was instrumental in preparing peasants to join Ukrainian cooperatives and the *Prosvita* (Enlightenment) societies when these were set up after the revolution of 1905.

The police suspected that the public associations for the spread of education would act as a front for national opposition activity and became particularly suspicious of the Ukrainian Enlightenment societies. The women who worked in the Kievan *Prosvita* were those who were active in the political rather than the community organizations. Because most of the Ukrainian women activists had a police record, they sometimes endangered the societies they joined. Lesia Ukrainka, the poet, could not get permission from the Ministry of Internal Affairs to open the Kiev

Prosvita Library.[17] Gender had little bearing on the decision. The police noted that the Society for the Propagation of Intermediate Education in Kiev had a Ukrainian on its board and maintained that it ought to be kept under particularly close watch. On the whole, the proclivity of Ukrainians to join societies for the spread of education made these societies suspect.[18]

During the revolution of 1905 there was also an attempt to make feminism a cause around which the various nationalities could rally. This aspect of the Russian feminist movement has been overlooked, first, because the whole movement was weak, and second, because it was identified politically with Russian liberals who did not openly espouse either national autonomy or women's equality. On occasion, of course, the liberals argued that the inclusion of women's and national equality was implied in the liberal program for basic political rights. Yet they also warned that both issues—sex equality and national rights—were divisive and weakened the struggle against absolutism.

Russian liberal women who founded the Union for Equality of Women (*Soiuz ravnoupravleniia zhenshchin*) in 1905 were not used to political work but quickly showed a keen understanding of the principles of democracy. The central board recognized the demands of its branches, and the union went on record in support of the principle of national autonomy. In Kiev the branch of the union made little headway. It showed no interest in specifically feminist concerns, its public meetings were run by males, and it reflected the liberal political program. In Kharkiv, on the other hand, the union concentrated on feminist concerns. It stressed the importance of joining the International Council of Women, it organized advanced academic courses for women, and it cooperated with the Society for Mutual Aid for Working Women.[19]

On the whole the women who joined this organization were politically moderate. Aleksandra Efimenko, the Russian historian of Ukraine who in 1910 became the first woman to receive a doctorate in Russia (an honorary one, from Kharkiv University), worked on ways in which existing legislation could be used to ensure the rights of women. The Kharkiv women also prepared leaflets explaining the need for equality for peasant women and agitated for equal land allotments for men and women.[20]

But the women who joined the union also demanded national rights. The issue emerged at the very first congress of the union, held from 6 to 9 May 1905. Three hundred women, sharing the excitement of the revolutionary changes, assembled to develop a political program. From the very start the Russian feminists were taken aback by the demand for national autonomy put forth by the Ukrainian, Jewish, Polish, Belorussian, and Lithuanian women who represented local branches of the union that threatened to withdraw unless the union acknowledged the principle of national and organizational autonomy and the right to cultural and national self-determination of all nationalities in the empire. The debates on the issue were heated and protracted. The arguments against the inclusion of the national rights plank that some women proposed were similar to the ones used against the inclusion of the women's rights plank in the political parties—it was considered divisive and untimely. But, because the liberals had not yet held their congress and had not formulated their official policies, the women reached their own conclusions. After the initial debates at the May congress, the delegates agreed that "for the oppressed nationalities the issue of national freedom was the most pressing one." Hence, the congress, with only four abstentions and no opposition, "acknowledged the right of the different nationalities which are part of Russia to political autonomy and national self-determination."[21] The connection was not obvious to all women, and the third congress of the union, held in October 1905, after resolutions from Lithuanian, Polish, and Ukrainian women and additional debate, ratified another statement to the effect that "the liberation of women is inseparably tied to the achievement of autonomy for their native land and its liberation from the yoke of russification." The last phrase was quite significant.[22]

Shared feminist goals, however, were not enough to break down national animosities. Russian feminists, smarting under the snubs they received from their male colleagues who would not commit themselves to suffrage, used their responsiveness to the nationality issue as proof of their political sophistication. "This question barely emerged in Russian society, and our association was one of the first to solve it," boasted the president.[23] But the members did not solve the issue peacefully. The amicable experiences of the Kiev and Kharkiv women on the community level were not reflected in the political arena, where ideological and national antagonisms prevailed.

In sheer numbers, the women's organizations compared favorably with those of the intelligentsia; in impact, the women were less influential than the major ideological groups, but in the amount of work performed, they were not inconsequential. Most important, however, the women's organizations illustrated the attempt to strengthen the civil society whose existence Marc Raeff has so ably characterized.

NOTES

1. There still is no satisfactory historical overview of Ukraine in any language. Of the available ones, Natalia Polons'ka-Vasylenko's two-volume *Istoriia Ukraiiny* (Munich: 1972–76) stresses the contributions of women to a greater degree than other histories. There are no satisfactory works on Ukrainian women. The few Soviet studies deal only with the contributions Ukrainian

women made to the building of socialism and the defense of the motherland. Non-Soviet Ukrainian works stress the achievements of a few exceptional women, usually in the promotion of the national cause. The best of these are Polons'ka-Vasylenko's *Vydatni zhinky Ukraiiny* (Winnipeg: 1969), and Sofiia Rusova's *Nashi vyznachni zhinky* (Kolomyia: 1934, reprinted in Winnipeg: 1945). The best introductions to the study of women in the Russian Empire are Richard Stites, *The Women's Liberation Movement in Russia: Feminism, Nihilism, and Bolshevism, 1860–1930* (Princeton: 1978); Linda H. Edmonson, *Feminism in Russia, 1900–1917* (Stanford: 1984); and Barbara Alpern Engel, *Mothers and Daughters: Women of the Intelligentsia in Nineteenth Century Russia* (New York: 1983). The general works on women's history to which I am greatly indebted are too numerous to mention here.

2. Historically, women have not been accustomed to seeing themselves as part of a community, nor have they been socialized into articulating a theoretical construct for defining their work. Many women active in women's organizations have shied away from the label *feminist*. Many also did not share the socialist conceptualization of the woman question. In my *Feminists Despite Themselves: Women in Ukrainian Community Life* (Edmonton, Alta.: 1988), I argue for the existence of a "pragmatic" feminism that differs from the liberal and socialist models. The unarticulated rationale for the community involvement of women is not the pursuit of equality but the contribution women make toward addressing issues of community concern. Both politics and tradition shaped the type of organizations developed by women. In Ukraine, in addition to the vestiges of frontier attitudes toward women that promoted their acceptance in nontraditional roles because every helping hand was needed, there was also the example of the Polish community, which, being a minority population in the Ukrainian territories, banded together into whatever societies they could establish. For instance, see the listing of various community and self-help organizations in the directory to the Kiev, Podillia, and Volyn regions, *Ves' Iugo-Zapadny Kray: Spravochnaia i Adresnaia Kniga*, published by the South-Western Section of the Russian Export Bureau (Kiev: 1913) under the overall supervision of M. V. Dovnar-Zapolski. The editor of this volume was A. I. Iaroshevich. On the Benevolent Ladies Society in Kiev see Nikolai Kolmakov, *Ocherk deiatel'nosti Kievskogo slavianskogo blagotvoritel'nogo obshchestva* (Kiev: 1894).

3. For instance, during the 1750s over three hundred schools were established in the Chernyhiv province alone as a result of local pressure. See M. K. Chaly, *Vospominaniia* (Kiev: 1890–95), 1, 85. It was local initiative that created the University of Kharkiv in 1805 and contributed to the establishment of the St. Vladimir University in Kiev in 1835. An overview is presented in Tatiana Kyshakevych, *University Education in Ukraine*, Ph.D. dissertation, University of Pittsburgh, 1976. Elementary schools are discussed in V. Y. Borysenko, *Borot'ba demokratychnykh syl za narodnu osvitu na Ukraiini v 60tykh–90tykh rokakh XIX stolittia* (Kiev: 1890). On the policies of the educational districts in Ukraine see Mikhail O. Kosinsky and V. V. Wessel (eds.), *O zhenskikh uchilishchakh: Svod zamechanii na VII glavu proekta ustava obshcheobra-*

zovatel'nykh uchebnykh zavedenii ministerstva narodnogo prosveshcheniia (St. Petersburg: 1864). General histories on higher education for women in the Russian Empire are E. O. Likhacheva, *Materialy dlia istorii zhenskogo obrazovaniia v Rossii*, 2 vols. (St. Petersburg: 1890–1901) and Sophie Satina, *Obrazovanie zhenshchin v dorevoliutsionnoi Rossii* (New York: 1966). Materials relating to the women's courses in Kiev are located in the Central State Archives of the Ukrainian Soviet Socialist Republic in Kiev (Tsentralny Derzhavny Istorychny Arkhiv, henceforth *TsDIA*). An overview of the courses is presented in a booklet published in a limited edition in Kiev in 1883, *Istoricheskaia zapiska i otchet o kievskikh vysshykh zhenskikh kursakh za pervoe chetyrekhletie, 1878–1882*, TsDIA, Kiev, f.707, op. 151, spr. 30.

4. Letter of M. N. Chertkov to A. E. Timashev, 25 September 1878, in TsDIA, Kiev, f. 442, op. 828, d. zb. 146, 16. The major women's gymnasia in Kiev at the time were the Fundukleevskaia and Leninskogo.

5. Ibid.

6. Report of the Kiev police chief, dated 26 December 1878, in ibid.

7. Reports in ibid., op. 835, od. zb. 121, 3, and op. 836, od. zb. 53, 3–10.

8. Requests for permission to hold the concerts, submitted between 2 January 1887 and 6 November 1887, in TsDIA, f. 442, op. 837, od. zb. 6, esp. 12.

9. Ibid., f. 274, op. 4, od. zb. 301, 493.

10. For a fuller discussion see M. I. Mukhin, *Pedahohichni pohliady i osvitnia diial'nist' Kh. D. Alchevs'koii* (Kiev: 1979). For an introduction to Alchevska see her *Peredumannoe i perezhitoe: Dnevniki, pis'ma, vospominaniia* (Moscow: 1912).

11. Alchevsky jumped to his death when his request for a loan that would have tided over his temporarily beleaguered tea trading business was denied. The financial setback proved to be temporary, and the family continued to be well off.

12. Letter dated 6 February 1908, in TsDIA, Kiev, f. 2052, op. 1, spr. 96.

13. Letter of the younger Khrystia Alchevska to Professor Sumtsov, 1910, in TsDIA, Kiev, f. 2052, op. 1, spr. 103.

14. *Exposition Universelle Internationale de 1889: Actes du Congrès International des Oeuvres et Institutions Féminines* (Paris: 1890), 301–7.

15. "Obshchestvo Vzaimnogo vspomozheniia trudiashchikhsia zhenshchin," in Tsentralnyi Gosudarstvennyi Istoricheskii Arkhiv (henceforth TsGIA), Moscow, f. 516, ed. khr. 5, 33. See also the journal *Soiuz zhenshchin* 3 (October 1907), 14. The poet Lesia Ukrainka, in a letter written 19 December 1905, commented on the extremely active life of Kharkiv when compared to the events in Kiev. Olha Kosach-Kryvyniuk, *Lesia Ukraiinka: Khronolohiia Zhyttia i Tvorchosty* (New York: 1970), 766.

16. The reports of the organization were published annually; many of them, as well as some pertinent police materials, are in TsDIA, Kiev, f. 442, op. 643, spr. 48.

17. The petition is on permanent display at the Museum of Lesia Ukrainka in Kiev.

18. TsGIA, Moscow, f. 102, D. O. op. 236/II, ed. khr. 194, no. 2, 1906, esp. 15–18.

19. Ibid., ed. khr. 99–47, 1905; also f. 516, ed. khr. 12, 11–17. Among the women active in Kharkiv was a Liudmila Orestovna Gabel, whose father had emigrated from Austria. See also *Soiuz zhenshchin* 3 (October 1907), 14.
20. TsGIA, Moscow, f. 102, O. O. 59–88 B 1911, 140, and O. O. 242 H 88 B 1912, 161–62.
21. Ibid., f. 516, ed. khr. 28, 28.
22. Ibid., ed. khr. 5, 37.
23. Ibid., 71. Mariia Chekhova was the president. Another member, Madame Shakhmatova, complained that the Constitutional Democrats gave the vote to "all the Samoed, Chukchi, Tungus, and Yakut, but denied it to women," ibid.

PART

Opposition To The Imperial Order

THE SUNGUROV AFFAIR, 1831

A Curious Conspiracy

John Keep

Historians have commonly looked on the first years of Nicholas I's reign as a time when censors and gendarmes rendered dissent all but impossible. The failure of the Decembrists and the severe repressive measures that followed brought about a reaction in Russian public opinion, and when Polish patriots in the Congress Kingdom rose in revolt in November 1830, there was a further swing toward the government. It was not until P. Ia. Chaadaev published his first "Philosophical Letter" in 1836—the famous "shot in the dark of the night," as Herzen called it—that the opposition movement in educated "society" began to recover.

This conventional view needs refinement. Discontent continued to simmer under the surface, notably in the universities. Student agitation over academic issues could easily become politicized, especially under the impact of news from the West. Nicholas exaggerated the extent of the dangers that this dissidence posed to his absolutist regime, but he did have some grounds for concern.[1] It is in this context that one should place the curious and little-known "Sungurov affair" of 1831, in which the principal actors were a small group of students at Moscow University and several Polish officers of the Lithuanian Corps who had been dispatched to the empire's second capital as a precautionary security move. Peter Squire dismisses the conspiracy—if such it can be called—as an "isolated instance of no political importance,"[2] and it is certainly true that its impact on contemporaries was minimal. Nevertheless, it did serve as a precedent: later clandestine "circles" (*kruzhki*) of Russian radicals would often emulate, albeit unwittingly, the attitudes and practices of this group.[3] Equally frequently, the authorities would respond to what they viewed as "subversion" in much the same clumsy and counterproductive fashion as Nicholas and his gendarmes. Perhaps the chief significance of the affair lies in the light it sheds on the nefarious role played by informing (delation) on both opponents and upholders of the tsarist regime.

It is still not possible to pass a definitive verdict on the "Sungurov affair," a designation that is in itself somewhat misleading, as we shall see. The main sources are the investigation and court-martial records[4] and the memoirs written in 1872 by the man who was really the principal activist, Jacob I. Kostenets'ky (1811–85).[5] The case has been studied by the prerevolutionary writer V. Eikhenbaum[6] and, more recently, by the Soviet historian L. I. Nasonkina.[7] The latter's interpretation is perceptive and generally convincing, but like most of her colleagues in this field she has little to say about the juridical aspects or the varied national backgrounds of the defendants.

In 1830–31 Moscow University students, especially those without private means (*kazennokoshtnye*), had ample reason for dissatisfaction. It was hard to make ends meet, clubs and associations were prohibited, the administration exercised a heavy-handed but inefficient surveillance, and teaching standards were often poor, especially since some faculty members were appointed for their political reliability rather than their professional competence. During the fall term the university had to close down for two months because of the cholera epidemic; when classes were resumed in January the authorities announced that students would receive no credit for their attendance during the current year. Few relished another twelve months of study before they could take their final examinations. This grievance became linked with complaints about the indifferent quality of canteen food.

As elsewhere, there was a tradition of "ragging" unpopular professors. Ia. A. Malov, who taught courses in the "ethical-political section" (which did duty for a law faculty), aroused irritation by his abrupt, haughty manner. On 16 March a number of his students organized a "demonstration," stamping their feet and rattling desks in unison to cries of "Out! Out!", whereupon the wretched pedagogue fled into the street, to the accompaniment of jeers, curses, and a hail of pebbles.[8] For reasons of their own the authorities did their best to hush up the incident. Malov was soon persuaded to resign, and the successful protest convinced its organizers that collective action was both feasible and effective.

Among the young agitators were Alexander Herzen and his acolyte Nicholas Ogarev. But the main activists were a group of students of Ukrainian origin. While still at school in Novgorod-Seversk, Kostenets'ky had made friends with Platon A. Antonovych. The former entered Moscow University in 1828 and the latter (after a year at Khar'kov) in 1830. Another schoolmate, Ivan N. Pollonin, who was two years older and of nonnoble status, did not take part in the Malov "scandal." Initially these students, as provincials, felt out of place among the Moscow sophisticates and so naturally sought each other's company. Kostenets'ky and Antono-

vych were both intelligent, sociable young men. They made the acquaintance of A. N. Topornin, a nineteen-year-old Russian in his third year,
and two students of German background, who were legally Prussian citizens: Julius P. Kohlreif, eighteen years old, son of a Protestant pastor in
Moscow, and A. F. Knobloch, twenty-one, whose father worked as an
architect in a German settlement near Tsaritsyn. They were an unusually
studious pair, and full of youthful romantic idealism. Once a month, they
decided, they would meet to check on the way each of them had spent his
time and to discuss an essay to be written on some important topic—a
scheme frustrated by the outbreak of the cholera epidemic.[9] They were
members of a regional association (*Landsmannschaft*) that comprised some
twenty German-speaking students who had transferred to Moscow from
Dorpat (now Tartu);[10] apparently they did not identify completely with
their comrades from the Baltic provinces and hence mixed more readily
with the Ukrainians—Kostenets'ky spoke German, and they addressed
one another by the familiar *Du*. Kohlreif's close friend, I. A. Tessin, nineteen, son of an official, was evidently another "Russian German" in the
same situation.

By the spring of 1831, Kostenets'ky began to think of setting up an
"association of friends" [*obshchestvo druzei*]. He conceived it primarily as a
device to raise its members' moral tone and clearly had the German students' *Landsmannschaft* in mind. As he explained later in evidence, he had
told his companions:

> we [students] have no morality, no [sense of] honor; we think nothing of
> offending others, whether they be our equals or inferiors. We can't keep our
> word; we boast of being in indecent places; we borrow money and don't
> return it; and so we're continually humiliated by the police. . . . Our failure
> to study and our jocular replies to [questions from] our professors lead them
> to despise us.[11]

The authorities, with their "loud measures," could bring about no improvement, whereas the association would impose its own standards of
conduct, formally breaking off relations with comrades who misbehaved
and in serious cases reporting (*donosit'*) them.[12] It was also to have charitable and artistic purposes, such as giving poorer students financial help
and practicing the violin, for Kostenets'ky, Antonovych, and Kohlreif
were all keen amateur musicians.

So was Pawel A. Kaszewski, eighteen, a student in the Medical Surgi-
cal Academy. Of Polish origin, his family had moved from Podolia to
Moscow and had accepted conversion to Orthodoxy.[13] Kostenets'ky later
described him as "a strikingly intelligent young man, with a firm, decisive

character, and imbued with the most patriotic aspirations."[14] He first planned to set up an association of his own, but on meeting the Ukrainian (through Kohlreif) gave up the idea as superfluous. Kaszewski introduced Kostenets'ky to some fellow students at the academy, including Oscar Barrieu, twenty, an orphaned Frenchman who came from Riga. In this way the group began to extend its links outside the immediate university milieu. It was, as Nasonkina puts it,[15] less a *kruzhok* than "an embryonic band of companions."

How politicized was it? All the young friends were sympathetic to Polish aspirations, but (except perhaps in Kaszewski's case) this sentiment owed more to a vague romantic identification with the oppressed than to any clearly articulated nationalist credo. Kostenets'ky referred to himself as a "Little Russian," but it would be anachronistic to label him an autonomist: he had grown up among the russified gentry of the left-bank Ukraine, and he was cautious in discussing this question.[16] In evidence he stated, apparently in good faith, that Russia had a right to rule the disputed western provinces and that, given the current international situation, Polish independence was impracticable.[17]

Similarly, members of the group had no coherent republican or democratic weltanschauung. It was easier for them to identify the evils in the present order of things—"despotism," by which they meant arbitrary and corrupt government, censorship, and so on—than to formulate an alternative, still less to agree on the methods whereby change might be effected. Kostenets'ky seems to have recognized that they needed to learn more about the workings of constitutional rule abroad before seeking its introduction into Russia:

> we all like to pronounce on important matters, on the country's interests and the policies of other states, without knowing them. . . . We often see irresponsible people who are excited by the words "liberty" and "independence" but don't understand what civic freedoms and independence amount to, but take them to mean anarchy, a chance to create all kinds of disorder. . . .[18]

He naturally stressed the moderation of his views in evidence. Nevertheless, he was a liberal reformist in later life, and the gradualism of his outlook at the time is corroborated by Kaszewski, who told the inquiry (rather confusedly) that "the aim of the society which Kostenets'ky set up was to introduce a constitution into Russia, precisely by enlightened activity upon the people, and so on."[19]

Kaszewski himself wrote some notes on international affairs that were confiscated and, as summarized by the investigators, suggest Bonapartist sympathies. Recent events in France, he stated, threatened other countries, including Russia, with revolution, and if this movement were directed by a genius it might unite Europe under French leadership. The Russian national character "could be molded like wax into the form desired."[20] However, his notes in the Central State Military-Historical Archive file convey a more nuanced impression. Kaszewski wanted international relations to be based on the principles of equality between states and popular sovereignty; yet he was willing to allow Russia sufficient "primacy" over her neighbors to safeguard her security needs.[21] In testimony he claimed that his initial sympathy for the Polish national cause had waned and that he now felt himself to be a loyal Russian[22]—but this characterization does not ring true.

A similar statement was made by Knobloch, who labeled Kaszewski a "Voltairean" and added that he himself preferred the philosophy of Spinoza; as for politics, he averred that "revolution would be a thousand times more harmful" than monarchy, as ancient and modern history made plain.[23] Knobloch was probably less liberal than his friend Kohlreif, who expressed republican sympathies in a student essay on ancient Rome and who in his diary welcomed the overthrow of Western European monarchs: "France is threatened by the [popular] desire for a republic, Belgium is exposed to stormy unrest, and in Germany one hears on every hand cries for freedom . . . . For two days I have clearly felt how many disadvantages Russia brings me"—a remark he had some trouble explaining. Eventually Kohlreif came up with the theory that, although the laws of reason demonstrated the superiority of republicanism, on practical grounds monarchy was not only superior but essential, because "spirit" had to be supplemented by "matter."[24] The investigators were not impressed by his lucubrations.

In general these young men may be characterized as reformists for whom constitutional government was at best a distant goal.[25] Socioeconomic concerns do not seem to have been featured prominently in their thinking, although their ideas might well have evolved, had not their fate taken an adverse turn.

For in April 1831, Pollonin introduced Kostenets'ky, his former schoolmate, to Fedor P. Gurov, who attended lectures as an external student (*vol'noslushatel'*). Gurov had already passed through the university in 1823–26 (without taking his degree) and had gone on to the *iunker* school in Mogilev, but had been discharged from military service because of poor health. Aged twenty-five, he was significantly older and more experienced in the ways of the world than any of Kostenets'ky's other associates. Gurov lodged with his cousin and near-namesake, Nicholas P. Sungurov, twenty-six, in the latter's own house. Sungurov's father had left him a small fortune; married to one of the family's serfs, he had two children, servants, and a carriage.[26] The pair's life-style was quite different from that of ordinary students, who depended on casual tutoring to support themselves. The Ukrainians soon accepted invitations to visit the house. Gurov was fond of jokes and scandalous stories; he struck the students as somewhat flippant and irresponsible. Sungurov seemed to have a dark side to his character. He was more reserved and self-important. Kostenets'ky noticed his eyes, which "darted hither and thither." It was not long before the merry conversation turned to politics. Both hosts spoke frankly about corruption in high places, the poverty of the people, and other evils.[27] Gurov was vehemently critical of the government's use of informers (whom he called, anachronistically, *fiskaly*), uttered "disrespectful remarks" about members of the imperial family, and read out some anticlerical verses he had written.[28]

Sungurov told his young visitors, in suitably conspiratorial fashion, that he belonged to an important clandestine society with constitutional goals, an outgrowth of the organizations set up by the Decembrists. He invited the students to adhere to it. The offer appealed to their romantic natures, but they were also disconcerted by Sungurov's refusal to reveal any details of the society's purposes or methods of operation until they had joined. As Kostenets'ky stated later, "I believed yet disbelieved him."[29] The Ukrainians turned for advice to Kaszewski, Topornin, and the two Germans. Why, they wondered, should Sungurov seek the aid of political neophytes if, as he claimed, he had very influential associates? Could he be lying and seeking to entrap them? Topornin was the most skeptical. He said he did not believe that any such society existed—as was indeed the case. The others decided that, to test Sungurov's sincerity, he and Gurov should be invited to a meeting and asked for further information.

Although Sungurov at first demurred, at the end of May the meeting duly took place in Knobloch's room, which was chosen purely for reasons of convenience.[30] Sungurov identified General A. P. Ermolov (until recently commander of Russian forces in the Caucasus, and known for his independent stance) as head of the supposed organization, but refused to say how or when it would act. He explained that the student members' role would be to spread constitutional ideas among their peers, to which Kostenets'ky replied that, given the students' current mood, such a task would be superfluous. Neither Sungurov's statements nor his conduct at the meeting reassured the younger men. Kaszewski thought he might be trying to manipulate them in pursuit of some personal ambition; Kohlreif found him antipathetic. Nasonkina writes that they decided to keep Sungurov at arm's length; Kostenets'ky alone was to maintain the contact, in a manner that would not arouse his suspicions.[31] This is putting it a little too definitely, for in the event Antonovych, who had not been present at this meeting, also went to see Sungurov on several occasions. Apparently the Ukrainians were more willing than the others to run risks.

Among those present at these encounters were a Russian ex-colonel, Dmitrii Kozlov—whom Sungurov once identified as his "contact" with the higher echelons of his supposed society—and several Polish officers in the group posted to Moscow. Kozlov had gotten to know Gurov ten years earlier.[32] It was Gurov, too, who initially established contact with the Poles, for he had met one of them, Sublieutenant Frants Siedlecki of the Troitskii infantry regiment, while in the army.[33] Through him the pair became acquainted with four of his comrades (Sublieutenants M. Moraczewski, S. Kiersnowski; the latter's brother, Cornet T. Kiersnowski; and Cornet Ciepliński). The officers were already in contact with two fellow-nationals in the university: Onufry Pietraszkiewicz, a library employee, and Kaspar Szianiawski, a medical student.

On 3 or 4 June Siedlecki and Moraczewski were present at a gathering at Tiufeleva's Grove, in the Moscow suburbs, where Sungurov apparently had rented a *dacha*. Later another meeting was arranged in the city center, at the Restaurant François—an enterprise of which Sungurov was part owner, evidently a convenient locale for such clandestine encounters.[34] According to Pollonin, Sungurov took a cautious attitude toward the Poles, regarding Moraczewski in particular as a dangerous hothead who "want[s] to act as soon as possible" whereas "we are not yet ready to begin."[35] The substance of their discussions was revealed to the investigators by Gurov, whose resistance eventually broke down under the strain. The officers said that the Polish insurgents urgently needed help from their sympathizers in Russia and suggested that it would not be very difficult to stage a coup in Moscow, because there were a number of Polish prisoners in the city who were marched about the streets on Fridays. Moreover, some Polish artillerymen were stationed at nearby Khoroshevo. Unless action were taken at once, they argued, the Polish officers might well be sent on to the Caucasus and a valuable opportunity lost. To this Szianiawski added that the atmosphere in Moscow University was regrettably unlike that in Warsaw, "where the students fought like lions."[36]

These notions appear to have had some impact, at least outwardly, on their interlocutors. At another meeting, on 13 June, this time held in Pollonin's quarters, Sungurov discussed with Antonovych and others a scheme very much in line with the Poles' ideas: having won control of Moscow by a coup, carried out with the aid of Polish troops, they should force the military governor-general to proclaim a constitution; distribute arms to the people and win their goodwill by promises of a share of confiscated state funds; coerce recalcitrants into submission; spread a false rumor that Grand Duke Constantine was leading an army from Poland to free the peasants; and then march on Tula to seize the arms works there.[37] Sungurov also said that it might be possible to raise a revolt in Siberia and that, if things went wrong, the conspirators could flee to Archangel, where the governor, V. S. Filimonov, would help them to make good their escape by sea.[38] There was an obvious element of lighthearted fantasy about such ideas, and it is improbable, as we shall see, that Sungurov entertained them seriously.

In any event the Polish officers distrusted his intentions. They had come to realize that little or no aid could be expected from their Moscow contacts and were turning to an alternative plan: to escape from the city and join the insurgents in Lithuania. To this end they accumulated money and weapons and made inquiries about a possible sanctuary en route. Through Pietraszkiewicz they obtained from an army noncommissioned officer and auditor, Kirshaev, forged travel documents, which were needed to pass through the quarantine cordon around the city. Sungurov learned, through Gurov and Siedlecki, of these preparations. He asked Gurov to try to persuade the Poles to remain, but actually their project fitted in with a new scheme he had devised: to denounce the Poles to the authorities, as a way of affirming his credit in their eyes.

We do not know exactly when he decided to take this drastic step. Possibly, his echoing of the officers' insurrectionary plans had been just a feint. Alternatively, he may have envisaged this as a possible course and kept both options open until deciding which one to select.

Cunning as his scheme was, Sungurov was outsmarted by an associate with even fewer scruples, Pollonin. The dénouement was melodramatic, as one denunciation followed another with breathtaking speed. On or about 12 June, when the *kazennokoshtnye* students were dining, a quarrel broke out over the Polish insurrection. The fiery Szianiawski struck one of the Russians present (presumably a student named Shubinskii); the latter reported the incident to the rector.[39] Sungurov, evidently fearing that his own activities would now come to light, approached Lieutenant-Colonel Mukhanov, an officer in the (civil) police with whom he had previously been in social contact (the students had seen him at his house), and told him of the Polish officers' escape plan. The city commandant, Major-General K. G. Staal, immediately had the officers arrested (16 June), bringing to light their cache of weapons and false documents. Sublieutenant Siedlecki was taken at Sungurov's house, where Pollonin happened to be present. On 17 June the Ukrainian, thoroughly alarmed, went to the local gendarme commander, Count Apraksin,[40] and denounced Sungurov and everyone whom he knew to have had any connection with him (including one or two individuals who were subsequently found to be quite innocent). All those named who were in Moscow were taken into custody, as was Pollonin himself. On 18 June he further alleged that members of Sungurov's society, with its manifold links in high places, had plotted to assassinate the tsar. Suddenly D. V. Golitsyn, the governor-general, was faced with what appeared to be a major conspiracy threatening the security of the state. He set up a five-man investigating commission under his own chairmanship, which started work on 21 June. St. Petersburg was duly informed. Nicholas would take a close interest in the case throughout and personally determine its outcome. However, neither he nor his aides appreciated its relative insignificance.

The commission met in secret session almost daily for about two months. Hearings commenced at 6 P.M. and continued until late at night—an additional tribulation for the prisoners, who were detained separately in various barracks scattered around the city and taken to the governor-general's residence under police escort for interrogation. They were not physically maltreated; Kostenets'ky later commented favorably on the food he was given and also commended Golitsyn and Staal for gestures of kindliness toward the accused. The latter, although not told of the charges against them (so that the term "accused" is inexact), sometimes managed to find out through informal channels what was going on.[41] The questioning was persistent, if not thorough or efficient. The investigators were mainly interested in finding evidence that would bolster their own preconceptions about the case, which were based largely on the delator Pollonin's testimony. They took this more seriously than it warranted and interpreted loose talk as sinister plotting. Much time was wasted in following up obvious red herrings (such as the implication of Filimonov, governor of Archangel, who was summoned to Moscow and interrogated). Yet important details—for instance, the dates and particulars of the various clandestine encounters—were not established precisely.

Initially, individual written and oral statements were taken, and then some of the accused were confronted with one another until their resistance was worn down and partial or full confessions obtained. Gurov's spirit was broken in the last week of July. Sungurov gave no substantial testimony until the following month and even then protested his innocence. By and large the defendants stood up manfully to the psychological pressure. None of them admitted to the bogus accusation of having plotted regicide. Kostenets'ky wrote later that he had made it a rule to admit only those actions or statements that he knew the investigators had already discovered from other testimony, and the record bears out his claim.[42] Not until 30 July, after Gurov had confessed, did Kostenets'ky reveal (and then only partially) the substance of his conversations with Sungurov.[43] Antonovych did not resist quite so firmly but took time and care in writing his responses.[44] The authorities learned a good deal from Knobloch, who (like Kostenets'ky and Topornin) had gone to the country after term ended. He was not arrested until 14 July and, when interrogated two weeks later, spoke quite frankly.[45] He had every reason to do so, because he had met Sungurov only once, and Kostenets'ky infrequently; neither he nor Kohlreif considered himself guilty of illegal activity. Yet by his sincere testimony Knobloch added to the burden of evidence against Kaszewski. By stating incautiously that Gurov "had threatened me with a horrible death" should he betray their secret, Knobloch reinforced the investigators' conviction that they were dealing with a group of dangerous terrorists, for similar evidence had previously been given against Sungurov by Pollonin. Moreover, Gurov himself admitted that the pair had discussed the use of poison against traitors.[46]

Sungurov's defense was ingenious. He claimed, in essence, that he had acted as a would-be informal *agent provocateur*. All his actions could be explained by the interpretation that he had sought to gather as much information as possible on disloyal elements in order to denounce them at the appropriate moment, just as he had informed on the Polish officers. His "secret society" was but a figment of his imagination. Cleverly he turned the interrogators' questions. Asked where "the" society had met, he replied that he had unfortunately been unable to discover this, since his research had been prematurely cut short by his arrest. Why had he told Kostenets'ky that he belonged to a secret organization with highly placed contacts? "In order to spread a rumor which I wanted to exploit in order to unearth some kind of secret evil-intentioned society."[47]

This argument was not easy for the investigators to deal with, the more so because it was partly true. His "society" had indeed consisted solely of him and Gurov, since the only genuine clandestine groups were Kostenets'ky's and the Polish officers'. Sungurov offered a plausible and circumstantial account of the way he and Gurov had gone about their self-appointed task of counter-espionage: first they had approached Pollonin, then Antonovych, followed by a certain staff-captain Petrov, but these probes had led nowhere. With Kostenets'ky they had had better luck, since he had introduced them to his young friends. Finally, Gurov had opened the trail that led to the Polish officers.[48] Time and again Sungurov patiently elaborated on the details of his story.

It had two major weaknesses. One was that Pollonin told the authorities that Sungurov had previously recommended it as the best line to take if they were arrested. He had once said, in the presence of Gurov and Antonovych:

Listen, gentlemen, if our society is somehow discovered and I am taken first, I assure you that I shall not give anyone away. . . . I have thought up a marvelous idea. . . . I shall say that we have heard that there are subversive societies in Moscow and have set up our own to uncover [them] and denounce them to the government.[49]

Both Gurov and Antonovych later confirmed this.[50] Such a line of defense could of course work only if no one revealed that it had been "preprogrammed." It also raised the issue of his failure to ask for official accreditation as an *agent provocateur*. To this, Sungurov, without mentioning his link to Mukhanov, explained weakly that he had feared such an offer would not be accepted.

The second major defect in Sungurov's evidence was that it made his cousin into the leading spirit in forging contacts with suspected subversives. This enabled the investigators to focus their attention on Gurov, who as the feebler character could be "turned" against his associate. On 29 July the tribunal received from him an abject confession abounding in recriminations against Sungurov, whom he charged with trying to pass his own guilt on to him:

I am a criminal! Execute me, in ghastly fashion, so that my death may serve as an example for all time and that children may shudder when they learn of it. Sungurov! When I came to you, my heart was not so corrupt [as now]. . . . Your vicious conversations, concealed by a [bogus] love for Tsar and Fatherland, have been my undoing. . . . You taught me to speak out brazenly in order to win the wrongdoers' confidence. . . . You used me as your vile instrument. . . . My lightheartedness and cowardice have been my ruin.

Sungurov, in short, had deceived him, just as he had the Polish officers, and had even harbored designs on his (Gurov's) life.[51] In an accompanying petition Gurov besought the tsar to have him put to death: "I shall die loyal to the throne and the realm." So distraught was he that, on returning from the tribunal to his place of detention, he tried to commit suicide.[52] In official eyes this act was additional evidence of guilt.

Although they did not credit Sungurov's defense, the investigators had to concede that Pollonin's testimony had not been fully substantiated. In particular there had been no conspiracy to assassinate the tsar. It was nevertheless clear that the accused had discussed and spread ideas that, in Nicholas's Russia, were seditious and therefore merited punishment. On 9 September the tribunal presented its report, which Golitsyn forwarded to St. Petersburg five weeks later.[53] The penalties that he recommended were relatively mild by contemporary standards: Sungurov should be condemned to "political death," that is, to loss of rank and privileges, and be sentenced to a term of imprisonment in a fortress, followed by indefinite enforced residence in a settlement (*na poselenie*) in Siberia; Gurov should be sent back to the army, to serve in some distant garrison; Kostenets'ky, Antonovych, and Kaszewski should be assigned to civil service jobs in Transcaucasia or Siberia and be kept under police surveillance; the two Germans and the Frenchman were to be expatriated; for the rest a simple police watch would suffice.

As the tribunal's work drew to a conclusion, conditions for the prisoners were improved: they could receive visitors and meet each other. Count S. G. Stroganov, a senior official with responsibilities in the educational field, told Kostenets'ky privately that he would come to no harm, and the Moscow civil governor, Nebolsin, even confided to him that "we all share your views on the form of government."[54] Evidently the commission members expected their recommendations to be endorsed without further ado. But they reckoned without Nicholas.

On 29 October Benkendorf relayed to Golitsyn "His Imperial Majesty's desire" that all those implicated be tried by court-martial.[55] The decision shocked the Moscow authorities and must have appalled the defendants. For it meant that the entire proceedings would be repeated in the less civilized atmosphere of the local ordnance depot, before a tribunal consisting wholly of army officers (one of them an auditor, formally empowered to see that justice was done, but lacking any real independence) who could not depart from the strict procedural rules and harsh penalties laid down in Peter I's Military Statute (1716), a code that subsequent legislation, at least since 1796, had done little to modify.[56]

The new proceedings began on 17 November, under Colonel Zherebtsov as president (*prezus*), and dragged on until the following April. The familiar allegations were trotted out; the accused repeated their earlier testimony and were once more confronted with one another; even Governor Filimonov had to reappear. Curiously, Gurov again lost his self-control and on 7 December exclaimed "with a great shout" that all the evidence, including his own, that had been given at the earlier inquiry was false. Told to calm down, he cried out: "Why should I give evidence—to knife my comrades?" He called Sungurov his "benefactor" and said that they had neither formed a clandestine society nor sought to expose wrongdoers; they had just been a group of friends, whose discussions Pollonin had crudely misrepresented. This was the truth, and very nearly the whole truth. But the court took the view that Gurov was suffering from "a darkening of moral forces"(sic) and had him examined by an army doctor. This functionary found him to be of sound mind but with "nerves weakened by fear."[57]

Sungurov stubbornly held to his previous line of defense, although its credibility was now close to nil. As in the earlier hearings, he was confronted (on 20 January 1832) with Mukhanov, the police official to whom he had reported on 16 June. Their testimony was directly contradictory. Sungurov claimed that he had told Mukhanov about his efforts to expose subversion among the students; the lieutenant-colonel maintained that Sungurov had denounced only the would-be Polish fugitive officers—and, moreover, that he had done so as a ruse, to cover up his own illegal activities.[58] As there were no witnesses to their encounter, the matter was left there. No one asked what had passed between the two men *earlier*, when Mukhanov had visited Sungurov's house. Nor did Sungurov volunteer any information on this score, although he did complain that, at the confrontation with the officer, he had been prevented by the court from saying all he wanted.

Displaying a remarkably detailed knowledge of the legal precedents, Sungurov invoked Catherine II's *Nakaz* and other edicts of 1801 and 1808, which, he argued, entitled him to clemency.[59] Unfortunately for him, military courts were not obliged to take account of all relevant legislation and in practice made an arbitrary selection from the norms they fancied, citing them without regard for their original context. The liberalism of the *Nakaz*, needless to say, was little to the taste of Colonel Zherebtsov and his fellow-judges, who knew what was expected of them on high. The record lists a large number of possible precedents (compiled by the auditor?), but twenty-six of them have been struck through in pencil—among them all those that Sungurov had indicated.[60] The court found that they were "quite remote from his crimes," all the more so since he had brought others into conflict with the law.[61] The sentence condemned Sungurov and Gurov (as well as Kozlov, whose case was examined concurrently) to execution "without mercy," after which their bodies were to be chopped into four pieces; eight of the accused, including the students, were to be hanged ("simple execution"); four others were "entrusted to the Will of God." The archaic language accorded with the venerable legal precedents, which went back to the 1649 *Ulozhenie*.

Definitive as this decision might seem, it was really no more than an elaborate judicial fiction. Eikhenbaum calls it "a *pro forma* [verdict] to intimidate the spirits [of the accused], a theatrical prop . . . of no use to anyone."[62] For like all court-martial sentences it now went its way up the hierarchical ladder of reviewing instances, each of which was free to draw its own conclusions as to the nature of the accused's offenses, the degree of their guilt, and the penalties they deserved—in short, to select what they wanted from the tomes of evidence so painstakingly accumulated. The first, and most liberal, of these interpreters was Commandant Staal. After reciting the charges (with slight but significant alterations in the wording), he gave his opinions (*mneniia*), which coincided precisely with those he had recorded the previous year. He expressed his scorn for the military court indirectly, by challenging the juridical basis of its verdict on Kozlov, who was charged with false denunciation.[63] On 16 June, one year to the day from the beginning of the affair, Golitsyn added his recommendations. He proposed Siberian exile rather than the death penalty for Sungurov and limited terms of military service for most of the other accused, "in the expectation that [this] will teach them to obey the authorities . . . and render them fit for socially useful service in future"; the foreigners were to be imprisoned before being deported.[64]

Once again Moscow had spoken. But St. Petersburg decided. The next reviewing instance was the auditor-general in the War Ministry. His officials took five months to reconsider the case before delivering judgment on 7 January 1833. Predictably, these recommendations were more severe than Staal's or Golitsyn's but less draconian than those of the military court. Sungurov and his cousin were to be sent to Siberia—but to forced labor (*katorga*); Kostenets'ky, Antonovych, Kaszewski, Kohlreif, and Knobloch were to lose their inherited rights and be sent into the army as privates for an indefinite term.[65] On 26 January Nicholas concurred in this verdict.[66]

Despite the veil of secrecy cast over it, the Sungurov affair continued for some time to send ripples through the bureaucracy. The auditor-general's department solemnly rebuked the court-martial board for three faults of procedure—none of which had any bearing on the quality of the "justice" they had dispensed.[67] On the other hand, several functionaries involved in the initial investigation were rewarded with cash grants, ranging from one hundred rubles for ordinary clerks to the equivalent of three years' salary for the chief auditor.[68]

Meanwhile, the prisoners were taken to a transit depot in the Sparrow Hills outside Moscow to be readied for dispatch to distant regions of the empire. Staal arranged for a relief fund to be set up, and enough money was collected to enable Kostenets'ky and Antonovych to buy some warm clothing, as well as a horse and cart, for their long journey to the Caucasus—which they at least did not have to complete on foot or in chains, as did the wretched convicts whom they accompanied. Some of their old friends, including Ogarev, came to bid them a tearful but convivial farewell.[69] Sungurov had fallen ill and remained a little longer in the transit prison. On 16 April, taking advantage of the relaxed surveillance measures,[70] he fled—only to be recaptured the next day, whereupon he tried to cut his throat with a razor blade. For this he was sentenced to a lashing with the knout before being sent into exile. He died some time later in Nerchinsk.[71]

Gurov fared rather better. After four years of forced labor he was transferred, on a petition by his father, a former officer, to the field forces in
the Caucasus. Wounded in action, he was promoted to noncommissioned
rank and then to that of ensign; in 1843 he obtained his discharge and
returned to live with his family near Tambov. Kostenets'ky and Antonovych were able to remain in touch with one another episodically while
serving in the Caucasus. Both reached officer's rank within six years and
subsequently secured staff jobs. The former was discharged in 1842 and
thereafter quietly farmed his estate in Chernigov province. The latter
made a remarkable career in state service. By 1861 he had become city
governor of Odessa, with a major-general's epaulettes, and in 1868 the
archconservative minister D. A. Tolstoi appointed him curator of Kiev
educational district. Such turns of fate were possible only in Russia. Even
odder was the career of Knobloch, the studious German. In the 1870s he
was commandant of the notorious Nerchinsk mines, worked largely by
convict labor![72] As for the delator Pollonin, he went back to the university,
where he was received coolly by the students; Benkendorf interceded to
find him a job—appropriately enough, in the Moscow city police.

The Polish officers, and those who had helped them try to flee, lost
their liberty for a lengthier span. In August 1831 Nicholas had ruled that
their cases should be dealt with separately, in effect by the Third Department. Court-martialed for treason, they were sentenced to deprivation of
rights and compulsory residence in Siberia.[73] They were more successful
than the others in keeping up contact. The Kiersnowski brothers, Moraczewski, and Pietraszkiewicz were all assigned to the same town, Tobol'sk, where three of them obtained civil service jobs. Only two men (T.
Kiersnowski and Szianiawski) managed to return home before 1856, when
the remainder benefited from the amnesty that Alexander II granted on
his coronation.[74]

The "Sungurov affair" is a misnomer, because the security threat to
Nicholas's regime, slight as it was, came from Kostenets'ky and his
friends, who opposed autocracy and sympathized with the Poles. Sungurov by contrast was more of an adventurer, motivated as much by his
own fantasies and ambitions as by any consistent principle. Gurov was
merely his instrument. Although Sungurov showed great courage in ad-
versity, he had a cynical, mendacious streak in his character. It was no
coincidence that both the students and the Polish officers distrusted him,
even though both these groups fell briefly under his spell, for he had
charisma as well as ambition.

Many years later Nechaev and Azev would display similar characteristics. Unlike Nechaev, Sungurov did not physically assault any of his

comrades, limiting himself to verbal threats, and then to betrayal. Unlike Azev, he does not seem to have been an agent provocateur in the literal sense, although his relations with the police are certainly puzzling.

In his memoirs Kostenets'ky advanced the hypothesis that, since Sungurov consorted with Mukhanov, he might have been his agent.

> If Mukhanov later repudiated the slightest solidarity with him, may this not be because Sungurov showed himself to be a bad police agent, who initiated action with such nullities [as the students] and, having failed to discover anything important, so soon allowed himself to become the object of a denunciation [by Pollonin]? Perhaps [Mukhanov] wanted him to penetrate the higher social spheres, not a society of students that held no interest for the government, and really to form a serious secret society which the police would then uncover, so displaying their constant vigilance.[75]

But the authorities *were* interested in mere students. And if Sungurov had been betrayed by Mukhanov, would he not have revealed details of their earlier cooperation to prove his good faith?

Nasonkina considers Kostenets'ky's theory "not unfounded" but too simple. She accepts Eikhenbaum's suggestion that Sungurov may have come to realize that he had overexposed himself by his rash talk and then tried to save himself by informing, only to be anticipated by Pollonin.[76] But this is not really in dispute. Then, rather inconsistently, Nasonkina tries to rehabilitate Sungurov's reputation as a revolutionary by speculating that he did indeed try to establish a genuine secret society, which he naively believed could "overturn Russia," in which historic event he hoped to play a leading part. When the Polish officers refused to fall in with his plans, he took revenge on them.[77] In my view Sungurov was more Machiavellian. He took an ambiguous line, building up links that he thought might fructify, while preparing to repudiate them if the risks became too great. Knowledge of the Polish officers' insurrectionary plans strengthened his "subversive" inclinations, but when this opportunity ceased to exist, he moved in the opposite direction.

Such duplicity can be explained only by the prevailing climate of anxiety, due in large measure to the inducements that officialdom offered to delators. In Nicholas's Russia, as in the oriental despotisms recently discussed by Roland Mousnier, "the population lived under constant surveillance, in perpetual fear of denunciations."[78] Sedition was defined narrowly, and even to contemplate political change was a sanctionable offense. It is not surprising that Kaszewski should have admitted to "thought-crime": "I know that every government is obliged for its security to eliminate thoughts inimical to it, and therefore I must expect to be punished."[79] It was tempting to escape the intense psychological stress by double-crossing one's associates. Delation was, so to speak, "in the air." Gurov stated in evidence that he had planned to inform on Sungurov, as he had wanted to emulate "the loyal deed of Shervud" (the informer who gave away Pestel' in 1825).[80] Knobloch and Kohlreif agreed to report their other contacts as soon as they could conveniently do so.[81] Kozlov tendered false information, and the investigating commission received a report from a prisoner that some foreigners in the local jail were plotting a mass escape.[82]

The great problem facing potential delators, apart from the moral dilemma, was to choose the right moment. If one acted too soon, one might not be able to adduce sufficient proof to support the allegations, as was required by law,[83] and might be charged with bearing false witness. If one delayed too long, one fell under suspicion of complicity with the culprit by failing to denounce him. In such circumstances it is a wonder that there were not more "Sungurov affairs." Perhaps there were. For historians have yet to explore systematically the tsarist police and military archives with a view to establishing the behavioral norms of either suspects or investigators.

NOTES

1. For a balanced view of his educational policies see M. Raeff, *Comprendre l'ancien régime russe: Etat et société en Russie impériale* (Paris: 1982), 155–59. (English translation: *Understanding Imperial Russia: State and Society in the Old Regime*, trans. by Arthur Goldhammer (New York: 1984), 149–52. See also C. H. Whittaker, *The Origins of Modern Russian Education: An Intellectual Biography of Count Sergei Uvarov, 1786–1855* (DeKalb, Ill.: 1984), 174–82.

2. P. S. Squire, *The Third Department: The Establishment and Practices of Political Police in the Russia of Nicholas I* (London and New York: 1968), 200.

3. See D. Brower, *Training the Nihilists: Education and Radicalism in Tsarist Russia* (Ithaca, N.Y. and London: 1975), 28: "A distinct radical style and set of beliefs [began] to emerge in a few small groups, baptized 'circles', particularly in Moscow University in the 1830s."

4. Tsentral'nyi Gosudarstvennyi Voenno-Istoricheskii Arkhiv (hereafter TsGVIA), fond 801, opis' 64, sv. 2, 1832 g., 4 parts (hereafter cited as *Delo*). Other papers are in Tsentral'nyi Gosudarstvennyi Arkhiv Oktiabr'skoi Revoliutsii (TsGAOR), fond 109, 1 eksp., d. 353, and fond 728, opis' 1, delo 2271, razriad IX: I did not see these. The court-martial verdict was published by [first name unknown] Sazonov as "Tainoe obshchestvo: voenno-sudnoe delo 1831 g.: po arkhivnym delam," *Russkii arkhiv* 12 (1912), 481–95.

5. "Vospominaniia iz moei studencheskoi zhizni, 1828–1833," *Russkii arkhiv* 1 (1887), 99–117; 2, 229–42; 3, 321–49; 5, 73–81; 6, 217–42.

6. "Tainoe obshchestvo Sungurova," *Zavety* 3 (1913), 15–37; 5, 45–63 (based on Third Department papers).
7. *Moskovskii universitet posle vosstaniia dekabristov* (Moscow: 1972), 211–59 (based on Moscow University records as well as Third Department papers). Nasonkina overlooked B. Andraka, "Kołko Sungurowa i polski aspekt jego działalności," *Slavia orientalis* 10, no. 3 (1961), 377–94. Neither of these historians evidently saw the TsGVIA records. There is a brief summary in V. G. Verzhbitskii, *Revoliutsionnoe dvizhenie v russkoi armii s 1826 po 1859* (Moscow: 1964), 104–10.
8. Kostenets'ky, "Vospominaniia," 336–42, 375; Nasonkina, *Moskovskii universitet*, 212–16; see also "Iz khroniki Moskovskogo universiteta: Istoriia s professorom Malovym," *Russkii arkhiv* 1 (1901), 316–24.
9. "Delo," 1, 514 (Kohlreif, 22 July).
10. The university authorities either deliberately permitted or turned a blind eye to this development, for reasons that are not clear: conceivably they felt it safe to relax the rules for students from this privileged region. There were differences of opinion within the administration on disciplinary policy.
11. "Delo," 1, 104 (27 June).
12. Ibid., 105; this is consistent with his later account: "Vospominaniia," 334.
13. Ibid., 94 (26 June).
14. Kostenets'ky, "Vospominaniia, " 78; Nasonkina, *Moskovskii universitet*, 225.
15. Nasonkina, *Moskovskii universitet*, 226.
16. "Delo," 1, 558 (Gurov, 22 July).
17. Ibid., 151–52 (30 June).
18. Ibid., 152v–153.
19. Ibid., 97v (26 June).
20. Ibid., 4, 475.
21. Ibid., 1, 247–310, esp. 250, 261–62.
22. Ibid., 95–97, 140–44 (26, 29 June); see Eikhenbaum, "Tainoe obshchestvo," 28.
23. Ibid., 605, 619v (28 July); see ibid., 4, 15 (Staal, 29 June 1832).
24. Ibid., 1, 515, 529, 554, 622, 649.
25. Soviet historians stereotype them as revolutionaries. See O. V. Orlik, *Rossiia i frantsuzskaia revoliutsiia 1830 g.* (Moscow: 1968), 101: "their bold antigovernment projects were shining testimony to the growth and development of revolutionary views among advanced students after December 14, 1825." Verzhbitskii calls Sungurov a "gentry revolutionary": *Revoliutsionnoe dvizhenie*, 108.
26. The police officer Mukhanov stated that he "lived in sin ("Delo," 1, 49), but the records contain their marriage certificate of 1826 (4, 1–2).
27. Kostenets'ky, "Vospominaniia," 73–74 (where Sungurov's age is wrongly given); Nasonkina, *Moskovskii universitet*, 228–29.
28. One piece, entitled "Joy in Heaven," tells of merrymaking among the celestial powers ("Delo," 1, 201–8). Its impiety shocked the investigators and contributed to the severity of his punishment. Gurov claimed that the author was

A. I. Polezhaev, another Moscow student who had been sent as a soldier five years earlier for versifying in a similar vein. (For his career see B. S. Meilakh et al. (eds.), *Istoriia russkoi literatury* 6 (Moscow: 1953), 460–71). Oddly, while still at Mogilev Gurov had been officially commended for some stanzas he composed in honor of Nicholas I, but these also helped to incriminate him in official eyes: "Delo," 1, 57, 3, 540; for the text, see 4, 62.

29. Kostenets'ky, "Vospominaniia," 77.
30. "Delo," 1, 618v (Knobloch, 28 July); in his reminiscences (79–80) Kostenets'ky dated it wrongly. Nasonkina (231) gives the date as 19 May.
31. Nasonkina, *Moskovskii universitet*, 232.
32. "Delo," 1, 214 (Gurov, 6 July). Kozlov's case became entangled with that of Sungurov but really should be considered separately, since he was not privy to the group's political discussions and his chief fault, in official eyes, was to have falsely alleged, when under arrest, that a disturbance was planned in Orenburg province in which certain senior local officials, with whom he was in conflict, were implicated. "Delo," 4, 419–21.
33. For his background see ibid., 1, 213 (Gurov, 6 July). See also Andraka, "Kołko," 381–82.
34. "Delo," 1, 108 (Ensign P. O. Lents, 27 June), 149 (Pollonin, 30 June), 209v (Gurov, 6 July).
35. Ibid., 150v.
36. Ibid., 644v–645v (Gurov, 29 July).
37. Ibid., 5v, 7v (Pollonin, 17, 18 June); Antonovych later confirmed the substance of this conversation (ibid., 485, 21 July).
38. Ibid., 343–44 (Antonovych, 9 July).
39. Eikhenbaum, "Tainoe obshchestvo," 17; Nasonkina (*Moskovskii universitet*, 235–36) defends this reaction on the grounds that Szianiawski was guilty of "nationalism" and lack of self-restraint.
40. Or possibly his subordinate, Volkov (Kostenets'ky, "Vospominaniia," 221); Apraksin's report to Golitsyn is dated 17/18 June.
41. Kostenets'ky, "Vospominaniia," 220, 222, 227.
42. Ibid., 221; Nasonkina (241) claims that this was true of *all* the defendants.
43. "Delo," 1, 680.
44. Ibid., 314, 321.
45. Ibid., 599–637.
46. Ibid., 22 (Pollonin, 21 June), 397 (Gurov, 15 July), 601 (Knobloch, 28 July).
47. Ibid., 160, 166 (1, 6 July).
48. Ibid., 187–90 (6 July).
49. Ibid., 312 (6 July).
50. Ibid., 391v (Gurov, 15 July), 487–91 (Antonovych, 21 July); they set the conversation in different locales.
51. Ibid., 643–46; also in Eikhenbaum, "Tainoe obshchestvo," 35. Adam Ulam calls revolutionaries' confessions and recantations "a uniquely Russian genre of literature." See his *In the Name of the People: Prophets and Conspirators in Prerevolutionary Russia* (New York: 1977), 40.

52. "Delo," 1, 639.

53. Eikhenbaum, "Tainoe obshchestvo," 52–56; Nasonkina, *Moskovskii universitet*, 250.

54. Kostenets'ky, "Vospominaniia," 226–27.

55. "Delo," 3, 39.

56. Alexander I's Field Regulations (1812) were concurrently in force and, contrary to their original intention, could be applied in peacetime conditions. Nicholas I codified Russian military law in 1839, but this "reform" scarcely improved the rights of the accused. For an introduction to the subject in English see J. P. LeDonne, "The Administration of Military Justice under Nicholas I," *Cahiers du monde russe et soviétique* 13 (1972), 180–91, and, more especially, V. Savinkov, *Kratkii obzor istoricheskogo razvitiia voennougolovnogo zakonodatel'stva* (St. Petersburg: 1869). See also Elise Kimerling Wirtschafter, "Military Justice and Social Relations in the Prereform Army," *Slavic Review* 44 (1985), 67–82, for a sensitive appreciation of soldiers' expectations from and reactions to the military-judicial system, and John L. H. Keep, "Justice for the Troops: A Comparative Study of Nicholas I's Russia and France under Louis-Philippe," *Cahiers du monde russe et soviétique* 28 (1987), 31–54.

57. "Delo," 4, 180–83.

58. Ibid., 3, 286–87. When informing on the Poles, Sungurov had also mentioned to Mukhanov the existence of a "Weisshaupt" society (a Masonic organization?), but as he could give no details of it this was construed as a deliberate effort to throw the police off the scent.

59. Ibid., 399.

60. Ibid., 528–37. Among these provisions: that in moderately governed states capital punishment was inflicted only for insurgency (*Nakaz*, § 114); that an accused must be allowed adequate means to defend himself (*ibid.*, § 116); and the right to present evidence in his favor, which the court was obliged to examine (I *Polnoe sobranie zakonov*, 26, 19968, 8 August 1801; 30, 23166, 18 July 1808, § 17).

61. "Delo," 3, 544ff.

62. Eikhenbaum, "Tainoe obshchestvo," 57.

63. "Delo," 4, 374–87.

64. Ibid., 3, 1–9, esp. 4v.

65. Ibid., 4, 430–33.

66. Ibid., 402.

67. Ibid., 457–58.

68. TsGVIA, fond 1, opis' 4, tom 1, delo 272, no. 55, 1832, ll. 19–20.

69. Kostenets'ky, "Vospominaniia," 237–38.

70. Nasonkina suggests (*Moskovskii universitet*, 256–57) that this laxity may have been deliberately contrived by Mukhanov, but this seems farfetched. Even if they had been *sub rosa* confederates, would the policeman have dared to let him go?

71. For the following see Kostenets'ky, "Vospominaniia," 239–41; Eikhenbaum, "Tainoe obshchestvo," 61–63; Andraka, "Kołko," 391–92; Nasonkina, *Moskovskii universitet*, 258–59.

72. His friend Kohlreif, after six years in the army, was transferred to the civil service as a result of ill health and died in 1844. Kaszewski's fate is unknown; he may have been killed in action in the Caucasus.

73. Except for Siedliecki, who after a few months' imprisonment was to be sent to the Caucasus. "Delo," 4, 72–73; fond 1 (see n. 68), l. 12.

74. Andraka, "Koko," 392–93.

75. Kostenets'ky, "Vospominaniia," 236.

76. Eikhenbaum, "Tainoe obshchestvo," 17.

77. Nasonkina, *Moskovskii universitet*, 253.

78. R. Mousnier, "Monarchies absolues en Europe et en Asie," *Révue historique* 272 (1984), 42.

79. "Delo," 1, 232 (7 July).

80. Ibid., 388v (10/15 July).

81. Ibid., 601v, 618v (28 July).

82. Ibid., 137 (29 June).

83. M. N. Tikhomirov and P. P. Epifanov (eds.), *Sobornoe Ulozhenie 1649 g.: posobie dlia vysshei shkoly* (Moscow: 1961), chap. 21, §§ 49, 57; see II *Polnoe sobranie zakonov* 4, 3033 (24 July 1829), §§ 8–13. For the antecedents: A. Kleimola, "The Duty to Denounce in Muscovite Russia," *Slavic Review* 31 (1972), 759–79.

Herzen, Herwegh, Marx

Judith E. Zimmerman

lexander Herzen traveled to Western Europe in 1847 as a radical sightseer. The sights soon turned out to be far more ex-
citing than he could have imagined, for he arrived just as the
European order created in 1815 by the Congress of Vienna
was giving way to revolutionary violence. He was an eyewitness to events in Italy in 1847–48 and was in Paris in time for the bloody
suppression of radical revolution in the French capital. His experiences
and observations convinced him that he should remain in the West and
dedicate his life to the revolutionary cause. In 1852 he settled in London,
where he embarked on his mature career of radical journalist.

During these first years abroad Herzen equipped himself to function as
an active member of an international radical community. He staked out a
position by defining his own beliefs and by identifying his friends, allies,
and enemies within the revolutionary camp. He established a reputation
by publishing important work in the French and German radical press.
He also made practical arrangements for life abroad by surreptitiously
transferring the bulk of his assets to the West and consigning them to the
care of the Paris Rothschild bank.

In this essay I wish to explore the process whereby Herzen found his
own place in the radical community. In searching out the network of contacts that he developed, I discovered that personal relations were far more
important in determining political position than was pure ideology.
Among the men Herzen counted as friends there was no uniformity of
belief, nor was there even consensus on proper strategy (a far more immediate and serious matter in the midst of revolutionary crisis). I found
that the key to Herzen's alliances was the web of contacts established by
Georg Herwegh over the preceding half-decade. Moreover, I discovered
that Herwegh's own network, as it crystallized in 1849, was itself defined
almost entirely by a generalized hostility to Karl Marx. Thus, even
though Marx and Herzen never met, Marx's own activities prior to and

during the revolutionary crisis, and his involvement with the workers' movement in Cologne, in particular, became a crucial part of Herzen's story.

In addition to developing a set of political friends, Herzen also attempted to find a political niche for himself. Generally speaking, the revolutionaries whom he met were fighting for change in their homeland; most of them had at least a chance to make a bid for power on some level during the revolutionary period. Herzen, as a Russian, had no realistic hope of a revolution at home. He tried, therefore, to define for himself a position of revolutionary internationalism that would unite radicals from across Europe in a common cause of liberation. Ultimately, he was unsuccessful in this effort; revolutionary internationalism, when it came, would come in Marx's version, not Herzen's. Nonetheless, there were some attempts to build the type of coalition Herzen sought; they are also part of this study of Herzen's first effort to define his position in the West.

Paris was the scene of Herzen's first activities as a European radical politician; the crucial period was the ebb tide of revolution, the winter of 1848–49. He had arrived back in the French capital from Italy in early May 1848 and remained there until June 1849.[1] These months saw the decline of the French Republic into authoritarianism, and the election of Louis Napoleon Bonaparte as president. Outside France, the revolutionary movements that had seemed so universal and invincible in the spring were defeated by the forces of the old governments. Popular protest was met with repression, and the radical leaders, after their brief moment of power, feared for their safety. Some were arrested, a few executed, and many took the road to exile.

Herzen's second Paris stay can be divided into two relatively distinct periods. During the summer of 1848, he remained essentially a bystander, observing the most dramatic and, for someone of Herzen's convictions, the most terrible events of the revolutionary process. At this time he functioned primarily within a small Russian colony of friends and friends of friends; together they saw the revolutionary sights and reacted to events. But at the end of the summer when most of the Russians returned home, the Herzens decided it was not yet time to go back. Over the next few months they decided to remain indefinitely in the West, a decision that forced them to break most of their personal ties with their own country and adopt the émigré community as their new home.

Paradoxically, this decision came only after Herzen had become thoroughly disillusioned about the prospects for revolution and democracy in the West, and in France in particular. He had viewed the events of 1848 from a position on the left of the political spectrum, close to that of the radical Paris clubs. This implied a nondoctrinaire socialism and a notion of "democracy" that legitimated political action by the participation of the organized and conscious working people. Disillusionment with the new government came almost immediately after his return to Paris, upon witnessing the *journée* of May 15, when radical crowds briefly invaded the National Assembly. He felt that the democratic members of the government should have supported the movement; their failure to do so proved to Herzen their incapacity or bad faith.[2]

Far more devastating was the uprising of the Paris workers of June, and its violent suppression by the forces of the Republic. Despite the perceptible development of a political crisis in the preceding weeks, the eruption of violence was sudden. Natalie Herzen was in the middle of a chatty letter, about friends at home and domestic concerns in Paris, when it began. As she told of her hopes and plans for their son Sasha, she commented, "Sometimes I feel that I am reliving my life. . . ." "At the word 'life'," she resumed six days later,

> I was interrupted by cannon fire, which continued—day and night!—*four days*, the city is still *en état de siège*, they say there are 8,000 dead. That's all. I haven't the spirit to go into detail. I am surprised that we are alive, but we are alive only physically. Tania, there were moments when I wished to be destroyed *with the whole family*. I do not know if we shall revive enough that anything in life will ever again be able to evoke a sincere smile.[3]

The Herzens could hear the firing squads from their apartment. Herzen himself had been seized as a suspected Russian agent as he made his way around the city under martial law. He was released after a few hours, but later his house was searched and his papers temporarily confiscated.[4] Thus the Herzen family saw the counterrevolutionary violence and shared with the Paris populace the political repression that accompanied the bloodiest episode of 1848. The spectacle of cannons raking the streets would affect Herzen's view of politics for the rest of his life.

The June days shredded the social fabric of France. Men of the Left, like Herzen and his friends, could see only the greed and ruthlessness of the propertied classes. Herzen had no other explanation of what appeared to him the furious slaughter of a defenseless population in the name of an "order" that benefited only the bourgeoisie. The Herzens were stunned, and any residual faith in the democratic potential of the revolution they might have retained was destroyed. All their correspondence in the following weeks tells of their helpless rage and horror. A nostalgia for Russia appears at the same time in Herzen's letters, as does the belief that only the Russian peasants and the Paris workers were true freedom-loving democrats by nature. Still, despite what he saw as the brutal unmasking of the real nature of bourgeois republican politics, the West remained freer than Russia; therefore it would be from the West that the struggle for Russian and European freedom would be waged. Despite his rage and disillusionment, Herzen had decided that he would dedicate himself to that struggle.

> O, *cari miei*, what I would give to be able to rest a little time with you; then [I] would take up my staff again and return to my place in the desperate struggle, to the place of the defeat of everything holy, everything human. . . . Sometimes I dream of returning, of our poor nature, the villages, our peasants, of life at Sokolovo⁵—and I feel like flinging myself at you like the prodigal son. . . who has lost all hopes. I desperately love Russia and the Russians—only they have a broad nature, the broad nature which I saw in all its brilliance and greatness in the French worker. These are the two peoples of the future (i.e., not the French, but the workers), for the sake of whom I cannot tear myself away from Paris.⁶

Natalie expressed this combination of distress and determination in even more extreme terms in a letter written at the same time:

> Our hopes are destroyed. We do nothing. We see nothing. We are living through our death, but I have not arrived at despair. There is still much to be done, and neither Cavaignac⁷ nor any force in the world will hinder me or destroy my barricade. Yes, Granovskii, I feel this, and know I could not live without it. Personal happiness is not enough, and there is no personal happiness without this [feeling]. I know I am building a strong barricade— my barricade is—my Sasha! Perhaps it too will be destroyed, but much will be saved behind it. Sometimes I can see prison, chains, the guillotine far away on the path along which I lead him, but my heart neither aches nor trembles. I hold him firmly by the hand and an inner voice keeps saying to me: "Marchons! Marchons!"⁸

Herzen's ideology helped him choose his weapon. He derived from his Feuerbachian philosophy⁹ an anarchism based on the premise that any setting up of an authority over oneself is a form of oppression and a diminution of the human personality. This position became codified in works dating from 1849 to about 1854 as the concept of "dualism," which linked religion and the state, regardless of its political form, in a single repressive system.¹⁰ In the aftermath of the June days, he began to formulate this idea:

> Lamartine, in his brochure "Trois mois au pouvoir," says that he and his comrades wished a *constitutional republic*, i.e., a monarchy without a king,

without hereditary power—and that kind of constitutional or, more frankly, *monarchical* republic was established. In fact, can a republic be distinguished from a monarchy solely by the fact that in it instead of a king, a motley crowd of representatives, invested with the same power as the banished king, reigns? There is nothing in the world more opposed and antipathetic than these two governmental forms. In a monarchy they *govern* the people, in a republic the people *governs* its own affairs. The model for monarchy is the master directing his workshop, the father, the guardian managing the property of minors. The model for a republic is the *artel'* of workers, which has its managers, but no master. Monarchy is based on authority; it needs hierarchy, religio-political ritual . . . it needs *vestments*, rather than clothing; at every step it must recall that the individual is insignificant before authority; it must demand submission. A republic demands only one thing of people—that they be people; it is based on confidence in the person; it is natural and therefore does not impose bonds, but establishes conditions which issue from the very essence of social life, to such an extent that to escape them is absurd or irrational. If it asks more than this, it is not a republic. . . . Monarchism is based on dualism, the government must never coincide with the people, the government is providence, spirit, holy rank; the people is matter, laymen, subjects; monarchism is essentially theocracy, it is solid only by *le droit divin;* . . . without a concept of Jehovah there is no tsar. . . . The inner principle of a republic is immanence and not dualism; it worships nothing; its religion is man, its god is man, "and there is no other god besides him"; a republic leads to atheism and anarchy. . . .[11]

The task of the revolutionary was to undermine the conservative institutions and instincts that held the old, oppressive system together, and simultaneously maintain faith in the validity and possibility of the goal of a free society and fight debilitating despair. The source of conservatism was in people's minds, and so the work of destruction would also have to operate on the level of intellect. The practical result of this position was that some time during his stay in Paris, Herzen finally chose his vocation. He would be a radical journalist and thereby contribute to the intellectual preparation for revolution.

This decision was also a natural outgrowth of Herzen's earlier activities; while still in Russia, he had been a writer, had dreamed of directing a journal, and wished to use his writing to further social and moral change. The difference was one of commitment—as he well knew, his entire future life would be shaped by this decision. The impulse probably came from the realization that in the West journalism provided more political options than in Russia. The freer press made it possible to express oneself openly, and the radical writers formed a network of influence and support considerably larger than the Moscow coteries Herzen had known and outgrown. The example of his friend Georg Herwegh, who shared his perceptions of current conditions and was an active journalist, was important.[12] So was the moral authority achieved by a man Herzen had long admired as a theoretician, Pierre-Joseph Proudhon, who as a journalist and member of the National Assembly won great stature as the most courageous spokesman against the excesses of counterrevolution.[13]

During this same winter of 1848–49, Herzen also decided to supplement his journalism with a foreign-based press that would disseminate his own and others' writings to his homeland.[14] Herwegh, Herzen's closest European friend, probably was the inspiration for this plan. Years before he had been able to galvanize the German opposition of the *Vormärz* through the operation of just such a press, established in Switzerland by Julius Fröbel primarily for the purpose of distributing the poet's *Gedichte eines Lebendigen*. Fröbel and his friends had intended to follow up the success of the press with a journal, and had appointed Herwegh editor. They hoped to use it to create a forum for opinion from all over Germany and here again foreshadowed Herzen's later program for *Poliarnaia zvezda*.[15]

A milieu in which Herzen could function politically began to take form toward the end of the summer of 1848. As the Russians departed, refugees from the rest of Europe arrived in Paris, their first step on what would become, for many, a long journey of exile. The new arrivals, whatever their achievements had been in the spring and summer, were now cut off from practical activity. Among them, Herzen was less an outsider than he was in the world of French politics; his activity and stature increased commensurately.

Entrée into this milieu was provided by his friendship with Herwegh. After the poet's return from the humiliating defeat of his German Legion,[16] the Herzen and Herwegh families had become inseparable. When the German forty-eighters arrived in Paris, they sought out Herwegh, whose house had long served as a center for radical émigré life. Now they found the poet discouraged and speaking of withdrawing from political concerns altogether in order to concentrate on natural science. Through him they met Herzen, whose perceptions of the present were just as bleak, but whose vivacity and humor were less depressing.[17] Soon the Herzens' house became a second haven for the refugees, many of whom arrived nearly penniless. Herzen's generosity to them became legendary. Thus, one friend from this period told of twenty extra places laid at each meal for the destitute émigrés, of anonymous contributions to anyone who was in need, and even of facilities provided for two Hungarian women to deliver their babies in the Herzen home.[18]

The identity of the refugees befriended in the first instance by Herwegh, and then by Herzen, was largely determined by Herwegh's previous political activity and by developments that took place within German radicalism, primarily during the revolutionary year. Ideology, in the sense of a fairly rigorous theoretical position and a consistent political strategy derived from it, turns out not to have been important in the pattern of these contacts. For Herwegh and Herzen, political friends were people who shared three characteristics: an internationalist perspective, a revolutionary mood, and personal antipathy to Karl Marx.

Revolutionary internationalism, the notion that a community of interests linked revolutionaries everywhere, that in fact there was a single struggle for progress and freedom against the united forces of the reactionary governments, was a perceptible, if minor, strain in the politics of 1848. For Herzen, however, it represented the aspect of revolution of most immediate relevance to his own situation. In 1849 the possibility of revolution in Russia was remote indeed, and so for a Russian who wished to be considered a participant in the movement, it would have to be perceived as an international enterprise. Hence his search for allies among radicals from many countries, and for an internationalist forum.

Revolutionism, the insistence that an acceptable polity could not be achieved by the government in place, was more a mood than a program. One form of revolutionism was involvement in violent revolutionary activity. Democratic nationalists with very moderate social programs, such as Mazzini and many of the Polish émigrés, were among the most implacable revolutionists of this type. Some of Europe's most radical social visionaries, on the other hand—Proudhon and Cabet, as well as Marx—either saw no need for violent revolution or believed that renewed attempts at uprisings were futile at the present time. Their revolutionism was expressed, instead, in their insistence that all existing governmental systems, even those produced by political revolutions, were inherently unable to bring about the social transformation they sought. Herzen's revolutionism had elements of both activism and socialist radicalism. Although he was opposed to revolutionary adventurism on each specific occasion when action was proposed, his rage at the defeats of 1848, his sense that all those who had participated in government had ended up compromised, and his vestigial romanticism produced sympathy and admiration for those who risked their lives for their beliefs. More consistently with his ideology, he also felt that the revolutionary process had not produced a framework that would make possible a truly radical social transformation.

The last characteristic that defines Herzen's friends, opposition to Marx, is the most surprising; for this reason it is the one that I wish to consider in detail in this paper. This also seems to be the characteristic that best accounts for the patterns of Herzen's later contacts, and it may also explain the exaggerated dislike of Marx and Herzen for each other, an antipathy that has never been satisfactorily explained.[19] To understand the hostility evoked by Marx among many radicals, it is necessary to review his activity before and during the revolutionary months of 1848.

In the early 1840s, German radical intellectuals had begun to move out of the university and into the nascent political arena. The first centers of activity were journals; in Cologne, Moses Hess and Karl Marx briefly controlled the liberal *Rheinische Zeitung*, while Arnold Ruge made two attempts to publish a democratic journal, first in Halle and then in Dresden (the *Hallische* and then the *Deutsche Jahrbücher für Wissenschaft und Kunst*). In 1844 the two sets of journalists coalesced, when Ruge brought Marx, Herwegh, Hess, and Michael Bakunin to Paris to establish the *Deutsch-Französische Jahrbücher.* These new émigrés by no means constituted an ideologically homogeneous group; indeed, none of them had yet elaborated a coherent position. Conflict over personality and life–style soon arose between Ruge, on the one hand, and Marx and Herwegh on the other. The antagonism probably also reflected the greater political radicalism of the two younger men. There is no indication that Marx and Herwegh were ever particularly close, but neither was there any disagreement between them. They remained on relatively good terms until 1848, when they broke over the issue of the German Legion.

Marx was expelled from France early in 1845 and went to Brussels. There he remained until the 1848 revolutions and, in collaboration with Engels, developed his mature style. Theoretically, he moved from the 1844 *Economic and Philosophical Manuscripts* to the *Communist Manifesto*. His intellectual development was not an independent phenomenon; it was inextricably linked to his other roles as organizer and polemicist. All were part of Marx's effort to politicize and then dominate his movement. On a practical level, he attempted to win control of existing working-class radical organizations. At the same time, his theoretical work fueled his remarkably acerbic polemics that served to undermine the sense of socialist solidarity and to drive real or potential middle-class rivals out of the movement.[20]

Marx's working-class base was the League of the Just, established in the 1830s, a secret society made up primarily of German artisans working in foreign countries. There were branches in Switzerland, Paris, and London, as well as the Rhineland cities. The leading figure in the League was a self-educated tailor, Wilhelm Weitling.[21] The League espoused a moralizing communism, its members believing that capitalist productive relations were evil and that workers' solidarity in the struggle for change was a moral imperative. In mood it was insurrectional, and the Paris branch had collaborated in the revolutionary attempt of 1839.

Marx's special style was displayed in his efforts to control the workers organized in the scattered branches of the League and to impose on them his own brand of socialism. He and Engels established a Communist Correspondence Committee in Brussels in 1846 and then attempted to transform existing branches of the League of the Just into "Communist League" affiliates that would be under the control of the new Committee.[22] They gained control of the committee by forcing out Weitling, charging him with theoretical vacuity and thoughtless leadership. It was the first time that socialist ranks had been purged, and Weitling was not the only one stunned by it. Moses Hess, appalled, wrote to Marx in order to dissociate himself from his former comrade's "party."[23]

In the years just prior to the revolution, the Paris branch of the League was the most important for Marx.[24] Its members resisted the nominal control of the Communist Correspondence Committee; they continued to seek in communism a moral community rather than a political force. Weitling remained popular among them, and they were also attracted by the German "true socialist" Karl Grün and the French socialists Proudhon and Cabet. Nonetheless, in the winter of 1847, with Engels on the scene in Paris, the League had officially become the "Communist League," giving Marx a shaky victory.[25] At the same time, on the theoretical level, Marx subjected his potential rivals to devastating polemical attack. Karl Grün and the "true socialists" were the victims of *The Holy Family*. Proudhon, who refused to enlist in Marx's campaign against the "true socialists," was the target of *The Poverty of Philosophy*.[26]

As a result of these bitter polemics, by the time revolution broke out in 1848 Marx could count Weitling, Moses Hess, Proudhon, and Ruge among his enemies. The Communist League, which he and Engels had labored to create and to link with themselves, was badly divided over his treatment of Weitling and his attacks on its former positions. Once the February Revolution began, these tensions split the German community in Paris. A German Democratic Association was established there immediately after the revolution, initiated apparently by Adalbert von Bornstedt, a former officer and Prussian government agent, a member of the Communist League and associate of Marx's in Brussels.[27] The first meeting of the Association, which was attended by about four hundred people, elected a governing committee, with Herwegh as president.

On 6 March a large public meeting took place with four thousand in attendance, most of them probably workers with some connection to one or another of the radical artisanal organizations. Herwegh and Bornstedt, vigorously supported by Michael Bakunin, proposed that the Democratic Association form a legion to carry revolutionary democracy back to Germany by force of arms. Marx, who had returned to the French capital and was present at this meeting, along with supporters from the London branch of the Communist League and representatives of the left wing of British Chartism, strongly opposed the plan. He sensibly pointed out the thorough futility of such a course of action and proposed instead that the Germans in Paris return to their homes individually and work from there for internal revolution.

After Herwegh and Bornstedt carried the day Marx pulled out of the Association, taking the Communist League faction with him. Soon his followers organized their own club, the *Ouvriers Allemands*, in opposition to the Democratic Association. They seem, however, to have constituted only a minority of the original Paris Communist League, while the majority, workers who still found the traditional communism of the League of the Just more compatible than Marx's brand of socialism, now left the League for the German Association and so demonstrated their resentment of the recent transformation of their organization.[28]

The Legion set off for Germany on 21 March, amid celebrations of revolutionary solidarity. Poles, Hungarians, and the Paris *Garde mobile* demonstrated their support before the departure. "An immense crowd made the air resound with cries of 'Vive the universal republic!'"[29] But once the ill-equipped, ill-informed legion crossed into Germany, its campaign became a tragicomedy of missed connections, futile marches and countermarches, constantly changing plans, and a single disastrous encounter with the Prussian army.[30] A defeated and humiliated Herwegh escaped capture and made his way back to Paris, where he renewed his contacts with the German democratic Left.[31] Despite the fact that most of the radicals agreed with Marx in dismissing the legion as futile and wasteful, Herwegh himself was not repudiated; unlike Marx, he remained a part of their community, despite a foolish and catastrophic error.

Marx soon left Paris for Cologne, which became one of the major centers of Left political action in 1848. From there, he continued his efforts to dominate the working-class movement and to eliminate potential rivals. In his bid for national prominence, he also managed to alienate many middle-class radical democrats. In the process he created more enemies, who in their turn became the friends of Herzen.

Cologne boasted an active branch of the Communist League, whose leaders had been in the forefront of the revolutionary action of 3 March (preceding the outbreak of revolution in Berlin by two weeks).[32] Marx's arrival soon split the Left along fault lines created by personal and political rivalries. The Communist League was led by a physician, Andreas Gottschalk, and included the former officers Friedrich Anneke and August Willich, who had become manual workers. All three were "true socialists," believers in the moral obligation of communism, the view excoriated by Marx in *The Holy Family.* Gottschalk was personally close to Hess.

In April, Gottschalk established an open Workers' Association *(Arbeiterverein)*, which soon displaced the conspiratorial League. Marx, upon his return to the city, attacked Gottschalk's Association and attempted to take over the League, but he failed to overcome the League majority loyal to its founder.[33] He had success in another arena, however; he beat out his rival, Hess, to become editor of the *Neue Rheinische Zeitung.* In this paper Marx followed a more moderate policy than that advocated by Hess and Gottschalk. Because he believed that a socialist revolution was impossible at the time, he called on the working class to support liberal democratic initiatives instead of seeking a more radical resolution of the current crisis.[34]

In addition to editing the *Neue Rheinische Zeitung*, Marx also became head of the Cologne Democratic Society, an umbrella group of liberals, democrats, and communists, which included the Workers' Association as its left wing.[35] In the late summer Gottschalk, along with Anneke, was arrested "for having preached communism before an assembled multitude of 8,000 citizens."[36] Two of Marx's lieutenants now took Gottschalk's place at the head of the Workers' Association, and Marx himself assumed leadership in October.[37] Despite an understanding that he was serving temporarily, he did not relinquish this post upon Gottschalk's release in December. The incident exacerbated the rivalry between Gottschalk and Marx and undermined still more unity on the Left. Gottschalk, offended, left Cologne, and in travels to Bonn, Paris, and Brussels, "he cultivated contacts with the poet Herwegh, Moses Hess, and others whom Marx had offended"; this led, in turn, to his repudiation by the Association.[38]

Gottschalk and his friends found Marx too conciliatory toward the liberal democrats. But the democrats themselves were offended by Marx's abrasiveness. As the summer progressed, there were a number of efforts within Germany to create a nationwide, relatively broadly based democratic movement. An early attempt was a meeting in Cologne, called by Marx, of a Congress of Democratic Associations. Among those in attendance was Carl Schurz, at that time a faithful disciple of the Bonn art historian and democrat Gottfried Kinkel. Schurz described the impression made by the outstanding socialist thinker of the century:

> He already was the recognized head of the advanced socialistic school. The somewhat thick-set man with his broad forehead, his very black hair and beard and his dark sparkling eyes at once attracted general attention. He enjoyed the reputation of having acquired great learning, and as I knew very little of his discoveries and theories, I was all the more eager to gather words

of wisdom from the lips of that famous man. This expectation was disappointed in a peculiar way. Marx's utterances were indeed full of meaning, logical and clear, but I have never seen a man whose bearing was so provoking and intolerable. To no opinion, which differed from his, he accorded the honor of even a condescending consideration. Everyone who contradicted him he treated with abject contempt; every argument that he did not like he answered either with biting scorn at the unfathomable ignorance that had prompted it, or with opprobrious aspersions upon the motives of him who had advanced it. I remember most clearly the cutting disdain with which he pronounced the word "bourgeois"; and as a "bourgeois," that is a detestable example of the deepest mental and moral degeneracy he denounced everyone that dared to oppose his opinion. Of course the propositions advanced or advocated by Marx in that meeting were voted down, because everyone whose feelings had been hurt by his conduct was inclined to support everything that Marx did not favor. It was very evident that not only had he not won any adherents, but had repelled many who might otherwise have become his followers.[39]

All this vigorous organizational activity soon came to an end. Repression of the Viennese revolution in the autumn sent the first wave of refugees fleeing to Paris. The failure of the Frankfurt Parliament to bring about a united, constitutional Germany led to the last, pathetic effort of democrats based in the Rhineland to defend democracy by force of arms. The Prussian army was everywhere easily victorious, and repression sent into flight radicals like Marx and Hess, as well as moderates like Schurz and Kinkel. For the moment, Paris offered refuge and political freedom.

The filtering process of the revolutionary months defined which among the refugees who made their way to Paris would contact Herwegh and through him become a part of Herzen's network. They were on the radical edge of the German political scene: from the far Left of the official assemblies (the Frankfurt Parliament and the constituent assemblies that met in the individual states) and beyond. But they also tended to be on the opposite side of a divide from Karl Marx, who had that summer antagonized so many people of so many different political persuasions. Politically, it was an ill-assorted group, for it ranged from quite moderate democrats to convinced communists; it was by no means a political party, merely a collection of people linked by their disappointed dreams and by their belief that all revolutionaries were part of a fraternity which was obliged to treat its members with a consideration that the intellectuals in Cologne so often seemed to lack. The émigrés' distrust of Marx and desire to avoid falling under his influence were explicit.[40]

Among the men with whom Herzen now became acquainted were Herwegh's and Marx's former colleagues from the Paris emigration, Moses

Hess and Hermann Ewerbeck.[41] Hess had the greatest respect for Marx's erudition and theoretical power and would later criticize Herzen for failing to incorporate Marx's materialism into his vision of revolution. But he also found Marx an impossible colleague, and this feeling too he transmitted to his Russian acquaintance.[42] Hermann Ewerbeck, a physician, had long been active in the radical organizations of the German workers in Paris. He had wavered between Grün and Marx in the first period of polemics, and, in his Marxist phase, had been the source for the rumor, printed by the *Neue Rheinische Zeitung*, that Bakunin was a Russian agent.[43] Ideologically, however, he remained closer to the communism of Cabet and Weitling than to the "scientific socialism" of Marx. During the summer of 1848 he had been in Cologne, and there he seems to have been a backer of Gottschalk.[44] Gottschalk himself arrived in Paris after his release from prison; he met and made a strong impression on Herzen.[45]

In January, a young Hegelian socialist, Friedrich Kapp, arrived in Paris. He had gone to Cologne shortly before the revolution and there had become active in the Communist League. It is likely that during 1848 he too had sided with Gottschalk against Marx and Engels.[46] Herzen, who always attempted to surround himself with representatives of the radical community, soon hired Kapp as Sasha's tutor and his own secretary and translator.

Among the more moderate German forty-eighters, Arnold Ruge, another of Marx's former colleagues and present enemies, met Herzen in June 1849, just after his arrival in the city and shortly before the Russian's hasty departure. They never became friends, but when Herzen arrived in London three years later looking for allies against Herwegh, he felt it appropriate to solicit the support of Ruge.[47] At that time he also sought out Kinkel, the radical democrat with fuzzy, philanthropic socialist tendencies, whom he had never met but who was, like many others, both a part of the radical community and a person offended by Marx. Through Kinkel, Herzen later became friendly with Carl Schurz,[48] as well as with a substantial segment of the moderate German colony in London. At the same time, a link with the German Left in London was provided by Herzen's admiring friendship with August Willich, one of Marx's radical opponents in the Cologne Communist League; in London, Willich headed the anti-Marx faction within the German working-class socialist organization. He opposed Marx from the Left, calling for new revolutionary uprisings.[49]

The influence of his new contacts can be perceived in Herzen's first venture into the world of Western European journalism, his flirtation with Adam Mickiewicz's newspaper, *La Tribune des Peuples*. Once he had burned his bridges as far as returning to Russia was concerned, had secured his property, and had found a group of contacts who provided him with a network and a sense of participation in a radical community, Herzen was ready to go to work. He was seeking a newspaper through which he could play a role, ideally one that would help provide a structure for the inchoate group of international radicals with whom he had become affiliated. Democracy, socialism, internationalism, and the provision of a platform for polemics with the Cologne radicals behind Marx were the most important programmatic considerations. The backing of a great "star" of international democracy would be an additional benefit.

La Tribune des Peuples is the first paper known to have approached Herzen for support. Its leading figure was a "star" of the very greatest magnitude, the Polish poet Adam Mickiewicz, who had attracted a wide following in France just before the revolution through his course on Slavic literature at the Collège de France. Prohibited from resuming his chair, Mickiewicz was enabled to undertake the direction of the newspaper through the generosity of his compatriot, Count Xavier Branicki.[50] Mickiewicz's ideology combined elements of Bonapartism and romantic Polish messianism, views that would make him a strange ally for Herzen, a proponent of atheistic, socialist anarchism. Indeed, the attempt to collaborate foundered on this divergence of views. As Herzen described the episode in *Byloe i dumy*, Charles Edmond Chojecki approached him about the journal and introduced him to Mickiewicz at a banquet. Herzen, however, found the obsequiousness of the mystical poet's followers offensive, and the political differences between Herzen and the Poles proved too great to be surmounted.[51]

A somewhat different picture emerges from piecing together other bits of evidence and examining the pages of *La Tribune des Peuples* itself. Division of opinion seems to have been built into the very structure of the paper. There was a rather shadowy Polish group exercising overall direction, but the paper's historian has been unable to define its activity or influence "with any precision."[52] Within the active editorial group, Mickiewicz and his friends controlled the general line, but at the start the correspondents were recruited by Charles Edmond Chojecki, a young, radical compatriot of the poet's. He had left his native country in 1844, fearing arrest for his participation in subversive groups. He went to Paris, where, under the name Charles Edmond, he became a contributor to opposition journals. In 1848 he fought on the barricades in February and then returned to Poland for several months, hoping to help spread the revolution. He attended the Prague Slav Congress and then in December 1848 returned to Paris. Philosophically Chojecki was a left Hegelian, and politically he was close to Proudhon.[53] Ladislas Mickiewicz, the poet's

son, believed he was imposed on the paper by Branicki, and that his
friends constituted the editorial board's left wing, a view not wholly accepted by the historian Kieniewicz. Ladislas Mickiewicz further stated
that Chojecki did not share Adam Mickiewicz's views and would gladly
have replaced the poet with Herzen.[54]

Chojecki and Mickiewicz agreed, however, on the revolutionary internationalism that was to be the paper's most basic ideological position, and
that explains the potential connection with Herzen. "Henceforth," Mickiewicz asserted in the first issue, "it has become impossible for one
people to march in isolation along the path of progress." The goal of the
paper would be to provide an international forum: "we call on all the
nations to come to this *Tribune*, each with its free word."[55] Not only was
La Tribune to be internationalist, but in line with Mickiewicz's own position, and in sharp distinction from the rest of the democratic press in
France, it was by no means anti-Russian, showing a unique ability to
distinguish the actions of the Russian state from the attitudes of the Russian people.

The openness to Russia was reflected in the paper's staff. Among the
collaborators was Herzen's old friend from his student days and member
of his first "circle," Nikolai Sazonov. Now he was at least a peripheral
member of Mickiewicz's circle, as well as Herzen's regular companion; he
was, thus, a potential link between the two.[56] His writing appeared in *La
Tribune* under the pseudonym "Iwan Woinof."[57] In an article in the first
issue, which by virtue of its position and length appeared to represent the
editorial view, he sharply differentiated between the Russian state and its
people and interpreted the Russian situation in a way that prefigured Herzen's later works:

> through its diverse oppressions and its successive revolts, under the iron
> Asiatic yoke, as under the European yoke of formulas, the Russian people
> knew how to hold intact its communal organization, which it has enjoyed
> from time immemorial. It allowed a foreign authority, a German adminis-
> tration to be established; it allowed itself to be oppressed and pillaged.
>
> On the other hand, the sentiment of liberty, which is developing ever
> more strongly in the civilized classes, has had its martyrs as well in the
> noble insurgents of December 14, 1825.
>
> At the same time, all of Russian literature offers us an uninterrupted
> series of intellectual martyrs in Pushkin, Griboedov, Lermontov, Polevoi,
> Belinskii.
>
> The two interests of civilization and of nationality, which hitherto have
> seemed opposed to each other in Russia, have found in these men a common
> symbol.
>
> One more effort, and the Russian people will shake off the yoke of a false

and obsolete order of things in order to reveal itself to Europe, young, strong, and free. We have complete confidence in the future of this people, and it is because we are persuaded . . . it will justify our confidence, that we ask for its admission into the fraternal circle of European peoples.[58]

Herzen would later search in vain for another paper so involved with the international movement, and so willing to hear a revolutionary Russian point of view.

During the brief period that Chojecki served as managing editor, there was considerable overlap between Herzen's circle and *La Tribune*, and it was possible to believe that the paper would not only be a forum for internationalism, but also provide a voice for Herzen's non-Russian friends. Chojecki secured the collaboration of Ewerbeck, and of Ramon de la Sagra, a Spanish former deputy whom Herzen admired and who was an acquaintance of Proudhon.[59] Ernst Haug, a former officer in the Austrian army who had joined the revolutionary forces, and who later became one of Herzen's staunchest friends, contributed an article condemning the narrow nationalism of the Hungarian revolutionary government.[60] Gottschalk, as late as May, hoped that the paper could be used as a platform for Marx's opponents.[61] This did not happen, however, and instead Chojecki was forced to resign. After his departure, *La Tribune* no longer had much in common with Herzen and his friends.

Herzen was correct about the difficulties of a possible alliance with Mickiewicz; Bonapartism and messianism could not mix with socialism and atheism. The episode is revealing, however, for it demonstrates an attempt by those socialists whom Marx had insulted or injured to find a common vehicle and to use Mickiewicz's name and resources for the purpose. Chojecki, the friend of Proudhon; Herzen, the friend of Herwegh; and Ewerbeck are known to have been involved. It is not clear that Chojecki himself perceived his collaborators as forming a potential anti-Marxian nucleus, but Gottschalk certainly hoped to use *La Tribune* in this manner and so informed Herzen's confidant Herwegh.[62]

Soon after Herzen's failure to find the vehicle for his activity in *La Tribune*, there was a major change in his own circumstances. He participated in the last of the insurrectionary demonstrations of the 1848 period, that of 13 June 1849, called to protest the French government's seizure of Mazzini's Roman Republic. The repression that followed convinced Herzen to leave France; he went to Geneva, and a new exile colony.

His ambitions were unchanged, however, and so were his political alliances. Soon Sazonov and Chojecki would invite him to participate in *La Voix du Peuple*, another daily newspaper, socialist but non-Marxian, headed by another of Marx's victims, Proudhon. Ramon de la Sagra of *La*

Tribune contributed to the new journal as well. Fröbel and Gottschalk were also potential contributors, Herzen told Proudhon.[63] Herzen was relatively unconcerned about the ideological differences that separated him from Proudhon, but he did attempt to push his new vehicle much further toward internationalism than the rather provincial Proudhon would have gone if left to his own devices.[64] The collaboration with Proudhon was, then, the logical culmination of Herzen's efforts to find a niche for himself within international radicalism, as well as the real start of his Western career.

NOTES

This essay is part of a larger study of Herzen and Western European radicalism which will appear in 1989 as Midpassage: Alexander Herzen and European Radicalism, 1847–1852, *published by the University of Pittsburgh Press.*

1. For biographical studies of Herzen during this period, see E. H. Carr, *The Romantic Exiles*, reprint ed. (New York: 1975); Ia. El'sberg, *Gertsen: Zhizn' i tvorchestvo*, 4th expanded ed. (Moscow: 1963); Allen McConnell, "Against All Idols: Alexander Herzen and the Revolutions of 1848: A Chapter in the History of Tragic Liberalism," Ph.D. dissertation, Columbia University, 1954; Barbara Sciacchitano, "The Exile World of Alexander Herzen: A View of Russia and the West," Ph.D. dissertation, University of Illinois at Chicago Circle, 1979. Especially important is Herzen's own autobiographical account, *Byloe i dumy*, in Aleksandr Gertsen, *Sobranie sochinenii v tridtsati tomakh* (Moscow: 1954–65), 8–11, esp. vol. 10. (This edition of Herzen's works will be cited as *Gertsen*.) For background on events in France, see Maurice Agulhon, *The Republican Experiment: 1848–1852* (New York: 1983); Georges Duveau, *1848: The Making of a Revolution*, trans. Ann Carter, intro. George Rudé (New York: 1968); Peter H. Amann, *Revolution and Mass Democracy: The Paris Club Movement in 1848* (Princeton: 1975); Daniel Stern [Marie d'Agoult], *Histoire de la Révolution de 1848*, 3 vols. (Paris: 1850, 1851).
2. Herzen to Moscow friends, 2–8 August 1848, Gersten, 23, 86–87.
3. Natalie Herzen to Tatiana Astrakova, 23–30 June 1848, ibid., 79.
4. On Herzen's arrest and the seizure of his papers, see ibid., 10, 29–35; Iwan Golownin, *Der Russische Nihilismus: Meine Beziehungen zu Herzen und zu Bakunin* (Leipzig: n.d.), 60.
5. The estate where the circle had spent the summers of 1845 and 1846.
6. Herzen to Moscow friends, 2–8 August 1848, Gertsen, 23, 79–80.
7. Commander of the forces that suppressed the June uprising.
8. Natalie Herzen to T. N. Granovskii, in N. P. Antsiferov (ed.), "N. A. Gertsen (Zakharina): Materialy dlia biografii," *Literaturnoe nasledstvo* 53 (1956), 382.
9. For Herzen's Left Hegelianism, see Martin Malia, *Alexander Herzen and the Birth of Russian Socialism: 1812–1855* (Cambridge, Mass.: 1961), 225–56.

10. See, for example, "Le Dualisme, c'est la monarchie," Gertsen, 12, 217–25; "La Russie et le vieux monde" (1854), ibid., 13, 135.

11. Ibid., 5, 363–64; see also Herzen to Moscow friends, 6 September 1848, ibid., 23, 95. On Herzen's anarchism, see Z. V. Smirnova, *Sotsial'naia filoso-fiia A. I. Gertsena* (Moscow: 1973), 99–100, 113–17.

12. Victor Fleury, *Le Poète Georges Herwegh (1817–1875)* (Paris: 1911), 147.

13. Proudhon's position in 1848 was by no means one of straightforward political radicalism; however, his distrust of the political Left, which by June had failed to democratize France, and his crusty independence won admiration. His positive program at this time was devoted almost entirely to the establishment of a "People's Bank" that would provide free credit and so, he thought, make possible the withdrawal of civil society from the state. Herzen was not interested in this at all. I deal in detail with the relationship between Proudhon and Herzen in my "Herzen, Proudhon, and *La Voix du Peuple:* A Reconsideration," *Russian History* 11, no. 4 (Winter 1984), 422–50.

14. "Vmesto predisloviia ili ob"iasneniia k sborniku," Gertsen, 6, 145–49.

15. Julius Fröbel, *Ein Lebenslauf: Aufzeichnungen, Erinnerungen und Bekentnisse*, 2 vols. (Stuttgart: 1890–91), 1, 95–97; Fleury, *Le Poète*, 85–95.

16. On the German Legion, see the following discussion.

17. On Herwegh's despair, see Edmund Silberner, *Johann Jacoby: Politiker und Mensch* (Braunschweig-Bonn, Bonn-Bad Godesberg: 1976), 209, drawing on letters from the summer of 1848; Gustav Rasch, *Aus meiner Festungszeit: Ein Beitrag zur Geschichte der preussischen Reaction* (Pest, Vienna, Leipzig: 1868), 23–24; on Herzen's rather despairing vivacity—"there is a revolution now, and soon it will be over, we do not wish to go home," he would say when staying out till five and six in the morning—see A. I. Gertsen, *Polnoe sobranie sochi-nenii i pisem*, ed. M. K. Lemke, 22 vols. (Petrograd: 1915–25), 5, 260 (henceforth cited as *Lemke*), quoting Ruge's correspondence for June 1849. Herzen already had a reputation in Germany as a writer of fiction. See B. F. Egorov, K. N. Lomanov, I. G. Prushkina, Ia. E. El'sberg (eds.), *Letopis' zhizni i tvor-chestva A. I. Gertsena: 1812–1870*, 2 vols (Moscow: 1974), 1, 473.

18. Gustav Rasch, commemorative article on Herzen, *Neue Freie Presse*, translated and quoted in Lemke, 5, 269–70. The account in Rasch's memoirs, *Aus meiner Festungszeit*, 20, is similar, but not quite so expansive.

19. On this hostility, see Gertsen, 11, 161, 166–67; editorial note, A. I. Gertsen, *Byloe i dumy* (Moscow: 1963), 2, 672–74; El'sberg, *Gertsen*, 391–95; Maksim Kovalevskii, "Gertsen i osvoboditel'noe dvizhenie na Zapade," *Vestnik Evropy* 47, no. 6 (June 1912), 221–36; Karl Marx and Friedrich Engels, *Werke*, 42 vols. (Berlin: 1956–67), 28, 344, 346, 432–36, 439, 461–62.

20. On Marx's early involvement in international workers' organizations see David McLellan, *Karl Marx: His Life and Thought* (New York: 1973), and David Felix, *Marx as Politician* (Carbondale, Ill.: 1983). Felix's argument that Marx is to be viewed primarily as a political actor rather than a theorist is in accord with my views, and his account of Marx's political maneuvers between 1845 and 1850 is the fullest available; however, I do not share his unfailing admiration of Marx's skill and foresight. The discussion of Marx's quarrels with

other socialists that follows is not intended to be exhaustive; only those whose victimization by Marx in some way impinged on Herzen's development are mentioned.

21. For an appreciation of Weitling and his role in the League of the Just see Hermann Ewerbeck, *L'Allemagne et les Allemands* (Paris: 1851), 592–93 and passim. See also E. Kandel' and S. Levtsova, "Marks i Engel's—vospitateli pervykh proletarskikh revoliutsionerov," in E. Kandel' (ed.), *Marks i Engel's i pervye proletarskie revoliutsionery* (Moscow: 1961), 10.

22. On this episode, in addition to McLellan and Felix, see Edmund Silberner, *Moses Hess: Geschichte seines Lebens* (Leiden: 1966), 254.

23. McLellan, *Karl Marx*, 155–59; Silberner, *Hess*, 257–58.

24. Ultimately, the London Branch, which was the group for whom the *Communist Manifesto* was written, and which provided Marx's base during the post-1848 years, was more important. However, before 1848, London (led by refugees from Paris, forced to flee after the 1839 uprising) was docile: Marx's polemical works were inspired by the need to win over Paris.

25. McLellan, *Karl Marx*, 160–66, 175–76; Oscar J. Hammen, *The Red '48ers: Karl Marx and Friedrich Engels* (New York: 1969), 154–56; Engels to Marx, 14 January 1848 in Marx and Engels, *Werke*, 17, 111; Felix, *Marx as Politician*, 68.

26. Pierre Haubtmann, *Proudhon, Marx et la pensée allemande* (Grenoble: 1981), 103–13.

27. Ibid., 173

28. Hammen, *Red '48ers*, 201; Marx to Engels, 16 March 1848, *Werke*, 28, 119; Herwig Foerder, Martin Handt, Jefim Kandel, Sofia Lewiowa (eds.), *Der Bund der Kommunisten: Dokumente und Materialen*, 1, *1836–49* (Berlin: 1970), 721–22, 747.

29. Communiqué of the Société allemand, *La Voix des Clubs*, 14, 25 March 1848, 3.

30. [Otto von] Corvin [-Wiersbitzkii], *Aus der Leben eines Volkskampfers: Erinnerungen*, 4 vols. (Amsterdam: 1861), 3, passim.; Carr, *Romantic Exiles*, 50–51; Jacques Droz, *Les Révolutions allemandes de 1848* (Paris: 1957), 236–42.

31. Fleury, *Le Poète* 147; Bruno Kaiser, *Der Freiheit eine Gasse: Aus den Leben und Werk Georg Herwegh* (Berlin: 1948), 44–45.

32. McLellan, *Karl Marx*, 194–95; Hans-Ulrich Wehler (ed.), *Friedrich Kapp: Vom radikalen Frühsozialisten des Vormärz zum liberalen Parteipolitiker des Bismarckreiches: Briefe 1843–1884* (Frankfurt am Main: 1969), 9–10; Friedrich to Johanna Kapp, 17 January 1848, ibid., 52.

33. Silberner, *Hess*, 285; Droz, *Les Révolutions*, 96–97; McLellan, *Karl Marx*, 196.

34. Silberner, *Hess*, 283–85; Felix, *Marx as Politician*, 86–87.

35. Loyd D. Easton, "August Willich, Marx and Left-Hegelian Socialism," *Cahiers de l'ISEA* (August 1965), 104, 109.

36. [Ewerbeck], "Germany (Extract from a Letter from Berlin)," *The Spirit of the Age*, 12, 14 October 1848, 182.

37. McLellan, *Karl Marx*, 20–22; Felix, *Marx as Politician*, 88–89.

38. Hammen, *Red '48ers*, 371; *Der Bund der Kommunisten*, 115–17; "Beschluss der I. Filiale des Kölner Arbeitervereins," Marx and Engels, *Werke*, 6, 585–87.

39. Carl Schurz, *The Reminiscences of Carl Schurz*, 2 vols. (New York: 1907–08), 1, 139–40.

40. Ewerbeck to Hess, Edmund Silberner (ed.), *Moses Hess, Briefwechsel* (The Hague: 1959), 209.

41. Marc Vuilleumier, Michel Aucouturier, Sven Stelling-Michaud, and Michel Cadot (eds.), *Autour d'Alexandre Herzen: Révolutionnaires et exilés du xixᵉ siècle: Documents inédits* (Geneva: 1973), 36.

42. Hess, "Briefe an Iscander," Hess, *Briefwechsel*, 239–63.

43. Haubtmann, *Proudhon, Marx*, 105; Marx to Engels, 3 September 1853, Marx and Engels, *Werke*, 28, 281.

44. Silberner, *Hess*, 150–51.

45. Herzen to Moscow friends, 27 September 1849, Gertsen, 23, 189. See also Georg to Emma Herwegh, in Marcel Herwegh (ed.), *1848: Briefe von und an Georg Herwegh*, 2d ed. (Munich: 1898), 275.

46. See note 29.

47. Paul Herrlich (ed.), Arnold Ruge, *Briefwechsel und Tagebuchblätter aus den Jahren 1825 –1880*, 2 vols. (Berlin: 1886), 2, 99. In 1852 Ruge wrote a play, *Die Neue Welt*, in which the plot, if not the characters, was largely based on the Herwegh-Herzen triangle. He sent a copy to Herzen for comments, which angered him. Gertsen, 25, 154–55. Ruge resented the Russian's reaction, which ignored, he claimed, the fact that his tragedy aroused general interest by posing the problems of the "freest people." Ruge to Herzen, 1854, Russian translation in Lemke, 8, 21–22.

48. Schurz, *Reminiscences*, 2, 53–54.

49. Easton, "August Willich," 113, 115.

50. Ladislas Mickiewicz, "Preface," Adam Mickiewicz, *La Tribune des Peuples* (Paris: 1907), 7.

51. Gertsen, 10, 38–41.

52. Stefan Kieniewicz, "Histoire de la 'Tribune des Peuples,'" *L'Indépendance et la question agraire: Esquisses polonaises du xixᵉ siècle: Opera Minora* (Warsaw: 1982), 136–37.

53. On Chojecki, see Zygmunt Markiewicz, "Charles Edmond, Voyageur et comparatiste oublié," *Connaissance de l'étranger: Mélanges offerts à la mémoire de Jean-Marie Carré* (Paris: 1964), 292–301; and Z. L. Zaleski, *Attitudes et Destinées: Faces et Profiles d'écrivains Polonais* (Paris: 1932).

54. Mickiewicz, "Preface," 9; Kieniewicz, "Histoire," 136.

55. Leader, *La Tribune des Peuples*, 1, 15 March 1849. Mickiewicz identification from Mickiewicz, *La Tribune des Peuples*, 54–58.

56. Mickiewicz, 11.

57. Franco Venturi, *Studies in Free Russia* (Chicago: 1982), 190.

58. Iwan Woinof, "De la Russie," *La Tribune des Peuples*, 1, 15 March 1849.

59. Mickiewicz, "Preface," 7; Kieniewicz, "Histoire," 136. Kieniewicz associates De la Sagra with the central, policy-defining group on the paper, which

would imply that he was Mickiewicz's appointee rather than Chojecki's. However, this does not square with Herzen's account of De la Sagra's open opposition to Mickiewicz's views at the paper's founding banquet. Gertsen, 10, 40–41.

60. "Réponse à M. Pulszky," *La Tribune des Peuples*, 3, 17 March 1849. The author was identified in the next issue.

61. Gottschalk to Herwegh, 1 May 1849, in *1848*, 267.

62. Chojecki apparently did leave papers, but they are in Poland, and I have not been able to consult them; they may shed some useful light on this question.

63. Herzen to Proudhon, 27 August 1849; Gertsen, 23, 175–76.

64. On the Proudhon collaboration, see my "Herzen, Proudhon, and *La Voix du Peuple*."

MICHAEL BAKUNIN AND HIS BIOGRAPHERS

The Question of Bakunin's Sexual Impotence

Marshall S. Shatz

The subject of this essay—the alleged sexual impotence of Michael Bakunin—may seem at first glance a trivial and even unseemly one for historical investigation. Indeed, it ought to be. The fact is, however, that it has been accepted unquestioningly and reiterated over and over again by a long line of biographers and historians. More important, for over two generations now it has played a considerable role in shaping the image of Bakunin, as a man and as a political figure, that has been projected in English-language historiography. Should it turn out, as I hope to demonstrate, that there is no reliable evidence whatsoever for this allegation, two conclusions of some significance follow. First, students of the Russian intelligentsia and of the Russian revolutionary movement should finally lay to rest a myth that has served only to distort and becloud our understanding of this major figure. Second, historians in general should take this as a cautionary tale, as a case study of the way unexamined speculation can establish itself as received wisdom.

The work most responsible for propagating the impotence theory in English-language scholarship is E. H. Carr's biography of Bakunin. First published in 1937, it was until recently the only full-length treatment of Bakunin in English, and it remains the most readable and accessible. Well-written, entertaining, and the work of a distinguished historian, it has been the standard biography, and the most influential, ever since its appearance. The theory of Bakunin's sexual impotence is central to Carr's interpretation. He states it early in the book, in explaining why Bakunin disclaimed any romantic interest in Natalia Beer, who, with her sister Alexandra, was a close friend of the Bakunin family and at one point developed a crush on Michael. Carr detects in Bakunin, who was not quite twenty-one at the time, "a strain of abnormality" and contends:

from this point his sexual development is strangely arrested. In later life, Michael was certainly impotent. When he was in his twenties, some of his contemporaries already suspected an incapacity of this kind; and he is not known to have had sexual relations with any women. No explicit statement on the subject, medical or other, has been preserved.[1]

This last sentence should at the very least give pause to the historian. Carr, however, not only accepts Bakunin's impotence as a fact, identifying it as a psychological product of hatred of his mother, but makes it the key to his political career:

His tumultuous passions, denied a sexual outlet, boiled over into every personal and political relationship of his life, and created that intense, bizarre, destructive personality which fascinated even where it repelled, and which left its mark on half nineteenth-century Europe.[2]

Carr strongly implies that if Bakunin had had a normal sex life he would not have developed into the kind of revolutionary he later became, although the psychological, or glandular, connection between sexual impotence and revolutionism is merely assumed, never explained. The further implication is that Bakunin's political ideas and activity need not be taken very seriously, as they were in large part the products of an individual character disorder. This underlying attitude is sustained throughout the rest of Carr's biography, the imputation of arrested sexual development being joined by the theme of infantilism, a repeated depiction of the mature Bakunin as a child who never grew up.[3]

Thanks to Carr, sexual impotence has become almost inseparably linked to Bakunin's name. It appears in Edward Brown's work on the Stankevich Circle ("Bakunin was impotent and had no 'normal' relations with women"), and, a bit more cautiously, in Evgenii Lampert's *Studies in Rebellion* ("the sexual impotence which most biographers ascribe to him").[4] The latter, however, soon abandons this caution, and, like Carr, draws a connection between Bakunin's sexual incapacity and his anarchist political ideology: "he could not or would not love, just as he could not and would not build, beget, preserve."[5] The impotence theory is a central theme in the popular biography of Bakunin by Anthony Masters, which is heavily dependent on Carr.[6] It reappears in the two most recent biographical studies. Aileen Kelly says merely that "he seems to have been sexually impotent"[7] and then concentrates on his intellectual development, but in her portrayal of Bakunin as a frustrated and divided individual seeking "personal wholeness" through revolution, she does not differ greatly from those who have based this image on a psychosexual approach. Finally,

Arthur Mendel, in the most extensive psychosexual analysis of Bakunin to appear, makes sexual impotence a crucial feature both of his life and of his politics (characterizing his philosophy of anarchism as a "rhetoric of impotence"),[8] along with revulsion against sexuality itself, Oedipal disorder, and pathological narcissism. Even those historians who have not emphasized the impotence theory have been influenced by it to the extent of regarding Bakunin as in some way abnormal. This tendency has left an indelible mark on the historical literature.

Although Carr was responsible for introducing the impotence theory into English-language historiography, he did not originate it. Its creator appears to have been Iurii Steklov, with the publication in 1920 of the first installment of his four-volume biography of Bakunin. Because Carr follows Steklov very closely, it will be useful first to look at the evidence Steklov offers, then to see what Carr and others may have added to it. As Carr was to do, Steklov introduces the theme with an expression of surprise that there was no element of physical love, at least for Bakunin's part, in his relationship with Natalia and Alexandra Beer. Each of the sisters in succession seems to have fancied herself momentarily in love with Michael, but he put them off, usually with philosophical sermons on the superiority of spiritual love over the "animal," or sensual element. Some of Bakunin's biographers have taken these passages as an expression of Bakunin's fear, and rejection, of sexuality itself.[9] It would be rash, however, to regard such statements as much more than exalted flights of idealist rhetoric. Not only Bakunin but the other members of the Premukhino Circle (Premukhino was the Bakunin family estate) saw themselves as special beings, morally and spiritually superior to the mundane world around them (a view that, among other factors, made it difficult for them to accept the conventional marriages and service careers their parents thought suitable for them). The letters of Bakunin's sisters and their friends in the 1830s, which A. A. Kornilov quotes extensively in the first volume of his biography of Bakunin,[10] are also steeped in an admixture of idealist philosophy and traditional Christian sentiments and to one degree or another exalt selflessness, spirituality, and universal love over materialism, "egoism," and so forth. The outpourings of these young people, cast in the idealist and romantic vocabulary of the day, should not be taken literally or with a great deal of psychological solemnity.

As far as Bakunin's relations with the Beer girls are concerned, it is at least possible that he simply was not attracted to them. Stankevich, for example, had also proved immune to Natalia's charms.[11] Nor was Bakunin averse to romance, for twice in his Moscow years he wrote to his sisters describing his strong feelings about other girls.[12] Nothing serious came of these episodes, but there is no obvious reason why his lack of passion for the Beers should be given more weight than the adolescent flirtations in which he did engage. It should also be kept in mind that Bakunin was forging a new life for himself and a new self-image, breaking with all the expectations of his family, class, and society, and a serious relationship at this time would have jeopardized the independence he was seeking.

Starting with Bakunin's relationship with the Beer sisters, Steklov then takes the very large step of asserting that "Bakunin did not allow himself to develop the feeling of love for a woman, and perhaps this came to him naturally, without being forced. His friends knew of this trait in Bakunin's character. . . ."[13] As examples of such knowledge, Steklov first cites Herzen, who wrote of Bakunin that "no woman played a large role in the life of this revolutionary ascetic: his love, his passion, belonged to something else." Asceticism, of course, is not the same as sexual incapacity or indifference; furthermore, Steklov fails to inform the reader that Herzen wrote these words in 1851, seven years before Bakunin married.[14] Next, Steklov claims that "Turgenev notes this same characteristic in Rudin, in whom he tried to depict the young Bakunin." Whatever the degree to which Bakunin may have served as a model for the hero of Turgenev's novel—and even Steklov concedes elsewhere that this is a controversial issue[15]—it is always risky to confuse fiction and biography. Moreover, the novel does not tell us that Rudin was sexually impotent. Rudin is a man of intellect rather than passion, of words not deeds, and he fails at love just as he fails at everything else in his life, but there is no indication that his failure is physical rather than purely emotional. Indeed, one might well ask why Turgenev would bother to write a novel about a man whose pathos reduced itself to an organic dysfunction. Finally, in a footnote to the reference to Rudin, Steklov asserts that Michael Katkov was probably referring to this same feature when, in the course of a quarrel, he allegedly called Bakunin a "eunuch." Steklov recounts this episode some pages later, and without further comment, but he has already prepared the reader to regard it as explicit confirmation of what was merely hinted at by Bakunin's other friends.

Carr follows Steklov's treatment of the subject step by step. As noted earlier, he too starts with Bakunin's relationship with the Beer sisters. Citing two letters from Bakunin to the sisters in April 1835, Carr finds them remarkable for "their outspoken rejection of sexual love."[16] It is difficult to see how the contents of these letters support such an interpretation. In the first letter, Bakunin assures the sisters of the constancy of his affection for them precisely because, he states frankly, he is not in love with either one. Had he experienced "passion for one of you, passion connected with feeling and not with the soul, fervent, stormy passion," he would at first have been blind to her faults, then inevitably disillusioned. Instead, he loves them for themselves, for "your beautiful souls," and therefore his friendship will not change.[17] In the second letter, he announces that he has a special "mission" in life: the hand of God has written in his heart that he will not live just for himself and will "sacrifice everything for this holy good." A lengthy idealist disquisition follows, its subject being love as the expression of the divine or eternal in man. He then devotes an entire paragraph to a disappointed love affair.

> You tell me that I have not known love. No, I have known it. I have known it in all its raptures . . . I have tasted all its happiness, all its hopes. . . . Oh, let us not speak of this! Why have I stirred up such burning memories, suffering, the terrible traces of which my lacerated heart still feels so keenly. Let us not speak about it. My beautiful days have come to an end![18]

He was probably alluding to his infatuation with Maria Voeikova, and one can readily agree with Steklov's comment in his edition of the letters that because Bakunin does not seem to have been as deeply wounded as he claims here, he was most likely just "showing off before the young ladies."[19] He was posing, as a twenty-one-year-old idealist and romantic might, as a man experienced in the ways of the heart but capable of rising above his emotional wounds to devote himself to higher things. As such, he proceeds to advise Natalia on her relationship with Stankevich, "for I also have suffered, for I also have experienced the sufferings of love."[20] Whatever one might think of Bakunin's sincerity or profundity in these letters, they do not constitute a renunciation of sexual love, either for himself or for anyone else.

Carr, like Steklov, presents only one further piece of evidence for the impotence theory: the quarrel in which Katkov called Bakunin a "eunuch." In fact, of the contemporaries who supposedly suspected this incapacity in Bakunin, Carr quotes only Belinskii, who witnessed this quarrel and wrote an account of it. And, like Steklov, Carr presents Belinskii's account without further comment, having already prepared the reader to take it as an allusion to Bakunin's sexual impotence. Because this is the one seemingly direct and explicit reference to the subject that any of Bakunin's biographers have been able to uncover, and is therefore the cornerstone of the entire theory, it needs to be looked at carefully.

In August 1840, Belinskii wrote a long letter to Vasilii Botkin in which he described a heated quarrel between Bakunin and Katkov that had taken place in Belinskii's St. Petersburg apartment on the eve of Bakunin's departure for Germany. Apparently Katkov held Bakunin responsible for spreading gossip about him and Nicholas Ogarev's first wife, Maria

L'vovna. Finding out that Bakunin was going to Belinskii's apartment, he confronted him there. As Belinskii related the incident to Botkin, the following exchange took place. To Katkov's accusation, Bakunin responded:

> "Facts, facts, I would like some facts, my dear sir!" "What facts do you need! You have sold me out over a trifle—you are a scoundrel, sir!"— B[akunin] leaped up. "You are a scoundrel yourself!"—"Eunuch [*skopets*]!"—this had a stronger effect on him than scoundrel: he winced as though from an electric shock.[21]

Bakunin and Katkov then traded a few blows, and there ensued a challenge to a duel, which, however, never took place.

There are a number of circumstances surrounding this narrative that in themselves should urge caution upon the historian. First, of course, common sense suggests that whenever, in the course of a quarrel, one young man accuses another of sexual inadequacy, a certain amount of skepticism is called for, even when nineteenth-century Russian idealists are involved. Second, we have only Belinskii's account of this incident. Bakunin in a letter home referred only to "a major and serious explanation with Mr. Katkov," and if Katkov left any description of the encounter Bakunin's biographers have failed to find it.[22] Third, Belinskii at this time was very hostile to Bakunin and had every desire to malign him; the entire letter is laced with venom. Therefore we cannot be certain that Belinskii was reporting Katkov's exact words and not his own embellishment of them. In fact, there is reason to suspect the latter.

This suspicion arises from the text of the letter itself, which neither Steklov nor Carr appears to have finished reading. A few pages beyond the passage quoted, Belinskii uses the word *eunuch* a second time. He tells Botkin that Bakunin subsequently brought him a note intended for Katkov, the gist of which was that it would be better to fight their duel in Germany, where both of them were headed, rather than in Russia, where dueling was illegal. Belinskii scornfully characterizes Bakunin's note as written "in the style of a masturbator and eunuch [*onanisticheskim i skopecheskim slogom*]."[23] One does not have to be a physiologist to suggest that it is really rather difficult to be both a "masturbator" and a "eunuch" at the same time. At least twice more in his letters to Botkin, Belinskii applies the epithet *skopets* to Bakunin, and these instances also raise doubts as to whether he is actually referring to sexual impotence. In a letter of 4 October 1840, Belinskii touches on a recent episode in his own life, possibly a love affair, that had stirred him deeply. It would be difficult to imagine anyone more unfortunate than he, Belinskii complains: "A passionate, loving nature—the thirst of a Tantalus, remaining eternally unsatisfied! Why am I not a eunuch by nature [*skopets ot prirody*] like M[ichael] B[akunin]!"[24] The context strongly suggests that Belinskii is alluding to what he considers to be Bakunin's self-centeredness, or lack of emotional depth, and not to sexual incapacity. Finally, in another letter a few months later, he remarks that Bakunin once accused him of vulgarity for using the phrase "to sleep with one's wife." That, Belinskii declares, "is the idealism of a eunuch and a masturbator,"[25] once again employing this improbable combination of insults.

If taken as a literal reference to sexual impotence, Belinskii's application of the term *skopets* to Bakunin makes little sense. There is no need to take it literally, however. D. N. Ushakov's Russian-language dictionary includes the following among its definitions of the word: "*fig.* A passionless, cold man (coll.)." The example Ushakov provides of this usage is from no less an authority than Pushkin: "At heart you are cold eunuchs."[26] In the figurative sense of someone who is lacking in emotional warmth, wrapped up in theories and abstractions, insensitive to the feelings of others, Belinskii's use of *eunuch* is entirely comprehensible, for it is an extension of the criticism of Bakunin's character that Belinskii had been making for several years.

Time and again in the course of their stormy friendship, which had begun in 1836, Belinskii accused Bakunin of being too intellectual, too abstract and philosophical, cut off from feeling, emotion, the living pulse of human life. In October 1838, for example, he writes to Bakunin that "an idea is dearer to you than a person." Further on in the same letter, he writes: "Your blood is hot and vital, but it . . . flows not in your veins but in your spirit; my spirit lives in my blood, hot and coursing . . . ."[27] He tells Stankevich that Bakunin "loves ideas, not people, he wants to dominate by means of his authority, not to love."[28] One of his favorite terms for Bakunin was "abstract hero," as in the following characterization in a letter to Botkin a few months before the Katkov affair: "An abstract hero, born to bring ruin on himself and others, a man with a marvellous head but decidedly without heart and with the blood of a rotten salt cod." In the same letter he warns Botkin not to trust Bakunin's literary judgments because nature has deprived him of aesthetic feeling: "he understands art, but with his head, without the participation of his heart . . . ."[29]

It is in this context that we must read another passage from Belinskii that Carr takes as an allusion to Bakunin's impotence—the only seemingly direct reference to the subject that Carr cites aside from the Bakunin-Katkov quarrel. On 10 September 1838, Belinskii wrote Bakunin a letter in which he criticized the latter's main faults. It included the following words, as Carr translates them: "In fact, you have not lived at all, you do not yet know what is well known to everyone even without going to school: the act of life, which is a mystery even apart from the feeling of love." Carr interprets these words as a reference to Bakunin's "lack of sexual experience," presumably taking the phrase "act of life" (*akt zhizni*) to mean sexual intercourse.[30] If so, it would be a peculiarly vague and oblique locution, uncharacteristic of the direct and somewhat earthy Belinskii. In fact, however, a more appropriate translation would be "act of living," which robs the phrase of any sexual connotations but makes considerably more sense in the context. For the sentence is embedded in a long passage in which Belinskii again criticizes Bakunin for immersing himself in abstract thought at the expense of genuine feeling. Belinskii complains that Bakunin sacrifices his own feelings to theoretical abstraction and, even worse, has persuaded his sisters to do the same.[31] It is Belinskii's constant refrain: Bakunin lacks spontaneity and naturalness; he refuses to live life as it comes rather than endlessly analyzing it and theorizing about it.

Perhaps there was some truth to Belinskii's characterization of the young Bakunin. Bakunin himself seems to have accepted it to some degree, wondering on occasion whether he were capable of loving deeply, or of being loved.[32] At the same time, Belinskii had every incentive to exaggerate this criticism of Bakunin, for it provided him with a convenient defense of his own wounded ego. One of the main sources of friction in the relationship between Bakunin and Belinskii was the latter's sense of intellectual inferiority. With a much sketchier education than the gentry intellectuals with whom he associated, lacking a knowledge of German and hence direct access to the philosophy that was all the rage in these circles, Belinskii came to resent Bakunin's intellectual domination, which, undoubtedly, was at times overbearing. What he could claim for himself, however, was a greater capacity for spontaneous feeling, for passion, for life experience, for "heart" as opposed to "intellect." A second factor impelled him in the same direction: his brief infatuation with Bakunin's sister, Alexandra. Nothing came of it, for a number of reasons, including Alexandra's father's opposition and what appears to have been Alexandra's own unenthusiastic response. Belinskii, however, chose to blame Bakunin's influence: he accused him of having infected his sisters with his abstract philosophizing, thereby stifling their natural instinct for feeling and emotion.[33] Again, whatever the validity of Belinskii's charge, it served also as a way of rationalizing his humiliation.

In the larger context of Belinskii's interpretation of Bakunin's character, his account of the Katkov episode takes on a significance quite different from the explicit reference to sexual impotence so many historians have found in it. It is noteworthy, for example, that Belinskii does not elaborate on Katkov's supposed use of the epithet "eunuch"—he simply states it and goes on. If Bakunin's sexual incapacity was such an open secret among his close friends, one might expect some discussion of it in such a hostile private letter. Finally, it should be mentioned that those historians who have placed such great emphasis on this passage have ignored other remarks in Belinskii's letters that seem to contradict it. At the beginning of 1838, for example, when Belinskii had already known Bakunin for two years and at a moment when he was well disposed toward him, he wrote to Botkin: "What a fellow! Truly, brother, this man is worthy of having the best woman on earth forget both herself and the world in love for him."[34]

In sum, Belinskii's account of the quarrel between Bakunin and Katkov cannot be taken as reliable testimony that Bakunin was sexually impotent. The adherents of this theory, however, have failed to provide any other evidence. If there are any unequivocal references to the subject in the letters of Bakunin's other intimates, his biographers have not found them. Carr, in fact, tells us that this was "a subject on which silence was rarely broken between Michael and his friends."[35] He does not explain why these intense young people, who in their correspondence analyzed the most intimate aspects of their own and each other's lives in almost painful detail, exhibited such uncharacteristic reticence in this case. But if, as Carr maintains, no explicit references to Bakunin's impotence have been preserved, and the subject was rarely even alluded to among those who knew about it, how can we know that it existed? Without further corroboration, there is no justification for continuing to claim that it did exist, or even that it might have existed.

This is not the end of the story, however. In 1852, from the depths of the Petropavlovsk Fortress, Bakunin wrote a long, rambling letter to his family (a letter that was in fact withheld by the tsarist authorities and never delivered). In this letter Bakunin addresses himself at length to his brother Alexander and the latter's recent bride, Liza. Among other things, he urges Alexander to renounce his philosophical interests lest he come to grief like his older brother. All he has achieved from his own study of philosophy, Bakunin declares, is a decided aversion to it, "and my philosophical dreams have ended not in the sweet realm of love, but in a narrow prison cell." He tells Alexander to devote himself instead to cultivating his marriage, which must be based on complete equality between husband and wife, and he dwells at length on the marital relationship. In addition, the letter contains an unmistakable erotic element: three times he refers to his new sister-in-law's sparkling eyes, which he has been told are a beautiful emerald green.[36] What could have been more natural than for the desperately lonely Bakunin, languishing in solitary confinement, to have concluded that he had sacrificed too much in the way of personal

fulfillment in his exclusive devotion first to philosophy and then to revolution? In 1858, just a year and a half after he was released from prison
and allowed to settle in Siberia, he married a comely eighteen-year-old of
Polish extraction, Antonia Ksaver'evna Kviatkovskaia (Kwiatkowska).
Bakunin's biographers have had to reconcile the fact of his marriage with
their belief that he was incapable of having normal sexual relations.

To the adherents of the impotence theory, Bakunin's marriage has
brought the proverbial "bad news and good news." On the one hand,
Bakunin did enter upon a formal relationship with a member of the opposite sex and sustained it until his death eighteen years later. On the
other hand, biographers have been able to argue that whatever Bakunin's
motivations in contracting it, the circumstances of the marriage actually
confirm the impotence theory, because, they maintain, it was a sexless
marriage—what the French call a *mariage blanc*.

To explain the inconvenient fact of the marriage, those of Bakunin's
biographers who have been persuaded of his incapacity for normal marital
life have resorted to a number of purely speculative hypotheses. Steklov,
for example, suggested that it was part of Bakunin's effort to gain respect-
ability in the eyes of the authorities and permission to move freely around
Siberia, in preparation for his eventual escape.[37] Bakunin did refer to the
necessity of supporting his wife when he petitioned to be allowed to travel
in Siberia,[38] but this would scarcely explain why he sent for her when he
reached Western Europe and remained with her for the rest of his life.
Steklov also speculates that perhaps Bakunin's "incapacity" was made
fully clear to him only after the marriage,[39] but if this were the case, how
could Katkov and Belinskii have been so certain of it back in 1840? Carr,
in what seems an utter non sequitur, tells us in a single paragraph that
Bakunin all his life enjoyed feminine adoration; that "his impotence had
saved him from the impulse to concentrate his emotion on a single object";
and that, lonely and adrift in Siberia, he would naturally fall in love with
the first young woman who would pay attention to him.[40] A closer look
at the marriage reveals that it was without doubt the object of a deep and
abiding emotional commitment for Bakunin, and, though we have less
evidence of Antonia's feelings, apparently for her as well.

Bakunin's letters from Siberia informing his family and friends of his
marriage reflect considerable depth of feeling. In a letter to Herzen at the
end of 1860, he wrote that while living in Tomsk he had become friendly
with a Polish family (Antonia's father was privately employed in the gold-
mining industry), had begun to teach the two daughters French, and had
won the "complete trust" of one of them. "I loved her passionately," he
told Herzen, "she loved me also—so I got married, and I've been married

for two years now and utterly happy. It's good to live not for oneself but for someone else, especially if that someone is a dear woman."[41] He even initiated a correspondence with Katkov, notwithstanding their quarrel of many years earlier, and, in a very matter-of-fact tone that cannot but add to our suspicion of Belinskii's report of that quarrel, informed him in one of his letters, "I got married three months ago and am utterly happy."[42] Elsewhere he refers to his wife as "a friend and angel" whom he will cherish as the flower of his old age.[43]

Having fled Siberia and made his way to London, Bakunin was prepared to move heaven and earth to bring Antonia to him. He bombarded his brothers and sisters, other relatives, and various friends and acquaintances with requests for money and assistance for Antonia's journey. In one letter asking his siblings for help, he assures them that they will love Antonia once they get to know her. But the real point, he adds, is that "I love her and I need her."[44] To Antonia herself, he writes: "My heart has pined for you. Day and night I see only you."[45] Steklov, in some bewilderment, devotes an entire chapter of his biography to Bakunin's efforts. He concedes that the "real passion" he displayed does not accord with "everything that we know about Bakunin's family life, if that is the term for it," but "apparently he loved his wife, at least at this time, with a real masculine love."[46]

But what of Antonia and her feelings? Steklov simply ignores the question, and Carr in effect dismisses it, along with Antonia herself. First, Carr writes that there were few eligible suitors in Tomsk. In fact, we do not know how many suitors may have been available to Antonia. We do know, however, that she was very attractive—visitors to the Bakunins in Italy a few years later testify to this[47]—and it might well be asked why a pretty eighteen-year-old felt it necessary to settle for a forty-four-year-old political exile, penniless and with as few prospects as he had teeth (thanks to the scurvy he had contracted in prison), even if he was a Russian nobleman. Carr then characterizes Antonia as a "naturally submissive woman" of the sort "who want nothing more than to let a man settle their destiny for them. . . ."[48] This seems an inappropriate description of the young woman who now left her family, to whom she was deeply attached; journeyed to Premukhino to meet a crowd of new in-laws whose approval of her could not be assured; went on to St. Petersburg, where she was required to sign a pledge that she would never return to Russia (though she was allowed back in 1872 to visit her family); then traveled alone to London, only to discover that her husband had gone to Stockholm, where she finally caught up with him.[49] Furthermore, neither Steklov nor Carr—nor, for that matter, anyone else—has asked why an attractive young woman, who by now would have had ample opportunity to find out that her husband was incapable of marital relations, nevertheless made such an effort to follow him into an émigré life fraught with grave uncertainties. Yet, she not only did so but in her letters to her in-laws upon her arrival in Western Europe expressed her great happiness at being reunited with her husband.[50] In the absence of any evidence to the contrary, we can only assume that the marriage was founded on a substantial degree of mutual attraction.

In the early years of the Bakunins' life together in Western Europe, friends and acquaintances sometimes expressed puzzlement over the marriage, but only because the couple seemed so mismatched. Herzen, for example, in an article written in 1865, declared that he could explain how Bakunin came to get married only on the grounds of "Siberian boredom." The passage in which he makes this statement, however, refers solely to Bakunin's gypsy habits, the unsettled, impecunious way of life of a perpetual student that seemed incompatible with the responsibilities of marriage.[51] Visitors to the Bakunins often remarked on how little they seemed to have in common: they differed in their interests, political commitment, age, and even size—the diminutive Antonia scarcely came up to Bakunin's chest, one observer wrote, rather like a pony and an elephant at the circus.[52] Another acquaintance, a young Russian named G. Vyrubov, went so far as to refer to a "pseudo-marital association," but, lest this phrase be misconstrued, it would be well to quote the entire statement:

> It was a strange marital, or, rather, pseudo-marital association. Why this perpetual vagrant, this typical homeless person, found it necessary to get married, he probably didn't know himself.
> "With your tastes and habits, how did it come into your head to get married?" I asked him when we had become better acquainted.
> "Somehow, it just happened."

Nevertheless, Vyrubov continues, Bakunin loved his wife very much and was very solicitous of her welfare. "Look at my Tosia," Bakunin said to him, "She's my little dummy [*ona u menia glupen'kaia*] and doesn't share my convictions at all, but she's very sweet, extraordinarily kind, and does a wonderful job of recopying important manuscripts for me when I need to keep my handwriting from being recognized."[53] As for Antonia, the few letters of hers from the 1860s reflect contentment with their life in Italy and confirm the picture of a warm and affectionate relationship between two very different individuals.[54] We have no way of knowing what the sexual content of the relationship was, but Bakunin's biographers have turned up no indications, even in the form of rumors or gossip, that this was a *mariage blanc*.

Nevertheless, the marriage has been taken as the ultimate proof that Bakunin was impotent, for, beginning in 1868, Antonia gave birth to three children whose father was not Bakunin but one of his Italian political associates, Carlo Gambuzzi, whom Antonia was to marry after Bakunin's death. That Gambuzzi was the father of Antonia's children seems fairly certain, though it is not entirely beyond doubt. Bakunin himself, who was very fond of them, sometimes referred to "her children," that is, Antonia's, but sometimes also to "our children."[55] Both James Guillaume and Armand Ross (Mikhail Sazhin), however, who were closely acquainted with Bakunin in his last years, state unequivocally that the children were Gambuzzi's.[56] The boy's name, Carluccio, also seems to point to Gambuzzi's paternity.

As far as can be determined, then, between 1868 and Bakunin's death in 1876, his wife bore three children of whom he was not the father. That is all that can be determined, however; the circumstances behind this situation, whether sexual or otherwise, remain unknown. This tells us nothing about the first ten years of the marriage or about why the Bakunins apparently did not have any children together. Those of Bakunin's associates who were aware of the family's circumstances make no allusion to impotence. Guillaume, for example, claimed to have been told that Bakunin had married his wife in Tomsk in order to save her from a compromising situation (there is no evidence that this was in fact the case). According to "some of Bakunin's most intimate Russian friends," Guillaume's account continues, he had told her that in accordance with the principles embodied in Chernyshevskii's *What Is to Be Done?*, he intended to respect her freedom absolutely.[57] Though Chernyshevskii's novel had not yet been published at the time of the marriage, it is not implausible that some such arrangement might have existed. Bakunin was a consistent advocate of the freedom and equality of women, from his youthful efforts to "liberate" his sisters from unsuitable marriages to his marital advice from prison to his brother Alexander.[58] It is at least possible, then, that the last years of Bakunin's marriage reflected the "progressive principles" popular among the Russian intelligentsia of the time.

If so, this marriage might not have seemed nearly as peculiar to Bakunin's contemporaries as it would today. Bakunin's peers displayed a marked taste for bizarre though amicable triangular relationships. E. H. Carr, in *The Romantic Exiles*, has described with considerable sympathy Herzen's London ménage, where Herzen, Ogarev, and Ogarev's wife all lived in the same house while Herzen fathered children by Mrs. Ogarev. (Gambuzzi paid visits to the Bakunins in Switzerland and gave them financial assistance, but at least they had the delicacy not to move him into the house with them!) There is also the case of Ivan Turgenev, who spent much of his life in love with the opera singer Pauline Viardot—an affair that may or may not have been consummated—while getting along famously with her husband and the rest of her family.[59] Given the vast differences between the Bakunins, Antonia's eventual liaison with a younger man is perhaps less remarkable than the bonds of affection and loyalty that held the marriage together until Bakunin's death. In 1872, for example, when Antonia and the children left to visit her relatives in Russia, Bakunin recorded sadly in his diary, "Separation; for how long? a year? forever?" And when they returned two years later he celebrated their arrival with a fireworks display.[60] For her part, although Bakunin's habitual insolvency subjected Antonia to considerable insecurity and humiliation and gave her a good deal of justification for seeking alternatives, she never abandoned him. At the time of his death in Berne she was in Italy making arrangements for the two of them to resettle there; hastening back to Switzerland but arriving too late for the funeral, she was described by an eyewitness as virtually prostrate with grief.[61]

In sum, we really know nothing about the sexual side of the Bakunins' marriage. What we do know about their life together, however, lends no more credence to the impotence theory than any of the other "evidence" that has been presented in its support.

Finally, it must be pointed out that the adherents of the impotence theory have not only failed to marshal any real evidence for it but ignored indications in the Bakunin literature that contradict it. In 1930 the widow of one of Bakunin's most assiduous biographers, A. A. Kornilov, published a compilation of letters of Bakunin's relatives and friends. Included was a brief quotation from a letter to the Bakunin family by Genrikh Kraevskii, a Pole with whom Bakunin had become acquainted in Siberia. Writing from Moscow on 16 February 1862, Kraevskii reported having learned that Bakunin had fathered a son whose present whereabouts were unknown. A footnote to the quotation relates that in the papers of A. A. Kornilov (who died in 1925) copies of documents were found indicating that Bakunin had in fact fathered a son in Siberia. The note then spelled out the details of the story.[62] In 1979, Natalia Mikhailovna Pirumova, Bakunin's Soviet biographer, in a letter to me provided a possible corroboration of that account and supplied some additional details. The story goes as follows.

On 1 November 1860, a newborn boy was abandoned at the home of a civil servant in Irkutsk named M. N. Maslovskii. Maslovskii adopted him, but records of the Ecclesiastical Consistory state that the godparents at the child's christening were "state criminal Mikhail Aleksandrovich Bakunin" and Ekaterina Petrovna Golenishcheva-Kutuzova, the wife of a retired official. The child received the given name *Mikhail* and the patronymic *Mikhailovich.* At the end of 1862 Maslovskii took the child to Moscow and placed him in the Foundling Home—possibly in connection with Bakunin's escape from Siberia, which would have interrupted the arrangements for the boy's support and drawn the attention of the authorities investigating the escape. The boy was subsequently given into the care of a peasant family on the estate of the Bagrianovskii family near Moscow. When it turned out that the child answered to the name Misha Bakunin he was adopted by the Bagrianovskiis, was educated at Moscow University, and became a lawyer in Moscow. He had four children, the eldest of whom, Mikhail Mikhailovich, became a music and theater critic who wrote under the name Bakunin-Bagrianovskii. The youngest son, Andrei Mikhailovich, also an expert on music, was still living in Moscow at the time Pirumova wrote to me and was the source of the information she furnished in her letter.[63]

We have no way of knowing whether, or to what degree, this story has any basis in historical fact. For our purposes, however, it hardly matters. What the story tells us is that the impotence theory is not only based wholly on conjecture, but on selective conjecture at that. The supposed allusions to Bakunin's sexual impotence must be weighed against the rumors that he sired a child, and the latter actually seem more substantial than the former. All the more reason, then, to bury the impotence theory at last.

Although the personal relationships of the young idealists of the 1830s began to interest Russian historians in the early years of the twentieth century, the impotence theory in regard to Bakunin was slow to make its appearance among them. Two prominent historians of the intelligentsia, Paul Miliukov and Ivanov-Razumnik, examined the tension between ideal love and earthly love in the intellectuals of the thirties without discerning any sexual dysfunction in Bakunin. This was the case also with A. A. Kornilov, whose two-volume biography, based on the Bakunin family archives, began to appear in serial form in 1909. Both Ivanov-Razumnik and Kornilov quoted Belinskii's account of the Bakunin-Katkov quarrel, but neither drew any sexual inferences from it.[64] It would appear, then, that the appearance in 1920 of the first edition of volume 1 of Steklov's monumental biography marks the debut of the impotence theory in Russian historiography.[65]

Once introduced, the theory proved remarkably resilient. It was accepted by Viacheslav Polonskii, who, along with Kornilov and Steklov, was the third major Soviet scholar of Bakunin in the 1920s. Referring to Bakunin's marriage, Polonskii wrote: "The question of Bakunin's family life is obscure. We know only that Bakunin had no children and could not have any."[66] It also figured in a curious debate between Polonskii and the literary scholar Leonid Grossman over the figure of Stavrogin in Dostoevskii's novel *The Possessed*. Composed of equal parts of erudition and academic venom, the debate raged through several literary societies and journals between 1923 and 1925. Grossman had somehow become convinced that Bakunin was Dostoevskii's real-life model for Stavrogin. He was adamantly opposed by Polonskii, who argued, more convincingly, that there was only the most superficial resemblance between Stavrogin and Bakunin and that the Petrashevist Nicholas Speshnev was a more likely historical source. One of the arguments Grossman used to support his position was that both Stavrogin (in his relationship with Liza Drozdova) and Bakunin were sexually impotent. On Bakunin, he cited Steklov's biography, Polonskii himself, and Belinskii's account of the quarrel with Katkov. Polonskii countered that although there was good reason to believe that Bakunin had been impotent, there was no indication in the novel that Stavrogin was![67] At this point the debate took a strange turn. In his rejoinder to Polonskii, Grossman backed off from his assertion about Bakunin. Referring only to "some available information," he now stated that the assertion that Bakunin was childless required reexamination, and that "his 'sexual deficiency' was apparently not a continual and unconditional phenomenon." Although he did not identify the source of the "information" or its content, one may surmise that he had heard from Kornilov, who was still alive at the time, the story of Bakunin's illegitimate son. Grossman refused to give up entirely, however, now contending that both Stavrogin and Bakunin could have suffered from intermittent, or temporary, impotence rather than a lifelong defect.[68]

Iurii Steklov was similarly unfazed, even after the publication by Kornilov's widow in 1930 of the details concerning Bakunin's reputed child. In the exhaustive commentaries to his four-volume edition of Bakunin's works and letters that appeared in 1934–35 (cut short when Steklov fell victim to Stalin's purges), he reiterated the impotence theory even more dogmatically than he had in his biography.[69]

The development of this theory reached a culmination of sorts in 1934 with the publication of a small book by Ivan Malinin, *The Oedipus Complex and the Fate of Michael Bakunin*. Malinin reiterated the allegation that Bakunin was impotent, relying, like so many others, primarily on Belinskii's letter,[70] but this theme was submerged, along with incest and infantilism, in the broader psychosexual interpretation announced in the book's title. Malinin saw Bakunin's unresolved struggle against his father as the real and immediate source not only of his distorted family relationships but of his political opposition to the Russian autocracy and his anarchist struggle against authority. Even Steklov, while taking Marx's side in the struggle

within the International, had given Bakunin considerable credit as a heroic rebel against the existing order. It was Malinin who first reduced
Bakunin's political and ideological position to the level of a personality
disorder. Bakunin was not a real revolutionary, he contended; his revolt
was of a purely psychological order, and his revolutionary struggle was
nothing but a symbolic projection of his internal, individual struggle.[71]
Although E. H. Carr did not cite Malinin's book, it was this reductionist
viewpoint that he incorporated into his 1937 biography, which lodged it
firmly in English-language historiography.

In view of the extreme flimsiness of the theory of Bakunin's sexual impotence, it should be asked why it has been repeated without closer examination by so many historians of such diverse ideological stripes and
historical interests. The answer seems to be simply that it made such a
good story. Here was the delicious paradox of a man who rejected power
as evil and was himself powerless in one vital regard; a man who urged
apocalyptic destruction of the external order but harbored a fundamental
internal passivity; a man who preached the liberation of mankind from all
authority but could not free himself of a crippling inner constraint. As an
apparent insight into this highly complex and contradictory individual it
has proved irresistible not only to historians repelled by Bakunin's political stance and eager to discredit it, but to those who merely savor the
ironies of history. If, however, this seeming paradox is founded on nothing more than a legend, it behooves future historians and biographers to
undertake the difficult search for a new key to the intricate interplay of
Bakunin's personality, anarchist thought, and revolutionary career.

It can at least be said, however, that the perpetrators of this legend have
had some illustrious company. Just as the theory of Bakunin's impotence
was developing, a very similar one was being created about the novelist
Henry James—and by no less a figure than Ernest Hemingway. In his
autobiography, James had referred to "an obscure hurt" that he suffered
at the age of eighteen. James was very vague about this injury, but, in the
words of his biographer Leon Edel, in the 1920s critics began to draw "a
relationship between the accident and his celibacy, his apparent avoidance
of involvements with women and the absence of overt sexuality in his
work." The result was a "theory" that the injury he had suffered
amounted to castration and had rendered him sexually impotent. Edel
identifies Hemingway as the creator of the legend, but it was subsequently accepted and repeated by such critics as R. P. Blackmur and Lio-
nel Trilling. According to Edel, James's account of his accident, lacking
in specifics and filled with inconsistencies, may have been no more than
a way of justifying his lack of participation in the Civil War; if it was a
real injury, it was probably nothing more than the recurrent backache he

complained about later in life. It was an obscure hurt, indeed, but it did not make James a eunuch.[72]

Many questions remain about Bakunin's personal life, and, given the historical documentation, we may simply have to forgo the hope of ever finding the answers. A biographical myth such as the impotence theory, however, is not an acceptable substitute for such answers. It tells us no more about the character and politics of Michael Bakunin than it does about the literary themes and prose style of Henry James.

NOTES

1. E. H. Carr, *Michael Bakunin* (New York: 1961), 24. This book was first published in 1937.
2. Ibid., 25.
3. Ibid., 255, 257, 272, 328, 498.
4. Edward J. Brown, *Stankevich and His Moscow Circle, 1830–1840* (Stanford: 1966), 66; E. Lampert, *Studies in Rebellion* (New York: 1957), 114.
5. Lampert, *Studies in Rebellion*, 124–25. Lampert accepts without reservation the assertion that Bakunin's later marriage was sexless (275, n. 26), a subject that will be dealt with later in this article.
6. Anthony Masters, *Bakunin: The Father of Anarchism* (London: 1974).
7. Aileen Kelly, *Mikhail Bakunin: A Study in the Psychology and Politics of Utopianism* (Oxford: 1982), 30.
8. Arthur P. Mendel, *Michael Bakunin: Roots of Apocalypse* (New York: 1981), 28, 360, 447–48, n. 75; see also his "Bakunin: A View from Within," *Canadian-American Slavic Studies* 10, no. 4 (Winter 1976), 466–87. By contrast with these English-language works, Bakunin's most recent Soviet biographer omits this theme entirely. See N. Pirumova, *Bakunin* (Moscow: 1970). In a curious, and instructive, variation on this theme, Barbara Alpern Engel in a recent work makes the statement that Bakunin "may have been homosexual, bisexual, or impotent" (*Mothers and Daughters: Women of the Intelligentsia in Nineteenth-Century Russia* [Cambridge: 1983], 22). Engel cites no sources for this statement, but her book draws both on Carr and on Philip Pomper's *Sergei Nechaev* (New Brunswick, N. J.: 1979). Pomper does not repeat the impotence theory, but he does recount a passage from Carr concerning a rumor that Bakunin once gave Nechaev a document promising him complete obedience, even to the point of forging banknotes if necessary, and, as a token of his submission, signed it with a woman's name, "Matrena." Pomper comments that this may have been "more significant" than Carr believed, although "it is virtually certain that no open homosexual relationship existed" (232). Pomper cites only Carr on the subject. Turning to the latter (392), we find him declaring that "the story is too lightly attested to warrant credence," and if Bakunin did use such a signature it "was not invested with the significance which rumor attached to it." Carr does not explain just what that sig-

nificance was, nor does he cite any source for the story. Iurii Steklov, on whose biography of Bakunin Carr relied heavily, did accept the authenticity of the note with the Matrena signature but refers to it only in passing, without commenting on it. *Mikhail Aleksandrovich Bakunin, ego zhizn' i deiatel'nost' (1814–1876)*, 4 vols., 1 (Moscow: 1920); 2–4 (Moscow-Leningrad: 1927), 3, 436. He does, however, identify the original source of the story: a note by M. P. Dragomanov in his edition of Bakunin's letters to Herzen and Ogarev. There, Dragomanov relates a rumor he heard in Russian émigré circles in Switzerland in the 1870s that this document had been found among Nechaev's papers after his arrest. As to the signature, Dragomanov says only that "As a mark of the complete renunciation of his own will Bakunin even signed this paper with a woman's name, Matrena if we are not mistaken." M. P. Dragomanov (ed.), *Pis'ma M. A. Bakunina k A. I. Gertsenu i N. P. Ogarevu* (Geneva: 1896), 343. If I have traced this chain of references correctly, it is a variation in miniature on the larger theme of this essay: vague rumors that Bakunin once signed a note to Nechaev with a woman's name eventually turn into the assertion that Bakunin may have been homosexual.

9. Steklov, *Bakunin*, 1, 36; Carr, *Michael Bakunin*, 25; Kelly, *Mikhail Bakunin*, 30; Mendel, *Michael Bakunin*, 28. Arthur Mendel, who finds in Bakunin's "revulsion towards sexuality" a leitmotif of his personality, detects even earlier evidence of it. At the age of fourteen, Bakunin was sent to the Artillery School in St. Petersburg, where he was very lonely and unhappy. According to Mendel (10), Bakunin in his letters home contrasted "the dark, filthy, and vile side of life" that the barracks taught him with "the pure and virginal" life he had known at Premukhino. These phrases actually occur not in a letter Bakunin wrote while at the school but in one to his parents nine years later, in 1837; he does not specify any sexual element in the "vileness" to which he refers, and what he actually wrote was: "Until now my soul and my imagination had been pure and virginal [or innocent: *devstvennyi*]." M. A. Bakunin, *Sobranie sochinenii i pisem*, Iu. M. Steklov (ed.), 4 vols. (Moscow: 1934–35), 2, 106. Having quoted these two phrases, Mendel then proceeds to repeat one or the other, or both, at least sixteen times, by my count: pp. 12, 22, 26, 29, 53, 67, 70, 71, 73, 88, 95, 109, 111, 112, 291, 449, n. 82. An inattentive reader might well forget that it is not Bakunin who is reiterating these phrases so many times and charging them with such significance, but Mendel.

10. A. A. Kornilov, "Semeistvo Bakuninykh," serialized in *Russkaia mysl'*, 1909–14, and published in book form as *Molodye gody Mikhaila Bakunina* (Moscow: 1915).

11. Carr, *Michael Bakunin*, 21–22.

12. One was a cousin, Maria Voeikova. See his letters to his sisters in the spring of 1833, *Sobranie sochinenii*, 1, 76–89. The other, in 1838, was another cousin, Sophia Murav'eva. See ibid., 2, 142, 152. In regard to the latter, he asked his sisters to keep his infatuation a secret from the Beers—Alexandra, like Natalia previously, now apparently had a crush on him. Ibid., 142, 445.

13. Steklov, *Bakunin*, 1, 36.

14. A. I. Gertsen, *Sobranie sochinenii v tridtsati tomakh* (Moscow: 1954–64), 7, 354.

15. Steklov, *Bakunin*, 1, 64–66; 4, 458–62. For a discussion of this issue, see Kelly, *Mikhail Bakunin*, 72–75.
16. Carr, *Michael Bakunin*, 25.
17. Bakunin, *Sobranie sochinenii*, 1, 166.
18. Ibid., 170.
19. Ibid., 452.
20. Ibid., 172.
21. V. G. Belinskii, *Polnoe sobranie sochinenii*, 13 vols. (Moscow: 1953–59), 11, 542.
22. Bakunin, *Sobranie sochinenii*, 2, 434. In their accounts of this episode, both S. Nevedenskii, *Katkov i ego vremia* (St. Petersburg: 1888), 59–63, and the more recent biography by Martin Katz, *Mikhail N. Katkov: A Political Biography, 1818–1887* (The Hague: 1966), 30, rely on Belinskii as their source.
23. Belinskii, *Polnoe sobranie sochinenii*, 11, 544.
24. Ibid., 559.
25. Ibid., 12, 31.
26. D. N. Ushakov (ed.), *Tolkovyi slovar' russkogo iazyka*, 4 vols. (Moscow: 1935–40), 4, col. 228. That Belinskii tended to employ such words metaphorically is indicated by his use—in reference to himself!—of the expression "moral masturbation" in a letter to Bakunin of 2 November 1837. *Polnoe sobranie sochinenii*, 11, 196.
27. Belinskii, *Polnoe sobranie sochinenii*, 11, 336, 346.
28. Ibid., 350.
29. Ibid., 522, 524.
30. Carr, *Michael Bakunin*, 72–73.
31. Belinskii, *Polnoe sobranie sochinenii*, 11, 291, 301. In a similar vein, Arthur Mendel twice states that Herzen described Bakunin in 1848 as an "old Joan of Arc," a "maiden" as she had been. *Michael Bakunin*, 448, n. 75; 493, n. 154. His source is not Herzen himself but Pavel Annenkov, and it is clear from the context that Herzen was referring jokingly to what he considered to be Bakunin's political innocence, not to his sex life. The following is the passage from Annenkov:

> Bakunin was always ready to exhort people to unsullied feats, to the immaculate life, to the idealistic conception of life's tasks. That was what prompted Herzen at that very time (1848) to dub him in jest "an old Joan of Arc," adding that Bakunin, too, was a "maid," though not *of* but *anti*-Orleans, inasmuch as he despised the king, Louis Philippe . . . of Orleans.

P. V. Annenkov, *The Extraordinary Decade: Literary Memoirs*, trans. Irwin R. Titunik (Ann Arbor: 1968), 27.
32. Bakunin, *Sobranie sochinenii*, 3, 98, 107, 110, 164, 166. It should be noted, however, that such expressions of loneliness and self-doubt seem to occur largely in 1842, a time when Bakunin, now permanently in emigration and turning to politics, was burning his bridges behind him. In 1845, he would write to one of his brothers that he was passionately in love. Ibid., 245.
33. Belinskii, *Polnoe sobranie sochinenii*, 11, 295–303; 12, 16.
34. Ibid., 11, 232.

35. Carr, *Michael Bakunin*, 72.
36. Bakunin, *Sobranie sochinenii*, 4, 210–14, 220, 222.
37. Steklov, *Bakunin*, 1, 354, and 3, 410; Bakunin, *Sobranie sochinenii*, 4, 570.
38. Bakunin, *Sobranie sochinenii*, 4, 286.
39. Steklov, *Bakunin*, 3, 410.
40. Carr, *Michael Bakunin*, 239.
41. Bakunin, *Sobranie sochinenii*, 4, 368.
42. Ibid., 296.
43. Ibid., 300.
44. Steklov, *Bakunin*, 2, 21.
45. Mikh. Lemke (ed.), "Vosemnadtsat' pisem M. A. Bakunina," *Byloe*, no. 7 (July, 1906), 196. Even before he reached London, in fact from the moment he set foot in the United States, where he spent two months after escaping from Siberia, he had begun making the arrangements that would reunite him with Antonia. See Paul Avrich, "Bakunin and the United States," *International Review of Social History* 24 (1979), pt. 3, 321, 328.
46. Steklov, *Bakunin*, 2, 20–21.
47. Ibid., 299, 300.
48. Carr, *Michael Bakunin*, 239.
49. Steklov, *Bakunin*, 2, 23–24.
50. E. Kornilova (ed.), "Pis'ma zheny M. A. Bakunina (Iz arkhiva sem'i Bakuninykh)," *Katorga i ssylka*, no. 3 (88) (1932), 116–17. Carr states (239) that only "one insignificant letter" of Antonia's has been preserved, but A. A. Kornilov's widow had published this series of letters, dating from 1863 to 1868, five years before Carr's book appeared.
51. "M. Bakunin i pol'skoe delo" (pub. 1871), in Gertsen, *Sobranie sochinenii*, 11, 361.
52. Steklov, *Bakunin*, 2, 378.
53. Ibid., 318.
54. See, for example, Antonia to the wife of Bakunin's brother Paul, 25/12 March 1866, in Kornilova (ed.), "Pis'ma zheny," 124; also Bakunin's letter to his brother Paul from Sorrento, 1865, quoted in Steklov, *Bakunin*, 2, 313.
55. For example, Steklov, *Bakunin*, 3, 411; 4, 334, 348. The oldest child was a boy, followed by two girls. Steklov in one place (3, 411) refers to the second child as a son, but this was evidently a mistake.
56. James Guillaume, *L'Internationale: documents et souvenirs (1864–1878)*, 4 vols. (Paris: 1905–10), 1, 181–82, 261; A. Ross, "Bakunin i ego villa 'Baronata'," *Golos minuvshego*, no. 5 (May 1914), 208. See also A. Bauler, "M. A. Bakunin nakanune smerti, " *Byloe*, no. 7/19 (July 1907), 76–78. Alexandra Bauler was a Russian student in Switzerland who came to know Bakunin in the last months of his life.
57. Guillaume, *L'Internationale*, 1, 108.
58. A letter to his brothers and sisters of 1 May 1845, for example, contains a ringing declaration of women's liberation:

> Women almost everywhere are slaves and we ourselves are slaves of their bondage; without their liberation, without their complete, unlimited freedom our freedom

is impossible. . . . A man loves only to the degree that he wishes and calls forth the freedom and independence of another—complete independence from everything, even, and especially, from himself.

Sobranie sochinenii, 3, 252.

59. E. H. Carr, *The Romantic Exiles* (Boston: 1961; first pub. 1933), chap. 8; Leonard Schapiro, *Turgenev: His Life and Times* (New York: 1978), esp. 70–72.

60. Steklov, *Bakunin*, 4, 211, 342.

61. Ibid., 442.

62. E. Kornilova (ed.), "Mikhail Aleksandrovich Bakunin v pis'makh ego rodnykh i druzei (1857–1875 g.g.)," *Katorga i ssylka*, no. 2(63) (1930), 68, n. 1. I wish to thank Dr. Miklós Kun of Loránd Eötvös University, Budapest, for bringing this neglected source to my attention.

63. Letter of N. M. Pirumova to the author, 18 June 1979. I am very grateful to Natalia Mikhailovna Pirumova and to Andrei Mikhailovich Bakunin-Bagrianovskii for their permission to use this information.

64. P. Miliukov, "Liubov' u 'idealistov tridtsatykh godov'," *Iz istorii russkoi intelligentsii: sbornik statei i etiudov*, 2d ed. (St. Petersburg: 1903; reprinted Hattiesburg, Miss.: 1970), 73–168; Ivanov-Razumnik, *Velikie iskaniia* (St. Petersburg: 1911), esp. 41–44, 167, n. 88; Kornilov, "Semeistvo Bakuninykh," *Russkaia mysl'*, 34 (June 1914), 27–28.

65. According to Kornilov (ibid., 28), Ivanov-Razumnik was the first to make use of the then unpublished letter from Belinskii to Botkin of 12–16 August 1840, the complete letter itself appearing only in 1914, in the collection of Belinskii's letters edited by E. A. Liatskii. This would help to explain why Steklov made no mention at all of sexual impotence in the brief biography of Bakunin that he published in Germany in 1913. See Georg Steklov, *Michael Bakunin: Ein Lebensbild* (Stuttgart: 1913).

66. Viacheslav Polonskii, *Mikhail Aleksandrovich Bakunin: zhizn', deiatel'nost', myshlenie*, 1, 2d ed. (Moscow-Leningrad: 1925; first pub. 1922), 455.

67. *Spor o Bakunine i Dostoevskom: stat'i L. P. Grossmana i Viach. Polonskogo* (Leningrad: 1926), 15–16, 53–54.

68. Ibid., 86. Arthur Mendel, also cognizant of the rumor of Bakunin's illegitimate son, makes the same argument (*Michael Bakunin*, 448). Surely, however, what is at issue here is not the nature of the affliction but whether it can be proved that Bakunin actually suffered from it.

69. Bakunin, *Sobranie sochinenii*, 2, 481; 3, 472–73; 4, 570.

70. I. Malinin, *Kompleks Edipa i sud'ba Mikhaila Bakunina: K voprosu o psikhologii bunta: Psikhoanaliticheskii opyt* (Belgrad: 1934), 66–71. See also the perceptive review of the book by V. Miakotin, "M. Bakunin, istolkovannyi po Freidu," *Poslednie novosti*, 5 May 1934, 2.

71. See esp. 9, 28–34.

72. Leon Edel, *Henry James: A Life* (New York: 1985), 57–61, 721–22.

THE ROOTS OF "JEWISH SOCIALISM" (1881–1892)

From "Populism" to "Cosmopolitanism"?

Jonathan Frankel

The term *Jewish socialism* as used in this article refers to those socialist individuals, groups, and emergent movements that sought, or at least hoped, to establish a political role for themselves or their ideas specifically within the Russian-Jewish world (which in the late-nineteenth century, of course, was still overwhelmingly Yiddish-speaking). The years between 1881 and 1892 represented a time of transition in the development of this phenomenon that, strictly speaking, was too inchoate and divided to be called a "movement" and can, perhaps, best be considered a subculture within the framework of the new Jewish politics. During the 1870s "Jewish socialism" was clearly identified with Aron Liberman and his extraordinary attempts to establish a Jewish section within the framework of the Russian and international socialist movement (the most notable of his undertakings, perhaps, being the publication of a Hebrew journal, *Ha–emet* [The Truth], aimed at disseminating socialist doctrines within the Pale of Settlement). From the mid-1890s "Jewish socialism" came to be represented in Russia primarily by the Vilna movement, which in 1897 officially established the Bund. No such clear focal point characterized the intervening period, which has attracted much less attention from the historians but nonetheless is not without intrinsic interest.[1]

As described in most histories of the subject, Jewish socialism in the 1880s and early 1890s (whether in the Pale of Settlement or among the immigrant masses in the West) was strictly "cosmopolitan" or "internationalist" in its ideology. Only by a long and complex process of evolution (so the argument goes) did the Bund and other parties eventually develop syncretic doctrines that combined socialism with some form of Jewish nationalism. This basic conception, for example, has always dominated Bundist historiography.

The fact that members of the intelligentsia were ready to make enormous efforts to organize Jewish workers in the Pale of Settlement, in the East End of London, or on the Lower East Side of New York is explained as the result of tactical and short-term considerations. In the one case, they were seeking to recruit agitators and propagandists to work in the Russian revolutionary movement; in the other, they had no choice but to work among the immigrant masses because they themselves hardly knew English. They were internationalists forced by circumstance, faute de mieux, to function within a narrow, Jewish framework.

It is, of course, true that among the *intelligenty* who laid the foundations of the Bund in Vilna were a number of men (such as Martov and Kremer) who had been forced to move there from St. Petersburg under the terms of their police exile. Both Shmuel Gozhanskii and Arkadi Kremer stressed in their memoirs that in the early 1890s the socialists saw the Jewish labor movement specifically as a training ground from which to recruit revolutionaries for the great industrial centers in the interior of Russia.[2] For his part, Abe Cahan (a delegate from the United Hebrew Trades in New York) could declare at the congress of the Second International held in Brussels in 1891 that the only reason and justification for an autonomous Jewish labor movement in the United States was the objective fact that the language of the immigrants was still Yiddish.[3] And, indeed, at the annual conferences of the movement in America, large signs on the walls read, "We are not Jewish, but Yiddish-speaking, socialists."[4]

Why, then (again according to the traditional historiography), did the Bund gradually move from "cosmopolitanism" to its own form of nationalism, adopting the demand for Jewish national autonomy in Russia at its fourth congress in 1901? This transformation is normally explained as the natural result of the decision taken in the early 1890s to transform the organization in Vilna from a small circle of *intelligenty* and workers into a mass movement. To broaden the social base inevitably meant to make concessions to Jewish nationalism. Or, as Martov put it as early as 1895:

> The more democratic our movement, the more materialist it becomes. . . .[5]
> The kind of worker we are seeking to influence is not the worker-*intelligent*
> but the average worker, a member of the masses with average demands. . . .[6] From the moment that we placed the mass movement at the
> center of our program we had no choice but to adapt our propaganda and
> agitation to the masses—that is, to make them more Jewish. As a result, we
> have won a new victory over attitudes borrowed from the bourgeois intelligentsia. . . .[7] We have to assign a more national character to our movement.[8]

This explanatory theory, however, is by no means as self-evidently logical as it might appear at first glance. Historical evidence does not support the view that simply because the Jewish proletariat was Yiddish-speaking, it was therefore ipso facto inclined to Jewish nationalism. And, conversely, the fact that the intelligentsia spoke Russian, for example, did not necessarily commit it to an "internationalist" weltanschauung. Furthermore, the ideological superstructure was not determined exclusively by the socioeconomic base. In reality, both in theory and in practice, the leaders and the masses interacted in complex and ever-changing ways.[9]

A natural result of the traditional approach has been the relative neglect of the 1880s in the historiography of emergent Jewish socialism. During those years, the movement developed primarily among the Jewish emigrants to England and the United States, and it has, for the most part, been considered axiomatic that it was essentially "internationalist" (or "assimilationist") in character. What was actually written at the time has rarely been subjected to critical scrutiny. Moreover, the socialist group in Vilna, the proto-Bund, which has attracted the greatest historiographical attention, was perceived as evolving according to its own inner dynamism, independently of the Jewish socialist groups in the West that were so far removed not only geographically but also—because of the different political environment—culturally. That the overseas "emigrations" could have exerted significant influence on the emergent movement within the Pale is a proposition that has not been systematically examined.

It is the intention of this article not to present new facts from the archives but to suggest a different framework for the interpretation of the published sources. Specifically, it will be argued that it is preferable to regard the years 1881–92 as constituting not one but rather two distinct periods in the history of Jewish socialism. In the years 1881–85, the radical *intelligenty* who sought ways to give a political lead to the Jewish masses in the Pale or in the immigrant communities in the West tended to think in terms that can be best characterized as "Jewish populism" or *narodnichestvo*. The populism of this period was in many essential ways similar to, and even influenced by, the so-called Hebrew socialism developed by Aron Liberman in the 1870s. But whereas Liberman had regarded himself as subordinate to the Russian populist movement (specifically to Lavrov's *Vpered!* group) this was by no means the case in the early 1880s, when Jewish politics increasingly came to be seen as autonomous.

The highly inchoate populism of 1881–85 gave way in the years 1885–92 to ideologies and organizations that were defined, and distinguished, with much greater clarity and sharpness. A process of polarization produced an ever-wider gap between the socialist (and anarchist) camp, which became militantly "internationalist," on the one hand, and that of Jewish nationalism, or proto-Zionism, which now developed as non-, or even anti-, socialist, on the other.

Nonetheless, there was not a total break dividing the two periods, and involvement with issues of specific concern to the Jewish people continued, albeit to a diminishing extent, to engage the attention of the "Yiddish-speaking socialists" even in the years 1885–92. The subsequent ideological development of the Vilna Group of Jewish Social Democrats (the proto-Bund) in the 1890s cannot be understood without taking into account the fact that a distinctive Jewish socialist movement had already evolved during the previous decade on the Lower East Side of Manhattan and in the East End of London; that this movement had its own distinct history; and that it exerted its own influence on the revolutionaries in the Pale of Settlement.

A number of general ideas (or, more exactly, trends of thought) were characteristic of Russian, and Russian-Jewish, "populism" as the term is used here. First, there was the belief that the true source of social wealth was physical labor, particularly farm work, and that this was the only legitimate source of livelihood. From this idea there followed the assumption that the intelligentsia owed a deep moral debt to the people (*narod*) and that it was therefore duty bound to devote itself to defending the interests, whether political or cultural, of the masses. Again, in accord with this same logic, there was a tendency to categorize the Jews in the Russian Empire as belonging for the most part to the stratum of the exploiters rather than to that of the exploited. The only safe escape route for the Jewish community was to reconstitute itself on totally new socioeconomic foundations, agricultural and egalitarian.

Beyond this, the *narodniki* tended toward voluntarism in their philosophical outlook and argued that both the individual and the "people" were ultimately free to decide their fate. In consequence, in general they assigned greater value to action than to thought, to praxis than to theory. They rarely constructed all-embracing or monistic ideological systems and opted for a self-conscious eclecticism, which drew freely on the ideas not only of Lavrov or Bakunin, for example, but also of Marx and Engels. Socialism and nationalism, in their view, did not necessarily contradict each other. On the contrary, so long as nationalism gave expression to folk culture and moved within the traditions of thought associated with, for instance, Rousseau, or Herder, it had a legitimate role to play. The future socialist order, so most *narodniki* believed, would permit the national peoples their own autonomy.

Once the general ideological framework within which the radical or left-wing Jewish intelligentsia developed is perceived to have been populist in character, no reason to expect hard-and-fast distinctions between socialism and Jewish nationalism during the period 1881–85 remains. On the contrary, there was bound to be a high degree of overlap.

Both the political movements that emerged in the years 1881–82 to work for an "exodus" from Russia, the Palestine-oriented Bilu and the Am Olam, which hoped to found a Jewish territory in the American west, can best be described as populist in character. During the period of the pogroms, the Jewish student youth in Odessa, Kiev, and other major cities entered the synagogues en bloc and in their uniforms (especially on the special days of fasting that were called at the time) in order to express solidarity and to offer their services to the Jewish people. On the one hand, these dramatic appearances can be seen as a gesture of mass repentance (*tshuva*) and thus, to some extent, as a renewal of a deep-rooted religious tradition. But, on the other hand, this was probably even more an example of a "going to the people" (*khozhdenie v narod*) in the best *narodnik* tradition. Indeed, at the time, M. I. Rabinovich (better known by his nom de plume, Ben Ami, "son of my people") applied this term to such demonstrations of support,[10] which culminated in the establishment of Am Olam in Odessa in 1881 and of the Bilu[11] in Kharkov in 1882.

Am Olam has been much neglected by the historians[12] of both Jewish socialism and of Zionism, presumably, in part at least, because its ideology was seen as essentially internationalist and alien to Jewish nationalism. However, in reality, there was a powerful strand of national consciousness in the movement. The goal of creating model cooperatives or communal colonies in the new world combined with the strong urge to "go to the people," to work on its behalf and in its name, to transform not only the world but also the Jewish nation. The choice of a Hebrew name, *Am Olam* ("Eternal People")—the title of a famous work of early Jewish nationalism published by Perez Smolenskin in 1872—itself illustrates this trend of thought within the movement.

At the time, in 1882, when large groups of the Am Olam were stranded in the Galician frontier town of Brody, many members (among them Ezra Shamraevskii and David Spivakovskii) made every effort to direct the movement to Palestine rather than to America.[13] Abe Cahan, who had joined the Am Olam in Balta, would later recall the mood prevailing among the young would-be colonists in Brody in 1882:

> We had arguments between us but the word "pogrom" united us all. Some were heading for Palestine; others to America. Some wanted to set up Jewish communes which would serve as a beacon for the entire world, while others did not even want to listen to such talk. But there was one feeling and one idea which we all shared: "The Jews in Russia are living day in and day out with their lives threatened by terrible danger. We are duty-bound to find a home for the Russian Jews. . . ." To the extent that we could, we worked together on behalf of our battered and bloodied people.[14]

As for the historiography of the Bilu movement, the trend has been in the other direction—to see it as essentially an integral subsector of the general nationalist, proto-Zionist (or Hibat Zion) camp. The existence of strongly radical tendencies within the group has been somewhat under-emphasized. In reality, one of the two dominant leaders of the Bilu, Moshe Mints, was known among his comrades in 1882 for his socialist inclinations.[15] And it is reasonable to assume that socialist ideas under-pinned his determination to ensure the establishment of a model collective farm where three hundred members of the group at a time could receive their agricultural training. True, the plan for the farm does not have to be seen as fully socialist, but there can be no doubting its strongly utopian character. Despite the insuperable difficulties, Mints refused adamantly to give up working for this grandiose project, which combined aspirations for radical change in both the social and the national spheres.[16] He stayed in Constantinople for over a year, exploring every channel in the hope of obtaining from the Ottoman government a decree (*firman*) that would grant the Bilu a sufficiently large tract of land. Together with other leaders of the group, he was even ready to consider accepting such a land grant in Syria should one not be obtained in Palestine. When he finally realized that this scheme had come to nothing, he and a group of his closest com-rades left Palestine in 1884. Three years later he initiated the publication of the first left-wing newspaper in Yiddish in New York (about which more will be said).

The pogroms in the early 1880s came as a traumatic shock to the Jewish student youth and intelligentsia in Russia and served to reinforce their populist impulse (except that the suffering *narod* was now perceived as Jewish rather than Russian). As a result, in this period, a measure of dialogue, interaction, and mutual influence between socialists and Jewish nationalists became characteristic in radical circles. The lines between the two camps became blurred. Ideas that they held in common—democra-tization, for example, or the self-liberation of the people—often appeared to be more important than the differences dividing them.

It was in 1882 that Pavel Axelrod wrote his brochure on socialism and the pogroms,[17] considered the possibility of mass Jewish settlement in Palestine, and even made efforts to ascertain Elisée Reclus's professional opinion about the technical feasibility of such colonization. Lev Deich, of course, strongly opposed the publication of the brochure, but he, too, in a letter to Axelrod, hinted that he might well agree to support the orga-nized emigration of the Jews to America.[18] Axelrod's close friend, Grigorii Gurevich, a veteran socialist, became a strong advocate of proto-Zionism in this period. And Gurevich began to compose Yiddish poetry out of a sense "of duty towards the democratic forces in Jewry—because of the need to develop the language of the masses as do Uspenskii and Zlatov-ratskii."[19]

In 1883, an exchange of letters between Elyohu Volf Rabinovich and Yehuda Lev Levin was published in the (Hebrew-language) paper *Hamagid*, which appeared in East Prussia. The two men were both well-known writers and had been associated in the 1870s with various episodes in the development of "Hebrew socialism." In the opening letter, Rabinovich expressed enthusiastic support for the idea of Jewish settlement in Palestine as one of the ways to solve the Jewish question. He identified, he wrote, with every nation fighting for its freedom. Nonetheless, he was afraid that the liberal leaders in the Hibat Zion (proto-Zionist) movement, such as Pinsker and Lilienblum, were too few and too weak to prevent its eventual domination by the forces of theocracy. The radical wing in Hibat Zion was clearly in the minority, and under such circumstances, he asked, did Levin believe that the movement had the moral right to call on the poverty-stricken Jewish masses to settle in Palestine, a country plagued by the harshest physical and economic conditions?

In response, Levin replied that before all else, the Jews had first to solve their specific national problem by the settlement of their own homeland. Once this essential goal had been achieved, they could then undertake to deal with socioeconomic issues and to construct a society based on the principles of justice: "Regardless of the quality of life in the Land of Israel, at least it will be one of independence."

> Now, let's consider what would happen if those many people who have dedicated themselves to the cause of mankind and to eternal justice were to succeed in bringing together the different nations into one fraternal union. Their entire effort would turn out to have been in vain if one large and entire nationality were to remain without independence, a mere appendix hanging on in part to one nation and in part to another. Such a development would serve as a real hindrance to the creation of a united human society living in peace and calm.[20]

This correspondence, which thus intermingled national and social (even utopian) themes, was in many ways typical of the thinking in Jewish radical circles at the time.

In 1884, a collection of articles on the new colonies in Palestine was published in St. Petersburg. In one of the essays, Iakov Rombro strongly opposed the negative attitude to Palestinian settlement adopted by the Alliance Israélite Universelle. He had expressed the same viewpoint in previous articles that he had published in the Russian-Jewish press. His argument was that "settlement in Palestine is the only way to realize the ancient ideals of Israel; and it [the center in Palestine] will have to be the full responsibility of the entire Jewish people."[21]

Rombro would become much better known in later years under the name Philip Krantz. In the early 1880s, he was already a veteran revolutionary, a onetime member of the Narodnaia Volia, who had been exiled as a political prisoner to Siberia. In 1883, he was among the founders of the Jewish Labor Society (Evreiskoe rabochee obshchestvo) in Paris, and in 1885 he was to be appointed as the first editor of the Yiddish-language socialist paper published in London, *Der arbeter fraynd*.

It was at this time, too, that Benjamin Feigenbaum first became politically active. Like Krantz, he too would gain his name primarily as a pioneer of the socialist press in Yiddish. But in the mid-1880s he was still publishing his articles in the Hebrew papers *Ha-magid*, *Ha-yom*, and *Ha-melits*, where he supported the idea of Jewish nationalism in modernized form. In his writings, he sought out universalist values and expressions of popular, or folk, creativity in Jewish history and in Judaism. He would later describe himself[22] as having been very close in his ideas in the mid-1880s to Asher Ginsburg, a proto-Zionist ideologist—better known as Ahad Ha-Am ("one of the people").

Within the leadership of the new proto-Zionist Hibat Zion movement, populist impulses were also at work in this period. The consistent backing that Pinsker and Lilienblum gave the Bilu group, in general, and its members who had set up the colony of Gedera, in particular, was motivated in large part by their conviction that their movement had to win the support of both the student youth and the popular masses. In his opening speech at the Kattowitz conference of Hibat Zion in 1884, Pinsker took as a central theme the vital necessity of transferring the Jewish people from urban to agrarian foundations, from trade in Europe to agriculture in Palestine.

> It is a fact that those who are hostile to us regard the [economic] activity of the Jews as opposed to justice and as illegitimate. For this reason alone—as well as to permit the steady development of our own potentialities—nothing could be better than to return the masses of our people who are degenerating as petty traders and artisans, to agriculture. The land willingly lets itself be exploited and even shows its gratitude to those who work it. It is more grateful than human beings, each of whom is ready to exploit his fellow men while denying to others, certainly to the Jews, the right to do the same to him. Things have come to such a pass, that our very existence in the world is regarded as exploitation.[23]

In the same year another leading figure in the movement, Yampolskii, wrote to Pinsker insisting that the latter's work, *Auto-Emancipation*, should long since have been translated into Yiddish, because "it is absolutely essential that the ideas included in it should reach the mass of the people [*seryi narod*]. If we could ensure that, we should not have to fear for the future of the people."[24]

On 1 February 1885, a new German-language journal, *Selbst-Emanzipation*, began to appear in Vienna, edited by Nathan Birnbaum. The name of the journal was borrowed from the title of Pinsker's book (which likewise had originally been published in German). One of the early issues of the journal contained an article that carried extensive quotations from *Rome and Jerusalem* by Moses Hess and argued that socialism could not possibly solve the Jewish question in the foreseeable future. But, the author granted, in the long run, "when the great struggle between capital and labor reaches its end, mankind will become one, and every individual aspiration will find its harmonious fulfillment within it."[25] Articles and news items that appeared in *Selbst-Emanzipation* were quoted frequently in the Yiddish journal, *Di tsukunft*, which had begun to appear in London in November 1884 (succeeding another Yiddish journal, *Der poylisher yidel*).

This latter publication has often been described (to use the words of Kalman Marmor, for example) as "the first socialist paper in the Yiddish language."[26] And this is understandable given the fact that in the 1870s Vinchevskii had been a supporter of Aron Liberman and would become known from the turn of the century as "the grandfather of Jewish socialism." He himself in his memoirs stated that *Der poylisher yidel* represented "the beginning of the Jewish socialist movement."[27]

However, it is more exact to characterize the journal as a vehicle for the populism that was then still the prevailing weltanschauung among important sections of the Jewish intelligentsia. Significantly, while Vinchevskii was the editor of the paper, the publisher was Elyohu Volf Rabinovich, who, as has already been noted, was tending at that time toward proto-Zionism. The two men reached an agreement to refrain from outright identification with the programs of Hibat Zion, on the one hand, and of the socialist movement, on the other.

This self-denying ordinance, however, did not mean that *Der poylisher yidel* was apolitical. The principles that guided Vinchevskii (with the acquiescence of Rabinovich) can be summarized succinctly. Modern, racial anti-Semitism had to be recognized as a grave threat to the very safety of the Jewish people. The pogroms in Russia were, then, not a transitory episode but rather symptomatic of a profound sociopolitical syndrome. The Jews had no choice but to find ways to grapple with this danger as effectively as they could. For its part, *Der poylisher yidel* aimed at raising the political consciousness of the Jewish immigrants from the Russian Empire who were then arriving in the East End of London. The immigrants, insisted the paper, needed their own organizations. To rail against political apathy was the primary duty that Vinchevskii took upon himself.

Given the collective danger facing it, the Jewish people had above all to form a united front. At the time of the pogroms in 1881–82, Jewish efforts to act as one had been impressive, but they had proved to be short-lived and had not culminated in any fundamental political change. *Der poylisher yidel* held up as a positive example "the Irish, the Poles, and other oppressed nationalities. They united behind a common goal; we unite only to provide aid and succor to each other."[28]

In the editorial article that he wrote for the first issue of *Der poylisher yidel*, Vinchevskii declared that "we regard the Jew from three angles: as a man, as a Jew, and as a worker."[29] He argued that these three characteristics of the immigrant masses were organically and inseparably linked. So, for example, he constantly called on the Jews to form trade unions in order to forestall accusations of undercutting the existing wage level. At the same time, he insisted that the Anglo-Jewish establishment set up public kitchens and hostels for the new arrivals and for the unemployed as a concrete expression of Jewish solidarity as well as respect for human dignity. Addressing the "Polish" Jews, he urged them not to be ashamed of, but rather to take pride in, their own culture and language. He granted that Yiddish had been formed out of "bits of Russian, Polish, and Lithuanian, interwoven with Hebrew, stitched on to some kind of old German, but nonetheless it is still a language just like any other."[30] And if the immigrants earned their living by manual labor, they had every reason to be proud of the fact, for, by so doing, they put paid to the slander that the Jews were nothing but parasites and profiteers.

Der poylisher yidel devoted much space to news of developments in the Jewish world, particularly to cases of anti-Semitism, pogroms, and blood libels, as well as to Jewish efforts to formulate effective modes of response. It carried many reports on the agricultural colonies set up by the Am Olam and other Russian-Jewish groups in America. And it also contained items, albeit less frequent, on the new settlements in Palestine. There was an entire series of articles on the history of English Jewry in the Middle Ages with heavy emphasis on the ceaseless persecution that had characterized that history.

In his important study of the Yiddish press in the East End of London in the 1880s, Elhanan Orren[31] states that Elyohu Volf Rabinovich emerged as a champion of Jewish nationalism in 1886—which is to say, after he ended his association with Vinchevskii. And it is true that only in that year did Rabinovich come out in full support for the proto-Zionism of the Hibat Zion movement. However, as against this, the populism that reached full expression in *Der poylisher yidel* and *Di tsukunft* under the joint control of Rabinovich and Vinchevskii can be regarded with every justification as in itself a specific form of Jewish nationalism.

However, it was in 1885 that populism first clearly began to lose its predominant hold on the radical intelligentsia involved in Jewish affairs. In July of that year another Yiddish journal, *Der arbeter fraynd*, was established in London. Philip Krantz (Rombro) was appointed as editor, and Vinchevskii became an active contributor.

Initially, Vinchevskii had been opposed to this new experiment, but a number of socialists belonging to the next generation had insisted on going ahead with it. The editorial statement in the first issue of *Der arbeter fraynd* made it crystal clear that it was committed to a policy very different from that followed hitherto by *Der poylisher yidel* and *Di tsukunft*. Its declared goal was "to disseminate the ideas of real socialism among the Jewish workers . . .; to bring about a fundamental change in the prevailing conditions of tyranny and injustice which permit the few to have millions of pounds, and the many to have nothing." [32] The gap between the new and the older surviving journal (*Di tsukunft*) grew from 1886 onward, producing an open, bitter dispute. *Der arbeter fraynd* insisted, for example, that nothing positive could be expected from national liberation movements such as that of the Irish, whereas, on the other side, *Di tsukunft* (now under the sole control of Elyohu Volf Rabinovich) gave enthusiastic support to the Hibat Zion movement.

In the United States, too, a similar evolution was to be observed during this same period, 1885–90. As a result, for example, the major left-wing Yiddish journals published in the East End and on the Lower East Side in the year 1890—*Der arbeter fraynd* in London, *Di arbeter tsaytung* and *Di fraye arbeter shtime* in New York—could maintain a demonstrative silence with regard to political issues of specifically Jewish interest.

In Russia, the radical and revolutionary Jewish youth did not produce any Yiddish journals at that time, but there, too, it is possible to observe a similar polarization that would result in a division, both clear-cut and hostile, between the camps of "international" ("cosmopolitan") socialism and Jewish nationalism.

This trend (observable alike in the Pale of Settlement and in the "emigrations") can best be explained by the changing character and fortunes of the Jewish nationalist experiments (including those with a populist character), on the one hand, and of the general socialist and anarchist movements in Europe and America, on the other.

By the late 1880s, the various national groups and parties that had sprung up in Russia in response to the pogroms of 1881–82 were in clear decline. The last of the surviving Am Olam colonies established in the United States, New Odessa in Oregon, broke up in 1887. Gedera, the settlement founded in Palestine by members of the Bilu, barely managed to struggle on with a mere handful of colonists. As for the colonies associated with the Hibat Zion movement, they had become totally dependent for their economic survival on the goodwill of, and the huge subsidies supplied by, Baron Edmund de Rothschild in Paris. And he insisted on the instant removal from the colonies of anybody suspected of radicalism or "nihilism" in any shape or form.

Moreover, the movement in Russia had come to rely on a constant series of compromises between the secular and modernizing leadership of Pinsker and Lilienblum and the traditionalist rabbis, such as Mohilever, Eliasberg, Berlin, and Spektor, who had identified themselves with Hibat Zion. Not one new colony was established in Palestine in the period 1886–90, and the claim of the movement to be able to solve the Jewish question was thus coming to seem utterly utopian, if not downright ridiculous. Even Ahad Ha-Am, who was emerging as a central ideologist of Hibat Zion, now came to the conclusion that the basic socioeconomic problem of East European Jewry (the question of "bread") would find its solution through massive emigration to the American continent. For its part, the proto-Zionist movement, as he saw it, could at best create no more than a relatively small "spiritual center" in Palestine, marked by quality, not quantity: a focal point for the Jewish people in the modern, postreligious world.

In marked contrast, while Jewish nationalism in its various manifestations was thus in clear disarray, the socialist and labor movements in general were enjoying a period of unprecedented success. In Germany, the Social Democratic party was gaining strength steadily, defying the severe restrictions imposed on it by Bismarck's exclusionary legislation. The anarchist movement in the United States likewise grew in public stature as the government acted against it—particularly when, after the Haymarket case in Chicago in 1886, a number of its members were executed. In 1889, the strike of the dock workers in England achieved mass support on an extraordinary scale.

It is thus hardly cause for surprise that many of the radical Jewish *intelligenty*, who had previously been drawn to populist amalgams of nationalism and socialism, should now conclude that the upsurge of specifically Jewish political action following the pogroms had been simply unrealistic and that the Jewish problem, like all other mere symptoms of social disease, could only be cured by striking at the root cause—by social revolution.

After the Haymarket affair, Vinchevskii published a Yiddish poem that gave authentic expression to the new sense of hope and confidence in the socialist future of mankind, *Es rirt zikh* ("On the Move"):

Hert ir, kinder, vi es rirt zikh,
Merkt ir az der sof komt?
Forverts kinder, s'marshirt zikh,
Lustik bay der royter fon?[33]

The existence of two tendencies on the socialist Left—the anarchist and the Marxist, which were crystallizing into two separate and rival movements during the 1880s—had the effect of discouraging everything that smacked of "particularism" or "nationalism." Within the Russian-Jewish intelligentsia the Marxists and the anarchists now increasingly competed with each other to demonstrate their complete commitment to the class war and to the cause of social liberation without regard to national differences.

Nonetheless, the polarization between Jewish nationalism and international socialism, however dominant in the period 1885–92, did not even then become all-encompassing. Thus, for example, during the first two years of its existence, *Der arbeter fraynd* (which was then still being published on the press of Elyohu Volf Rabinovich) continued to devote considerable space to issues of specifically Jewish concern. True, the political line was now strictly socialist, but the editors were ready enough to conduct polemical disputes against the Hibat Zion movement and its ideology.

Morris Vinchevskii, Joseph Jaffe, and Isaac Stoune published many articles that set out to prove that the tsarist regime and not the Russian people had been responsible for the pogroms, and that a fundamental improvement in the situation of the Jews in the Pale would therefore result from the revolutionary overthrow of the established political and social order. Vinchevskii even went so far as to argue that the swing of the masses toward Jewish nationalism in the wake of the pogroms was comparable to the betrayal of Moses by the Children of Israel in the desert, making and worshipping the Golden Calf. In these articles the Jewish question was still central, but the solutions were proletarian and universalist.

In 1886, Ilya Rubanovich published an article entitled "What Should the Jews Do?" in the journal of Petr Lavrov, *Vestnik "Narodnoi voli."* He there maintained that the Hibat Zion movement had aroused messianic expectations that had proved false, and that the only solution to the Jewish question was the social revolution. But at the same time, Rubanovich (who at the turn of the century would become a prominent member of the

Socialist Revolutionary party and who in 1883 had been among the founders of the Jewish Labor Society in Paris) described the new colonies in Palestine in a favorable light and even toyed with the idea that they might be able to act as a base for the revolutionary movement in Russia:

> It is a cause for satisfaction that beyond the frontiers of Russia, a number of well-established Jewish colonies have been set up. Just as the Irish emigrants offer help [to Ireland], so [these colonies] can aid their co-nationals in Russia in their struggle against those economic conditions which make it impossible for all the Jews, tied down there as they are, to begin to live as human beings.[34]

In 1886, as mentioned previously, Moshe Mints (until shortly before one of the leaders of Bilu), established the first labor paper in Yiddish in the United States, *Di nyu yorker yidishe folkstsaytung*. This journal was strongly reminiscent of *Der poylisher yidel* in its ideological approach. In the opening editorial, Mints declared unequivocally that the Jewish question had to be seen as a distinctive issue in its own right and not as a mere aspect of the social problem in general. The working Jew, he wrote, "has, as a worker, many brothers; but as a Jew he has only a few. The Jewish problem is very important, and it demands the investment of great thought if we are to find the right solution."[35] In this editorial he assured the readers that much space would be devoted to issues of Jewish concern and to Jewish history.

Despite the clearly populist tone that suffused the journal, it was well received in left-wing circles on the Lower East Side, and Mints became one of the central figures in the Jewish Labor Union (Der yidisher arbeter ferayn). This measure of latitudinarianism, in decline throughout the late 1880s, was narrowed still further in 1890 with the appearance of two new Yiddish journals, the one Marxist or Social Democratic and the other anarchist, which struggled hard against each other to attain hegemony on the Left. (The *Folkstsaytung* had closed down in 1889.)

However, even in the period of radicalized conflict between the Marxists and the anarchists, there were still cases of young *intelligenty* who saw Yiddish-language socialism as a way for them to express certain Jewish loyalties rather than simply as a concession imposed by technical problems, a second best.

Benjamin Feigenbaum describes in his memoirs how in 1887, as a young socialist then in Belgium, he reached the conclusion independently that the time had come to create a socialist journal in the Yiddish language. He was overwhelmed with excitement when he discovered that such a paper, *Der arbeter fraynd*, was already in existence, and he at once wrote a letter to Philip Krantz. Soon afterward, he and his wife moved to London and he began work as a writer for the paper.[36]

Again, Shmuel Rabinovich, the son of the well-known *maskil* ("enlightener") and proto-Zionist Shaul Pinhas Rabinovich, invested enormous efforts in the attempt to have S. Dikshtein's socialist booklet, *From What Does Man Live?* (originally published in Polish), brought out in a Yiddish translation. Eventually he managed to do so, thanks to active assistance offered by Petr Lavrov and the well-known leader of the Polish socialist movement, Stanisław Mendelson.[37] The booklet was printed on the press of *Der arbeter fraynd* in London and appeared in 1887 under the imprint of the Yiddish-Language Socialist Library.[38] (It is worth noting here, too, that Vinchevskii had already brought out his agitational brochure, *Let There Be Light*, in Yiddish, translated from Hebrew, in 1885 under the imprint of The Jewish People's Library [Yidishe folks-bibliotek].[39])

Word of Rabinovich's "Library" reached Haim Zhitlovskii in the town of Vitebsk. He reacted with great enthusiasm and looked for ways to join the group that (he assumed) stood behind the enterprise.[40] In the same year, 1887, Vinchevskii published as a Yiddish booklet the speech in which Petr Lavrov had declared that internationalist socialism was particularly attractive to Jews because of factors deeply rooted in their collective history such as faith in the Messianic age and their age-old dispersion among the nations of the world.[41]

Such phenomena, which still carried the clear mark of Jewish populism, became, as already noted, ever less frequent toward the late 1880s and early 1890s. While the "Yiddish-speaking" movement, with its trade unions and rapidly burgeoning press, was growing by leaps and bounds, active interest in Jewish affairs went into sharp decline. But there was never a time without some exceptions to the rule. Strict "internationalism" (or "cosmopolitanism") never became universally accepted by the Left on the Lower East Side or in the East End.

The most consistent in their rejection of Jewish particularism in every shape and form were the anarchists, who prided themselves on their total rejection of everything established. In contrast, the Marxists, the Social Democrats, were in favor of participation in the existing political system including elections—if only as an agitational device—and they therefore tended to show greater flexibility in their search for the mass vote. Abe Cahan, for example, was determined to win an ever-larger reading public for the socialist journals that he edited and insisted that the Yiddish be popular in style and the contents of wide appeal. In his memoirs he would describe his work in the Jewish labor movement as "going to the people."[42] Thus, it is not surprising that it was Cahan who placed the subject of anti-Semitism on the agenda of the congress of the Second

International in 1891—nor, likewise, that in his paper, *Di arbeter tsaytung*, he chose not to report on the fact that the congress condemned not only anti-Semitism but also "philo-Semitism."

Cahan and the group of "Yiddish-speaking" Social Democrats to which he belonged had no specific program dealing with the Jewish question, but, at the same time (unlike the anarchists), they were not committed to ignoring the creative aspects of Jewish life. Even in the years 1891–92, for example, Cahan could write extensive criticism of Yiddish literature and Yiddish drama. His pen name, the "Proletarian *Magid* [Preacher]," suggests the duality characteristic of his attitude to "socialist cosmopolitanism."

The socialists who defined themselves loosely as "social revolutionaries" (as opposed to both the "anarchists" and the Social Democrats) tended to retain somewhat more of the populist ethos. This fact found public expression when the anarchists in 1891 gained control of *Der arbeter fraynd* in London, turning it into their "party" journal. In response, Vinchevskii, Feigenbaum, K. Liberman, and others of like mind set up a rival journal in which they criticized "internationalism" in its then prevailing form. K. Liberman could write there, for example:

> We have to be Jewish and, on no account, to be ashamed of that. We have to be somewhat national; to be Jewish patriots a bit. Of course, such patriotism must not be exaggerated. We cannot be Palestinian patriots. We should unite with all the socialists who advocate internationalist ideas, and yet we should still remain national (not nationalistic). Have you ever heard, for example, of an English trade union which calls itself "International"? But among the Jews it is customary to use this term in naming all unions . . . . The Jewish socialists behave in this way as though by so doing they can change the length of their noses and their Pinsk habits.[43]

In the same year, 1892, Haim Zhitlovskii's book, *A Jew to the Jews*, was also published in London, albeit in Russian. Zhitlovskii there, of course, rejected in toto the idea that socialist work among the Jewish masses should be regarded as of secondary importance and of merely auxiliary value. He, too, belonged to the camp of "social revolutionaries," dogged eclectics in a period of hardening doctrinalism.

It is known that many of the Yiddish journals published in the West, including *Der poylisher yidel* and *Di nyu yorker yidishe folkstsaytung*, reached the socialist circles in Vilna from at least as early as 1887–88, and that they were received there with true enthusiasm.[44] This fact should surely be given its due weight in explaining the clearly nationalist ideas that are to be found in two of the earliest doctrinal statements to issue from the

Vilna Group of Jewish Social Democrats—Gozhanskii's "Letter to the Agitators" of 1893 and Martov's May Day address (quoted previously) of 1895. By then, after all, a radical and socialist press in Yiddish—initially populist in character—had been in continuous existence in the Russian-Jewish centers of the West for some ten years. As a potentiality, a synthesis between socialist internationalism and Jewish nationalism was there waiting to be discovered, especially but not only in the journals that appeared in the years 1884–85. The motto of *Der poylisher yidel* came from Psalms: "When thou eatest the labor of thy hands, happy shalt thou be" (128:2) and was printed in Hebrew. *Der arbeter fraynd* also carried a motto in Hebrew: "If I am not for myself, who will be? And if I am for myself alone, what am I?" ("Ethics of the Fathers," 1:14).

NOTES

This article (in somewhat different form) was originally a paper delivered at the World Congress of Jewish Studies held in Jerusalem in 1981 and was subsequently published in Hebrew: "Shorshei ha-sotsializm ha-yehudi (1882–1890)—me-amoniyut (narodnichestvo) yehudit le-kosmopolitiut," Proceedings of the Eighth World Congress of Jewish Studies: Panel Sessions: Jewish History: Hebrew Section (Jerusalem: 1984), 21–33.

1. By far the most important historical research on Jewish socialism and the labor movement in the 1880s was that carried out by Elyohu Cherikover in the YIVO Institute primarily before the Second World War. Without the documents and articles that he (and other colleagues, most notably Abraham Menes) then published, much less would be known about this period. See, for example, Cherikover et al. (eds.), *Historishe shriftn* 3 (Warsaw and Vilna: 1939), and E. Cherikover (ed.), *Geshikhte fun der yidisher arbeter bavegung in di fareynikte shtatn*, 2 vols. (New York: 1943–45). (Abbreviated English edition: *The Early Jewish Labor Movement in the United States*, translated and revised by A. Antonovsky [New York: 1961]).

2. A. Kremer, "Mit 35 yor tsurik," *Undzer tsayt* 2 (February 1928), 83; S. Gozhanskii, "Evreiskoe rabochee dvizhenie nachala 90-kh godov," *Revoliutsionnoe dvizhenie sredi evreev*, introduced by S. Dimanshtein (Moscow: 1930), 82.

3. See, for example, "Rabochee dvizhenie v 1891 godu," *Sotsial-Demokrat* 4, no. 2 (1892), 105.

4. S. P. [Peskin], "Vi fun yidish-shprekhende sotsyalistn vern mir yidishe sotsyalistn," *Forverts*, 3 June 1903, 4.

5. [L. Martov (Iu. O. Tsederbaum)], *Povorotnyi punkt v istorii evreiskogo rabochego dvizheniia* (Geneva: 1900), 11.

6. Ibid.

7. Ibid., 18.

8. Ibid., 21.

9. For a fuller discussion of this point, see J. Frankel, *Prophecy and Politics: Socialism, Nationalism and the Russian Jews 1862–1917* (Cambridge: 1981), 171–200.

10. M. [M. I. Rabinovich], "Vliianie protivuevreiskikh bezporiadkov na evreev," *Volnoe slovo* 37, 15 May 1882, 11.

11. Bilu is an acronym based on the verse "House of Jacob, come ye and let us go" (Isaiah 2:5). The name first adopted by the group was *Dabyu*, also an acronym, drawn from another Biblical phrase: "Speak unto the Children of Israel that they go forth" (Exodus 14:15).

12. The two best known articles on Am Olam in Russia are A. Menes, "The Am Oylom Movement," *YIVO Annual of Jewish Social Science* 4 (1949), 9–33, and H. Turtel, "Tnuat 'am olam'," *He-avar* 10 (1963), 124–43. See also E. Mendelsohn, "The Russian Roots of the American Jewish Labor Movement," *YIVO Annual of Jewish Social Science* 16 (1976), 150–77.

13. D. Spivak, "Erinerungen fun Kahan's grine tsaytn," in *Yubileum-shrift tsu Ab. Kahans 50-stn geburtstog* (New York: 1910), 30; E. Raevskii, "Mayn ershte bagegenish mit Ab. Kahan," ibid., 24. See also A. Druianov (ed.), *Ktavim letoldot hibat tsiyon ve-yishuv erets yisrael*, 1 (Odessa: 1919), 33.

14. A. Cahan, "Kishinev! Kishinev!" *Forverts*, 19 May 1903, 4.

15. See, for example, the letter from Vladimir (Zeev) Dubnov to his brother, Simon, in *Ktavim le-toldot hibat tsiyon . . .* , 3 (Tel-Aviv: 1932), 497.

16. In her very important study, based in large part on previously unexplored archival materials, Shulamit Laskov argues that in general the statutes of Bilu reflected not socialist, or social, but only nationalist aspirations (a determination to advance the plans for Jewish agricultural settlement). However, when they are seen against the contemporary background of Russian radicalism, the plans for a model colony would appear, rather, to be suffused with populist modes of thought. See S. Laskov, *Ha-biluim* (Tel Aviv: 1979), 160–63.

17. P. B. Axelrod, "O zadachakh evreisko-sotsialisticheskoi intelligentsii," V. S. Voitinskii, B. I. Nikolaevskii et al. (eds.), *Iz arkhiva P. B. Akselroda (Materialy po istorii revoliutsionnogo dvizheniia II)* (Berlin: 1924), 215–27. On this episode, see A. Ascher, "Pavel Axelrod: A Conflict between Jewish Loyalty and Revolutionary Dedication," *Russian Review* 24 (1965), 249–65.

18. L. G. Deich (ed.), *Gruppa "osvobozhdenie truda" (Iz arkhivov G. V. Plekhanova i L. G. Deicha)* 1 (Moscow: 1923), 153, 160.

19. G. E. Gurevich [Gershon Badanes], "Sredi revoliutsionerov v tsiurikhe," *Evreiskaia letopis'* 4 (1926), 102–3.

20. Yehuda Lev Levin [Yahalel], "Miktav le-Or: mi-ze ehad u-mize ehad," *Hamagid* no. 20, 23 May 1883, 164. See also *Ktavim le-toldot hibat tsiyon*, 3, 556–59.

21. Y. Rombro [P. Krantz], "'Alians' i Palestina," *Palestina: sbornik statei i svedenii o evreiskikh poseleniiakh v sv. zemle* (St. Petersburg: 1884), 127.

22. B. Feigenbaum, "Dos letstes vort: vegn der Dreyfus geshikhte un der gmore," *Di arbeter tsaytung*, 16 October 1898, 4.

23. *Ktavim le-toldot hibat tsiyon*, 1, 278.

24. Ibid., 126.

25. M. Lion, "Was thun?" *Selbst-Emanzipation*, 8, 18 May 1885, 2.

26. K. Marmor, *Moris Vintchevski: zayn lebn, virkn un shafn* (published as vol. 1 of Vinchevskii's *Gezamelte verk*) (New York: 1928), 103.

27. M. Vinchevskii, *Erinerungen*, 2 (vol. 10 of *Gezamelte verk*) (New York: 1927), 122.

28. "Yidishe akhdes," *Der poylisher yidel* 5, 8 August 1884, 21.

29. "An der lezer," ibid., 1, 25 July 1884, 1.

30. "Yidish," ibid., 3, 8 August 1884, 9.

31. E. Orren, "Ha-publitsistika ha-yidit be-mizrah london ba-shanim 1883–1887," *Ha-tsiyonut* 2 (1971), 47–73 (see specifically 59–60); E. Orren, *Hibat tsiyon be-britanya* (Tel Aviv: 1974).

32. "Fun der redaktsyon," *Der arbeter fraynd* 1, 15 July 1885, 1. On the Jewish socialists and anarchists in London in this period, see, for example, L. P. Gartner, *The Jewish Immigrant in England, 1870–1914* (London: 1960), 106–37; and W. S. Fishman, *East End Jewish Radicals 1875–1914* (London: 1974), 135–214.

33. K. Marmor, *Moris Vintchevski; zayn lebn, virkn un shafn*, 134. A free translation would be "Do you hear, children, how things are moving? Don't you see that the end is coming? Forward, children, march along, gladly under the red flag."

34. I. Il'iashevich [Rubanovich], "Chto delat' evreiam v Rossii?" *Vestnik "Narodnoi voli"* 5 (1886), 114.

35. "Di programe fun di N. y. yidishe folkstsaytung," *Di nyu yorker yidisher folks-tsaytung* 1, 25 June 1886, 1. (See E. Lifschutz, "Ha-'yidishe folks-tsaytung' be-nyu york," *M'asef* 7 [1975], 4–48.)

36. B. Feigenbaum, "Dos letstes vort . . . ," *Di arbeter tsaytung*, 16 October 1898, 4.

37. S. Rabinovich, "Mit 50 yor tsurik—fragmentn fun zikhroynes," *Historishe shriftn* 3, 329–36.

38. Jan Młot [S. Dikstein], *Von vos eyner lebt?* (published by the Sotsyalistishe bibliotek in yidish-deytsh) (London: 1887).

39. M. Vinchevskii, *Yehi or: eyn unterhaltung iber di farkerte velt mit zayn fraynd Hayman* (London: 1885).

40. H. Zhitlovskii, *Zikhroynes fun mayn lebn* 3 (New York: 1940), 145.

41. *Peter Lavrov un di yidishe arbeter* (London: 1887). See, too, E. Cherikover, "Peter Lavrov and the Jewish Socialist Émigrés," *YIVO Annual of Jewish Social Science* 7 (1952), 132–45.

42. A. Cahan, *Bleter fun mayn lebn* 3 (New York: 1926), 198.

43. K. Liberman, "Di yidishe arbeter in England un di yidishe sotsyalisten," *Di fraye velt* 4 (September 1892), 93.

44. See, for example, T. M. Kopelzon, "Di ershte shprotsungen (zikhroynes)," *Arbeter luekh* 3 (Warsaw: 1922), 67; S. Rabinovich, "Mit 50 yor tsurik . . . ," *Historishe shriftn* 3, 329; *Di geshikhte fun der yidisher arbeter bavegung in rusland un poylen* (Geneva: 1900), 20; [Y. Mil], "Varshe," *Der yidisher arbeter*, 2–3 (February 1897), 21.

GERMAN SOCIALISTS AND THE RUSSIAN
REVOLUTION OF 1905

Abraham Ascher

I t is a commonplace in the historical literature that the Russian revolution of 1905 served as a catalyst in radicalizing the German
Social Democratic party (SPD), the largest and most influential
workers' movement in the world. The standard account runs as follows: Surprised and overjoyed at the courage, persistence, and
achievements of the workers who demonstrated in large masses throughout the Russian Empire, German activists on the Left and industrial laborers came to believe that they, too, must adopt militant tactics to
promote their cause. "The news of Bloody Sunday in St. Petersburg (22
January 1905)," wrote Carl Schorske, "shook the socialist world of Germany." At last, the Marxist intellectuals' faith in the possibility of revolution appeared to be justified.[1] J. P. Nettl, the biographer of Rosa
Luxemburg, made a similar observation and in addition claimed that
"German Social Democracy developed a distinct feeling of solidarity with
the proletariat in Russia; here and there even muted calls for emulation
could be heard. . . . The party as a whole undoubtedly moved to the
left."[2] According to the historian Richard Reichard, the growing dissatisfaction in 1905 of a "large part of the German working class . . . with
the pace of progress toward socialism" must be attributed to the magne-
tism of the Russian revolution. Socialist leaders "of all varieties of belief,
who were in contact with the masses and had no particular reason to emphasize the Russian revolution as against their own efforts," readily acknowledged this at the time.[3]

For Communist historians the thesis of the revolution's powerful impact
on the German Left has been an article of faith, derived from the more
general contention that in 1905 Russia was "transformed into the real center of revolutionary thought and of the revolutionary cause."[4] Thus, in
a recently published book S. V. Tiutiukin contends that in 1905 the
German proletariat "in practice sought to apply 'Russian' methods of

struggle" not only by staging an increasing number of strikes but also by adopting "extra-parliamentary methods of political struggle."[5] An East German historian has argued that despite its ultimate failure, the Russian revolution "showed [the Germans] the way, gave them the necessary schooling . . . [and was] the touchstone for the revolutionary convictions of the German worker, for the conduct of the German Social Democratic Party."[6] Another historian has asserted that "the Russian Revolution of 1905 evoked an enthusiastic echo among the German working class" and that the Russian proletariat provided the workers in Germany with a "forceful example of revolutionary struggle."[7]

Although some evidence can be cited to support such sweeping generalizations, a careful examination of the assessments by German socialists of events in Russia in the period from 1904 to 1907 indicates that the Left's reactions to the upheaval were much more complicated. Despite their scorn for tsarism and admiration for Russian revolutionaries, prominent spokesmen from all wings of the SPD—revisionists, centrists, and radicals—voiced serious doubts about the tactics of their comrades in the east and rejected the notion that the strategies pursued by Russian socialists should be applied in Germany. With very few exceptions, scholars have ignored these reactions to the policies of the Left in Russia.[8] Yet it can be argued that the German socialists' reservations about the conduct of the Russian Leftists were a more accurate reflection of sentiment within the SPD than expressions of enthusiastic support that historians tend to emphasize. Certainly, the SPD's policies and behavior in the years from 1917 to 1920, when revolution again swept over Russia, support such a conclusion. To be sure, it would be an oversimplification to consider those reservations as the only cause of the SPD's unwillingness to emulate the Bolsheviks or even to come to their aid, two developments that shocked Lenin and his followers. By the same token, the behavior of most German socialists in that turbulent era cannot be attributed simply to a sudden change of heart by the SPD or to the treacherous behavior of leaders of the German working class. The truth is that from the moment that Russian Marxists became a political force of consequence in 1905, a substantial sector of the SPD recoiled from their maximalism. Perceptive observers of the debates over strategy and ideology within the German party should not have been surprised by its antipathy toward the Bolshevik system of rule after 1917.

It is likely that historians have been influenced in their interpretations of the impact of the revolution of 1905 on the SPD by the fact that the German Left to a man despised the autocratic regime in Russia and enthusiastically hailed the efforts to bring it down. *Vorwärts*, the main newspaper of the German Social Democratic party, reflected those sentiments in the coverage it gave to the upheaval. Six days after Bloody Sunday, when the strike movement of industrial workers spread to numerous urban centers, the paper cheerfully predicted that the people would most probably succeed in "casting off the chains of tsarism."[9] In the fall, *Vorwärts* declared that "The year 1905 is a wonderful year. It is as though the world has been transformed. Whereas previously it took several years to change fundamentally the relations between states and people, this has now happened in one stroke. . . . The Russian revolution, which under the leadership of Social Democracy is becoming a more powerful factor, has made possible that which even a short time ago was believed to be impossible."[10]

Moreover, *Vorwärts* sympathized with the views of the most militant segments of the Russian opposition. Thus, it deprecated the October Manifesto, which promised civil liberties and the election of a representative body with an important role in passing legislation for the empire. The editors of the paper declared that the manifesto was insignificant and that the revolutionary opposition must prepare for the next battle. Like the Leninists, they predicted that most liberals would now leave the proletariat in the lurch and would secure the rights promised by the tsar only for themselves. The liberals' slogan, *Vorwärts* declared, would be "calm and order," on the pretext that the manifesto signified the opposition's complete triumph over the old order. But the "class conscious proletariat" must not allow itself to be duped. Its slogan must be "Keep the powder dry, the sword unsheathed."[11] When the armed uprising occurred in Moscow in December 1905, the paper printed articles encouraging the insurgents in their struggle against the government.

Occasionally, a local socialist newspaper even predicted that the revolutionary fervor of the Russian masses would spread to other countries. "The gush of blood," wrote *Volksstimme* in Magdeburg on 22 January, "flows like a wide stream across the German border"; it would, *Volksstimme* stated, have the effect of rousing the masses in Germany from their apathetic mood.

The SPD expressed support for the revolution in various ways. Party congresses unanimously adopted resolutions to send socialist literature into Russia, collect money for victims of tsarist repression, urge the German government to end its friendly relations with Russia, and in general to offer "all possible moral, personal, and material support." The party congress at Jena in 1905 declared that "Russian despotism has through [its] barbaric furies condemned itself in the eyes of the civilized world, and it has therefore justified every means that is used to bring about its destruction."[12] Mass meetings in support of the revolution were held in numerous regions of Germany and by September 1907 almost 340,000 marks had been collected for the Russian Left.[13]

But the party's and the socialist newspapers' effusions of support were only one part of the story. The theoretical journals of the SPD analyzed the revolution and the pronouncements of Russian Marxists in great detail and came up with appraisals much more nuanced than those that appeared in the daily press or that were voiced at mass meetings. To be sure, the *Neue Zeit*, the most authoritative journal of international socialism, treated the Russian militants sympathetically and regularly ran articles on the revolution by such activists as Leon Trotsky, Parvus (Alexander Helphand), Iulii Martov, and Fedor Dan. But at the same time, it frequently carried long articles by Germans who, though orthodox Marxists, nevertheless took issue with Russian colleagues who believed in the imminence of a socialist revolution or who favored intransigent tactics.

Karl Kautsky is a good case in point. The preeminent theorist of German and international socialism, Kautsky took a keen interest in Russian affairs. Several leaders of Russian social democracy were close friends and went to great lengths to keep him informed about developments in their party and country. As was his wont, Kautsky reached conclusions that were at once bold and restrained: bold in their theoretical thrust and restrained in their practical implications.[14] On the one hand, he argued that the revolution was "not a local but an international event,"[15] and declared that "No regime in Europe resembles as closely the one in Russia as the German," suggesting that he believed that his country, too, could soon expect a revolution.[16] Indeed, the European bourgeoisie "instinctively feels" that the upheaval in the East will provoke "reactions" in the West and that the victories over the old regime by the Russian proletariat will strengthen the proletariat of the entire world. Kautsky agreed with that assessment and was sure that before long the "Russian revolution would pose the most difficult problems for the proletariat of all of Europe": they would have to decide how to help their colleagues in the East.[17]

But Kautsky also asserted that it was the peculiar conditions in Russia that had made it possible for the working class to emerge as a powerful political force. The Russian revolution could not be compared to the "great French revolution" or other upheavals in Western Europe, where the petty bourgeoisie, located primarily in the large cities, was the "leading class," the driving force, in the revolutionary movement. In Russia there was no comparable petty bourgeoisie; the liberals were predominantly landowners, who could not be counted upon to favor a genuine revolution for the simple reason that they feared the peasantry, the vast majority of the population. The peasantry yearned for more land, which it could secure only by confiscating the estates of the landowners. The liberals would never agree to that; only the socialists did not shrink from a massive redistribution of the land. Thus, Russia lacked the preconditions for bourgeois democracy: in contrast to the situation in the West, no

social class considered it to be in its interest to create a party that would
lead a joint campaign for political freedom by the bourgeoisie and proletariat. Consequently the industrial proletariat in Russia was "not an ap-
pendage to, or instrument of, the bourgeoisie"; it was an independent
class with independent aims.

Nevertheless, Kautsky asserted that it would be incorrect to designate
the revolution in Russia as a socialist revolution. "Under no circumstances
must the proletariat take power alone, [and] establish a [class] dictatorship.
For that, the proletariat of Russia is too weak and too underdeveloped."[18]
Kautsky did not rule out the possibility that the Social Democrats might
attain power in the near future, but he insisted that this could only happen
if they aligned themselves with another class, the peasants. And if that
came to pass, the Social Democrats would not be able to implement a
socialist program, for the peasants did not favor it. It seemed to Kautsky,
therefore, that the Russian revolution should be regarded as neither bourgeois nor socialist, but rather as a unique event that defied traditional
categories. It would fulfill tasks that were partially bourgeois and partially
socialist and would prepare the way for the full triumph of the latter. He
predicted that the revolution would "carry all of humanity in the capitalist
world a mighty step forward in its [progressive] development."[19]

In speaking of an alliance between the proletariat and peasantry Kautsky sounded very much like Lenin, who favored precisely that strategy
for the Social Democrats. But Kautsky was more insistent and outspoken
than Lenin in rejecting the possibility of an immediate turn to socialism.[20]
On occasion, however, he was carried away by his enthusiasm for revolution as such. Thus, after the December uprising in Moscow, he spoke
glowingly of the insurgents and, to the dismay of some of his colleagues
in his own party, suggested that Social Democrats were wrong to assume
that pitched battles against the authorities were now unfeasible. He repudiated Friedrich Engels's suggestion in his introduction to Marx's *Class
Struggles in France, 1848–1850*, published in 1895, that violent street
battles may no longer be the most effective means for the proletariat to
achieve power. "Only the era of the *old* battles at barricades has passed."
Kautsky declared. "That was demonstrated by the battle in Moscow,
where a small group of insurgents succeeded in holding on for two weeks
against superior forces equipped with all means of modern artillery."[21]

But German socialists who feared that Kautsky might now advocate
violent tactics for their party misread his intentions. Kautsky was quite
cautious about drawing lessons from Russia for Germany. A few months
before the Moscow uprising, he had in fact given a rather tame reply to
his own question of what should be done "to help our struggling brothers
in Russia: . . . For the time being, to be sure, we can do very little. The

most important thing we can do is to collect money; no less important, we must pull the mask from the face of all allies of the tsar and possibly make it more difficult for them to carry on with their dirty work."[22]

And in the spring of 1906 Kautsky also adopted a fairly moderate position on the duma, the representative institution granted by Tsar Nicholas. It is true that Kautsky expressed understanding for those socialists (Bolsheviks, Socialist-Revolutionaries, and Bundists) who insisted on boycotting the elections, which were based on a very limited suffrage. In a recent, unflattering portrayal of Kautsky, an East German historian, Hans-Jürgen Mende, praises him for this stand.[23] But in doing so, Mende ignores the fact that immediately after making certain critical statements about the duma, Kautsky developed a theme that closely reflected the position of right-wing Mensheviks, most notably Pavel Axelrod, who opposed the boycott of the elections. Kautsky argued that because a revolutionary situation still prevailed in Russia, the duma was bound to develop into the center of opposition to the autocracy. This would be highly desirable, because it would at last lead to a "revolution that was centralized" and therefore better capable of dealing out blows at the centralized government. "The logic of the situation will always drive the duma forward, or, in other words, the peasants and proletariat will always and with increasing intensity and vehemence prod the members of the duma [to take action], will always strengthen the left wing [of the duma, and] will always weaken their opponents, paralyzing them, and finally sweep them away." Under the circumstances, the boycott of the duma seemed to Kautsky to be "senseless."[24]

Rosa Luxemburg, the stormy petrel of the German Left, formulated her views more stridently than Kautsky, but her analysis of the revolution in Russia did not differ substantially from his. She also noted the absence of a progressive, urban petty bourgeoisie (*Kleinbürgertum*) in Russia, which necessarily placed the industrial working class in the position of the leading force in the upheaval. And, like Kautsky, she insisted that the revolution could not proceed beyond a bourgeois-democratic form of government.[25] But Luxemburg was much more inclined than Kautsky to view the militancy of the Russian workers—in particular their resort to mass strikes—as a model to be followed by the German proletariat. This was true even before she returned to Warsaw to participate in the revolution late in December 1905. Thus, at the congress of the German party in September 1905 she threw down the gauntlet to her more cautious colleagues during a discussion of the tactic of the mass strike (about which more later): "We see the Russian Revolution and we would be donkeys if we did not learn anything from it."[26]

Franz Mehring, the eminent historian and theorist of Marxism, appeared to echo most closely the views of the militant Marxists in Russia. On 1 November 1905, he published an article, "Die Revolution in Permanenz," in the *Neue Zeit*, whose very title overjoyed the editors of *Nachalo* ("The Beginning"), a journal that was even more radical than comparable publications put out by the Bolsheviks. It was in *Nachalo* that Trotsky and Parvus, among others, contended that Russia was in the throes of a socialist revolution. Eager for support, the editors interpreted Mehring to be saying the same thing and consequently published a translation of his piece in their journal. In a footnote they gleefully asserted that the article showed "that this outstanding historian and publicist of the German Social Democratic Party accepts a point of view on the Russian revolution that our sycophants and philistines try to depict as anarchism and Jacobinism."[27] But a close reading of Mehring's piece discloses that he did not agree with the arguments in *Nachalo*, even though he spoke glowingly of the achievements of the working class in Russia. He emphasized that the Russian proletariat did not possess the power "to jump over stages of historical development and to create in one moment a socialist society out of the tsarist autocracy." The new conditions prevailing in the country would not permit them to impose "a dictatorship of the proletariat" in Russia. At best, they could shorten and ease the path of their struggle for emancipation. Moreover, unlike many of the authors in *Nachalo*, Mehring did not deprecate the contributions of the liberals to the political emancipation of Russia. On the contrary, he insisted that the freedoms the liberals had gained for themselves should be extended to the working class and that this would be a progressive and significant step forward.[28]

The moderates and revisionists within German Social Democracy, a force to be reckoned with, were even more skeptical about a socialist revolution in Russia in the foreseeable future. This is not to say that they were any less pleased with the outbreak of the revolution in Russia. The *Sozialistische Monatshefte*, the organ of the revisionists, carried many accounts of developments in Russia, and the tone was thoroughly hostile to the old order. In the summer of 1904, for example, an anonymous article defended the assassination of the minister of the interior, Viacheslav Plehve. "The terror of the oppressed is directed at the terror of the autocratic government. It is downright superfluous to engage in investigations of whether or not assassinations of individuals are excusable or useful. They may not be either; they are simply the expressions of deep despair, and as such we must approve of assassinations in Russia."[29] Shortly after Bloody Sunday, Richard Calwer, one of the more vocal spokesmen of revisionism, contended that *all* means were justified in the struggle against the autocracy.[30] Early in 1906 an unsigned article in the *Sozialistische Monatshefte* depicted the Moscow uprising as a heroic event that spelled the beginning of the end of the autocratic regime. The significance of the violence in Moscow was not its immediate result, according to this article, but rather the fact that it took place at all. For Moscow was symbolically as important for Russia as Rome for the papacy. "What would have remained of the papacy if Rome had been destroyed by the Turks? And what will remain of tsarism if Moscow, the holy city of Russian Orthodoxy, is turned into the holy city of the Revolution? . . . Tsarism would cease to exist!" The author was convinced that the uprising would prove to be the turning point in the history of the Russian Empire.[31] It was a farfetched analysis, noteworthy only because it resembles the later contention of Soviet writers that without the insurrection in Moscow in 1905 the Bolsheviks' seizure of power in 1917 would not have been possible.

But even while lauding the most extreme tactics of the revolutionaries in Russia, the revisionists always insisted that they were not sanctioning mass violence in principle. Russia was a special case and the tactics appropriate in that country were not necessarily suitable to other countries, and most certainly not to Germany. In a constitutional state, Calwer argued, a revolution was "as senseless as it is unavoidable in a despotic [state]."[32] He did not so much as hint at the desirability of German socialists' emulating their Russian colleagues.

Eduard Bernstein, the founder and intellectual leader of revisionism, provided the most extensive commentary on events in Russia. His assessments in the *Sozialistische Monatshefte* can be said to have been at all times consistent with the basic thrust of revisionism, which was avowedly antirevolutionary. Bernstein was no apologist for tsarism. Nor did he fail to appreciate the broader implications of developments in Russia. "The question of the outcome of the Russian revolution," he wrote in March 1906, "is not simply a concern of the Russians. The entire political development of Europe will be influenced by it."[33] For precisely that reason, however, he considered it his duty to speak candidly and to point out the errors that, he believed, the Left was committing in Russia.

Like other German socialists, Bernstein contended that although the revolution in the East was different from those in the West in the seventeenth and eighteenth centuries, it could not lead to a socialist transformation of the country in the near future. To be sure, the cities and industrial centers were "playing the leading role" in the upheaval, but Russia's class structure and system of production were such that "any thought that the impending revolution would assume a socialist character appears to be hopeless utopianism." It could not be expected to achieve more than a "bourgeois-liberal-democratic" polity.[34] Bernstein placed the greatest value on such a polity and warned statesmen in the West against intervening in Russian affairs to prevent its emergence. Any attempt by them to do so should be met with rigorous action by "European democracy led by German Social Democracy."[35]

Bernstein criticized not only the immediate goals of the ultra-Left in Russia, but also its intransigence and lack of realism concerning its real strength. "Revolutionary optimism is a very good thing, but when it grows into fantasy, then it becomes dangerous for no one except the fighters themselves." The concentration on violence seemed to him to be senseless, for he could think of no example in history that demonstrated the possibility that people could artificially create a revolutionary situation. And he was appalled, early in 1906, by the arguments of socialists in Russia that the Moscow uprising was a laudable "step in the development" of the revolution and that preparations should be made for another such insurrection. True, at the beginning of the uprising in Moscow the chances for success appeared to be strong, because the tsar's troops seemed to be demoralized. But if that was really the case, Bernstein asked, why did the insurrection fail? If it was the result of a shortage of arms, then it was the "greatest mistake to initiate the uprising." If that was not the reason, then the revolutionaries committed an even more serious blunder. For it would mean that they had grossly misjudged the correlation of forces in the country and the temper of the people.[36]

In any case, it was evident to Bernstein that the failure of the uprising had "at least temporarily" strengthened the government. Under the circumstances, it seemed to him extremely unwise for the Left in Russia to focus on violent methods of struggle and to abjure the opportunity to participate in the political process. Bernstein was thinking of the elections to the duma, scheduled to take place in the spring of 1906, which the Bundists wanted to boycott in the hope of scuttling them.[37] If the tactic had any chance of success, Bernstein argued, it would be appropriate to adopt it, because the electoral arrangements amounted to an "unworthy fraud" for the working class. But it was clear to Bernstein that the elections would be held and that if the proletariat shunned them, it would be deprived of any influence in the new representative institution. Moreover, in the unlikely event that the revolutionary Left succeeded in preventing the elections, the bourgeoisie, which strongly favored them, would be driven to the Right, into the arms of tsarism. Bernstein urged the advocates of a boycott to abandon their quest for "absolutes" and to take part in the duma, where they should form a "bloc of all democratic elements in contemporary Russia." To clinch his argument, Bernstein quoted Marx on the Left's lack of realism: "No party is more given to exaggerating its means than the democratic [party], none deceives itself more recklessly about its situation."[38]

During the second period of the revolution, from the spring of 1906 to mid–1907, the *Sozialistische Monatshefte* ran a series of articles increasingly critical of the revolutionary Left in Russia, now charged with irresponsible conduct tinged with anarchism. Although the previous apologies for violence were not formally withdrawn, it is clear that the contributors to the journal had undergone a change of heart. The critical factor seems to have been the refusal of the Russian Left to alter its tactics in light of the tsar's concessions. "The childishness of the Leninists, who await salvation only from an armed uprising, must not confuse the sensible Social Democrats," declared one anonymous article. "Social Democracy must not squander its strength on adventures."[39] Another article blamed the Left Social Democrats for the failure of the masses to respond to a call for a general strike in protest against the dissolution of the first duma in July 1906. Why, asked the author, should they have come to the defense of an institution that the extremists had discredited? "How could workers decide to join a general strike for a treacherous duma?"[40] The writer singled out the liberals, now known as the Kadets, for special praise as a political group that had fought courageously in the electoral campaign and that had "acted very nobly" toward the socialists.[41]

In July 1907, shortly after the fifth congress of the Russian Social Democrats, at which the Leninists emerged as the strongest faction in the party, the editors of the *Sozialistische Monatshefte* published their most extensive and sharpest criticism of their Russian colleagues. An anonymous writer charged that instead of seeking to unite all progressive forces against the autocracy, the revolutionary Left devoted its energies to discrediting the very "idea of an institution representing the people" and to waging a fierce battle against the bourgeois Left, a tactic that was bound to isolate the socialists. By causing a rift within the opposition to the autocracy, the Social Democrats had played into the hands of the enemy, the tsarist regime. "It cannot be said," concluded the article, "that Russian Social Democracy at its party congress . . . gave evidence of political maturity."[42]

A principal argument of the historians who have stressed the linkage between the revolution in Russia and the leftward drift of German Social Democracy has been that only late in 1905 did the German party bring itself to adopt a resolution favoring a political mass strike.[43] The issue had been debated for some time, but its proponents had lacked the strength to prevail within the party. But at the Jena congress in September 1905 August Bebel, the party chairman, who had not previously indicated his own position, introduced a motion sanctioning the tactic of the mass strike and delivered a three and one-half hour address in its support. The motion did not fully satisfy the radicals, for it was not a call for a revolutionary offensive against the government but rather an affirmation of the mass strike as a defensive weapon. The resolution stated that if the government sought to undermine universal suffrage or the right of association, the working class would be justified in resorting to "every suitable means," the most effective of which would be a mass strike.[44] Nevertheless, the adoption of the resolution by an overwhelming majority of the delegates (287 to 14) was widely interpreted as a sign of the party's radicalization. Lenin was among those who perceived it in this way.[45]

But it is doubtful whether the votes of the party's congress can by themselves be considered an accurate barometer of the political mood of the German workers in 1905 or as a correct indication of the impact of the Russian revolution on the SPD in Germany. The behavior of German workers and of the party was simply too variegated and even contradictory. It is true that many workers turned militant that year, as is attested to by the fact that in 1905 alone more laborers participated in work stoppages than in the entire decade from 1890 to 1899. But the militancy had manifested itself *before* Bloody Sunday, in the intense labor conflicts that broke out in the Ruhr in the first days of January 1905. Indeed, four months after the onset of industrial unrest in Russia, news of which had made the headlines all over Germany, trade unionists displayed remarkable moderation. A congress of unionists at Cologne in May 1905 overwhelmingly voted for a resolution branding the general strike as "undiscussible" and urging workers not to allow themselves to be diverted "from small day-to-day tasks of building up the organizations of labor." A number of unions vehemently opposed the resolution, but no evidence has been produced to show that the protesters were influenced by the Russian revolution.[46] For organized labor, conditions in Germany seem to have been a more pressing concern than developments in distant Russia.

Perhaps more to the point, speakers for the resolution on the mass strike at the party congress in Jena—and again a year later in Mannheim, where the issue was also debated—only fleetingly referred to the revolution in Russia. This suggests that they did not believe they could sway many minds by dwelling on the successes of the Russian proletariat. Indeed, Bebel went out of his way to dismiss the relevance of events in Russia to the situation in his country. And it is also noteworthy that in their attempts to discredit the mass strike the opponents of the resolution, too, only rarely referred to the revolution. Although the revolution in Russia clearly did not loom very large in the thinking of most delegates at the party congress, it is instructive to examine the lessons the two sides drew from that upheaval in the debate over the mass strike.

The most fervent radicals, a mere handful, viewed the militancy of the Russian labor movement as a worthy model for the Germans. At Jena,

Rosa Luxemburg made the comment about "donkeys" that has already been quoted. Beyond that, she merely asked the delegates, rhetorically, whether they "really lived in the year of the glorious Russian revolution" or at a time "ten years before it." It seemed to her that the delegates read the news reports coming out of Russia but "had neither eyes to see nor ears to hear [what was happening]."[47] A year later, at Mannheim, she predicted that the "magnificent Russian revolution" would be the "teacher for the revolutionary movement of the proletariat for decades to come." When she again touched on the delegates' unwillingness to learn from the Russian experience, she was interrupted with hostile cries of "Quite right."[48]

At the suggestion of the Social Democratic organizations of Hamburg, Luxemburg had written *Mass Strike, Party and Trade Unions*, which proposed a revolutionary tactic for the party and was designed to win the support of the delegates at the Mannheim congress for the mass strike. The pamphlet was the most important theoretical statement to emerge from the ruminations of German socialists about the Revolution of 1905. But, as Schorske points out, it "failed miserably of its immediate purpose," though by 1910 that work, more than any other, may be said to have been the credo of the "left radical" wing of the party.[49]

Other supporters of the mass strike simply echoed Luxemburg, if they mentioned Russia at all. Dr. Robert Michels, who a few years later achieved eminence as the author of the seminal sociological work *Political Parties*, complained at Jena that "many of us regard the Russian revolution as merely a sensational event."[50] Luise Zietz of Hamburg urged her colleagues "to look at Russia" in considering the potential effectiveness of the mass strike: "There, workers have readily gone out on strike for such a long time; everywhere strikes break out and everywhere they appear again after they have stopped for a while, and everywhere the masses participate even though they have no organizations."[51] Finally, Karl Liebknecht contended that the revolution in Russia had inspired anew "an understanding of evolution by means of catastrophes." In 1906, when the government again had the upper hand, he held that the Russian workers had spilled their blood "for us, the proletariat of the entire world" and that German workers must not stand idly by. "It should not be recorded in world history that the Russian liberation movement was crushed because the German people, which has both the largest and most powerful organization, [failed to act]."[52]

The opponents of the mass strike expressed radically different views about the situation in Russia. Robert Schmidt, a delegate from Berlin, branded the mass strike as a weapon of despair and warned that if the SPD resorted to it, "We will . . . have Russian conditions and even worse, because we have a completely different system of administration and a much more highly concentrated military establishment. It would be a trifle for our bourgeoisie to drive us into the ground."[53] Eduard David, delegate from Mainz, thought that Luxemburg had blundered in bringing up the Russian revolution. For it seemed to him that the revolution did indeed "teach us a great deal, but precisely the opposite from that which Rosa Luxemburg is trying to make us believe." Conditions in the two countries were entirely different, and "what may be suitable over there may be wrong for us, and it is sheer madness to draw conclusions from Russian conditions about tactics that are necessary for us."[54]

The theme of different political paths for Russia and Germany was developed most extensively by Bebel himself, even though he did not dwell on the subject until some time after his long speech in favor of the mass strike. In fact, at Jena, Bebel hardly mentioned Russia. At one point in his speech he simply referred to the fear of "our rulers" that the revolution might spill over into Germany, and at another he casually compared the disorders in Russia with those in France during the June days of 1848 and the Commune of 1871.[55] It may well be that Bebel said so little about the revolution in Russia because he was much less sanguine about its chances of success than most of his colleagues. On 16 September 1905, he privately told a friend that from the beginning of the upheaval he had been skeptical about its "ultimate achievements." Bebel lauded the proletariat for behaving splendidly, but he did not believe that it could prevail in the face of the peasant masses, the enormous distinctions in the social structure, and the "hodgepodge of nationalities and races."[56]

In 1906, when the idea of the mass strike came under heavy attack from the trade union delegates at the national congress, he felt called upon to emphasize that his advocacy of that weapon did not mean that he favored a revolution on the Russian model. By this time, the trade union and party leaders had actually jettisoned the resolution adopted at Jena. Late in 1905 and early in 1906 a series of street demonstrations, mass meetings, and clashes between workers and police had erupted spontaneously in a number of cities in protest against moves by local governments to place further restrictions on the franchise at the provincial level. Alarmed at the prospect that the disturbances might get out of hand, leaders of the unions and the party secretly reached an agreement that stated, among other points, that the party would not campaign for a mass strike and would even do its utmost to prevent one from taking place.[57]

Bebel's approval of the agreement is not as startling as it might seem. Neither a revisionist nor a radical, Bebel was essentially a centrist who had attained the position of preeminent leader of the party by virtue of his remarkable skills as a politician. In the 1870s and 1880s he had belonged to the doctrinaire wing of the movement, and although he occasionally still paid obeisance to radicalism, his main concern now was with practical affairs. He wanted to maintain the SPD as a unified party, strengthen labor organizations, and hold on to middle-class supporters, who amounted to about 15 percent of the party's vote.[58] Despite his misgivings about parliamentarism, he recognized that his party had thrived under it, and consequently he had become its champion. Given Bebel's concerns and political predilections, it can be presumed that his remarks about Russia were designed to appeal to the largest number of Social Democrats and "fellow travelers." As such, they are probably a good indication of the attitude of the rank-and-file party member and party supporter toward the "Russian question."

Some seven months before the Mannheim party congress of 1906, Bebel had already announced in the Reichstag that the German workers did not intend to follow the path taken by the Russian proletariat. Shortly after the first anniversary of Bloody Sunday, when hundreds of thousands of Germans publicly demonstrated their sympathy for their Russian colleagues at numerous meetings throughout the country, he proudly declared that not a single meeting was disorderly and that "nowhere [was there] the slightest excess. . . .We shall not drive our people against your bayonets," Bebel predicted. That would be "stupid" because it would play into the hands of the conservatives itching to crush the labor movement.[59]

During the debate on the mass strike at the Mannheim congress Bebel elaborated on the theme of the German working class's political moderation. He drove home his point by stressing the different conditions in Russia and Germany. Russia was economically and politically backward, and consequently the struggle in that country was a "revolutionary struggle" for the most elementary human and political rights. The working class had chosen the technique of the mass strike because that was the "only possible weapon" available to it. But in Germany the masses had long since gained those rights. "The question for us is not the transformation of the entire political superstructure of bourgeois society." Indeed, if the working class in Germany decided to resort to the mass strike for the conquest of new political rights, it would call for a work stoppage only in north Germany, where universal and equal suffrage had not yet been introduced. It was self-evident to Bebel that the workers in the southern states would not participate in such a strike, for they already enjoyed equal suffrage in the elections to local legislatures. They could be expected to do no more than offer moral and material support. In short, Bebel conceived of the mass strike as a weapon to wrest limited political concessions from the government, or, as he had pointed out a year earlier, to defend political rights that the masses now exercised. The mass strike,

Bebel insisted, should be invoked only as the ultimate weapon, but even then "only as a peaceful mode of struggle. We have never declared that we want to stage a revolution."

In an obvious ploy to calm the radicals, Bebel went on to say that because only the ruling classes cause revolutions, he could not rule out for all time the possibility of a violent upheaval. But the thrust of his argument was patently antirevolutionary, and his aim was clearly to reassure the party faithful that he did not favor the tactics that Russian Social Democrats had used in their country.[60] The delegates at Mannheim, following Bebel's lead, executed a volte face by adopting a resolution (386 to 5) that in effect gave the trade unions the right to veto any decision by the party in favor of a mass strike.[61] The vote was a resounding defeat for the radicals. The influence of the Russian revolution over the SPD, such as it was, was therefore short-lived, lasting at best one year.

The thesis that the Russian revolution of 1905 influenced the German party in a fundamental way is also weakened by the fact that Bernstein strongly supported the mass strike as a defensive weapon, despite his categorical rejection of orthodox Marxism and militant tactics. Early in 1906 he granted that the strikes in Russia had helped to popularize the idea of a mass strike in Germany, but he warned Social Democrats not to assume that the weapon could be applied in the same way in the two countries. Like Bebel, he pointed out that the "Russian proletariat considers itself to be opposed to a thoroughly discredited, highly paralyzed state authority and a bourgeois class that is incapable of creating an organization that can provide effective leadership." That the working class under those circumstances was able to mount endless strikes should be seen less as a sign of the strength of the proletariat than as evidence of the temporary impotence or lack of energy of the other social classes and the authorities. Where such conditions did not prevail, strikes on a massive scale would be impossible. And "no one can maintain that political conditions in Germany are similar or almost similar to those in Russia." As a general rule, "the greater the amount of freedom in a country, the freer it is from great political confrontations." Still, Bernstein favored the political mass strike in the event that an attempt was made to "rob the workers of important rights." But he would not support it as a "revolutionary sport" (*Revolutionsspielerei*), that is, as the initiation of a violent seizure of power.[62]

Our survey of the reaction of German socialists to the Russian revolution of 1905 suggests three conclusions. First, they all welcomed the revolution as a justifiable attempt to eliminate a reactionary and barbarous regime and applauded the activism of Russian workers, who played a more dynamic role in 1905 than had the working class in any previous European revolution. But—and this is the second conclusion—when the militants within the Russian Left insisted on armed uprising as the only appropriate tactic for the opposition and spoke of such maximalist aims as the immediate transformation of Russia into a socialist order, a sizable number of German socialists became critical of their colleagues in the east. In particular, the refusal of several revolutionary groups to participate in the elections to the duma early in 1906 struck many Germans as senseless intransigence. And, third, only a handful of German socialists on the extreme Left of the political spectrum believed that their movement could draw useful lessons from the Russian experience for their country.

In short, German socialists tended to make a clear distinction between a revolution against tsarism, which they favored, and a revolution to establish socialism in the immediate future, which they opposed. If a few German socialists were radicalized by the upheaval of 1905, many more were confirmed in their conviction that in their country revolution and political maximalism were unnecessary and ineffective, if not counterproductive. In the long run, the latter reaction to 1905 was far more important than the former. There were several reasons for German Social Democracy's failure to emulate the Bolsheviks after the latter's seizure of power in 1917 and for the party's refusal to provide moral and material support to the Leninists. But not the least important was the fact that as a movement it never seriously regarded the strategy and tactics of the Russian Left as suitable models. That was amply demonstrated in the three years from 1905 to 1907.

NOTES

1. Carl E. Schorske, *German Social Democracy, 1905–1917: The Development of the Great Schism* (Cambridge, Mass.: 1955), 36.
2. J. P. Nettl, *Rosa Luxemburg* (London: 1966), 296–97.
3. Richard W. Reichard, "The German Working Class and the Russian Revolution of 1905," *Journal of Central European Affairs* 13 (1953), 147–48. See also Klaus Meyer, "Die russische Revolution von 1905 im deutschen Urteil," in Uwe Liszkowski (ed.), *Russland und Deutschland* (Stuttgart: 1974), 274, and H. Schurer, "The Russian Revolution of 1905 and the Origins of German Communism," *Slavonic and East European Review* 39 (1960–61), 459–71.
4. S. V. Tiutiukin, *Pervaia Rossiiskaia Revoliutsiia i G .V. Plekhanov* (Moscow: 1981), 3. This theme is repeated in all Soviet histories of 1905.
5   V. I. Bovykin et al. (eds.), *Rabochii klass v pervoi Rossiiskoi Revoliutsii 1905–1907 gg.* (Moscow: 1981), 364–65.
6. Rudolf Sauerzapf, "Die Haltung der deutschen Sozialdemokratie zur russischen Revolution von 1905," *Wissenschaftliche Zeitschrift der Martin-Luther-Universität Halle-Wittenberg* 3 (1953–54), 209.
7. Leo Stern et al. (eds.), *Archivalische Forschungen zur Geschichte der Deutschen Arbeiterbewegung*, 2d series, 2/1 (Berlin: 1954–61), lxxiii–lxxvi.

8. Two works with a more nuanced interpretation of the impact of the revolution on the German Left come to mind: Peter Lösche, *Der Bolschewismus im Urteil der Deutschen Sozialdemokratie* (Berlin: 1967), 34–47, and J. L. H. Keep, *The Rise of Social Democracy in Russia* (Oxford: 1963), 274–75.
9. *Vorwärts*, 28 January 1905.
10. Ibid., 9 November 1905.
11. Ibid., 2 November 1905.
12. *Dokumente und Materialien zur Geschichte der Deutschen Arbeiterbewegung*, 4 (Berlin: 1967), 159; see also 119–21, 136–37, 152–53, 195–99.
13. *Protokoll über die Verhandlungen des Parteitages der Sozialdemokratischen Partei Deutschlands, 1907* (Berlin: 1908), 61 (hereafter *Protokoll SPD*).
14. For a perceptive analysis of Kautsky's role in the SPD, see Erich Matthias, "Kautsky und der Kautskyianismus: Die Funktion der Ideologie in der deutschen Sozialdemokratie vor dem ersten Weltkriege," *Marxismusstudien* 2 (1957), 151–97.
15. Karl Kautsky, "Triebkräfte und Aussichten der russischen Revolution," *Neue Zeit* 15, no. 1 (1906–07), 331 (hereafter "Triebkräfte").
16. Karl Kautsky, "Der Kongress von Köln," *Neue Zeit* 23, no. 2 (1904–05), 315.
17. Karl Kautsky, "Die zivilisierte Welt und der Zar," ibid., no. 1, 615, 617 (hereafter "Die zivilisierte Welt").
18. Kautsky, "Triebkräfte," 331.
19. Ibid, 333.
20. Karl Kautsky, "Die Bauern und die Revolution in Russland," *Neue Zeit* 23, no. 1 (1904–5), 675–76, and "Die zivilisierte Welt," 615. In 1905 Lenin did not stress the likelihood of an immediate turn to socialism, but he did not altogether rule out that possibility. See Keep, *Rise of Social Democracy*, 193–98.
21. Karl Kautsky, "Aussichten der russischen Revolution," *Vorwärts*, 28 January 1906. Italics are mine.
22. Ibid., 614.
23. Hans-Jürgen Mende, *Karl Kautsky-vom Marxisten zum Opportunisten* (Berlin: 1985), 86.
24. Karl Kautsky, "Die russische Duma," *Neue Zeit* 24, no. 2 (1905–6), 243–44.
25. Rosa Luxemburg, "Die Revolution in Russland," *Neue Zeit* 23, 1 (1904–5), 577–78, and "Nach dem ersten Akt," ibid., 610–14.
26. *Protokoll SPD, 1905*, 320.
27. Franz Mehring, "Nepreryvnaia revoliutsiia," *Nachalo* 10 (25 November/8 December 1905), 2.
28. Franz Mehring, "Die Revolution in Permanenz," *Neue Zeit* 24, 1 (1905–6), 169–72.
29. *Sozialistische Monatshefte* 1 (1906), 769.
30. Richard Calwer, "Russland," *Sozialistische Monatshefte* 2 (1905), 113.
31. *Sozialistische Monatshefte* 1 (1906), 174.
32. Calwer, "Russland," 113; see also *Sozialistische Monatshefte* 2 (1904), 769.
33. Eduard Bernstein, "Fragen der Taktik in Russland," *Sozialistische Monatshefte* 1 (1906), 211 (hereafter "Fragen").
34. Eduard Bernstein, "Revolutionen und Russland," *Sozialistische Monatshefte* 1 (1905), 292.

35. Ibid., 295
36. Bernstein, "Fragen," 215.
37. Bernstein apparently did not know that the Leninists and Socialist-Revolutionaries also opposed participation in the elections, for he criticized only the Bundists.
38. Bernstein, "Fragen," 217.
39. *Sozialistische Monatshefte* 2 (1906), 973.
40. Ibid., 800.
41. Ibid., 1, 425.
42. Ibid., 2 (1907), 568–69.
43. See, for example, Bovykin, *Robochii Klass*, 364.
44. *Protokoll SPD, 1906*, 284–85.
45. V. I. Lenin, *Sochineniia*, 3d ed. (Leningrad: 1926–37), 8, 235.
46. See Schorske, *German Social Democracy*, 37–42, for the factual data, which he interprets differently.
47. *Protokoll SPD, 1905*, 320.
48. *Protokoll SPD, 1906*, 261.
49. See Schorske, *German Social Democracy*, 53–58. For a detailed discussion of the pamphlet, see Nettl, *Rosa Luxemburg*, 496–513.
50. Ibid., 325. Michels was a delegate from Marburg.
51. Ibid., 326.
52. Ibid., *Protokoll SPD, 1906*, 282.
53. *Protokoll SPD, 1905*, 319.
54. Ibid., 328.
55. Ibid., 298, 305.
56. Victor Adler, *Briefwechsel mit August Bebel und Karl Kautsky*, ed. Friedrich Adler (Vienna: 1954), 468.
57. Schorske, *German Social Democracy*, 45–49; Gary P. Steenson, *Karl Kautsky, 1854–1938: Marxism in the Classical Years* (Pittsburgh: 1978), 149.
58. William H. Maehl, *August Bebel: Shadow Emperor of the German Workers* (Philadelphia: 1980), 401–2, 388.
59. Ibid., 410.
60. *Protokoll SPD, 1906*, 231–33.
61. Ibid., 131–32.
62. Eduard Bernstein, "Politischer Massenstreik und Revolutionsromantik," *Sozialistische Monatshefte* 1 (1906), 17, 19.

V. M. Eikhenbaum (Volin)

Portrait of a Russian Anarchist

Paul Avrich

Volin, the pseudonym of Vsevolod Mikhailovich Eikhenbaum, was one of the most gifted and remarkable figures in the Russian anarchist movement. He played an active part in both the 1905 and the 1917 revolutions, as well as in the revolutionary movement in exile. In 1905, as a Socialist-Revolutionary, he was one of the founders of the St. Petersburg Soviet, and in 1917 he edited *Golos Truda* ("The Voice of Labor"), the principal anarcho-syndicalist journal of the revolutionary period. During the Civil War he helped found the *Nabat* ("Alarm") Confederation in the Ukraine, edited its newspaper of the same name, and was an important figure in the partisan movement of Nestor Makhno.

Volin was a prolific writer and lecturer, the theorist of "united anarchism," and the author of the most impressive anarchist-inspired history of the Russian Revolution, which has been translated into many languages. Speaker and editor, historian and journalist, educator and poet, Volin was a versatile man. His life, laden with hardship, was punctuated by arrests, escapes, and a number of brushes with death. One of the most effective critics of the Bolshevik dictatorship, he was twice imprisoned by the Soviet secret police and, Trotsky having ordered his execution, only narrowly escaped with his life. In prison and exile, in propaganda and action, he remained a devoted revolutionary, possessed of both moral and physical courage. He was, in Victor Serge's description, "completely honest, rigorous in his thinking, full of talent, of eternal youth and joy in struggle."[1] His nom de guerre, formed from the Russian word *volia*, "freedom," fittingly evokes the ideal to which he dedicated his life.

Volin was born on 11 August 1882 into an educated family of assimilated Russian-Jewish intellectuals, who lived near the city of Voronezh in the black earth region of south-central Russia. His paternal grandfather, Iakov Eikhenbaum, was a mathematician and poet;[2] his parents were both doctors in comfortable circumstances, employing Western tutors for the education of their two sons. Accordingly, Volin and his younger brother were brought up with a knowledge of French and German, which they could speak and write almost as fluently as their native Russian. The brother, Boris Eikhenbaum (1886–1959), was to become one of Russia's most distinguished literary critics, a founder of the formalist school and an authority on Tolstoi and other Russian writers.

Volin himself might have followed a similar path. He attended the gymnasium at Voronezh and enrolled in the law school of St. Petersburg University. There, however, he became immersed in revolutionary ideas. In 1904, to his parents' distress, he abandoned his studies to join the Socialist-Revolutionary party and engage in full-time agitation among the workers of the capital, with whom he had established tentative contact three years before, when he was nineteen. Volin devoted all the strength of his idealistic nature to his new cause. He organized workers' study groups, started a library, and drew up a reading program, while giving private lessons to earn a living.[3] On 9 January 1905, he took part in the great protest march on the Winter Palace that was fired on by tsarist troops, leaving hundreds of victims in the snow. This was the famous "Bloody Sunday," which marked the beginning of the 1905 Revolution. He also took part (while still a Socialist-Revolutionary) in the formation of the first St. Petersburg Soviet and in the Kronstadt rising of 25 October 1905, as a result of which he spent a short term in the Peter and Paul Fortress. Soon after his release, he became the object of a manhunt in the reaction that followed the revolution. Captured by the Okhrana in 1907, he was thrown into prison and ordered deported to Siberia, but succeeded in escaping to France.[4]

Volin's flight to the West opened a new phase in his political and intellectual development. In Paris he became acquainted with both French and Russian anarchists, including Sébastien Faure (with whom he was later to collaborate on the four-volume Encyclopédie Anarchiste) and Apollon Karelin, who presided over a small libertarian circle called the Brotherhood of Free Communists (Bratstvo Vol'nykh Obshchinnikov). In 1911 Volin joined Karelin's group, quitting the Socialist-Revolutionary party in favor of anarchism, to which he remained unswervingly devoted for the rest of his life.

A staunch antimilitarist, Volin in 1913 became an active member of the Committee for International Action Against War. After the outbreak of the First World War in August 1914, he stepped up his antimilitarist agitation, to the intense displeasure of the French authorities, who in 1915 decided to intern him for the duration of hostilities. Warned by friends, however, Volin fled to the port city of Bordeaux and shipped out as quartermaster aboard a freighter bound for the United States, leaving behind his wife and children.

Arriving in New York in early 1916, Volin joined the Union of Russian Workers of the United States and Canada, an anarcho-syndicalist organization with more than ten thousand adherents. A capable writer and speaker, he joined the staff of its weekly newspaper, *Golos Truda*, and debated and lectured at many of its clubs and meeting halls, in both Canada and the United States. In December 1916, for example, he embarked on a tour of Detroit, Pittsburgh, Cleveland, and Chicago, speaking on such subjects as syndicalism, the general strike, the world war, and the labor movement in France.[5] With the outbreak of the February Revolution, however, Volin resolved to return to Russia at the first opportunity. In May 1917, assisted by the Anarchist Red Cross, the staff of *Golos Truda*, Volin among them, packed up their equipment and sailed home by the Pacific route, arriving in Petrograd in July. The following month they resumed publication of *Golos Truda* as the weekly organ of the Union of Anarcho-Syndicalist Propaganda, which spread the gospel of revolutionary syndicalism among the workers of the capital.

Volin now emerged as one of the leading anarchist intellectuals of the revolutionary period. At rallies and in factories and clubhouses he was a popular speaker, calling for workers' control of production in place of both capitalism and reformist trade unionism. Though he was of medium height and frail physique, his handsome, intelligent face with its prematurely graying beard and piercing dark eyes made him an impressive-looking figure. With his cogent argumentation and emphatic gestures and witty, at times shattering, repartée—he reminded Victor Serge of the French rebel Blanqui—he held his listeners spellbound. Beginning with the second issue, he also assumed the editorship of *Golos Truda* (the first number was edited by Maksim Raevskii, who, for reasons still unexplained, suddenly dropped out of the movement). Under Volin's able direction, *Golos Truda* became the most influential anarcho-syndicalist journal of the Russian Revolution, with an estimated readership of twenty-five thousand. A selection of his own articles—which appeared in nearly every issue—was published in book form in Kharkov in 1919 under the title *Revoliutsiia i anarkhizm* ("Revolution and Anarchism").

Volin, meanwhile, had come into conflict with the fledgling Bolshevik administration. "Once their power has been consolidated and legalized," he wrote in *Golos Truda* at the end of 1917, "the Bolsheviks, as state socialists, that is as men who believe in centralized and authoritarian leadership, will start running the life of the country and of the people from the top. Your soviets. . . . will gradually become simple tools of the central government. . . . You will soon see the inauguration of an authoritar-

ian political and state apparatus that will crush all opposition with an iron
fist. . . . 'All power to the soviets' will become 'all power to the leaders of
the party.'"[6]

In March 1918 he was sharply critical of the Treaty of Brest-Litovsk,
by which Russia ceded to Germany more than a quarter of its population
and arable land and three-quarters of its iron and steel industry. Lenin
insisted that the agreement, severe as it was, provided a desperately
needed breathing spell in which to consolidate Bolshevik power. For the
anarchists, however, the treaty was a humiliating capitulation to the forces
of reaction, a betrayal of the worldwide revolution. Volin denounced it as
a "shameful" act and called for "relentless partisan warfare" against the
Germans.[7] Soon after this, he relinquished the editorship of Golos Truda
and left for the Ukraine, stopping in his native district to visit his relatives, whom he had not seen in more than a decade.

Spending the summer of 1918 in the town of Bobrov, Volin worked in
the educational section of the local soviet, helping to organize a program
of adult education, including a library and a people's theater. In the fall
he moved to Kharkov, where he became the guiding spirit of the Nabat
Confederation and the editor of its principal journal. He also played a key
role in its first general conference, held at Kursk in November 1918,
where he attempted to draft a declaration of principles that would be acceptable to all schools of anarchist thought, individualist as well as communist and syndicalist.[8]

Ever since he left Golos Truda, Volin had been moving from anarcho-
syndicalism toward a more ecumenical position that he called "united anarchism" (edinyi anarkhizm), a theory that would encourage all tendencies
of the movement to work together in a spirit of mutual respect and cooperation within the framework of a single, unified, but flexible organization—a sort of model for the future libertarian society itself. Many of his
former comrades, notably Grigorii Maksimov and Mark Mrachnyi, found
"united anarchism" a vague and ineffectual formula to which they were
unable to subscribe. Mrachnyi, although he thought Volin "a fluent
speaker and very knowledgeable," perceived "a certain shallowness in
him. He spoke and wrote easily, but always on the surface and without
real substance."[9]

Volin pressed forward with his idea. He saw the embodiment of united
anarchism in the Nabat Confederation, with its center in Kharkov and
branches in Kiev, Odessa, and other large southern cities, a single organization embracing all varieties of anarchism and guaranteeing autonomy
to each individual and group. Apart from publishing the Nabat, the confederation issued several regional papers, as well as brochures and proclamations, and sponsored a flourishing youth organization in addition

to a Union of Atheists. It presented an alternative social model to both the Bolsheviks and the Whites, who, needless to say, endeavored to suppress it.[10]

In the summer of 1919, as the Bolsheviks intensified their persecution of the anarchists and began to close their newspapers and meeting places, Volin went to Guliai-Pole and joined the insurrectionary army of Makhno, for which the Nabat Confederation supplied ideological guidance. Volin, along with Peter Arshinov and Aaron Baron, served in the cultural and educational section, editing the movement's newspapers, drafting its proclamations and manifestoes, and organizing its meetings and conferences. Volin headed the educational section (as he had in the Bobrov Soviet) during the summer and fall, besides serving for six months on the Military Revolutionary Council. The following year the Bolsheviks offered him the post of commissar of education for the Ukraine, which he abruptly refused, just as his mentor Kropotkin had refused Kerenskii's offer to become minister of education in the Provisional Government of 1917.[11]

In December 1919 the Military Revolutionary Council sent Volin to Krivoi Rog to counter Ukrainian nationalist propaganda disseminated in the area by Semyon Petliura. On the way, however, he was stricken with typhus and forced to stop at a peasant village, whose inhabitants labored to revive his health. On 14 January 1920, while still bedridden, he was arrested by the Fourteenth Red Army and handed over to the local Cheka. Trotsky, whom he had repeatedly criticized in *Nabat*, issued orders for his execution. But anarchists in Moscow, among them Alexander Berkman, recently arrived from the United States, circulated an appeal for his transfer to Moscow and presented it to Nikolai Krestinskii, secretary of the Communist party. Krestinskii, though he had known Volin as a fellow student at St. Petersburg University, rejected the appeal, insisting that Volin was a counterrevolutionary. But, under pressure from the anarchists and their sympathizers (Victor Serge among them), he finally yielded and ordered Volin transferred to Moscow's Butyrki prison.[12]

This occurred in March 1920. Seven months later, as part of an accord between the Red Army and Makhno's Insurgent Army of the Ukraine, Volin was released. Having recovered from his bout with typhus, he went to the town of Dmitrov, north of Moscow, to pay his respects to Kropotkin, before returning to Kharkov to resume the publication of *Nabat*. Once back in the Ukraine, he began preparations for an All-Russian Congress of Anarchists to meet at the end of the year. In late November, however, Trotsky tore up his agreement with Makhno and ordered an attack on Guliai-Pole, while the Cheka rounded up members of the Nabat Confederation assembled in Kharkov for the congress. Volin, with Baron and others, was carried off to Moscow and locked up again in Butyrki, from which he was transferred in turn to Lefortovo and Taganka, names that figure in Solzhenitsyn's writings on Soviet prisons.

Volin remained behind bars for more than a year. In July 1921, when the Red International of Trade Unions (the Profintern) was created in Moscow, a number of foreign delegates, disturbed by the persecution of the anarchists and the suppression of the Kronstadt rebellion, were persuaded by Emma Goldman, Alexander Berkman, and Alexander Schapiro to protest to Lenin and Dzerzhinskii, the head of the Cheka. The French anarchist Gaston Leval, then a young delegate to the Profintern Congress, was permitted to visit Volin in prison, and the latter, speaking in flawless French, regaled him for over an hour with the story of his odyssey in the Ukraine.[13] Soon afterward, Volin, Maksimov, and other anarchists staged an eleven-day hunger strike to dramatize their incarceration. Lenin finally agreed to release them, on condition of their perpetual banishment from Russia, and in January 1922 they left for Berlin.

In Berlin, Rudolf Rocker and other prominent German anarchists helped Volin and his family get settled. Though only forty, Volin, with his receding hair and grizzled beard, looked much older, but his animated gestures and rapid movements quickly dispelled this impression. Rocker, who had to closet himself in his private study when he wanted to write, envied Volin's facility for concentration; he could go on with his writing, Rocker recalled, in the same small attic where he and his wife and five children had to eat and sleep and carry on their daily lives.[14]

Volin stayed in Berlin for about two years. There he published seven issues of *Anarkhicheskii Vestnik* ("The Anarchist Herald"), an organ of "united anarchism" in contrast to Maksimov's specifically anarcho-syndicalist journal *Rabochii Put'* ("The Workers' Road"), which appeared at the same time. Together with Alexander Berkman, he engaged in relief work to aid his imprisoned and exiled comrades. In 1922 he edited a slim but important volume called *Goneniia na anarkhizm v Sovetskoi Rossii* ("The Repressions of the Anarchists in Soviet Russia"), published in French and German as well as Russian and providing the first documented information to the outside world of Bolshevik persecution of the anarchists. He also wrote a valuable preface to Arshinov's history of the Makhno movement and helped translate the book into German.[15]

In 1924 Volin was invited by Sébastien Faure to travel to Paris and collaborate on the anarchist encyclopedia he was preparing.[16] Volin accepted, moved to Paris, and wrote a number of major articles for the encyclopedia, some of which were published as separate pamphlets in several languages. Over the next dozen years, moreover, he contributed to a range of anarchist periodicals, including *Le Libertaire* and *La Revue*

Anarchiste in Paris, *Die Internationale* in Berlin, and *Man!*, *Vanguard*, *Delo Truda*, and the *Fraye Arbeter Shtime* in the United States. He also published a volume of poetry,[17] dedicated to the memory of Kropotkin, who had died in 1921, and began to work on his monumental history of the Russian Revolution.[18]

Volin, however, was not immune from the factional quarrels that plagued the Russian anarchists in exile. In 1926 he broke with his old comrades Arshinov and Makhno over their controversial *Organizational Platform*, which called for a General Union of Anarchists with a central executive committee to coordinate policy and action.[19] In the dispute, Volin ranged himself with Alexander Berkman, Emma Goldman, Sébastien Faure, Errico Malatesta, Rudolf Rocker, and other notable anarchists from various countries. With a group of associates, he issued a scathing reply to Arshinov the following year, arguing that the *Organizational Platform*, with its appeal for a central committee, clashed with the basic anarchist principle of local initiative and was a clear reflection of its author's "party spirit" (Arshinov had been a Bolshevik before joining the anarchists in 1906).[20] Volin felt vindicated in 1930 when Arshinov returned to the Soviet Union and rejoined the party—only to be purged by Stalin a few years later. With Arshinov gone, Galina Makhno urged Volin to visit her ailing husband, fatally stricken with tuberculosis. In 1934, on the eve of Makhno's death, the old friends were briefly reconciled, and Volin saw to the posthumous publication of the second and third volumes of Makhno's memoirs, to which he contributed prefaces and notes.[21]

During the late 1920s and the 1930s, Volin continued to denounce the Soviet dictatorship, labeling Bolshevism "red fascism"and likening Stalin to Mussolini and Hitler.[22] In his small Paris apartment he conducted an informal class on anarchism that attracted young comrades of several nationalities, Marie Louise Berneri among them. To support his family, meanwhile, he tried his hand at a variety of jobs, working, among other things, as an agent for a newspaper clipping service and collaborating with Alexander Berkman on a Russian translation of Eugene O'Neill's *Lazarus Laughed*, commissioned by the Moscow Art Theater.[23]

After the outbreak of the Spanish Civil War in 1936, Volin accepted an invitation from the Confederación Nacional del Trabajo (CNT) to edit its Paris-based French periodical *L'Espagne Anti-Fasciste*. He quit soon afterward, however, when the CNT endorsed the popular front and supported the loyalist government. At this point, his life never easy, always poised on the edge of poverty,[24] Volin suffered a series of misfortunes, of which the death of his wife, following a nervous collapse, was the worst. Shortly afterward, in 1938, he left Paris for Nîmes, to which his friend André Prudhommeaux, a well-known libertarian writer and the manager of a printing cooperative, had beckoned him. Volin took a seat on the editorial board of Prudhommeaux's weekly paper, *Terre Libre*, while continuing his study of the Russian Revolution, which he completed in Marseilles in 1940, soon after the outbreak of the Second World War.

Volin's book, *The Unknown Revolution*, is the most important anarchist history of the Russian Revolution in any language. It was written, as we have seen, by an eyewitness who himself played an active part in the events that he describes. Like Kropotkin's history of the French Revolution, it explores what Volin calls the "unknown revolution," that is, the social revolution of the people as distinguished from the seizure of political power by the Bolsheviks. Before the appearance of Volin's book, this theme had been little explored. The Russian Revolution, as Volin saw it, was much more than the story of Kerenskii and Lenin, of Social Democrats, Socialist-Revolutionaries, or even anarchists. It was an explosion of mass discontent and of mass creativity, elemental, unpremeditated, and unpolitical, a true social revolution such as Bakunin had foreseen half a century before.

As a great popular movement, a "revolt of the masses," the Russian Revolution needed a Volin to write its history "from below," as Kropotkin and Jean Jaurès had done for France. "It is the whole immense multitude of men who are finally entering the limelight," Jaurès had remarked.[25] Such was the case in Russia between 1917 and 1921, when the country underwent a vast upheaval embracing every area of life and in which ordinary men and women played an essential part. A similar phenomenon occurred in Spain between 1936 and 1939. Russia and Spain, indeed, experienced the greatest libertarian revolutions of the twentieth century, decentralist, spontaneous, and egalitarian, not led by any party or group, but largely the work of the people themselves.

The most striking feature of this "unknown revolution," in Volin's interpretation, was the decentralization and dispersal of authority, the spontaneous formation of autonomous communes and councils, and the emergence of workers' self-management in town and country. Indeed, all modern revolutions have seen the organization of local committees—factory committees, housing committees, educational and cultural committees, soldiers' and sailors' committees, peasant committees—in an efflorescence of direct action on the spot. In Russia the soviets, too, were popular organs of direct democracy until reduced by the Bolsheviks to instruments of centralized authority, rubber stamps of a new bureaucratic state.

Such is Volin's central thesis. In rich detail he documents the efforts of the workers, peasants, and intellectuals to inaugurate a free society based on local initiative and autonomy. Libertarian opposition to the new Soviet dictatorship, above all in Kronstadt and the Ukraine, receives extensive treatment. Volin presents a deeply sympathetic account of the Makhno movement, yet without glossing over its negative aspects, such as Makhno's heavy drinking (which made him violent and intractable) and the formation of what some regard as a military camarilla around Makhno's leadership. (Volin, it has been noted, broke with Makhno over the *Organizational Platform*, and the resulting antagonism never completely abated.)

The book, however, is not without its shortcomings. In discussing the historical antecedents of the Russian revolutionary movement, Volin mentions the great peasant and cossack rebellions of the seventeenth and eighteenth centuries only in passing, without taking account of their strongly antistatist character. For all their "primitive" qualities, the risings of Razin and Pugachev were antiauthoritarian movements for a decentralized and egalitarian society. Oddly enough, moreover, Volin omits the anarchists from his chapter on the 1905 Revolution, although it was in 1905 that the Russian anarchists first emerged as a force to be reckoned with. (Volin, it is worth recalling, was a Socialist-Revolutionary at the time, not converting to anarchism until 1911.)

Furthermore, Volin's discussion of the social revolution in 1917 needs amplification. Little is said of the worker and peasant movements outside Kronstadt and the Ukraine. The book also neglects the individualist anarchists, a fascinating if relatively small group, as well as the role of women in the anarchist and revolutionary movements. Surely the activities of women—on bread lines and picket lines, in strikes and demonstrations, on the barricades and in guerrilla units, in winning over the soldiers and their male and female workmates, in creating free schools and day-care centers, in their overall drive for dignity and equality—form a major part of the "unknown revolution" with which Volin was so deeply concerned.

The book, it must be added, suffers from deficiencies of style. Volin, as George Woodcock has noted, was "not an elegant writer in the literary sense." He tended, rather, toward prolixity, and his history would have benefited from condensation.[26] Yet, for all these blemishes, *The Unknown Revolution* is an impressive work. It is a pioneering history of a neglected aspect of the Russian Revolution. With the partial exceptions of Arshinov's history of the Makhno movement and Maksimov's history of the Bolshevik repressions, there is no other book like it. It should be read by every person interested in the anarchist movement and the Russian Revolution.[27]

Volin, as noted earlier, completed *The Unknown Revolution* in 1940 while living in Marseilles. When Victor Serge met him there that year, he was working in the office of a small movie house and living on practically nothing. After the Nazi invasion and the formation of the Vichy government, his position became increasingly precarious. He went from hiding place to hiding place, living in extreme poverty and in constant fear of arrest. Yet he refused to seek refuge across the Atlantic, hoping to take part in the coming events in Europe, about which, noted Serge, he cherished a "romantic optimism."[28] Two of Volin's comrades, Mollie Steimer and Senya Fleshin, met him in Marseilles in 1941. They begged him to go away with them to Mexico, but to no avail. He was needed in France, Volin insisted, to meet with the youth and "prepare for the revolution when the war is over."[29]

Pursued by the authorities both as an anarchist and as a Jew, Volin somehow managed to evade their clutches. When the war finally ended he returned to Paris, but only to enter a hospital. For he had contracted tuberculosis and his days were numbered. He died on 18 September 1945. His body was cremated and the ashes interred in the Père-Lachaise Cemetery, not far from the grave of Nestor Makhno, who had succumbed to the same disease eleven years before. The old comrades were thus reunited in death, their remains resting by those of the martyrs of the Paris Commune.

NOTES

1. Victor Serge, "In Memory: Boris [sic] Voline," *Politics* 3, no. 2 (February 1946), 62.
2. In 1840, according to one authority, Iakov Eikhenbaum published an acclaimed Yiddish poem about a chess game. Harold Schefski, "Eikhenbaum, Boris Mikhailovich," *The Modern Encyclopedia of Russian and Soviet Literature*, ed. Harry B. Weber (Gulf Breeze, Fla.: 1977–), 6, 110.
3. M. S. [Mollie Steimer], "Life of a Russian Anarchist," *Freedom*, 17 November 1945. On Volin's life and career see also Mollie Steimer, "A Memorial Tribute to Vsevolod Eikhenbaum Voline," in *Fighters for Anarchism: Mollie Steimer and Senya Fleshin*, ed. Abe Bluestein (New York, 1983), 70–79; G. P. Maksimov, "Vsevolod Mikhailovich Eikhenbaum (Volin)," *Delo Truda-Probuzhdenie*, January 1946; and Rudolf Rocker, preface to Volin, *The Unknown Revolution, 1917–1921* (Detroit: 1974), 9–15.
4. See his poem, "Vision," written in St. Petersburg prison in 1907, *An Anthology of Revolutionary Poetry*, ed. Marcus Graham (New York: 1929), 336–37.
5. *Delo Truda-Probuzhdenie*, July 1963.
6. Quoted in Daniel and Gabriel Cohn-Bendit, *Obsolete Communism: The Left-Wing Alternative* (New York: 1968), 218–19.
7. Ibid., 127.
8. *Pervaia konferentsiia anarkhistskikh organizatsii Ukrainy "Nabat": Deklaratsiia i rezoliutsii* (Buenos Aires: 1922).
9. Interview with Mark E. Clevans (Mrachnyi), New York City, 15 February 1974. Emma Goldman, it might be noted, considered Volin "a highly cultured man, a gifted writer and lecturer." Goldman, *My Disillusionment in Russia* (London: 1925), 240.

10. See Paul Avrich, *The Russian Anarchists* (Princeton: 1967), 205–8; and Anthony D'Agostino, *Marxism and the Russian Anarchists* (San Francisco: 1977), 195–220.

11. Avrich, *The Russian Anarchists*, 136.

12. Emma Goldman, *Living My Life* (New York: 1931), 786–87; G. P. Maksimov, *The Guillotine at Work* (Chicago: 1940), 121.

13. *Ni Dieu, Ni Maître*, ed. Daniel Guérin, 4 vols. (Paris: 1970), 4, 113.

14. Rocker, preface to Volin's *Unknown Revolution*, 14.

15. P. A. Arshinov, *Istoriia makhnovskogo dvizheniia (1918–1921 gg.)* (Berlin: 1923).

16. *Encyclopédie anarchiste*, ed. S. Faure, 4 vols. (Paris: n. d. [1934]).

17. V. Eikhenbaum, *Stikhotvoreniia* (Paris: 1927).

18. Volin began his analysis of the revolution as an eyewitness and participant during 1917. His views, first evolved in *Golos Truda*, were elaborated in the early 1920s in *Anarkhicheskii Vestnik* and *La Revue anarchiste* and afterward in such essays as "La Révolution russe," in *La véritable révolution sociale*, ed. S. Faure (Paris: 1935), 105–227, and Voline, *La Révolution en marche* (Nîmes: 1938).

19. *Organizatsionnaia platforma vseobshchego soiuza anarkhistov* (Paris: 1926).

20. *Otvet neskol'kikh russkikh anarkhistov na Organizatsionnuiu Platformu* (Paris: 1927).

21. N. I. Makhno, *Pod udarami kontr-revoliutsii (aprel'-iiun' 1918 g.)* and *Ukrainskaia revoliutsiia (iiul'-dekabr' 1918 g.)* (Paris: 1936–37). See also Volin's sympathetic obituary of Makhno, "Der shtendik-farfolgter," *Fraye arbeter shtime*, 12 October 1934.

22. Voline, *Le fascisme rouge* (Brussels: 1934).

23. Interview with Ernesto Bonomini, an Italian anarchist who attended Volin's classes, North Miami Beach, Florida, 16 January 1985; Alexander Berkman to Michael A. Cohn, 11 April 1927, archives of the Jewish Scientific Institute (Yivo), New York City.

24. Emma Goldman, in a letter to a German comrade, described Volin as being "almost destitute." Goldman to Augustin Souchy, 27 July 1937, in David Porter, ed., *Vision on Fire: Emma Goldman on the Spanish Revolution* (New Paltz, N. Y.: 1983), 43.

25. Quoted in Arthur Lehning, *From Buonarroti to Bakunin* (Leiden: 1970), 15.

26. George Woodcock, "The Anarchists in Russia," *Freedom*, 8 May 1954.

27. The original French version, *La Révolution inconnue (1917–1921)*, was published by the Friends of Volin in Paris in 1947, two years after its author's death. It has since appeared in Spanish, Italian, German, Japanese, and Korean translations. An incomplete English version, *The Unknown Revolution (1917–1921)*, was published in two volumes in 1954–1955, and a full edition, in one large volume of over seven hundred pages, in 1974, restoring the omitted sections.

28. Serge, "In Memory," 62.

29. Mollie Steimer to Paul Avrich, 9 December 1974.

MARC RAEFF

A Bibliography (1946–1987)

Compiled by Edward Kasinec

with Molly Molloy and Elliot S. Isaac

This bibliography is a complete listing of Marc Raeff's publications through December 1987. It is based on notes, offprints, and carbon copies kept in his own papers.* Each of the items listed below was seen and described *de visu*. An attempt has been made to describe each item *as fully as it appears in the original publication*. Certain changes, however, have been made when citing Professor Raeff's reviews: the given names of the author of the work being reviewed are always cited first and the imprint information standardized throughout to give the place of publication first and then the publishing or printing house. In most cases the number of the periodical volume is given in Arabic rather than in Roman numerals. Professor Raeff's original monographic works and articles are always listed first under their year of publication; reviews follow in the alphabetical order of the author's or editor's surname. Entries preceded by an asterisk also appear in the final section, "Reprints and Translations."

The compilers wish to express their appreciation to a number of individuals who contributed their efforts towards the compilation of this work: first, to James Cracraft, University of Illinois at Chicago, who initially suggested its undertaking; to Olga Kavochka Mayo, Harvard University, who did much to assist us in locating titles at Harvard; and, to Frank T. Brechka, University of California at Berkeley, Brenda Meehan-Waters, University of Rochester, Kevin O'Brien, University of California at Berkeley, and Robert H. Davis, New York Public Library, all of whom read an early draft of this bibliography and made constructive suggestions for its improvement.

*An earlier version of this bibliography covering 1947–82 was published in *Russian Review* 41 (4): 454–71, 1982, O. Used with permission.

ABBREVIATIONS

AHR—*American Historical Review*
ASEER—*American Slavic and East European Review*
BA—*Books Abroad*
CMRS—*Cahiers du monde russe et soviétique*
CSS/CASS—*Canadian Slavic Studies/Canadian-American Slavic Studies*
CSP—*Canadian Slavonic Papers*
CSSH—*Comparative Studies in Society and History*
HUS—*Harvard Ukrainian Studies*
HT—*History Today*
JEH—*Journal of Economic History*
JGO—*Jahrbücher für Geschichte Osteuropas*
JMH—*Journal of Modern History*
JUS—*Journal of Ukrainian Studies*
LH—*Labor History*
NL—*New Leader*
NYT—*New York Times*
NYTM—*New York Times Magazine*
NZh—*Novyi zhurnal*
OB—*Obozrenie*
OSP—*Oxford Slavonic Papers*
PC—*Problems of Communism*
PNWQ—*Pacific Northwest Quarterly*
PSQ—*Political Science Quarterly*
RES—*Revue des études slaves*
RH—*Russian History*
RHMC—*Revue d'histoire moderne et contemporaine*
RM—*Russkaia mysl'*
RU—*Russia*
RR—*Russian Review*
SEER—*Slavonic and East European Review*
SR—*Slavic Review*
TLS—*Times Literary Supplement*

BIBLIOGRAPHY

1946

1. Review:"'Na modnuiu temu: frantsuzskaia kniga o russkoi diplomatii.' A review of C. de Grunwald: *Trois siècles de diplomatie russe*. Paris, 1945," *Novoe russkoe slovo*, 37 (12,458): 4, Je 7.

1948

2. Review: [Mark Véart]. "'On Russian Spirituality.' A review of: *A Treasury of Russian Spirituality*. Edited by G. P. Fedotov. New York: Sheed and Ward. 501 pp.," *NL*, 31 (49): 10, D 4.

1949

*3. "An Early Theorist of Absolutism: Joseph of Volokolamsk," *ASEER*, 8(2): [77]–89, Apr. [Also see no. 264]

1950

4. *The Peasant Commune in the Political Thinking of Russian Publicists: Laissez-faire Liberalism in the Reign of Alexander II*. Unpublished Ph.D. dissertation, Harvard University. 239 pp.

5. Review: [Mark Véart]. "'A 16th Century Russian Despot.' A review of Hans von Eckardt. *Ivan the Terrible*. Alfred A. Knopf," *NL*, 33(8):12, F 25.

1951

6. "Russia after the Emancipation. Views of a Gentleman-Farmer," *SEER*, 29(73):470–85, Je.

7. Review: "P. A. Zajončkovskij, ed., *Dnevnik D. A. Miljutina 1873–1875 (Diary of D. A. Miljutin 1873–1875)*, Volume I. Moscow: Gosudarstvennaja Ordena Lenina Biblioteka SSSR imeni Lenina, Otdel rukopisej, 1947. 253 pp. 15 rubles," *ASEER*, 10 (3):232–34, O.

1952

8. "Georges Samarin et le commune paysanne après 1861," *RES*, 29 (1–4): [71]–81.

9. "A Reactionary Liberal: M. N. Katkov," *RR*, 11 (3):157–67, Jl.

10. Review: "P. A. Zajončkovskij, ed. *Dnevnik D. A. Miljutina (Diary of D. A. Miljutin)*, Volume II, 1876–1877. Moscow: 1949. 290 pp. 15 rubles. Volume III, 1878–1880. Moscow: 1950. 324 pp. 12 rubles. Volume IV, 1881–1882. Moscow. 1950. 202 pp. 10 rubles. All published by Gosudarstvennaja Ordena Lenina Biblioteka SSSR imeni Lenina, Otdel rukopisej," *ASEER*, 11 (3): 241–43, O.

1953

11. "An American View of the Decembrist Revolt," *JMH*, 25(3):286–93, S.

12. "The Philosophical Views of Count M. M. Speransky," *SEER*, 31 (77):[437]–51, Je.

13. "The Political Philosophy of Speranskij," *ASEER*, 12(1):[1]–21, F.

1954

14. Review: "V. V. Zenkovsky. *A History of Russian Philosophy*. 2 vols. George L. Kline, tr. New York: Columbia University Press, 1953. xiv + 947 pp. $15.00," *BA*, 28(2):227–28, Spring.

1955

15.   Review: "Don Aminado. *Poezd na tret'em puti*. New York: Chekhov, 1954. 352 pp. $2.75," *BA*, 29(2): 243, Spring.

16.   Review: "Alexei Khomyakov. *Izbrannye sochineniia*. Nicholas Arseniev, ed. New York: Chekhov, 1955. 415 pp. $3.00," *BA*, 29(4):486, Autumn.

17.   Review: "Horace G. Lunt, et al., eds. *Harvard Slavic Studies*, II. Cambridge: Harvard University Press, 1954. vi, 390 pp. $6.00," *BA*, 29(1):102, Winter.

18.   Review: "Sergei Makovskii. *Portrety Sovremennikov*. New York: Chekhov, 1955. 415 pages. $3," *BA*, 29(4):487, Autumn.

19.   Review: "Vladimir Nabokov. *Drugie berega*. New York: Chekhov, 1954. 269 pp., $2.25," *BA*, 29(3):307, Summer.

20.   Review: "Georg von Rauch, *Russland: Staatliche Einheit und nationale Vielfalt*. (*Veröffentlichungen des Osteuropa-Institutes München*, Band 5). München: Isar Verlag, 1953. 235 pp.," *ASEER*, 14(1):130–32, F.

21.   Review: "Kniazhna Ol'ga Trubetskaia. *Kniaz' S. N. Trubetskoi- vospominaniia* [-*sic*] *sestry*. New York: Chekhov, 1953. 271 pages. $2.25," *BA*, 29(3):366, Summer.

22.   Review, "Martin Winkler, ed. *Slavische Geisteswelt. I: Russland*. Darmstadt: Holle, 1955. 367 pp. 14 dm," *BA*, 29(4): 439–40, Autumn.

23.   Review: "V. S. Yanovsky. *Portativnoe bessmertie*. New York: Chekhov, 1953. 270 pages. $2.50," *BA*, 29(3):365–66, Summer.

24.   Review: "Boris Zaitsev. *Chekhov: literaturnaia biografiia*. New York: Chekhov, 1954. 261 pp. $2.50," *BA*, 29 (2):243, Spring.

1956

25.   *Siberia and the Reforms of 1822*. Seattle: University of Washington Press. (*University of Washington Publications on Asia*). 210 pp.

26.   Review: "Ivan Bunin. *O Chekhove (Nezakonchennaia rukopis´)*. New York: Chekhov, 1955. 412 pp. $3.00," *BA*, 30 (3): 289–90, Summer.

27.   Review: "Nicolas Evreinov. *Istoriia russkogo teatra—s drevneishikh vremen do 1917 goda*. New York: Chekhov, 1955. 413 pp. $3.00," *BA*, 30 (1):110, Winter.

28.   Review: "Wilhelm Lettenbauer. *Russische Literaturgeschichte*. Frankfurt am Main: Humboldt, 1955. 431 pp. 16.50 dm.," *BA*, 30 (4): 18, Autumn.

29.   Review: "A. M. Osorgina. *Istoriia russkoi literatury (S drevneishikh vremen do Pushkina)*. Paris: YMCA Press, 1955, 266 pp.," *BA*, 30 (4): 464, Autumn.

30.   Review: "Vladimir Seduro. *The Byelorussian Theater and Drama*. Edgar H. Lehrman, ed. New York: Research Program on the U.S.S.R., 1955. xxii, 516 pp.," *BA*, 30(2): 226–27, Spring.

31.   Review: "Sergei Shcherbatov. *Khudozhnik v ushedshei Rossii*. New York: Chekhov, 1955. 409 pp. $3.00," *BA*, 30(3): 349–50, Summer.

32.   Review: "Eugene Zamiatin. *Litsa*. New York: Chekhov, 1955. 285 pp. $2.50," *BA*, 30(2): 241, Spring.

1957

33.   "Education in the U.S.S.R.: Soviet System Declared Based on Slow Accumulation of Knowledge," *NYT*, 107 (36,460):34, Wednesday, N 20.

34. *Michael Speransky: Statesman of Imperial Russia, 1772–1839.* The Hague: Martinus Nijhoff. viii, 387 pp.

35. "The Russian Autocracy and Its Officials," *Harvard Slavic Studies, IV. Russian Thought and Politics.* Hugh McLean, Martin E. Malia, George Fischer, eds. Cambridge, Massachusetts: Harvard University Press. Pp. 77–91.

36. Review: "W. H. Bruford. *Anton Chekhov.* New Haven, Conn.: Yale University Press, 1957. 62 pp. $2.50," *BA*, 31(4):419, Autumn.

37. Review: "R. D. Charques. *A Short History of Russia.* New York: E. P. Dutton & Co., 1957. 284 pp., $3.95; Paul Sethe. *A Short History of Russia.* (Gateway Editions), Chicago: Henry Regnery Co., 1957. 192 pp., $1.25; C. Jay Smith, Jr. *The Russian Struggle for Power, 1914–1917: A Study of Russian Foreign Policy During the First World War.* New York: Philosophical Library, 1957. xv, 553 pp., $4.75," *SEEJ*, 15(3): 220–21, Fall.

38. Review: "Walther Kirchner, ed. *Eine Reise durch Sibirien im achtzehnten Jahrhundert (Die Fahrt des Schweizer Doktors Jakob Fries). (Veröffentlichungen des Osteuropa-Institutes München,* Band X). München: Isar Verlag, 1955. 126 pp.," *ASEER*, 16(2): 221–22, Apr.

39. Review: "*Littératures soviétiques. 1: Introduction aux littératures soviétiques: Contes et nouvelles.* Paris: Gallimard, 1956. 299 pp. 780 fr," *BA*, 31(2):155, Spring.

40. Review: "Rudolf Neumann, *Ostpreussen, 1945–1955.* Frankfurt M. and Berlin: Alfred Metzner Verlag, 1955. 112 pp.," *ASEER*, 16(2): 220–21, Apr.

41. Review: "V. S. Varshavsky. *Nezamechannoe pokolenie.* New York: Chekhov, 1956. 388 pp. $3.00," *BA*, 31(4): 437, Autumn.

42. Review: "Velikii [sic] Kniaz' Gabriil [sic] Konstantinovich. *V Mramornom dvortse.* New York: Chekhov, 1955. 412 pp. $3.00," *BA*, 31(1): 98, Winter.

1958

43. "Report on Russia's Big Red Schoolhouse," *NYTM*, 107(36,674, sec. 6): 5, 37–40, Je 22.

*44. "We do not teach them how to think," *NYTM*, 107(36,527, sec. 6): 7, 58–59, Ja 26. [Also see no. 265]

45. Review: "George Fischer. *Russian Liberalism.* [Cambridge, Massachusetts:] Harvard University Press, 1958. 240 pp. $4.50" "Victor Leontovitsch. *Geschichte des Liberalismus in Russland.* Frankfurt am Main: Vittorio Klostermann, 1957. 426 pp. DM 34," *RR*, 17(4):307–10, O.

46. Review: "Hans Rosenberg. *Bureaucracy, Aristocracy, and Autocracy. The Prussian Experience 1660–1815.* Cambridge, Massachusetts, 1958. (*Harvard Historical Monographs,* XXXIV), ix, 247 pp.," *CSSH*, 1: 396–99, 1958–1959.

47. Review: "Donald W. Treadgold. *The Great Siberian Migration: Government and Peasant in Resettlement from Emancipation to the First World War.* Princeton, New Jersey: Princeton Univ. Press, 1957. xiii, 278 pp., $5.00," *SEEJ*, 16(3):266–68, Fall.

1959

48. "Professors' Prose. Flight From Time," *Clark Scarlet*, 25(11):3–4.

*49. "Some Reflections on Russian Liberalism," *RR*, 18(3): 218–30, Jl. [Also see no. 266]

50. "Staatsdienst, Aussenpolitik, Ideologien. Die Rolle des Institutionen in der geistigen Entwicklung des Russischen Adels in 18 Jahrhundert," *JGO*, 7(2): [147]–81.

51. Review: "Robert F. Byrnes, *Bibliography of American Publications on East Central Europe, 1945–1957*. (*Slavic and East European Series*, XII.) [Bloomington:] Indiana Univ. Pubs., [1958]. xxx, 213 pp., $2.50," *SEEJ*, 17 (New Series) (3):280–81, Fall.

52. Review: "Jaroslaw Iwaszkiewicz. *Der Höhenflug.* Kurt Harrer, tr. München: Langen/Müller, 1959. 114 pp. 6.80 dm," *BA*, 33(4): 432, Autumn.

53. Review: "W. G. F. Jackson. *Seven Roads to Moscow.* New York: Philosophical Library, 1958. 334 pp. $7.50," *RR*, 18(4): 348–49, O.

54. "Gleb Struve. *Geschichte der Sowjetliteratur.* München: Isar, 1957. 595 pp. 38 dm," *BA*, 33(2): 189, Spring.

55. Review: "Donald W. Treadgold. *The Great Siberian Migration: Government and Peasant in Resettlement from Emancipation to the First World War.* Princeton: Princeton University Press, 1957. xiii, 278 pp., $5.00," *JEH*, 19(2): 323–25, Je.

56. Review: "Mikhail Zetlin. *The Decembrists.* Tr. George Panin. Preface Michael M. Karpovich. New York: International Univ. Press [c. 1958]. 349 pp., $5.00," *SEEJ*, 17 (New Series) (3): 303–4, Fall.

1960

57. "State and Nobility in the Ideology of M. M. Shcherbatov," *ASEER*, 19(3):[363]–79, O.

58. Review: "Hans Rogger. *National Consciousness in Eighteenth-Century Russia.* Cambridge, Mass.: Harvard University Press, 1960. viii, 319 pp. (*Russian Research Center Studies*, 38)," *JGO*, 8 (Neue Folge) (4):445–48.

1961

59. "Le climat politique et les projects de réforme dans les premières années du règne d'Alexandre Ier," *CMRS*, 11(4):415–33, O–D.

60. Review: "Jerome Blum. *Lord and Peasant in Russia from the Ninth to the Nineteenth Century.* Princeton: Princeton University Press, 1961. 656 pp. $12.50," *PSQ*, 77(2):307–10.

61. Review: "M. M. *Speranskii, Proekty i zapiski*, edited by S. N. Valk. Moscow-Leningrad: Akademiia nauk, Institut istorii, Leningradskoe otdelenie, 1961. 244 pp. 75k.," *SR*, 20(4):706–7, D.

1962

62. "L'état, le gouvernement et la tradition politique en Russie Impériale avant 1861," *RHMC*, 9: [295]–307, O–D.

*63. "Home, School, and Service in the Life of the 18th-Century Russian Nobleman," *SEER*, 40 (95):295–307, Je. [Also see no. 267]

64. Review: "Michael Cherniavsky. *Tsar and People: Studies in Russian Myths.* New Haven and London: Yale University Press, 1961. xix + 258 pp. $6.00," *SR*, 21(2):344–46, Je.

65. Review: "A Child of His Times. A review of Martin Malia: *Alexander Herzen and the Birth of Russian Socialism, 1812–55.* Harvard. 486 pp. $10.00," *NL*, 45(4):28–29, F 19.

66.   Review: "Anatole G. Mazour. *Russia: Tsarist and Communist*. Princeton, N.J.: D. Van Nostrand, 1962. x + 995 pp. $9.00," *SR*, 21(4):737–38, D.

1963

Ed 67.   Editor, *Peter the Great—Reformer or Revolutionary?* (*Problems in European Civilization*). Boston: D. C. Heath. xviii, 109 pp.

68.   Review: "*Eighteenth Century Russian Publications in the Library of Congress: A Catalog*. Prepared by Tatiana Fessenko. Washington, D. C. Government Printing Office, 1961. xvi + 157 pp. $1.00," *SR*, 22(1):185–86, Mr.

69.   Review: "Horst Jablonowski and Werner Philipp (eds.), *Forschungen zur osteuropäischen Geschichte (Historische Veröffentlichungen des Osteuropa-Instituts an der Freien Universität Berlin)*. Vol. I[1954], II[1955], III[1956], IV[1956], V[1957], VI[1958], VII[1959], VIII[1962]. Wiesbaden: Otto Harrassowitz," *SR*, 22(4):[751]–53, D.

70.   Review: "*Siberian Journey down the Amur to the Pacific, 1856–57*. Ed. by Charles Vevier. Madison: University of Wisconsin Press, 1962. ix, 370 pp. $6.00," *PNWQ*, 54(3):128, Jl.

71.   Review: "Jacob Walkin. *The Rise of Democracy in Pre-Revolutionary Russia: Political and Social Institutions under the Last Three Czars*. New York: Frederick A. Praeger, 1962. ix, 320 pp. $6.50," *SR*, 22(2):334–35, Je.

1964

72.   "The 150th Anniversary of the Campaign of 1812 in Soviet Historical Writing," *JGO*, 12(2):[247]–60, Jl.

* 73.   "Russia's Perception of Her Relationship with the West," *SR*, 23(1): [13]–19, Mr. [Also see no. 267]

74.   Review: "J. L. H. Keep. *The Rise of Social Democracy in Russia*. Oxford: Clarendon Press, 1963; Richard Kindersley. *The First Russian Revisionists; A Study of "Legal Marxism" in Russia*. Oxford: Clarendon Press, 1963; Arthur P. Mendel. *Dilemmas of Progress in Tsarist Russia—Legal Marxism and Legal Populism*. Cambridge, Massachusetts: Harvard University Press, 1963," *PC*, 13(4): 48–50, Jl–Ag.

75.   Review: "*Hans Lemberg: Die nationale Gedankenwelt der Dekabristen*. Köln, Graz: Herman Böhlau, 1963. viii, 168 pp. DM 16.50. (Kölner Historische Abhandlungen, Band 7)," *JGO*, 12(1):124–27, My.

76.   Review: "Friedrich von Schubert. *Unter dem Doppeladler: Erinnerungen eines Deutschen in russischen Offiziersdienst, 1789–1814*. Edited by Erik Amburger. Stuttgart: K. F. Koehler Verlag, 1962. viii, 388 pp.," *SR*, 23(1):139–40, Mr.

77.   Review: "Alexander Vucinich. *Science in Russian Culture: A History to 1860*. Stanford, Calif.: Stanford University Press, 1963. xv, 463 pp. $10.00," *JMH*, 36(4):450–51, D.

1965

78.   Review: "Horst Jablonowski and Werner Philipp, eds., *Forschungen zur osteuropäischen Geschichte*. Berlin and Wiesbaden: Otto Harrassowitz, 1963. 304 pp. (*Historische Veröffentlichungen des Osteuropa-Instituts an der Freien Universität Berlin*, Vol. IX)," *SR*, 24(1):130–31, Mr.

79. Review: "V. A. Maklakov. *The First State Duma (Contemporary Reminiscences)*. Bloomington: Indiana University Publications, 1964. 251 pp. $6.50," *RR*, 24(1):76–77, Ja.

80. Review: "Andre Mazon. *Deux russes écrivains français*. Paris: Didier, 1964. 427 pp. (*Études de littérature étrangère et comparée*, Vol. LI)," *SR*, 24(3):559–60, S.

81. Review: "Igor Smolitsch. *Geschichte der russischen Kirche, 1700–1917*. Vol. I. Leiden: E. J. Brill, 1964. lvii, 734 pp. 96 Dutch guilders. (*Studien zur Geschichte Osteuropas*, Vol. IX)," *SR*, 24(3):578–80, S.

1966

82. Editor. *The Decembrist Movement*. Englewood Cliffs, N. J.: Prentice-Hall, [1966]. (*Russian Civilization Series*). Michael Cherniavsky and Ivo J. Lederer, eds. x + 180 pp.

83. *Origins of the Russian Intelligentsia: The Eighteenth-Century Russian Nobility*. New York: Harcourt, Brace and World. 248 pp.

84. Editor. *Plans for Political Reform in Imperial Russia, 1730–1905*. Englewood Cliffs, N. J.: Prentice-Hall, [1966]. (*Russian Civilization Series*). Michael Cherniavsky and Ivo J. Lederer, eds. xi, 159 pp.

*85. Editor. *Russian Intellectual History: An Anthology*. With an introduction by Isaiah Berlin. (*The Harbrace Series in Russian Area Studies*). New York: Harcourt, Brace, and World. x, 404 pp. Also published: [Atlantic Highlands] N.J.: Humanities Press; Sussex: Harvester Press. [Also see no. 268]

86. Review: "Mathias Bernath, Horst Jablonowski, and Werner Philipp, eds. *Forschungen zur osteuropäischen Geschichte*. Berlin and Wiesbaden: Otto Harrassowitz. (*Historische Veröffentlichungen des Osteuropa-Instituts an der Freien Universität Berlin*. Vol. X[1965]. 356 pp. XI[1966]). 175 pp.," *SR*, 25(4):688–91, D.

1967

87. "Filling the Gap between Radishchev and the Decembrists," *SR*, 26 (3):[395]–413, S.

*88. "La jeunesse russe à l'aube du XIXe siècle—André Turgenev et ses amis," *CMRS*, 8(4):[560]–86, O–D. [Also see no. 269]

89. "Les Slaves, les Allemands et les 'Lumières,'" *CASS*, 1(4):[521]–51, Winter.

*90. "The Style of Russia's Imperial Policy and Prince G. A. Potemkin," *Statesman and Statecraft of the Modern West: Essays in Honor of Dwight E. Lee and H. Donaldson Jordan*. Gerald N. Grob, ed. Barre, Mass.: Barre Publishers. pp. 1–51. [Also see nos. 270 and 271]

91. Review: "Erik Amburger. *Geschichte der Behördenorganisation Russlands vom Peter dem Grossen bis 1917*. (*Studien zur Geschichte Osteuropas*, Number 10). Leiden: E. J. Brill, 1966. xxxii, 622 pp. 86 gl," *AHR*, 72(2):646–47, Ja.

92. Review: "Thornton Anderson. *Russian Political Thought: An Introduction*. Ithaca, N. Y.: Cornell University Press, 1967. xiii, 444 pp. $9.75," *AHR*, 73(2):541, D.

93. Review: "Martin Katz. *Mikhail N. Katkov: A Political Biography 1818–1887*. (*Studies in European History*, Number 6). The Hague: Mouton & Co., 1966. 195 pp. 24 gl.," *AHR*, 72(4): 1450, Jl.

94. Review: "E. Lampert. *Sons against Fathers: Studies in Russian Radicalism and*

Revolution. Oxford: The Clarendon Press, 1965. x, 405 pp. 63 S.," *The Historian,* 29(3):471–73, My.

95. Review: "Vladen Georgievič Sirotkin. *Duel' dvuch diplomatij. Rossija i Francija v 1801–1812 gg. (Le Duel de deux Diplomaties. Russie et France en 1801–1812).* Moscow: Izdat. Nauka, 1966. 206 pp. DM4," *JGO,* 15(3): 442–43, S.

1968

96. "Correspondance," *Annales: Économies, Sociétés, Civilisations,* 23(5): 1178–79, S–O. [Response to Michael Confino's review of *Origins of the Intelligentsia,* "Histoire et psychologie: A propos de la noblesse russe au XVIIIᵉ siècle," *Annales: Économies, Sociétés, Civilisations,* 22(6): 1163–1205, N–D, 1967.]

97. "Introduction," Alexander Israel Wittenberg. *The Prime Imperatives: Priorities in Education.* Preface by George Polya. Toronto, Vancouver: Clarke, Irwin & Company Limited. Pp. xi–xiv.

98. Review: "I. A. Fedosov. *Iz istorii russkoj obščestvennoj mysli XVIII stoletija* [*A Contribution to the History of Russian Social Thought*]. M. M. Ščerbatov. Moscow: Izdat. Moskovskogo Universiteta, 1967. 258 pp. DM 6, 10," *JGO,* 16(1):150, Mr.

99. Review: "Robert E. MacMaster. *Danilevsky: A Russian Totalitarian Philosopher.* Cambridge, Mass.: Harvard University Press, 1967. ix, 368 pp. $7.95," *PSQ,* 83(1):107–9, Mr.

100. Review: "Hugh Seton-Watson. *The Russian Empire, 1801–1917.* Oxford: Clarendon Press, 1967. 813 pp. $10.00," *RR,* 27(1):88–90, Ja.

1969

101. *Michael Speransky—Statesman of Imperial Russia, 1772–1839.* The Hague: Martinus Nijhoff. 2d rev. ed. ix, 394 pp.

102. "Some Translations of Surveys and Sources in Russian History," *CSS,* 3(3):556–64, Fall.

103. Review: "François-Xavier Coquin. *La Sibérie—Peuplement et immigration paysanne au XIXᵉ siècle.* Paris: Institut d'études slaves. Université de Paris. (*Collection historique,* No. XX). 1969. 789 pp. 60 F," *CSS,* 3(3):586–88, Fall.

104. Review: "Alton S. Donnelly. *The Russian Conquest of Bashkiria, 1552–1740: A Case Study in Imperialism (Yale Russian and East European Studies,* 7), New Haven and London: Yale University Press, 1968. x, 214 pp. $6.50. (Distributed in Canada by McGill-Queen's University Press, Montréal)," *CSS,* 3(4):750–52, Winter.

105. Review: "*Karlik favorita. Istorija žizni Ivana Andreeviča Jakubovskogo, karlika Svetlejšega Knjazja Platona Aleksandroviča Zubova, pisannaja im samym. Der Zwerg des Favoriten/ Die Lebensgeschichte Ivan Andreevič Jakubovskijs, des Zwerges des Fürsten Platon Aleksandrovič Zubov, von ihm selbst verfasst. S predisloviem i primečanijami grafa V. P. Zubova i poslesloviem Ditricha Gerchardta. Mit einem Vorwort und Anmerkungen von Valentin Graf Zubov sowie einem Nachwort von Dietrich Gerhardt.* Wilhelm Fink München 1968. 424 S. DM 68, (*Slavische Propyläen. Texte in Neu- und Nachdrucken* Band 32)," *JGO,* 17(1):112–13, Mr.

106. Review: "Forrestt A. Miller. *Dmitrii Miliutin and the Reform Era in Russia.*

Nashville, Tenn.: Vanderbilt University Press, 1968. iv, 246 pp. $7.50," *CSS*, 3(2):429–31, Summer.

1970

107. "The Domestic Policies of Peter III and His Overthrow," *AHR*, 75 (5):1289–1310, Je.

108. "Pugachev's Rebellion," *Preconditions of Revolution in Early Modern Europe*. Ed. with an introduction by Robert Forster and Jack P. Greene. Baltimore and London: The Johns Hopkins Press. Pp. 161–202.

109. Review: "John T. Alexander. *Autocratic Politics in a National Crisis: The Imperial Russian Government and Pugachev Revolt, 1773–1775* (*Russian and East European Series*, vol. 38). Bloomington and London: Indiana University Press for the International Affairs Center, 1969. xii, 346 pp. $8.50," *SR*, 29(3):507–8, S.

110. Review: "Robert F. Byrnes. *Pobedonostsev: His Life and Thought*. Bloomington and London: Indiana University Press, 1968. xiii, 495 pp. $15.00," *PSQ*, 85(3):528–30, S.

111. Review: "James R. Gibson. *Feeding the Russian Fur Trade—Provisionment of the Okhotsk Seaboard and the Kamchatka Peninsula 1639–1856*. Madison: University of Wisconsin Press, 1969. xix, 337 pp. $15.00," *CSS*, 4(1):118–19, Spring.

112. Review: "Patricia Kennedy Grimsted. *The Foreign Ministers of Alexander I: Political Attitudes and the Conduct of Russian Diplomacy, 1801–1825*. (*Russian and East European Studies*). Berkeley and Los Angeles: University of California Press, 1969. xxvi, 367 pp. $9.50," *AHR*, 75(5):1493–94, Je.

113. Review: "Hans-Bernd Harder. *Schiller in Russland. Materialen zu einer Wirkungsgeschichte. 1789–1814*. Verlag Gehlen Bad Homburg v.d.H., Berlin, Zürich, 1969. 234 S. DM 30 (*Frankfurter Beiträge zur Germanistik*, Band 4)," *JGO*, 18(3):450–52, S.

114. Review: "Michael Jenkins. *Arakcheev: Grand Vizier of the Russian Empire*. New York: The Dial Press, 1969. 317 pp. $5.95," *CSS*, 4(1):119–20, Spring.

115. Review: "Miriam Kochan. *Life in Russia under Catherine the Great*. (*European Life Series*, edited by Peter Quenell). London: B. T. Batsford Ltd. and New York: G. P. Putnam's Sons, 1969. ix, 182 pp. (Distributed in Canada by the Copp Clark Publishing Co., Toronto)," *CSS*, 4(3):619–20, Fall.

116. Review: "A. Walicki. *The Controversy over Capitalism. Studies in the Social Philosophy of the Russian Populists*. Oxford: Clarendon Press, 1969. 197 pp. 45 S. $7.25. (Distributed in Canada by Oxford University Press, Don Mills, Ontario)," *CSS*, 4(1):120–21, Spring.

1971

117. "Eighteenth- and Nineteenth-Century Russia" in Norman F. Cantor's *Perspectives on the European Past: Conversations with Historians*. New York and London: The Macmillan Company and Collier-Macmillan Limited. Pp. 242–66 [Section II, Chapter 28].

118. *Imperial Russia 1682–1825: The Coming of Age of Modern Russia*. New York: Alfred A. Knopf. xi, 176 pp.

119. "Patterns of Russian Imperial Policy Towards the Nationalities," in *So-*

viet Nationality Problems. Edward Allworth, editor. New York-London: Columbia University Press. Pp. [22]–42.

120. "Random Notes on the Reign of Catherine II in the Light of Recent Literature," *JGO*, 19(4):[541]–56, D.

121. Review: "Mathias Bernath, Horst Jablonowski,and Werner Philipp, eds. *Forschungen zur osteuropäischen Geschichte*, vol. XV. (*Historische Veröffentlichungen des Osteuropa-Instituts an der Freien Universität Berlin*) Berlin and Wiesbaden: Otto Harrassowitz, 1970. 306 pp. DM 78," *SR*, 30 (2):385–88, Je.

122. Review: "Peter Yakovlevich Chaadaev. *Philosophical Letters & Apology of a Madman.* Trans. and introd. Mary-Barbara Zeldin. Knoxville: The University of Tennessee Press, 1969. xi, 203 pp. $7.50; Raymond T. McNally. *The Major Works of Peter Chaadaev; A Translation and Commentary.* Introd. Richard Pipes. Notre Dame & London: University of Notre Dame Press, 1969. xix, 261 pp. $7.95," *CSS*, 5(1):129–30, Spring.

123. Review: "Peter K. Christoff. *The Third Heart: Some Intellectual-Ideological Currents and Cross Currents in Russia, 1800–1830.* (*Slavistic Printings and Reprintings*, 77). The Hague and Paris: Mouton, 1970. 130 pp. 34 Dutch guilders," *SR*, 30(2):393–94, Je.

124. Review: "Robert O. Crummey. *The Old Believers and the World of Antichrist. The Vyg Community and the Russian State, 1694–1855.* Madison: The University of Wisconsin Press, 1970. xix, 258 pp. $10.00," *CSS*, 5(3):433–34, Fall.

125. Review: "Annelies Lauch. *Wissenschaft und kulturelle Beziehungen in der russischen Aufklärung—Zur Wirken H. L. Ch. Bacmeisters.* Deutsche Akademie der Wissenschaften zu Berlin. (*Veröffentlichungen des Instituts für Slawistik*, 51). (H. H. Bielfeldt, Herausgeber). Berlin: Akademie-Verlag, 1969. 444 pp. (paper)," *CSS*, 5(3):435–36, Fall.

126. Review: "Norman E. Saul. *Russia and the Mediterranean, 1797–1807.* Chicago and London: The University of Chicago Press, 1970. xii, 268 pp., Sh 79," *JGO*, 19(2):293–95, Je.

1972

127. Editor. *Catherine the Great: A Profile.* New York: Hill and Wang. xiii + 331 pp. (*World Profiles.* Aida DiPace Donald, general editor).

128. "First Soviet-American Historical Colloquium," *SR*, 31(4):969–71, D.

129. Editor. *Peter the Great Changes Russia.* Lexington: D. C. Heath, 1972. (*Problems in European Civilization*, John Ratté, ed.) xxiv, 199 pp. [A new and revised edition of *Peter the Great—Reformer or Revolutionary?* Boston: D. C. Heath, 1963.]

130. Review: "François-Xavier Coquin. *La grande commission législative, 1767–1768. Les Cahiers de doléances urbains (Province de Moscou).* Preface by Victor L. Tapié. *Publications de la Faculté des lettres et sciences humaines de Paris-Sorbonne.* (Série "Recherches," vol. 67) Paris and Louvain: Béatrice Nauwelaerts, 1972. ix, 258 pp.," *SR*, 31(3):663–64, S.

131. Review: "James Cracraft. *The Church Reform of Peter the Great.* Stanford, California: Stanford University Press, 1971. 336 pp.," *RR*, 31(1):77–79, Ja.

132. Review: "'Revolution—Then.' Sam Dolgoff, editor and translator.

Bakunin on Anarchy: Selected Works by the Activist-Founder of World Anarchism. Alfred A. Knopf. Leon Trotsky. *1905.* Translated by Anya Bostock. Random House," *Yale Review,* 61(4):625–28, Summer.

133.   Review: "I. A. Fedosov, I. I. Astaf'ev, I. D. Koval'chenko, eds. *Isto-chnikovedenie istorii SSSR XIX-nachalo* [sic] *XXv.* Moscow. *Izdatel'stvo Moskovskogo Universiteta (Istoricheskii fakul'tet, Kafedra istorii SSSR—period kapitalizma),* 1970. 469 pp. 1 ruble 37 kopeks," *CASS,* 6(1):149–50, Spring.

134.   Review: "N. M. Lisovskii, comp. *Russkaia periodicheskaia pechat' 1703–1900 gg. (Bibliografia i graficheskiia tablitsy)* St. Petersburg 1895–Petrograd 1915. (Nachdruck by Zentral-Antiquariat der Deutschen Demokratischen Republik, Leipzig 1965) 267 pp. & Tables. $51.00; S. A. Vengerov, comp. *Russkiia knigi—s biograficheskimi dannymi ob avtorakh i perevodchikakh (1708–1893).* St. Petersburg, 1897–1899 (I. A-Babadzhanov; II. Babaev-Bogatyr'; III. Bogatyr'-Vavilov). (Nachdruck by Zentral-Antiquariat der Deutschen Demokratischen Republik, Leipzig, 1967). vii, 476 pp., iv, 472 pp. $81.00," *CASS,* 6(1):150–51, Spring.

135.   Review: "K. A. Papmehl. *Freedom of Expression in Eighteenth Century Russia.* The Hague: Martinus Nijhoff, 1971. xvi, 166 pp. 26 Dutch guilders," *JGO,* 20(3):446–47, S.

1973

136.   "The Enlightenment in Russia and Russian Thought in the Enlightenment," *The Eighteenth Century in Russia.* J. G. Garrard, Editor. Oxford: Clarendon Press. Pp. [25]–47.

137.   "Introduction," *Zhizn' i prikliucheniia Andreia Bolotova: opisanie samim im dlia svoikh potemtsev.* Cambridge, Eng.: Oriental Research Partners. 3v. in 1. *(Memoir Series)* Pp. iii–[viii]. Reprint of the 1931 ed. published by Academia, Moskva.

138.   Review: "*Forschungen zur osteuropäische Geschichte (Werner Philipp zum 65. Geburtstag von seinen Schülern). (Historische Veröffentlichungen des Osteuropa Institut an der Freien Universität Berlin).* Berlin: In Kommission bei Otto Harrassowitz Wiesbaden, 1973. 151 pp.," *CASS,* 7(4):545–46, Winter.

139.   Review: "Joseph T. Fuhrmann et al. *Essays on Russian Intellectual History.* Foreword by James P. Hart. Introduction by Sidney Monas. Edited by Leon Borden Blair. *(The Walter Prescott Webb Memorial Lectures,* Number 5.) Austin: University of Texas Press for the University of Texas at Arlington, 1971. 123 pp. $5.00," *AHR,* 78(2):464–65, Apr.

140.   Review: "Helmut Grasshoff and Ulf Lehmann, eds. *Studien zur Geschichte der russischen Literatur des 18. Jahrhunderts.* 3 vols. (Deutsche Akademie der Wissenschaften zu Berlin. *Veröffentlichungen des Instituts für Slawistik,* Nr. 28. Herausgegeben von H. H. Bielfeldt). Berlin: Akademie Verlag, 1963–1968. 187 pp., 492 pp., 664 pp. 25, 46, 65 DM.; *A. N. Radiščev und Deutschland; Beiträge zur Literatur des ausgehenden 18. Jahrhunderts. (Sitzungsberichte der sächsischen Akademie der Wissenschaften zu Leipzig. Philologisch-historische Klass,* Band 114, Heft 1). Berlin: Akademie Verlag, 1969. 132 pp. 9.50 DM," *CASS,* 7(1):118–19, Spring.

141.   Review: "Friedhelm Berthold Kaiser. *Die russische Justizreform von 1864. Zur Geschichte der russischen Justiz von Katharina II bis 1917.* Leiden: E. J. Brill, 1972. 552 pp.," *RR,* 32(3):318–19, Jl.

142.   Review: "Klaus Meyer. *Bibliographie zur osteuropäischen Geschichte. Ver-*

zeichnis der zwischen 1939 und 1964 veröffentlichten Literatur in westeuropäischen Sprachen zur osteuropäischen Geschichte bis 1945. Unter Mitarbeit von J. H. L. Keep, K. Manfrass, A. Peetre. Herausgegeben von Werner Philipp. (*Bibliographische Mitteilungen des Osteuropa Institut an der Freien Universität Berlin.* Heft 10). Berlin: Osteuropa Institut an der Freien Universität Berlin, 1972. xlix, 649 pp.," *CASS,* 7(4):544–45, Winter.

143. Review: "*La Russie et l'Europe XVe–XXe siècles.* Paris-Moscou: Bibliothèque général de l'École Pratique des Hautes Études-VIe Section, S.E.V.P.E.N., 1970. 326 pp.; *Au Siècle des Lumières.* Paris-Moscou: École Pratique des Hautes Études-Sorbonne-VIe Section: Sciences Économiques et Sociales; Institut d'Histoire Universelle de l'Académie des Sciences de l'U.R.S.S., 1970. 310 pp.;" *CASS,* 7(1):120–21, Spring.

144. Review: "Tamara Talbot Rice. *Elizabeth: Empress of Russia.* New York and Washington: Praeger Publishers, 1970. xvi, 231 pp. $8.50," *CASS,* 7(1):122, Spring.

145. Review: "George L. Yaney. *The Systematization of Russian Government: Social Evolution in the Domestic Administration of Imperial Russia, 1711–1905.* Urbana, Chicago, London: University of Illinois Press, 1973. xvi, 430 pp. $13.50," *SR,* 33(2): 345–47, Je.

1974

146. "The Empress and the Vinerian Professor: Catherine II's Projects of Government Reform and Blackstone's Commentaries," *OSP,* 7(New Series): [18]–41.

147. "Michael Cherniavsky," *JGO,* 22 (Neue Folge) (1):159.

148. "Russia and the Soviet Union—II. A History of the Eighteenth Century." *Encyclopedia Britannica (Macropaedia).* 15th ed. Chicago and other places, vol. 16, pp. 49–57.

149. Review: "Valentin Boss. *Newton and Russia: The Early Influence, 1698–1796.* (*Russian Research Center Studies, 69*) Cambridge, Mass.: Harvard University Press, 1972. xviii, 309 pp. $19.00," *AHR,* 79(1):196–97, F.

150. Review: "Peter K. Christoff. *An Introduction to Nineteenth-Century Russian Slavophilism.* Volume 2, I. V. Kireevskij. (*Slavistic Printings and Reprints, 23/2*). The Hague: Mouton, 1972. x, 406 pp. 68gls," *AHR,* 79(2):534–35, Apr.

151. Review: "Karp Emel'janovič Džedžula. *Rossija i Velikaja francuzskaja buržuaznaja revoljucija konca XVIII veka (Russia and the Great French Bourgeois Revolution at the End of the 18th Century).* Kiev: Izdat. Kievskogo Universiteta, 1972. 449 pp. DM 14.70." *JGO,* 22 (*Neue Folge*)(3):433–35.

152. Review: "Shmuel Galai. *The Liberation Movement in Russia, 1900–1905.* Cambridge at the University Press, 1973. x, 325 pp. $22.50," *The Historian,* 36(2):329, F.

153. Review: "Hans-Jürgen Krüger, editor. *Archivalische Fundstücke zu den russisch-deutschen Beziehungen. Erik Amburger zum 65. Geburtstag. Giessener Abhandlungen zur Agrar- und Wirtschaftsforschung des europäischen Ostens.* (*Osteuropa Studien der Hochschulen des Landes Hessen.* Reihe 1). Berlin: In Kommission bei Duncker & Humblot, 1973," *CASS,* 8(4):597, Winter.

154. Review: "Alexander V. Muller, translator and editor. *The Spiritual*

Regulations of Peter the Great. (Publications on Russia and Eastern Europe of the Institute for Comparative and Foreign Area Studies, Number 3). Seattle and London: University of Washington Press, 1972. xxxviii, 150 pp. $10.00," *CASS*, 8(2):327–28, Summer.

155. Review: "S. O. Petrov, compiler. *Knyby braždans'koho druku vydani na Ukrajini XVIII–perša polovyna XIX stolittja: Kataloh (Books in Civil Type Published in the Ukraine in the Eighteenth and First Half of the Nineteenth Centuries: A Catalogue)*. Xarkiv: Vydavnyctvo "Redakcijno-vydavnyčyj viddil Knyžkovoji palaty URSR," 1971. 297 pp. 1400 copies," *Recenzija*, 5(1): 25, Fall–Winter.

156. Review: "S. Frederick Starr. *Decentralization and Self-Government in Russia, 1830–1870*. Princeton, N. J.: Princeton University Press, 1972. xiii, 386 pp. $15.00," *American Political Science Review*, 68(1):332–33, Mr.

157. Review: "Robert C. Tucker. *Stalin as Revolutionary 1879–1929. A Study in History and Personality*. New York: W. W. Norton & Company, 1973. xx, 519 pp.; Stephen F. Cohen. *Bukharin and the Bolshevik Revolution. A Political Biography 1888–1938*. New York: Alfred A. Knopf, 1973. xix, 495 pp.," *NZb*, 115:267–71, Je.

1975

*158. Review Essay: "*Iz pod glyb i istoriia Russkoi obshchestvennoi mysli*," *NZb*, 119:[191]–203, Je. [Also see no. 272]

*159. "The Well-Ordered Police State and the Development of Modernity in Seventeenth and Eighteenth Century Europe: An Attempt at a Comparative Approach," *AHR*, 80(5):1221–43, D. [Also see no. 273]

160. Review: "G. R. V. Barratt. *Voices in Exile: The Decembrist Memoirs*. Montreal: McGill-Queen's University Press, 1974. xxi, 381 pp. $18.50.; Anatole G. Mazour. *Women in Exile: Wives of the Decembrists*. Tallahassee, Florida: The Diplomatic Press, 1975. x, 134 pp. $15.00," *CSP*, 17(2&3):528–29, Summer and Fall.

161. Review: "Wolfgang Gesemann. *Die Entdeckung der unteren Volksschichten durch die russische Literatur (Zur Dialektik eines literarischen Motivs von Kantemir bis Belinskij)*. Wiesbaden: Otto Harrassowitz, 1972. 315S. (*Veröffentlichungen des Osteuropa-Institutes München*, Band 39)," *Zeitschrift für Slavische Philologie*, 38(1):197–201.

1976

162. "Imperial Russia: Peter I to Nicholas I," *An Introduction to Russian History*. Robert Auty and Dimitrii Obolensky, eds. With the editorial assistance of Anthony Kingsford. Cambridge: Cambridge University Press. Pp. 121–95. [Chapter 4.]

163. "Introduction," S. G. Pushkarev. *Krest'ianskaia pozemel'noperedel'naia obshchina v Rossii*. Newtonville, Mass.: Oriental Research Partners. Pp. i–v.

164. "Peter I," *The American Peoples Encyclopedia*, 14: 450–51. [Originally published in 1966]

165. "Russia's Autocracy and Paradoxes of Modernization," *Ost-West-Begegnung in Österreich. Festschrift für Eduard Winter zum 80. Geburtstag.* Herausgegeben von Gerhard Oberkofler und Eleonore Zlabinger. Wein-Köln-Graz: Böhlau Verlag. Pp. 275–83.

166. "Sergei Martynovich Troitskii, 1930–1976," *SR*, 35(3):595–96, S.

167. Review: "Adriano Cavanna. *La codificazione penal in Italia. Le origini lombarde.* Milano, A Giuffré ed., 1975. (*Università degli Studi di Milano Facoltà di Giurisprudenza. Pubblicazioni dell'Istituto di Storia del Diritto Italiano*, 5), 317 pp.," Trad. di Angelo Torre. *Rivista storica italiana*, 88(4):881–87, D.

168. Review: "Anton Denikin. *The Career of a Tsarist Officer: Memoirs, 1872–1916.* With an annotated translation by Margaret Patoski. Minneapolis: University of Minnesota Press, 1975. xxii, 333 pp. $17.95," *The Historian*, 38 (4):752–53, Ag.

1977

169. "Uniformity, Diversity, and the Imperial Administration in the Reign of Catherine II," *Osteuropa in Geschichte und Gegenwart. Festschrift für Günther Stökl zum 60. Geburtstag.* Herausgegeben von Hans Lemberg, Peter Nitsche und Erwin Oberländer unter Mitwirkung von Manfred Alexander und Hans Hecker. Köln-Wien: Böhlau Verlag. Pp. 97–113.

170. "Zum Problem der Sowjetsprache und ihrer Rolle in der sowjetischen Geschichtswissenschaft" *Die Interdependenz von Geschichte und Politik in Osteuropa seit 1954–Protokoll der Historiker Fachtagung in Bad Wiessee 1976.* Stuttgart: Deutsche Gesellschaft für Osteuropakunde e. V. Pp. 26–31.

171. Review: "'An opening to the West.' A review of Harold N. Ingle: *Nesselrode and the Russian Rapprochement with Britain, 1836–1844.* 196 pp. University of California Press. £8.20," *TLS*, 3904: 8, Je 7.

172. Review: "Wolfgang Knackstedt. *Moskau: Studien zur Geschichte einer mittelalterlichen Stadt. (Quellen und Studien zur Geschichte der östlichen Europa,* [vol. 8].) Wiesbaden: Franz Steiner Verlag, 1975. x, 285 pp. Maps. DM56, paper," *SR*, 36(4):[676]–77, D.

173. Review: "S. S. Landa. *Dukh revoliutsionnykh preobrazovanii . . . Iz istorii formirovaniia ideologii i politicheskoi organizatsii Dekabristov, 1816–1825* [The spirit of revolutionary transformations . . . from the history of the formation of the ideology and political organization of the Decembrists, 1816–1825]. Moscow: Izd-vo "Mysl'," 1975. 379 pp. 1.37 rubles," *RR*, 36(1):86–87, Ja.

174. Review: "W. H. Roobol. *Tsereteli—A Democrat in the Russian Revolution: A Political Biography.* Translated from the Dutch by Philip Hyams and Lynne Richards. (*International Institute of Social History, Amsterdam, Studies in Social History,* 1). The Hague: Martinus Nijhoff, 1976, xii, 273 pp. Illus. 80 Dglds.," *SR*, 36(4):681–82, D.

175. Review: "'The rise of the intelligentsia.' A review of Nicholas V. Riasanovsky: *A Parting of Ways. Government and the Educated Public in Russia, 1801–1855.* 323 pp. Oxford: Clarendon Press. 12 pounds," *TLS*, 3930: 839, Jl 8.

176. Review: "*Russkaia religiozno-filosofskaia mysl' XX veka: sbornik statei.* Edited by N. P. Poltoratskii. (*Slavic Series,* 2). Pittsburgh: Department of Slavic Languages and Literatures, Faculty of Arts and Sciences, University of Pittsburgh, 1975. 413 pp. Paper," *SR*, 36(1): 132–33, Mr.

177. Review: "Jeremiah Schneiderman. *Sergei Zubatov and Revolutionary Marxism: The Struggle for the Working Class in Tsarist Russia.* Ithaca and London: Cornell University Press, 1976. 401 pp. $18.50," *Labor History*, 18 (3):460–63, Summer.

178. Review: "Adam B. Ulam. *In the Name of the People: Prophets and Conspirators*

in Prerevolutionary Russia. New York: The Viking Press, 1977. xii, 418 pp. $15.00," *PSQ*, 92(2):358–60, Summer.

179.   Review: "Alexander Vucinich. *Social Thought in Tsarist Russia: The Quest for a General Science of Society, 1861–1917*. Chicago: University of Chicago Press, 1976. ix, 294 pp. $15.50," *CSP*, 19(2):223–25, Je.

180.   Review: "'Analysing the Realm of a Russian Utopia.' A review of A. Walicki: *The Slavophile Controversy*, 1975," *CASS*, 11(3):[431]–37, Fall.

1978

181.   "Russian Intellectual History and Its Historiography: Critical Remarks," *Forschungen zur Osteuropäischen Geschichte*, "*Werner Philipp zum 70. Geburtstag*," 25:297–303.

182.   Review: "'O knige Alena Bezansona.' A review of Alain Besançon: *Les origines intellectuelles du Léninisme*. Paris: Calmann-Lévi, 1977," *NZh*, 130: [219]–28, Mr.

183.   Review: "Astrid von Borcke. *Die Ursprünge des Bolschewismus—Die Jakobinische Tradition in Russland und die Theorie der Revolutionären Diktatur*. Munich: Johannes Berchmans, 1977. 646 pp. DM 89," *RR*, 37(2):224, Apr.

184.   Review: "*Landmarks: A Collection of Essays on the Russian Intelligentsia 1909: Berdyaev, Bulgakov, Gershenzon, Izgoev, Kistyakovsky, Struve, Frank*. Edited by Boris Shragin and Albert Todd. Translated by Marian Schwartz. New York: Karz Howard (200 East 84th Street, New York, N.Y. 10028), 1977. lx, 210 pp. $12.75," *SR*, 37(1):128–30, Mr.

185.   Review: "'What Became of the Liberal Tradition?—Comments on *Samosoznanie*.' A review of P. Litvinov, M. Meerson-Aksenov, and B. Shragin: *Samosoznanie: sbornik statei*. New York: "Khronika," 1976. 320 pp. $9.00," *SR*, 37(1):[116]–19, Mr.

186.   Review: "'Intelligentsia et nationalisme ruthènes.' A review of P. R. Magocsi: *The shaping of a national identity. Subcarpathian Rus'. 1848–1948*. Cambridge, Mass.: Harvard University Press, 1978. xiii, 640 pp.," *CMRS*, 19(4):451–52, O–D.

187.   Review: "George F. Putnam. *Russian Alternatives to Marxism: Christian Socialism and Idealistic Liberalism in Twentieth Century Russia*. Knoxville: University of Tennessee Press, 1977. xii, 233 pp.," *NZh*, 131: 288–90, Je.

188.   Review: "N. V. Reviakina. *Problemy cheloveka v ital'ianskom gumanizme vtoroi poloviny XIV– pervoi poloviny XV v.* (*Problems of Man in Italian Humanism in the Second Half of the XIVth and the first Half of the XVth Centuries.*) Moscow: Nauka Publishing House, 1977. 272 pp. 1 ruble 14 kopecks; A. Kh. Gorfunkel'. *Gumanizm i naturfilosofiia ital'ianskogo Vozrozhdeniia*. (*Humanism and Natural Philosophy in the Italian Renaissance.*) Moscow: Mysl' Publishing House, 1977. 359 pp. 1 ruble 67 kopecks," *Renaissance Quarterly*, 31(3):373–78, Fall.

1979

189.   Review Essay. "The Bureaucratic Phenomenon of Imperial Russia, 1700–1905," *AHR*, 84(2):399–411, Apr.

190. "Codification et droit en Russie impériale. Quelques remarques comparatives," *CMRS*, 20(1):5–13, Ja–Mr.

191. Review: "Isaiah Berlin. *Russian Thinkers*. Edited by Henry Hardy and Aileen Kelly. Introduction by Aileen Kelly. New York: Viking Press, 1978. xxiv, 312 pp. $14.95," *SR*, 38 (1): 106–7, Mr.

192. Review: "*Russland, Deutschland, Amerika: Festschrift für Fritz T. Epstein zum 80. Geburtstag*. Edited by Alexander Fischer, Günter Moltmann, and Klaus Schwabe. (*Frankfurter Historische Abhandlungen*, vol. 17). Wiesbaden: Franz Steiner Verlag, 1978. xviii, 441 pp. DM 58, paper," *SR*, 38(3) 485–86, S.

1980

193. "Catherine II, Empress of Russia (Catherine the Great)," *Academic American Encyclopedia*, v.4, pp. 209–10. Princeton, N.J.: Aretê Publishing Company.

194. "Russia/Union of Soviet Socialist Republics, history of," *Academic American Encyclopedia*, v.16, pp. 351–60. Princeton, N.J.: Aretê Publishing Company.

195. Review: "J. L. Black. *Citizens for the Fatherland: Education, Educators, and Pedagogical Ideals in Eighteenth Century Russia* (With a Translation of *Book on the Duties of Man and Citizen*, St. Petersburg 1783). (*East European Monographs*, no. 53). Boulder, Colo.: East European Quarterly, 1979. xiii, 273 pp. $16.50. Distributed by Columbia University Press," RH, 7(3):364.

196. Review: "Alex De Jonge. *Fire and Water: A Life of Peter the Great*. New York: Coward, McCann & Geoghegan, 1980. 279 pp. $12.95; Robert K. Massie. *Peter The Great: His Life and World*. New York: Alfred A. Knopf, 1980. xii, 909 pp. $17.95," RR, 40(1):58–60, Ja.

197. Review: "John B. Dunlop. *The New Russian Revolutionaries*. Belmont, Mass.: Nordland Publishing Company, 1976. 344 pp. $18.50," *SR*, 39 (1): 124–25, Mr.

198. Review: "Manfred Hildermeier. *Die Sozialrevolutionäre Partei Russlands—Agrarsozialismus und Modernisierung im Zarenreich (1900–1914)* (*Beiträge zur Geschichte Osteuropas*, Dietrich Geyer and Hans Roos, editors, Band 11). Köln-Wien: Böhlau Verlag, 1978. xviii, 458 pp.," *CASS*, 14 (4): 560–61, Winter.

199. Review: "Hartmut Klinger. *Konstantin Nikolaevič Bestužev-Rjumins Stellung in der russischen Historiographie und seine gesellschaftliche Tätigkeit. (Ein Beitrag zur russischen Geistesgeschichte des 19. Jahrhunderts)*. Frankfurt/M: Peter D. Lang, 1980. 244 pp. SFr.45," *RR* 40(3): 342–43, Je.

200. Review: "'Was Peter all that great?' A review of Robert K. Massie: *Peter the Great: His Life and World*. New York: Alfred A. Knopf, 1980. 909 pp. $17.95," *New York Review of Books*, 28 (4): 49–50, Mr 19.

201. Review: "James C. McClelland. *Autocrats and Academics: Education, Culture, and Society in Tsarist Russia*. Chicago: University of Chicago Press, 1979. xiv, 150 pp. $14.00," *RR*, 39(2): 239–40, Apr.

202. Review: "*Russian Officialdom: The Bureaucratization of Russian Society from the Seventeenth to the Twentieth Century*. Edited by Walter McKenzie Pintner and Don Karl Rowney. Chapel Hill, N.C.: University of North Carolina Press, 1980. xviii + 396 pp. $20.00 hardcover, $12.00 paperback," *HUS*, 5(1):125–29, Mr.

203. Review: "*Russian Orthodoxy under the Old Regime*. Edited by Robert L.

Nichols and Theofanis G. Stavrou. Minneapolis: University of Minnesota Press, 1978. xi + 261 pp.," CMRS, 21(1): [123]–25, Ja–Mr.

1981

204. "O tsarstvovanii Nikolaia I v svete noveishei istoriografii," *Russkii al'manakh*. Edited by Zinaida Shakhovskaia, Rene Gerra, Evgenii Ternovskii. Parizh: L'Almanach russe. Pp. 302–14.

205. Review: "Erik Amburger. *Ingermanland: Eine junge Russlands im Wirkungsbereich der Residenz und Weltstadt St. Petersburg-Leningrad*. 2 vols. *(Beiträge zur Geschichte Osteuropas*, vol. 13). Cologne and Vienna: Böhlau Verlag, 1980. xvi, 1947 pp., 16 pp. plates. Maps. DM 278," *SR*, 40 (3):468–69, Fall.

1982

206. "Beseda s istorikom Markom Raevym," *Vestnik russkogo khristianskogo dvizheniia*, 136(1/11):290–95. [K vykhodu v svet na frantsuzkom iazyke lektsii M. Raeva—*Comprendre l'Ancien Régime* (Poniat' staryi rezhim), Seuil, 1981, 320 p.]

*207. *Comprendre l'Ancien Régime russe: État et société en Russie impériale: Essai d'interprétation*. With a preface by Alain Besançon. Paris: Editions Du Seuil, 247 pp. [Also see nos. 274, 275]

208. Review: "J. Michael Hittle. The Service City: State and Townsmen in Russia, 1600–1800. Cambridge, Mass.: Harvard University Press, 1979. vii, 297 pp. $20.00," *LH*, 23(2):307–10, Spring.

209. "Intelligentsiia i kruzhki v Peterburge v nachale XIX veka," *OB.*" 1:10–18, O.

210. "Seventeenth-Century Europe in Eighteenth-Century Russia? (Pour prendre congé du dix-huitième siècle russe)," *SR*, 41(4): [611]–619, Winter; and "Reply," *SR*, 41(4): [634]–38, Winter.

211. "Some Remarks on the Pipes-Nove Exchange," *RU*, 5–6:124–26.

212. "Voina 1812 goda i russkaia obshchestvennost' v tsarstvovanie Aleksandra pervogo," *RM*, 3438: 10–11, Thursday, N 11.

213. Review: "*Russia in the Age of Catherine the Great*. By Isabel de Madariaga. New Haven, Conn.: Yale University Press, 1981. Pp. xii + 698," *JMH*, 54(3):635–38, S.

214. Review: "Heinz Ischreyt, series editor. *Studien zur Geschichte der Kulturbeziehungen in Mittel- und Osteuropa* (Im Auftrage des Studienkreises für Kulturbeziehungen Mittel- und Osteuropas, herausgegeben von Heinz Ischreyt). Volume V: Heinz Ischreyt, general editor. Eva H. Balazs, Ludwig Hammermayer, Hans Wagner, Jerzy Wojtowics, editors. *Beförderer der Aufklärung in Mittel- und Osteuropa (Freimaurer, Gesellschaften, Clubs)*. Berlin: Verlag Ulrich Camen, 1979. 347 pp. Volume VI: Wolfgang Kessler, general editor. B. I. Krasnobaev, Gert Robel, Herbert Zeman, editors. *Reisen und Reisebeschreibunger im 18. und 19. Jahrbundert als Quellen der Kulturbeziehungsforschung*. Berlin: Verlag Ulrich Camen, 1980. 403 pp.," *RH*, 9(2–3): 402–4.

215. Review: "*Russophilie und Konservatismus: Die russophile Literatur in der*

Deutschen Öffentlichkeit 1831–1852. By Peter Jahn. Geschichte und Theorie der Politik. Unterreihe A: Geschichte, vol. 2. Stuttgart: Ernst Klett Verlag, 1980. viii, 333pp.; *Das veränderte Russland: Studien zum deutschen Russland-verständnis im 18 Jahrhundert zwischen 1725 und 1762*. By Eckhard Matthes. Europäische Hochschulschriften. Series 3: Geschichte und ihre Hilfswissenshaften, vol. 135. Frankfurt/Main, Bern, and Cirencester: Peter D. Lang, 1981. 566 pp.," *SR*, 41(3): 541–42, Fall.

216. Review: *"Rethinking Ukrainian History*. Edited by Ivan L. Rudnytsky. With the Assistance of John-Paul Himka. Edmonton: The Canadian Institute of Ukrainian Studies and the University of Alberta (Distributed by the University of Toronto Press), 1981. x, 268 pp. $14.95 cloth; $9.95 paper," *HUS*, 6(1):100–103, Mr.

217. Review: "Orest Subtelny, *The Mazepists—Ukrainian Separatism in the Eighteenth Century*.viii, 280 pp. $20.00. *East European Monographs*. Boulder, Colo. Distributed by Columbia University Press, 1981," *HUS*, 6(3):415–17, S.

218. Review: "Alexander Yanov. *The Origins of Autocracy: Ivan the Terrible in Russian History*. Translated by Stephen Dunn. Berkeley: University of California Press, 1981. xvi, 339 pp. $19.95," *RR*, 41(4):474–76, O.

219. Review: "Dymitri Zlepko. *Der grosse Kosakenaufstand 1648 gegen die polnische Herrschaft. Die Rzeczpospolita und das Kosakentum in der ersten Phase des Aufstandes*. Veröffentlichungen des Osteuropa-Institutes München. Herausgeber: Georg Stadmuller. Band 49. Wiesbaden: Otto Harrassowitz, 1980. 132 pp. $19.50," *RH*, 9(1):129.

1983

220. "Academic Exchanges with the Soviet Union: Intellectual, Political, and Moral Dilemmas," *Proceedings. General Education Seminar. Columbia University*. Vol. 1: *Educational Frontiers and the Cultural Tradition in the Contemporary University*. 1982–83. Pp. 73–76.

221. "Na puti k revoliutsii v Rossii," *OB*, 4:30–31, Apr.

222. "The Russian Nobility in the Eighteenth and Nineteenth Centuries: Trends and Comparisons," *The Nobility in Russia and Eastern Europe*. Edited by Ivo Banac and Paul Bushkovitch. New Haven: Yale Concilium on International and Area Studies. (*Yale Russian and East European Publications*; 3). Pp. [99]–121.

223. *The Well-Ordered Police State: Social and Institutional Change through Law in the Germanies and Russia, 1600–1800*. New Haven and London: Yale University Press. ix + 284 pp.

224. Review: "Richard Hellie, *Slavery in Russia 1450–1725*. Chicago & London. University of Chicago Press. 1982. xix-776 pp, "*LH*, 24 (3): 471–75, Summer.

225. Review: *"Russlands erste Nationalitäten: Das Zarenreich und die Völker der mittleren Wolga vom 16. bis 19. Jahrhundert*. By Andreas Kappeler. Cologne and Vienna: Böhlau Verlag, 1982. vii, 571 pp. Maps. DM 158," *SR*, 42(1):103–4, Spring.

226. Review: "Neil B. Weissman. *Reform in Tsarist Russia: The State Bureaucracy*

and Local Government, 1900–1914. New Brunswick, N.J.: Rutgers University Press, 1981. x, 292 pp. $19.50," *RH*, 10(1):109–11.

1984

*227. "Foreword," Alexander Davydoff, *Russian Sketches-Memoirs.* Introduction by John M. Dax; [translated from the Russian by Olga Davydoff-Dax]. Tenafly, N.J.: Hermitage. Pp. 9–11. [Also see no. 276]

228. "Proniknovenie zapadnykh idei v Rossiiu," *OB*, 11:33–37, S,

229. Review: "Aileen Kelly. *Mikhail Bakunin: A Study in The Psychology and Politics of Utopianism.* Oxford (Clarendon Press). 1982. Pp. 320," *SR*, 43(4):678–79, Winter.

230. Review: "*Neopublikovannye proizvedeniia.* By V. O. Kliuchevskii. Moscow: Nauka, 1983. 416 pp. 2.20 rubles," *SR*, 42(2):[291]–92, Summer.

231. Review: "Heinz-Dietrich Löwe. *Antisemitismus and reaktionäre Utopie—Russischer Konservatismus im Kampf gegen den Wandel von Staat and Gesellschaft 1890–1917.* Hamburg: Hoffman und Campe Verlag, 1978. Reihe: Historische Perspektiven, Band 13. 304 pp. DM 58," *Studies in Contemporary Jewry.* Vol. 1. Edited by Jonathan Frankel. Bloomington: Published for the Institute for Contemporary Jewry, the Hebrew University of Jerusalem, by Indiana University Press. Pp. 496–500.

232. Review: "*Art and Culture in Nineteenth-century Russia.* Edited by Theofanis George Stavrou. Bloomington: Indiana University Press, 1983. xix, 268 pp. $27.50 £17.88," *SR*, 42(2): 357–58, Summer.

1985

233. "'*Novyi Grad*' and Germany: A Chapter in the Intellectual History of the Russian Emigration of the 1930s," *Felder und Vorfelder russischer Geschichte: Studien zu Ehren von Peter Scheibert.* Herausgegeben von Inge Auerbach, Andreas Hillgruber und Gottfried Schramm. Freiburg im Breisgau: Rombach. Pp. 255–65.

234. "O pervoi russkoi emigratsii," *OB*, 16:29–33, S.

235. Review: "*Religion and Rural Revolt.* Edited by Janos M. Bak and Gerhard Benecke. Manchester: Manchester University Press, 1984. x, 491 pp. £39.50," *CASS*, 19(2):239–40, Summer.

236. Review: "Franz Basler, *Die Deutsch-Russische Schule in Berlin 1931–1945: Geschichte und Auftrag.* Wiesbaden: Otto Harrassowitz, 1983. 98 pp. DM 20, – = Osteuropa-Institut an der Freien Universität Berlin. Slavistische Veröffentlichungen. Vol. 54," *JGO*, 33 (Neue Folge) (2) :312.

237. Review: "C. R. Bawden, *Shamans, Lamas and Evangelists—The English Missionaries in Siberia* (London: 1985)," *TLS*, 4279: 381, Apr. 5, Friday.

238. Review: "Dietrich Beyrau, *Militär und Gesellschaft im vorrevolutionären Russland. (Beiträge zur Geschichte Osteuropas*, Band 15). Köln/Wien: Böhlau Verlag, 1984. x, 504 pp. DM 138,00," *CASS*, 19(1):65–67, Spring.

239. Review: "Mikhail Geller, *Mashina i vintiki* (London: Overseas Publications Exchange, 1985)," *OB*, 15:42–43, Jl.

240. Review: "*The Image of Peter the Great in Russian History and Thought.* By

Nicholas V. Riasanovsky. New York and Oxford: Oxford University Press, 1985. ix, 331 pp. Illustrations. $29.95," *SR*, 44 (3):538–40, Fall.

241.   Review: "Edward C. Thaden. *Russia's Western Borderlands, 1710–1870.* Assisted by Marianna Forster Thaden. Princeton: Princeton University Press, 1984. Pp. xi, 278," *AHR*, 90(5):1239–40, D.

1986

242.   "Dvesti let imperii: Popytka istoricheskogo analiza," *OB*, 19:10–16, Mr.

243.   "Foreword," V. S. Yanovsky, *Elysian Fields: A Book of Memory.* DeKalb: Northern Illinois University Press. Pp. ix–xv.

244.   "Preface," Carol A. Leadenham, comp. *Guide to the Collections in the Hoover Institution Archives Relating to Imperial Russia, the Russian Revolutions and Civil War, and the First Emigrations.* (*Hoover Press Bibliographical Series*, no. 68) Stanford: Hoover Institution Press. Pp. xi–xii.

245.   Review: "Manfred Hildermeier, *Bürgertum und Stadt in Russland 1760–1870: Rechtliche Lage und soziale Struktur.* Köln, Wien: Böhlau Verlag, 1986. XIX, 689 pp., 2 maps. DM 208,—Beiträge zur Geschichte Osteuropas. Vol. 16," *JGO*, 35 (Neue Folge) (2):258–61.

246.   Review: "Westward the Course of Empire. John L. H. Keep. *Soldiers of the Tsar: Army and society in Russia 1462–1874.* 432 pp. Oxford: Clarendon Press. £35 019822575x. William C. Fuller, Jr. *Civil-Military Conflict in Imperial Russia 1881–1914.* 295 pp. Princeton University Press. £28.40 0691054525," *TLS*, 4339:601, May 30.

247.   Review: "Jo Ann Ruckman. *The Moscow Business Elite: A Social and Cultural Portrait of Two Generations, 1840–1905.* DeKalb: Northern Illinois University Press. 1984. Pp. xiii, 275. $24.00," *AHR*, 91(1):152–53, F.

248.   Review: "*Russian Studies.* By Leonard Schapiro. Edited by Ellen Dahrendorf. Introduction by Harry Willets. Elizabeth Sifton Books. New York: Viking, 1986. 390 pp.," *SR*, 46(1):132–34, Spring.

1987

249.   "Introduction," *Russia in the Twentieth Century: The Catalog of the Bakhmeteff Archive of Russian and East European History and Culture.* Boston: G. K. Hall & Co. Pp. vii–ix.

250.   "Letter to the editor," *RR*, 46(2):[224], Apr. [This concerns Robert Himmer's "On the Origin and Significance of the Name 'Stalin,'" *RR*, 45(3):269–86, Jl, 1986.]

251.   "Muscovy Looks West," *HT*, 36:16–21, Ag.

252.   "What Is European History?," *HT*, 36:46–48, Ja.

253.   "Russie—1796–1825" & "Spéransky, Michel—Mikhail Mikhailovitch" in Jean Tulard, *Dictionnaire Napoléon.* Paris: Fayard. Pp. 1485–93 and 1587–88, resp.

254.   Review: "*Russia* by Edward Acton, xiii + 342 pp. (*Longman*, The Present and the Past Series, £17.50 hardback, £8.95 paperback)," *HT*, 37:53–54, F.

255.   Review: "*No East or West.* By Paul B. Anderson. Edited by Donald E.

Davis. Paris: YMCA Press, 1985. iii, 175 pp. Photographs. Cloth," *SR*, 45(2):337, Summer.

256.   Review: "*1905: La première revolution russe. Actes du colloque international organizé du 2 au 6 juin 1981.* Edited by François-Xavier Coquin and Céline Gervais-Francelle. Série internationale, no. 26. Collection historique de l'Institut d' études slaves, vol. 32. Paris: Publication de la Sorbonne, 1986. 568 pp. 280 F.," *SR*, 46(2): 304–5, Summer.

257.   Review: "*Aristocrats and Servitors: The Boyar Elite in Russia, 1613–1689.* By Robert O. Crummey. Princeton, N. J.: Princeton University Press, 1983. Pp. xvi + 315. $30.00," *JMH*, 58(1):378–80, Mr.

258.   Review: "*The Ukrainian Impact on Russian Culture, 1750–1850.* By David Saunders. Canadian Library in Ukrainian Studies. Edmonton, Alberta: Canadian Institute of Ukrainian Studies, 1985. x, 415 pp. $14.95, paper. Distributed by the University of Toronto Press, Ontario, Toronto," *SR*, 45(4):767–68, Winter.

259.   Review: "*Russian Studies.* By Leonard Schapiro. Edited by Ellen Dahrendorf. Introduction by Harry Willetts. Elisabeth Sifton Books. New York: Viking, 1986. 390 pp.," *SR*, 46(1): [132]–34, Spring.

260.   Review: "Peter Scheibert, *Lenin an der Macht—Das russische Volk in der Revolution 1918–1922.* Weinheim: Acta Humaniora, 1984. xx, 730 pp. DM 220,00—," *CASS*, 20(1–2):186–87, Spring–Summer.

261.   Review: "*Na sluzhbe Rossii: ocherki po istorii NTS.* By A. P. Stolypin. Frankfurt a.M.: Possev, 1986. 302 pp. DM 33, paper.," *SR* 46(2):307–8, Summer.

262.   Review: "Orest Subtelny, *Domination of Eastern Europe—Native Nobilities and Foreign Absolutism, 1500–1715.* Kingston and Montreal: McGill-Queen's University Press; Gloucester: Alan Sutton, 1986. xii, 270 pp.," *JUS*, 11(2):93–95, Winter.

263.   Review: "*A Radical Worker in Tsarist Russia: The Autobiography of Semën Ivanovich Kanatchikov.* Translated and edited by Reginald E. Zelnik. Stanford: Stanford University Press, 1986. 472 pp. $39.95," *LH*, 28(2):262–63, Spring.

Reprints and Translations

264.   "An Early Theorist of Absolutism: Joseph of Volokolamsk," *Readings in Russian History,* Volume 1: *From Ancient Times to the Abolition of Serfdom.* Compiled by Sidney Harcave. New York: Thomas Y. Crowell Company, 1962. Pp. 177–87. [Also see no. 3]

265.   "Enseñemos a ponsar a nuestros alumnos," *La Educacion,* 10(3):47–48, Apr–Je, 1958. [Also see no. 44]

266.   "Einige Überlegungen zum russischen Liberalismus," in Lothar Gall, comp. *Liberalismus* (Köln: Kiepenheuer & Witsch, [1976]. Pp.[308]–18. [Translated by Anemone Bronecke] [Also see no. 49]

267.   *The Structure of Russian History: Interpretive Essays.* By Michael Cherniavsky. New York: Random House, 1970. Pp. 212–23 ["Home, school, and service . . ."], pp. 261–66 ["Russia's Perception . . ."].[Also see nos. 63, 73]

268.   Editor. *Russian Intellectual History: An Anthology.* With an introduction by

Isaiah Berlin; sponsored by the Russian Institute of Columbia University. [Atlantic Highlands] N.J.: Humanities Press, 1978, x, 404 pp. [Also see no. 85]

269.   "Russian Youth on the Eve of Romanticism, André I. Turgenev and His Circle," *Revolution and Politics in Russia; Essays in Memory of B. I. Nikolaevsky*. Ed. by Alexander and Janet Rabinowitch with Ladis K. D. Kristof. Bloomington-London: Indiana University Press for the International Affairs Center. *(Russian and East European Series*, vol. 41), 1972. Pp. 39–54. [Also see no. 88]

270.   "Der Stil der russischen Reichspolitik und Fürst G. A. Potemkin," *JGO*, 16(2):162–93, Je, 1968. [Also see no. 90]

271.   "In the Imperial Manner," *Catherine the Great: A Profile*. New York: Hill and Wang, 1972. xiii, 331 pp. (*World Profiles*. Aida DiPace Donald, general editor). Pp. 197–246. [Also see no. 90]

272.   Review Essay: "*Iz pod glyb* and the History of Russian Social Thought," *Iz pod glyb: Sbornik statei* [From Under the Rubble: A Collection of Articles]. Paris: YMCA Press, 1974, 276 pp.," *RR*, 34(4):476–88, O. [Also see no. 158]

273.   "Der Wohlgeordnete Polizeistaat und die Entwicklung der Moderne im Europa des 17. und 18. Jahrhunderts und ein Versuch eines vergleichenden Ansatzes," Ernst Hinrichs, comp. *Absolutismus* (Frankfurt am Main: Suhrkamp, 1986. 398 pp. (Suhrkamp-TB Wissenschaft, 535). [Also see no. 159]

274.   *Understanding Imperial Russia*. Translated by Arthur Goldhammer; foreword by John Keep. New York: Columbia University Press, 1984. xix, 248 pp. [Also see no. 207]

275.   *La Russia degli zar*. Translated by Giovanni Ferrara. Bari: Editori Laterza, 1984. (*Storia et Società*). xv + 240 pp. [Also see no. 207]

276.   "Préface," Aleksandr Davydov, *Images russes: souvenirs*. Traduit du russe par Olga Davydoff Dax; introduction par Jean Dax. Lausanne, Suisse: L'Age d'Homme, © 1984. Pp. 7–9. [Also see no. 227]

APPENDIX: DOCTORAL THESES SPONSORED PRINCIPALLY BY
MARC RAEFF

Flynn, James T. "The Universities in the Russia of Alexander I." Clark University. 1964. 454 pp.
Mendelsohn, Ezra. "The Jewish Labor Movement in Czarist Russia, from Its Origins to 1905." Columbia University. 1966. 301 leaves.
Fisher, Alan Washburn. "The Russian Annexation of the Crimea, 1774–1783." Columbia University. 1967. 265 leaves.
Zimmerman, Judith Elin. "Between Revolution and Reaction: The Russian Constitutional Democratic Party, October 1905–June 1907." Columbia University, 1967. ii, 402 leaves.
Bohachevsky-Chomiak, Martha. "Sergei N. Trubetskoi, a Study in the Russian Intelligentsia." Columbia University. 1968. 302 leaves.
Shatz, Marshall S. "Jan Waclaw Machajski and 'Makhaevshchina,' 1866–1926: Anti-Intellectualism and the Russian Intelligentsia." Columbia University. 1968. 244 leaves.
Allen, Samuel E., Jr. "The Zemstvo as a Force for Social and Civic Regeneration in Russia: A Study of Selected Aspects 1864–1905." Clark University, 1969. 274 pp.
Robbins, Richard G. "The Russian Famine of 1891–1892 and the Relief Policy of the Imperial Government." Columbia University. 1970. 406 leaves.
Ramer, Samuel Carroll. "Ivan Pnin and Vasily Popugaev: A Study in Russian Political Thought." Columbia University. 1971. 365 leaves.
Freeze, Gregory Lee. "The Russian Parish Clergy: Vladimir Province in the Eighteenth Century." Columbia University. 1972. 389 leaves.
Leventer, Herbert Michael. "Tatishchev: Science and Service in Eighteenth Century Russia." Columbia University. 1972. 290 leaves.
Rhinelander, Laurens Hamilton. "The Incorporation of the Caucasus into the Russian Empire: the Case of Georgia, 1801–1854." Columbia University. 1972. 380 leaves.
Schlafly, Daniel Lyons. "The Rostopchins and Roman Catholicism in Early Nineteenth Century Russia." Columbia University. 1972. 233 leaves.
Seltzer, Robert Melvin. "Simon Dubnow: A Critical Biography of His Early Years." Columbia University, 1970 (© 1973). ix, 312 leaves.
Thurston, Gary J. "The Franco-Russian Entente, 1856–1863: P. D. Kiselev's Paris Embassy." Columbia University. 1973. 404 leaves.

Valkenier, Elizabeth Kridl. "The Peredvizhnik School of Painters Against Their Social and Cultural Background, 1860–1890." Columbia University. 1973. 314 leaves.

Frieden, Nancy Mandlker. "Physicians and the State: The Development of the Russian Medical Profession, 1856–1896." City University of New York. 1974. 331 leaves.

Russo, Paul Anthony. "Golos, 1878–1883: Profile of a Russian Newspaper." Columbia University. 1974. 422 leaves.

Bushkovitch, Paul. "The Merchant Class of Moscow, 1590–1650." Columbia University. 1975. 318 leaves.

Eichrodt, Joan Beecher. "Anarchy and Culture: Dmitrii Merezhkovsky and the Kairos." Columbia University. 1975. 413 leaves.

Weinbaum, Alexandra Tamara. "N. I. Novikov (1714–1818): An Interpretation of His Career and Ideas." Columbia University. 1975. 390 leaves.

Roosevelt, Priscilla Reynolds. "T. N. Granovskii: Universal Historian and Russian Intelligent." Columbia University. 1976. 762 leaves.

Heuman, Susan Eva. "Bogdan Kistiakovskii and the Problem of Human Rights in the Russian Empire, 1899–1917." Columbia University. 1977. 250 leaves.

Morrison, Daniel. "'Trading Peasants' and Urbanization in Eighteenth Century Russia: The Central Industrial Region." Columbia University. 1981. 415 leaves.

Kimerling, Elise. "A Social History of the Lower Ranks in the Russian Army, 1796–1855." Columbia University. 1983. 454 leaves.

Melton, Herman Edgar Jr. "Serfdom and the Peasant Economy in Russia: 1780–1861." Columbia University. 1984. 203 leaves.

CONTRIBUTORS

Abraham Ascher is professor of history at the Graduate School of the City University of New York.

Paul Avrich is professor of history at Queens College of the City University of New York.

Martha Bohachevsky-Chomiak is a program officer in the Division of Research Programs of the National Endowment for the Humanities. She received her doctoral degree from Columbia University in 1968 under Marc Raeff's supervision.

James Cracraft is professor of history at the University of Illinois at Chicago.

Jonathan Frankel is professor of Russian studies and at the Institute of Contemporary Jewry of The Hebrew University of Jerusalem.

Gregory L. Freeze is professor of history at Brandeis University. He received his doctoral degree from Columbia University in 1972 under Marc Raeff's supervision.

Edward Kasinec is chief of the Slavic and Baltic Division of the New York Public Library.

John Keep is professor of history at the University of Toronto.

Allen McConnell is professor of history at Queens College of the City University of New York.

Ezra Mendelsohn is professor of Russian studies and at the Institute of Contemporary Jewry of The Hebrew University of Jerusalem. He received his doctoral degree from Columbia University in 1966 under Marc Raeff's supervision.

Samuel C. Ramer is associate professor of history at Tulane University. He received his doctoral degree from Columbia University in 1971 under Marc Raeff's supervision.

Richard G. Robbins, Jr., is associate professor of history at the University of New Mexico. He received his doctoral degree from Columbia University in 1970 under Marc Raeff's supervision.

Marshall S. Shatz is professor of history at the University of Massachusetts at Boston. He received his doctoral degree from Columbia University in 1968 under Marc Raeff's supervision.

Hans J. Torke is professor of Russian and East European history at the Osteuropa-Institut of the Free University of Berlin.

Elise Kimerling Wirtschafter is assistant professor of history at California State Polytechnic University, Pomona. She received her doctoral degree from Columbia University in 1983 under Marc Raeff's supervision.

Richard Wortman is professor of history at Columbia University.

Judith E. Zimmerman is professor of history at the University of Pittsburgh at Greensburg. She received her doctoral degree from Columbia University in 1967 under Marc Raeff's supervision.